Creative
management

Creative management

MALCOLM GOODMAN

PRENTICE HALL

London   New York   Toronto   Sydney   Tokyo   Singapore
Madrid   Mexico City   Munich

First published 1995 by
Prentice Hall International (UK) Limited
Campus 400, Maylands Avenue
Hemel Hempstead
Hertfordshire, HP2 7EZ
A division of
Simon & Schuster International Group

Typeset in 9.5/12pt Sabon
by Dorwyn Ltd, Rowlands Castle, Hants

Printed in Great Britain by T.J. Press Ltd, Padstow, Cornwall

Library of Congress Cataloging-in-Publication Data

Goodman, Malcolm.
    Creative management/Malcolm Goodman.
        p.   cm.
    Includes bibliographical references and index.
    ISBN 0–13–312059–7
        1. Creative ability in business.   2. Industrial management
I. Title
HD53.G664 1995
658.4'09—dc20   94–46627
                                                                CIP

British Library Cataloguing in Publication Data

A catalogue record for this book is available from
the British Library

ISBN 0–13–312059–7

1   2   3   4   5   99   98   97   96   95

Contents

Prologue   1
Acknowledgements   4

PART I **The management dilemma: a contextual review**   7

1 The context for change   11

    1.1   Introduction   13
    1.2   Ages, periods and times   14
    1.3   Wealth-creating activities   16
    1.4   The creative spark   19
    1.5   External influences   21
    1.6   Summary   32
        Questions   32
        References   32

2 The response to change   35

    2.1   Introduction   37
    2.2   Backwards into the future   37
    2.3   Forward into the future   48
    2.4   Focusing intelligence   50
    2.5   Organizational response patterns   52
    2.6   Summary   54
        Questions   54
        References   54

PART II **Journey in search of a new management approach**   61

3 Learning a new approach   65

    3.1   Introduction   67
    3.2   The evolution of management thought   67
    3.3   Traditional management competencies   71

3.4 Process of management   75
3.5 Time for a new management response   77
3.6 Creative management response   78
3.7 Summary   79
    Questions   80
    References   80

4 The individual: discovering, experiencing and using creativity   83
4.1 Introduction   85
4.2 What is creativity?   86
4.3 Encouraging creativity   90
4.4 Capturing creativity   93
4.5 The incredible machine   101
4.6 Discovering creative personal problem solving   114
4.7 Getting to grips with creative personal problem solving   116
4.8 The toymaker: from lone apprentice to master craftsperson   121
4.9 Obstacles to personal creativity   125
4.10 Summary   130
    Questions   130
    References   131
    Appendix 4.1: Management styles questionnaire   133
    Appendix 4.2: Personal creativity audit   133
    Appendix 4.3: The Peking Express   136
    Appendix 4.4: Exercises   137

5 Creative groups   141
5.1 Introduction   143
5.2 Group behaviour   143
5.3 Helping others to experience creativity   150
5.4 Establishing a creative climate   155
5.5 Building up a creative problem-solving tool kit   158
5.6 Creative problem-solving tools   164
5.7 Creative group problem solving: Master Guides   182
5.8 Obstacles to group creativity   185
5.9 Group creativity audit   186
5.10 Summary   187
    Questions   188
    References   189
    Note   190
    Appendix 5.1: Group creativity audit   190
    Appendix 5.2: Introductory CPS tool kit   193
    Appendix 5.3: Practical creative problem solving   195

6 Organizations and creativity   197
6.1 Introduction   199
6.2 Management thinking   199

6.3 Harnessing systems thinking   206
6.4 Hard systems   206
6.5 Soft systems   208
6.6 Cybernetics   218
6.7 Organizational responses   218
6.8 Organizational tools   226
6.9 Creative organizational problem solving: Master Guides   228
6.10 Summary   229
6.11 Organizational creativity audit   230
     Questions   230
     References   231
     Appendix 6.1: Organizational creativity audit   233

PART III **The CMR model: bridging the gap**   239

7 **The creative management approach**   243
  7.1 Introduction   245
  7.2 Approaching creative management I – the diagnosis   246
  7.3 Approaching creative management II – the journey   250
  7.4 Creative management response model   252
  7.5 Top gear   261
  7.6 Summary   265
       Questions   266
       References   266
       Appendix 7.1: Creative management response model   266
       Appendix 7.2: Creative management response model – factor codes   274
       Appendix 7.3: CMR model – factor code cards   278

PART IV **CMR applications: a management approach for the 1990s**   297

8 **The creative management response in action**   301
  8.1 Introduction   303
  8.2 Reviewing organizational behaviour   304
  8.3 Managing the interfaces   304
  8.4 Individual and group issues   315
  8.5 Organizational issues   318
  8.6 Summary   325
       Questions   326
       References   326

9 **Future issues**   329
  9.1 Introduction   331

9.2 The purpose of hunter individuals: self-satisfiers or social builders? 331

9.3 The purpose of teamwork: fact or fantasy? 333

9.4 The purpose of organizations: the big inside or the big outside? 334

9.5 The purpose of management: short-termism or long-termism? 335

9.6 The purpose of goverment: redistribution of wealth or increasing national wealth levels? 337

9.7 Summary 340

Questions 340

References 341

10 Case studies 343

10.1 Introduction 345

10.2 Analysis guide 346

10.3 *Case study 1* Hallstead and Partners 348

10.4 *Case study 2* Project control: walking on eggshells! 349

10.5 *Case study 3* T. L. Rose plc 351

10.6 *Case study 4* NJK plc 353

10.7 *Case study 5* Millbank Foods plc 358

10.8 *Case study 6* DHG Products plc 362

Appendix 10.1: Internal and external interface templates 382

Epilogue 402

Author index 405

Subject index 408

Prologue

The prime objective of the book is to address the problem of *how* Western managers can manage when their operating fields are subjected to mounting chaos, as the contextual factors that impact on their operations change dramatically. The text is presented in four parts. See Figure P.1 for a routemap through the text.

The management dilemma

Part I explores the reasons for the mounting pressures on Western wealth-creating and wealth-distributing activities and reviews general management responses since the Second World War in the light of the developing pattern of contextual changes. The diagnosis is that the wealth-creation arena is now a global one and that traditional ways of managing in the West will need to give way to a 'new approach' to management that is relevant to our time.

Journey in·search of a new management approach

Part II argues that a 'creative approach' to management holds great promise, and sets out to help the reader understand the concept, context and practice by the adoption of an experiential approach. The author believes that personal experiences of creativity powerfully promote its acceptance as a legitimate management pursuit and builds individual confidence. The practical application of creativity both by individuals and groups is developed through exercises in the text that introduce key tools and technical principles which are used to build up an *introductory creative problem-solving tool kit*. The organizational context is approached via a review of management thinking that focuses on the benefits to be derived from the adoption of softer systemics. Audits for taking stock of individual, group and organizational thinking in relation to creativity concepts and values are included in the appendices.

Introducing creative management

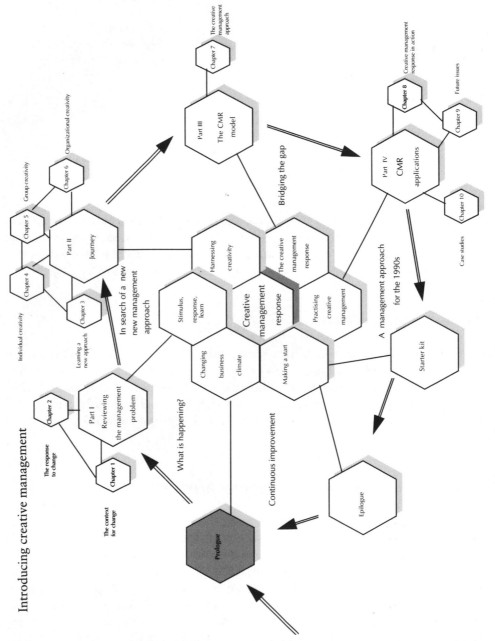

Figure P.1 Approaching creative management: text route map

The CMR model

Part III presents the author's *creative management response (CMR) model* together with its secondary and tertiary components, and stands as a bridge between the situational analysis – the *what* – and the response – the *how* – of creative management that follows in Part IV.

CMR applications

Part IV is largely intended for practitioners. It illustrates how the CMR model can be introduced into the lives of individuals, groups and organizations, and provides case study material, exercises and practical advice.

The book is designed to appeal to undergraduates, postgraduates and practitioners. It is offered not as a judgement of the traditional Western management approach but to provide experienced managers and students with a new vision and a set of creative management tools and principles to enable them to face the future with confidence.

Throughout this book the pronoun 'he' is intended in the generic sense to refer to 'person' (he/she) rather than to the male.

Acknowledgements

A text such as this is the product of the individual and collective effort of several people. Many have given up their time to assist in a number of ways, including academic discussion, practical management training, general project support and preparation assistance. It is fitting to place on record my appreciation of all these contributions.

An especial recognition is due to Kevyn Smith of Tyneside TEC and to my wife and family for their support. Kevyn invested many long hours in discussion and debate as the basic ideas and format of the text emerged.

Thanks are also due to key academic colleagues at Durham University Business School. Professor (Emeritus) Charles Baker and Professor David Kirby for their consistent support and encouragement. Bill Ferguson and John Ritchie for their sustained interest. Within the broader community of the University appreciation is due for the unflinching support given by Bob Williams, the Principal of St Aidan's College who also warmly hosted the initial meetings of the newly formed Creativity Society. Further, appreciation is also due to Professor E. Appleton of the Department of Engineering for his backing to include creative management in the Second Year undergraduate management course, Professor K. Bennett for his enthusiasm and early support and to Professor R. Layton of the Department of Anthropology for his learned discussion. Appreciation is also due to Dr M. Holgate of the Department of Engineering for general support and practical assistance in the development of early visual aids.

Sincere thanks also to Mr Clive Ritches of Durham School for allowing me to trial several of the key themes featured in this text in a series of workshops held at Durham School.

Thanks are also due to Northern Electric plc for supporting the practical development of the creative management model.

The production of the written material proved to be an exhausting task but was made possible by the professional expertise of Clare Griffen, Joan Kingston and Jorg Walther.

Now for the publisher! Thanks are also due to Jo Dodd, John Yates, Richard Fidczuk and Steven Scott of Prentice Hall for their enthusiasm and sound advice as the text has emerged.

To finish I express my gratitude for comments given by Sir John Harvey-Jones. For a lifetime of wise counsel from Arthur Conway, freelance journalist, and for the welcome support given by Professor A. Cockerill, the newly appointed Director of Durham University Business School.

St. Aidan's College
University of Durham
January 1995

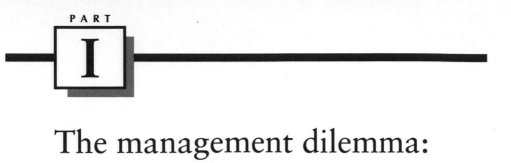

The management dilemma: a contextual review

Approaching creative management

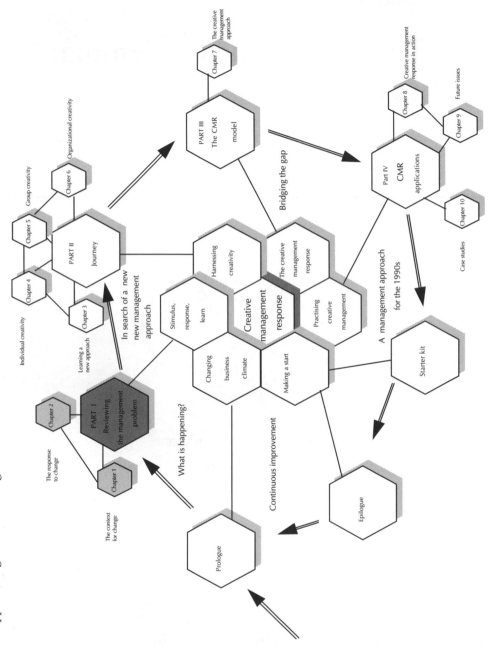

Introduction

Throughout history Man has been preoccupied with surviving the impact of continuous change on his environment. He has progressed from being a simple hunter gatherer to become a sophisticated creator of wealth by applying his native skill in order to respond to the environmental conditions (contextual stimuli) that impact on wealth creation and to use the available resources of his times. If the aim of management is to make the most from a given set of resources, then it is a process skill practised in the dynamic setting of change.

Part I

The first part of this text presents an overview of the complex pattern of external factors or *contextual stimuli* that influence wealth creation. It is particularly concerned to help the reader think about the appropriateness of individual and organizational *responses* to complex, sustained and ever-quickening changes in these patterns. In simple terms, are organizations managing effectively? Or do they need to rethink their response behaviours in the light of rapid and important changes in the contextual stimuli that affect their operations?

Part I closes with an invitation to the reader to explore a new dynamic approach to management, which, it is believed, holds considerable potential for modern managers charged with the responsibility of effectively using the resources at their disposal. It is a practical 'hands-on' approach that demands a willingness to suspend premature judgement and to 'have a go'. This text does not offer an immediate solution to management problems but it does introduce readers to some powerful tools and techniques which form the content of the *creative management response model* described in the text.

Chapter 1 – The context of change

We set out to discover *what* contextual factors impact on organizations, and identify two key groups of stimuli: in the background, the historical influences on wealth creation (time dimension); and in the foreground, the real-time external influences (macro and environmental stimuli) that impact on the day-to-day business of individuals and organizations. The interaction of these two groups of stimuli produces the mix of *contextual stimuli* that impact on Western wealth creation in the 1990s.

Chapter 2 – The response to change

In this chapter we look at *how* the contextual factors influenced wealth creation, by briefly surveying the characteristic management responses to changes in contextual stimuli since the Second World War. As the years progress, so we enter our own real time. The chapter finishes with a short discussion of organizational response patterns to discover whether contemporary responses will serve managers' needs as we approach the year 2000. This process builds a strong contextual basis for the rest of the text which addresses the skill responses of individuals and organizations in times of change.

1

The context for change

CONTENTS

1.1   Introduction   *13*

1.2   Ages, periods and times   *14*

1.3   Wealth-creating activities   *16*

1.4   The creative spark   *19*

1.5   External influences   *21*

1.6   Summary   *32*

Questions   *32*

References   *32*

Map: Chapter 1

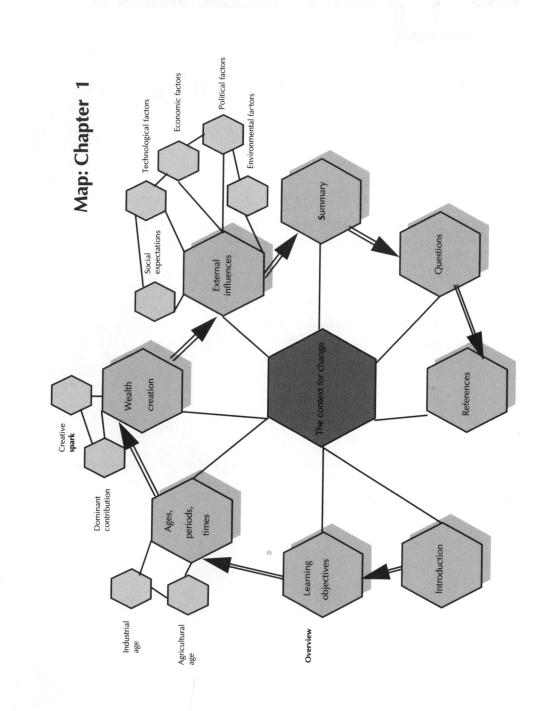

1.1 Introduction

Manipulating scarce resources effectively in real-time competitive conditions to achieve predetermined goals is a prime objective of both individuals and organizations. The key process ideas in this statement are, effectively, in *competitive conditions* and in *real time*. Management is a process skill that, like driving a car, riding a bicycle or swimming, is capable of constant improvement. This is well known to the dedicated racing driver, Olympic cyclist and swimmer, who practise daily to keep their skills highly tuned. However, in the case of management skills many of us so easily slip into a false sense of security by failing to keep our skills up to scratch. As with sports pursuits, management is a competitive activity. Practitioners who fail to practise and train will experience fading performance standards. Furthermore competitive activities happen within a clearly defined time context. The racing driver performs in a Grand Prix, the Olympic sports people in race meetings. In these cases the time dynamic is both present – the race – and continuous – the need to prepare for the next race.

Management is a continuous race. It is a long-distance activity in which fading performance often presents the competition with a real opportunity. To maintain high levels of performance, managers have to consciously devote time to polishing both their response skill patterns – *their game* – and their ability to read the situation or context – the *competitive game*. A good collection of skills is not enough. What counts is to know when and in what combination to use them. This chapter explores some key *contextual* issues that have a direct bearing on good management performance, while Chapter 2 presents an overview of how management seems to have responded to these *stimuli* in the period since the Second World War.

The purpose of Chapter 1 is to stress the importance of the external factors or stimuli that affect management performance. Operating conditions are influenced significantly by both *broad* and *specific stimuli* patterns. *Broad* stimuli refers to the historic perspective of wealth-creating activities as typified by the agricultural and industrial ages. The *specific* stimuli relate to the external, contextual influences on contemporary times as represented by social expectations, and by technical, economic and political factors.

LEARNING OBJECTIVES

After reading this first chapter the reader will have gained an appreciation of:

- The importance of the influence of external, contextual stimuli on the wealth-creating activity of individuals and organizations.
- The ages of wealth creation.
- The changing contributors to wealth creation.
- The creative role of man.
- How external contextual influences impact on wealth creation.

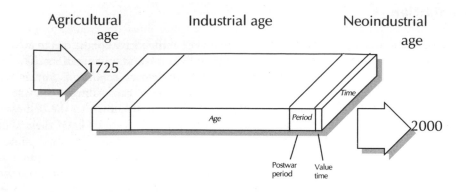

Figure 1.1   The ages, periods and times of wealth creation

1.2   Ages, periods and times

1.2.1   Time dimensions

Historians the world over habitually refer to terms such as age, period and time to describe the passage of history. An *age* displays distinct characteristics over many years before it is succeeded by another new age. The ages of geological history spring to mind as examples of this thinking. *Periods* are shorter intervals of time within ages: for example, royal dynasties such as that of the Tudor and Stuarts or the geologist's glacial periods. *Time* is used to describe distinctive groupings of consecutive years that form part of *periods*. Applying these terms to the study of the history of wealth creation highlights a number of great ages that have formed significant intervals in the development of trading societies (see Figure 1.1).

1.2.2   The agricultural age

From the earliest of times people have sought to create wealth: first, to satisfy the basic human needs, and then to provide for a progressive increase in their standard of living. To begin with, peoples turned their attention to the land and sea around them. In the early years of Western civilization people in the islands of modern Britain and on the continent of Europe gradually built wealth-creating systems to cater for their needs. As history unfolded and reached the medieval period, so these systems developed in complexity. Simple hunter–gatherer communities learnt how to store their wealth, and then how to trade it for accepted mediums of exchange. The advent of a common currency of exchange – money – led to the development of modern market-based economic systems.

Land and people to work it formed the backbone of the wealth-creating systems of these early years. Gradually more and more early machines and tools were introduced to improve efficiency: to plough the ground and gather in the crops; to catch and kill game plucked from the land or the sea. Life was heavily dependent on the regular progression of the seasons. Trade caravans and the development of shipping prospered the mercantile class and provided some variety to the seasonal fare for those who could afford it. The *agricultural age*, in order of importance, drew on the resources of land, labour and capital and characterized much of Western society's wealth-creation activity from the pre-medieval period to the late eighteenth century.

1.2.3   The industrial age/neoindustrial age

A progression of inventions and discoveries of new sources of power heralded the dawn of a new age that has become known as the *industrial age*. The first operations specifically designed to reduce costs – by setting out to achieve the optimum relationship between Man and machine – occurred in the English textile industry in the late eighteenth century. The process evolved out of the invention and development of five machines that transformed the industry, as follows:

1. John Kay's flying shuttle in 1733, which made it possible to weave larger widths of cloth at speed;
2. Edmund Cartwright's power loom in 1785;
3. James Hargreaves' spinning jenny in 1764;
4. Richard Arkwright's water frame in 1769; and
5. Samuel Crompton's spinning mule in 1779.

A sixth by James Watt, who invented the steam engine, was the key to further rapid development, as it signalled the progressive replacement of human, animal and water power by motive power.

Over the last three centuries the industrial age has revolutionized the pattern of wealth creation and trading in Europe and the United States. The early times of the new age saw the flight of labour from the nation's estates to the new factories that were mushrooming in rural and urban areas. Labour and capital challenged land as important wealth-creating factors and in the 1850s became the leading contributors to the country's wealth.

The concepts of division of labour, machine-assisted manufacture and the assembly of standardized parts boosted wealth creation. The onward march of transport technology as the road, rail and barge networks were expanded gave a further encouragement to industrial development. Exports boomed with the adoption of the steamship, which opened up overseas markets. From time to time the growth markets, ushered in by what has popularly become known as the Industrial Revolution, slowed under the influence of a series of wars, slumps, and mounting competition caused by the industrialization of other countries led by Germany and the United States. A catastrophic world war from 1914 to 1918 seriously damaged the wealth-creating capacity of most of Europe. Recovery from the devastation caused by the First World War was slow and the Wall Street Crash of 1929 ushered in a decade of depressed wealth-creating activity that in turn provided an important trigger for the Second World War. This too devastated the wealth-creating systems of the protagonists, and when the guns fell silent it was time once again to reconstruct the economies of the nations that had taken part.

With the aid of American loans and recovery plans, economies were gradually rebuilt. Since 1945 the industrial age has passed through three distinct *times*:

1. the *task-oriented* time;
2. the *product/service design-oriented* time; and
3. The *systems-oriented* time.

A fourth, the *value-oriented time*, heralds the transition to a new wealth-creating age – the *neoindustrial age*.

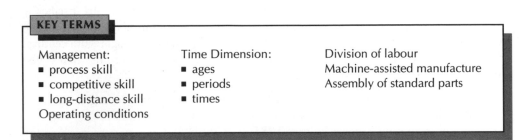

KEY TERMS

Management:
- process skill
- competitive skill
- long-distance skill
Operating conditions

Time Dimension:
- ages
- periods
- times

Division of labour
Machine-assisted manufacture
Assembly of standard parts

1.3   Wealth-creating activities

Dominant contribution – from agriculture to services

The dominant contributor to the early economies was the developing agricultural sector, with small but increasingly significant contributions coming from the fledgling industrial and service sectors. As the industrial sector developed and matured it gradually became the dominant contributor to the national wealth. The small service sector was boosted by industrialization and the agricultural sector achieved productivity gains as the new technologies were applied to the traditional agricultural pursuits. Just as the agricultural sector declined as the dominant contributor to the nation's wealth as the agricultural age was succeeded by the industrial age, so the coming of the neoindustrial age was heralded by a similar decline in the industrial sector. Figure 1.2 illustrates the changing contributions of the leading wealth creating sectors, using three indicative pie charts. The first two cover the heyday of the agricultural and industrial ages and the third depicts the position as the industrial age nears its end.

As the industrial base declined imports of manufactured goods increased, and despite exports of finished products increasing in value, the surplus in the balance of trade steadily declined into deficit. The United Kingdom emerged at the height of the industrial age as a premier trading nation and much of the country's prosperity over the last two hundred years stems from a healthy export activity. In current times this country, in

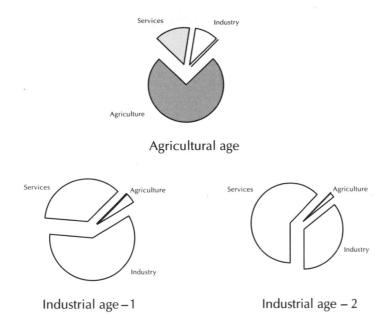

Figure 1.2 Main contributors to wealth creation in the United Kingdom

common with the United States, is critically dependent on a vibrant core industrial sector. Alarm in the 1970s and 1980s in both countries at the accelerating decline of the manufacturing sector encouraged a view that this sector was no longer important. According to this argument (Reich, 1991), the future of the advanced economies lay in de-industrialization and the sustained growth of the service sector. In both the United Kingdom and the United States the service sector now contributes almost two-thirds of the national wealth. As the agricultural age gave way to the industrial age, so those employed in agriculture declined steadily. However, the decline in employment was counterbalanced by an impressive growth in productivity as creative minds applied the inventions of the age to the agricultural sector. Similarly, the industrial sector has experienced a rapid decline in employment as technological advances have automated most manufacturing operations. For years pundits and sci-fi writers have been predicting the arrival of the knowledge-based economy. An impressive array of high-tech achievements in recent years has made this less of a dream and more of a forecast. Within the last ten to fifteen years dramatic advances have been made in a number of fields (including computer technology, telecommunication systems, semiconductors, biotechnics, automation and control) to sound the arrival in a big way of the knowledge-based industries (Toffler, 1990). When these really get underway in the developed market economies they will further tip the balance away from the traditional factors of production towards information and people as the dominant factors in wealth creation. However, this may not necessarily lead to increased general employment opportunities.

Many expect that the knowledge-based industries will require fewer conventional general managers and some, such as Drucker (1989) predict that their number will decline by as much as 50 per cent. Drucker uses the metaphor of a modern orchestra to describe the emerging knowledge-based organizations. The employees are all self-directed specialist contributors whose efforts are co-ordinated by the efforts of the conductor as well as by commonly available information such as the sheet music. In addition to playing the new technical tunes the knowledge-based organizations will improvise, skirt over the prevailing mind-sets and paradigms, and so gain competitive advantage. They will create their own music.

Such new music, or dropping the metaphor, new information will usher in a host of development possibilities as the information is creatively decoded into new products and processes that are of use to individuals. This trend is neatly illustrated in the work of the Japanese electronics multinational, Sharp, as summarized in Example 1.1.

EXAMPLE 1.1

Wizard of Oz

The Wizard is a 7 × 3.7 inch, 10-ounce personal organizer based on the displays and semiconductors that were originally designed for Sharp calculators. It is designed to appeal to business people on the move who have a lot of information to manage, and was launched in the United States in 1988. The Wizard, in the words of Richard Schaffer, editor of the American *Computer Letter* magazine, 'essentially created a market that others dismissed as toys. Computer makers think everything is an office machine. The big payoff comes in finding a machine for the people who say no to the question "Do you need a computer?"'   (*Fortune*, 1992)

The onward march of technology has boosted the development of a variety of support services that were required by modern industrial corporations: teams of specialized engineers to look after the machines, bureaucracies to run the organizations, as well as a host of specialist commercial services such as legal, financial, insurance, freight forwarding, transportation, and so on. Furthermore the increased wealth generated by this activity triggered increasing demand for a variety of private services such as health care, private education, private insurance, investment plans, and so forth. Increased levels of disposable income also boosted growth in leisure services such as sport, holidays and restaurants.

The rapid expansion of the service sector on both sides of the Atlantic has provided employment opportunities for some who were displaced by the mechanization and decline of the industrial sector. Increasingly, however, relatively low-skilled as well as part-time labour has been recruited. Whilst a first glance might indicate considerable employment potential in the service sector – as both the United Kingdom and the United States seek to replace traditional industrial activity by modern 'state of the art', technology-based industries – a second glance reveals some disappointing news. These industries tend to involve higher skill levels and produce greater added-value. Mounting competitive pressures, as product life cycles get shorter and shorter, are likely, in the short term, to lead to fewer rather than more full-time jobs. Little joy is likely to come from retailing, since sustained competition and advances in technology will probably reduce full-time jobs. Thus real unemployment levels seem destined to rise as the industrial sector continues to decline and public sector budgets are trimmed.

There is a danger in believing that Western trading economies, such as that of the United Kingdom, can function effectively without an efficient wealth-creating industrial base. If the native skill levels run down, as more and more goods are imported and are left behind by rapid advances in technology, it will become increasingly difficult to build competitive products in the United Kingdom. The logical conclusion from this is that the country is in danger of losing complete industry segments. Some have argued that this loss of wealth creating capacity can be replaced by the service industries. The lesson from across the Atlantic shows that the United States has paid a heavy price for partially entertaining this belief. The service sector is not independent of the industrial sector but complementary to it, as the industrial sector is both a service sector customer and creates wealth that supports the purchase of other services.

As nations progress through history, so their wealth-creating portfolio expands. From early times to the dawn of the industrial age the prime wealth creating sector was that of agriculture. The industrial age did not replace the agriculture sector's contribution to the national wealth but built on it. Similarly, the service sector should be seen as an additional contributor to the output of the agricultural and industrial sectors.

KEY TERMS

Wealth creation activities
- agriculture
- industry
- services
- knowledge-based industries

Ages
- agricultural
- industrial
- neoindustrial

1.4   The creative spark

If the main stimuli to wealth-creating activity since the medieval period have been the agricultural and industrial ages, what is it that has influenced progress in each age and triggered the progression from one age to another? The evolution and invention of farming tools and techniques has changed the appearance of the countryside. Life in general and wealth creation in particular has concerned societies ever since they abandoned the life of the simple hunter and gatherer. Man is a tribal animal that is distinctively endowed with a remarkable thinking ability, for he possesses the capability to think about how he lives and how he creates wealth. Given a highly developed power of original thought and the ability to learn from his own experiences and those of others, Man possesses the potential to be knowingly constructive – to create wealth – and destructive – to go to war. Some might think that war making is also wealth making though, strictly speaking, military conquests are really a matter of redistributing wealth.

However, the basic sustained wealth-creating or value patterns that have evolved over time seem to have been suddenly energized by extraordinary bursts of positive creative thought. Once creativity is in the air it stimulates man's curiosity and tends to spread rapidly like a forest fire. Sustained extraordinary creative activity triggers significant changes to dominant wealth-creating patterns – in the case of the United Kingdom, a movement from a dependence on agriculture to a dependence on industrial activity, and then to a dependence on the service sector. The unceasing searches for use advantage or utility and for cost effectiveness or productivity are the primary motivators of wealth-creating activity. In competitive times (either in peace or war time) the pace of technological development picks up, heralding the arrival of new market opportunities.

In the agricultural age quality clothes were expensive. The creative genius that brought the dawn of the industrial age expanded the domestic and foreign markets for such clothes as the price of cotton and woollen materials fell. The creative thought that produced the first desktop computer revolutionized conventional office work. The ever-increasing rate of technological development since the Second World War has led consumers to expect more and more sophisticated products and services. The power of competition has meant that products are progressively marketed to meet the specific *value-sets* of individuals. Now that customers usually have a considerable choice of potential suppliers they are becoming more and more demanding in the *value in use* that they expect from businesses. To succeed, organizations now have to do more than merely supply effectively: they have to apply creative thought and design in value for their prospective customers. The *value time* represents a significant shift from the dominant 'supply and buy' guarantee that sustained the industrial age for so long. A new era, the neoindustrial age is beckoning.

At this point in the Industrial Revolution, the methods and procedures used to organize human labour, to plan and control the flow of work, and to handle the myriad of details on the shop floor were largely informal and were based on historical patterns and precedents. One American, F. W. Taylor (1911) changed all that as he looked creatively at the process of manufacturing operations. He argued that managers should collect all the knowledge possessed by workmen and analyze it and codify it in a system of rules, laws and formulae. This should be followed by a search for the optimum technology or 'know-how' and then workmen should be scientifically trained to master best-practice skills. Planning and scheduling that had hitherto been carried out by the workers he saw as being strictly management tasks.

1.5   External influences

1.5.1   Two sets of stimuli

In addition to the stimuli resulting from the ages discussed above and to the constant presence of Man's key skill, his creativity, wealth-creating activity has developed into a complex global system. The countries and organizations that will prosper in the global markets and industries of the twenty-first century must be able to appreciate and come to terms with the predominant macro stimuli that are inherent in such a system. The main stimuli demanding a considered response fall into two distinct but interrelated groups (see Figure 1.3):

1. *STEP factors*   These describe the traditional external influences on wealth creation:
   (a) **Social expectations.**
   (b) **Technological factors.**

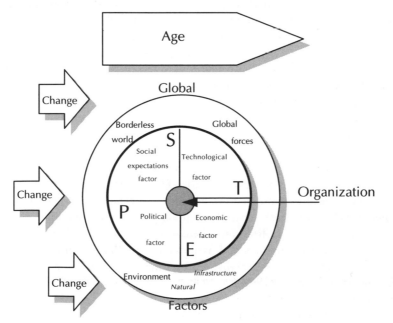

Figure 1.3   External influences affecting wealth creation

(c) Economic factors.

(d) Political factors.

For long periods of time the leading wealth-creating countries of the world, such as the United Kingdom and the United States, largely imposed these external influences on world markets. They set the social expectations, were the leading pace makers in technological development, and possessed the economic and political muscle to dominate the world. In the latter half of the twentieth century, and especially in the last twenty years or so, wealth-creating activity has become a global rather than a nationally dominated process. The emergence of Japan and the South East Asian countries as industrial powers caught the traditional wealth-creating nations by surprise.

2. *Global factors*   These factors focus on the impact of global wealth-creating and environmental trends.

(a) Global factors – the borderless world.

(b) Global business – forces organizational response.

(c) Environmental pressures – natural.

1.5.2   STEP factors

Social expectations

The agricultural age was dominated by subsistence – people in markets needed the basics to support human life. The evolution and development of the industrial age provided an opportunity for many people to earn more money and so be in a position gradually to improve their standard of living. This triggered demand for a variety of goods and services that the new technologies started to develop at prices many could afford. The perfection of mass production technology in the pre-First World War years of the twentieth century progressively reduced prices, thus fuelling demand. Rising demand encouraged further technological progress, which in turn provided many with more and more goods at realistic prices.

For a time it seemed possible that as the industrial age matured it would economically enfranchise all. To the disappointment of many the poor seemed to get poorer and the rich richer. This law or, as Professor Charles Handy (1994) calls it, paradox characterized the agricultural age and seems to have been in evidence throughout the whole of human history. However, the industrial age did improve the lot of many. Whilst progress might in the long term have been incremental, it was none the less significant. Local markets became national markets and national markets became international markets. As international markets became global markets the promise of ever-rising standards of living for the populace of the United Kingdom and the United States started to slow and then to decline. Simply speaking, both countries are getting relatively poorer as their industrial sectors feel the pinch of competition from expanding overseas industrial development. The first to reap the benefits of the sellers' markets both at home and

Table 1.1   **The threat of unemployment in the UK and US economies**

Country	1990	1991	1992	1993
UK	6.8	8.7	9.9	10.2
USA	5.4	6.6	7.4	6.8

Note: Figures are expressed as a percentage of the workforce.

Source: OECD Main Economic Indicators, Cot, 1993, *The Economist.*

overseas, as a result of the benefits of the industrial age, have become the first to suffer the effects of buyers' markets supplied by overseas organizations. As real unemployment rises on both sides of the Atlantic (see Table 1.1) the warning bells are becoming louder. Sustained complacency will lead to a steady fall in living standards. The Atlantic Alliance will go backwards into the future.

Given the desire of most wealth-creating societies to increase their standard of living, there has from the earliest of times been a need for societies to be good stewards of their resources. As local wealth creation developed in complexity there arose a need to administer and govern their affairs. When central government effectively assumed the main responsibility for this task – occasioned by the need to raise direct and indirect taxes – administering business affairs had clearly become an important matter. The central and local government officers charged with matters connected with wealth creation were afforded a high degree of importance and recognition.

However, in Britain the day-to-day responsibilities of businessmen and women, as they sought to create wealth, were not generally afforded the same recognition in society as the local and national government officials. This has become a cultural tradition in Britain which led Lord Kearton to complain, at a seminar held by the Institute of Mechanical Engineers in 1990, that 'Britain's cultural conditions generally speaking did not regard businessmen very highly and engineers hardly at all'. This is in marked contrast with the United States and most of Britain's chief overseas competitors. This may, in part, explain why many postgraduate courses in business management in Britain are Masters of Business Administration degrees. Whilst in reality the MBA title crossed the Atlantic it does echo the British cultural suspicion of the act of wealth creation. In the fiercely competitive global economies of modern times Britain needs to adjust her attitude to wealth creation. Business must become a part of contemporary culture if the country is to find a way of successfully trading in the new neoindustrial age.

Technological factors

Ever since the sustained burst of creative thought that triggered the Industrial Revolution, technological development has been a prominent contributor to the development of the industrial age. Taking rapid transport as an example; it took nearly four millennia for society to replace the horse with the car and just a few decades to replace the car with jet aircraft. In current times the economies of both Europe and the United States are constantly affected by the slipstream of the global technological roller-coaster. What is more, the pace of technological change is increasing as every year goes by.

If the technological advances made by rapid transport are impressive, this is dwarfed by the rate of technological change in the computer industry. In the quarter of a century to 1994 computer memory chips have developed from 1,000 bits of dynamic RAM to volume production of one million bit memory chips. In his book *Brief Time, Long March*, Gazis (1992: 48) of the IBM Research Centre wrote: 'we are able to quadruple the density of memory chips roughly every three years. And progress is accelerating.' Such momentous advances will enable smart organizations to translate better information into decisive competitive advantage. For example, Toyota has gained a demonstrable market edge by adding electronics to an efficient, low-tech, information-reporting system. Womack, Jones, and Roos (1990) describe how Toyota has used computer intelligence to develop an existing information-reporting system in its distribution system. Hewlett-Packard has stressed the importance of information technology in its charter, 'Getting the right information to the right people at the right time to achieve our business objectives'.

Economic and political factors

These factors are usually closely intertwined and are difficult to separate. Since the 1980s many of the world's largest economies have undergone considerable change as national governments in Japan, Asia, Latin America and Europe have followed the fashion of the United Kingdom in deregulating their economies and denationalizing state-controlled industries. This was undertaken in the common political belief that it would inject some sorely needed impetus into their economies. Ill-considered and sudden wide-scale abandonment of state intervention in key economic sectors may well carry a heavy price in the long-term effects on national economic infrastructures.

The political belief in releasing market forces impacted on the European communist countries which collapsed like dominoes in the late 1980s. Poland led the charge in 1989 and was quickly followed by a host of other Soviet satellite countries including the former Czechoslovakia, Hungary, Bulgaria and the dramatic absorption of East Germany into the West German market economy. The trend was boosted by the later collapse of the Soviet Union and the subsequent call for economic reforms in many of her constituent republics. As the world approaches the twenty-first century the dominant wealth-creating systems around the globe are characterized by deregulated market economies. Only China so far stands aloof but is increasingly showing signs of changing its policies.

To survive in the fiercely competitive global marketplace, individual nation states have sought protection from the economic and political power of dominant wealth-creating nations by the formation of defensive trading blocks. Six European nations established the European Community (EC) in 1957 to allay the power of the United States economy and to provide a springboard to recover lost trading ground. Over the period 1938 to 1985 the EC countries' share of global business declined from 37 per cent to 22 per cent. As the Europeans sought reasons for their trading decline the Japanese were developing their master plan to secure a leading role in the world's wealth-creating activity. Despite having few natural advantages in terms of the traditional factors of production, Japan focused its resources on the development of brain capital in wealth creation. It developed lean processes that enabled it to produce high-quality, high-valued-added goods. Perhaps the most familiar example of the Japanese success is the dramatic impact that they achieved in the automotive industry (Porter 1990). However, similar impressive miracles were recorded by Japanese companies in a variety of other industries including cameras (Nikon, Canon, Olympus), consumer electronics (Casio, JVC, NEC, Sharp and Sony), and motorcycles (Honda and Yamaha). Events were now in train for a dramatic transformation in the balance of global economic and political power.

A further significant force at work was the rise of the Pacific Rim economies. They include Japan and a variety of peoples and cultures held together by a common desire to achieve economic growth. This economic region is now achieving the highest rates of economic growth in the world, approaching 4.3 per cent annually against that of 3.0 per cent of the United States and Canada and 3.5 per cent for the EC group of countries. Furthermore the so called 'little dragons' of Asia (Hong Kong, Taiwan, Singapore and South Korea) rapidly industrialized and achieved an impressive sustained annual growth rate in excess of 6 per cent. Close behind the 'little dragons' are the rapidly developing economies of the ASEAN-4 Group (Indonesia, Malaysia, the Philippines and Thailand).

The emergence of these powerful geographical trading blocks throughout the 1970s and 1980s led to them becoming distinct centres of wealth-creating activity. Kenichi Ohmae (1985) termed this development the 'Global Triad' in full recognition that it represented an important shift in world economic power. The historical economic powers of the West were now being severely challenged by the growing strength of the Pacific Rim economies.

The creative spark that fired the Industrial Revolution transformed the United Kingdom from a primarily agricultural economy into an industrial trading economy. For several decades Britain was the workshop of the world and benefited from a sellers' market. The rapid industrialization of other developed nations, such as Germany and the United States, reduced the United Kingdom's absolute advantage to a comparable advantage in many export markets. Gradually at first, and then at an ever increasing pace, the British lost their pre-eminent position in world markets. Furthermore the cumulative impact of two world wars heavily damaged the country's economy and its ability to regenerate. It took nearly 40 years for the economy to recover after the Second World War and to improve its competitiveness significantly. In 1971 the United Kingdom, realizing that it could not survive in the long term on its own, joined the European Community and now enjoys one of the best growth rates and productivity ratings of the leading industrial nations.

The 1992 devaluation and the labour market reforms of the 1980s should ensure that Britain holds on to its position as the fastest growing economy in Europe and maintains its place as the second best performer of the G7 countries after Japan. However, all this could be prejudiced if the government returns to a policy of high interest rates, high taxes, or a high exchange rate. As a player on the global business field the United Kingdom is vitally affected by the contextual forces impinging on world trade. These include the age-old problem of other nations acting in restraint of trade, key raw material scarcities (for example, the 1971 oil crisis), and the complications brought by overseas political instability.

The infrastructure of an economy has an important contextual effect on the level and quality of wealth-creating activity. Traditionally it has been the state that has accepted the responsibility for building and maintaining the national infrastructure in the United Kingdom. The main transport networks (road and rail); the postal service, the power services, the telephone service, the big public services, and so on, have progressively since the 1980s been privatized as the national Treasury has sought to lessen the demand on its funds. It is important for all economies first to preserve and where essential to modernize their infrastructures. Failure to do so may secure short-term savings but is likely to be very expensive in the future. Privatization, however well regulated, may well result in an essentially short-term approach being taken to the matters that affect the upkeep of the country's infrastructure as corporations seek to please their investors.

If governments of the time are tempted to run down that part of the infrastructure still under their control, there is a risk that private organizations will progressively seek to invest in overseas locations with superior infrastructures. This conflict between macro or government and micro or organizational interest could have a serious debilitating affect on the future of the economy. For example, sustained cutbacks in educational and training expenditure by the private and public sectors for short-term cost saving could damage the leading edge of the country's skills for a generation or more. As a trading nation that is crucially dependent on a viable industrial sector, the United Kingdom should be seeking ways of building up its capability to exercise its native creativity to invent and produce hi-tech goods. To rely too heavily on the export of services is fraught with danger. How many French people prefer English accountants?

As manufacturing labour has progressively been replaced by technology more and more people have been released into the service trades. Just under half the population is in the labour force with the highest proportion of employees (over two-thirds) being in the service sectors (particularly financial services and distribution) . Manufacturing has consistently declined and now only accounts for about 20 per cent of the national workforce. The number of part time workers has increased considerably.

The United States, the world's largest and traditionally unregulated economy, although in good shape after the recent recovery – the weakest in modern American history – is showing signs of a slowing in its overall rate of growth. Other, mainly Pacific Rim countries are challenging the American share of world trade. Thus in addition to the external economic factors referred to above an increasing contextual threat to the business of the United Kingdom and the United States is increasing and sustained competition from other economies. The Clinton Administration has been forced to go slow on the implementation of their manifesto policy of 'Putting People First' as Congress pushes to reduce the federal debt. Beyond their own shores both economies can suffer disruption to their trading activities as a result of unfriendly actions and the general hurly-burly of international politics.

1.5.3 Global factors

Global factors – the borderless world

The last two decades have seen the emergence of a borderless world as wealth-creating activity has spread beyond the traditional political boundaries (Ohmae, 1990). International

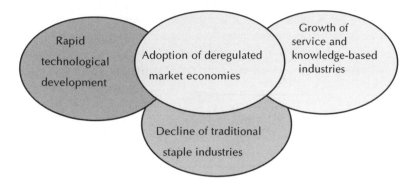

Figure 1.4 Factors affecting the development of the new global economic pattern

alliances are gradually taking over the mantle of the old national policies in all of the STEP factors. The advent of modern communication systems and the development of international business and tourism has led to common global expectations concerning living standards. The pace of technological development has both quickened and assumed an ever-rising cost, thus encouraging the formation of international alliances to exploit potential in many industries. This development is clearly to be seen in the case of the automotive industry in such key components as engines and body shells. Economically the world is increasingly seen as a total wealth-creating system rather than a collection of individual states. Whilst the degree of interdependence varies from country to country the world is going through a period of economic restructuring that is generating a new global economic pattern. This is challenging orthodox political beliefs and increasingly countries are abandoning political isolation and adopting global policies. Four core themes have assumed an especial dominance as national economics adjust to the borderless world:

1. The emergence of the market-driven, deregulated and decentralized economy as the widely accepted *modus operandi* for national wealth creation.
2. The rapid rate of technological advancement that has forced the restructuring of many national economies.
3. The decline of the traditional staple industries as prime contributors to wealth creation in many developed economies.
4. The mounting importance to many countries of the intangible growth industries (e.g. services and knowledge-based industries) as prime contributors to national wealth creation.

These forces are illustrated in Figure 1.4 The decline of the traditional staple industries and the subsequent rise of the service and knowledge-based industries has been discussed in section 1.3 on wealth-creating activities.

Global business – the organizational response

For centuries overseas trade has basically been a matter of trading in either raw materials or narrow product lines in a few localities. Multinational organizations were the

Figure 1.5   Characteristics of global corporations

exception rather than the rule. Since the mid-1970s this pattern has changed dramatically. More and more companies have shed their relatively narrow export activity in place of a broader transnational approach to overseas markets. The world has steadily become a single marketplace that ambitious organizations sought to penetrate by adopting a truly global approach. The 1980s saw the beginnings of the successful global organizations of today that can be distinguished by four key characteristics (see Figure 1.5):

1. They see the whole world as their marketplace – the *global contextual* view.
2. They have become economic superpowers.
3. They are actively engaged in world-class management practices.
4. They have negotiated strategic alliances with other organizations.

Originally many multinational organizations expanded overseas from a strong domestic base. The global organization adopts a wider view and sees the world as a single, highly segmented, market that it seeks to penetrate by an integrated set of global strategies – or in the apt words of the American General Electric corporation 'number one or number two globally'. These strategies are designed to firmly establish positions in the leading core markets within the Global Triad. The severe pressures placed on these organizations by the emerging buyers' markets in the key trading arenas of the world have prompted them to seek world-class management skills.

Such organizations literally operate on a global basis. They raise capital, conduct research, purchase materials, manufacture and market all around the world. The sun never sets on their operations. They transcend the traditional political frontiers and lines on the map.

Other key players in the global automotive industry, such as Honda, Nissan and Toyota, have decided to set up production plants in each sector of the Global Triad

Figure 1.6   The top ten global superpowers (Source: *Fortune*, 1992)

Industry	Global superpower	Country of origin	Turnover ($m.)	Turnover ranking
Automotive	General Motors	USA	123,780	1
Oil	Royal Dutch/Shell	UK/Netherlands	103,835	2
Computers	IBM	USA	65,394	3
Metals	IRI	Italy	64,096	4
Electronics	General Electric	USA	60,236	5
Food & Tobacco	Philip Morris	USA	48,109	6
Chemicals	E.I. Du Pont de Nemours	USA	38,031	7
Aerospace	Boeing	USA	29,314	8
Industrial & Farm Equipment	ABB Asea Brown Boveri	Switzerland	28,883	9
Soaps, cosmetics	Procter & Gamble	USA	27,406	10

(Womack, Jones and Roos, 1990). Global corporations command considerable economic power and their turnovers are sometimes greater than the gross domestic product of some of the smaller sovereign states. Figure 1.6 ranks the top ten global superpowers in terms of turnover.

EXAMPLE 1.2

Global pride

The South Korean Kia automotive corporation buys materials in the Pacific Rim, manufactures in South Korea and Germany and markets its products aggressively across the globe. In the United Kingdom they have achieved considerable success with their super-mini the Kia Pride launched in 1990 which they followed with the Mentor, a mid-range family saloon, in August 1994. Earlier in the year they announced their intention of building four-wheel-drive sports/utility vehicles in Germany after concluding a deal with Karmann, the German automotive engineering group. Furthermore they have recently launched their cars into the American market for the first time under their own brand name.

The Kia operation is a joint venture involving the South Koreans, the Japanese (Mazda) and the Americans (Ford).

The leading global organizations need to sustain their competitive positions in today's volatile markets and so tend to support *state-of-the-art* management practices. Most have shown interest in and have later integrated into their management systems such techniques as *kanban*, just-in-time (JIT), computer-integrated manufacture (CIM), lean production manufacturing, and business re-engineering which are discussed further in Chapter 2 (pp. 43–46). The prime purpose of the management of these organizations is to finely tune their operations in order to produce quality goods that customers want, and to use their workforces to deliver the kind of value that will positively differentiate their operations from those of their competitors. The importance of matching the people input with the expectations of the people in the market is a demanding challenge. To trade successfully in global markets organizations are having to innovate continuously to stay ahead in the race for custom. The buyers' markets keep supplier organizations on their toes and force them to find ways to react creatively to fast-changing patterns of demand. The old-fashioned trading styles of supply and collect the money are long since gone. Modern international business has to look for custom in chaotic conditions. This is a complex undertaking that demands the best management skills.

As the 'global pride' cameo in Example 1.2 illustrates, many serious global players are tending to negotiate strategic alliances with key support organizations so as to better their chances of competing successfully. Not so long ago such relationships were relatively rare. Daimler-Benz (Germany) has linked up with Matsushita (Japan), GEC (UK) with Bosch (Germany), and Pratt & Witney (USA) with Rolls-Royce (UK), while Japanese Aero Engines (Japan), Motoren Turbinen Union (Germany) and Fiat (Italy) have formed a joint venture known as International Aero Engines (IAE) to research and produce a new jet engine for medium-sized aircraft.

These are just a few examples chosen from many that strongly illustrate the machinations of global business. Organizations need each other's expertise and support to succeed. As these alliances proliferate and become more complex, so too does the task of management. Furthermore these alliances tend to enjoy relatively short lives and often come to an abrupt end as evidenced by the Rover (UK, now part of the German BMW organization) and Honda (Japan) connection that effectively finished when Rover was sold to BMW by the British Aerospace Company. Organizations seek global alliances with other organizations for a variety of reasons. Womack, Jones, and Roos (1990) postulated five reasons that seemed to predominate in all the cases that they researched:

1. As protection from unfriendly trade barriers and currency fluctuations.
2. As a means of obtaining new products to match market fragmentation.
3. As a way of achieving increased management sophistication as a result of exposure to different environments.
4. As a counter to regional economic cycles.
5. As a means of checking the impetus of competitors.

The implications of the impact of this complex set of external stimuli on modern management are profound. As the decade gets underway, more and more managers will discover that world business activity needs to be constantly at the forefront of their minds. The Global Triad will be of prime importance to any aspiring organizations seeking to secure a significant presence on the world business stage. This will necessitate competing vigorously in all three centres of activity and making sure that ground is not surrendered in domestic markets (Porter, 1990). This is no mean challenge, as, for example, the American and British automotive industries can testify. Successful global organizations of the early twenty-first century will demonstrate both a keen contextual sensitivity and truly world-class management in terms of their strategic and visionary activity.

Environmental pressures – natural

The last of the main contextual influences on business is the result of an increasing national and international concern for the natural environment. Rising levels of pollution are a legacy of the industrial age. In the past, governments have often accepted pollution as a consequence of accelerated wealth creation. Rapid advances in science and technology have alerted peoples to the dangers of pollution and provided the means to do something about it. Good environmental housekeeping in current times will do much to protect the environment for current and future generations. The world does seem to be becoming more responsible as modern means of communication enable scientists to warn of the seriousness of environmental damage caused by air, water and land pollution.

An important event in the history of environmental protection was the publicity afforded to the *greenhouse effect*. The consequences of this effect were chillingly listed by UNEP, a United Nations environment agency:

- Continued emissions of carbon dioxide, methane, CFCs and nitrous oxides at the present rate will increase the average surface temperature of the earth by 0.3 °C every decade.
- This means that at the end of the twenty-first century the average temperature of the earth will be around 3 °C higher than it is today.
- The effect of the rise in temperature will be that the oceans will rise by between 20 centimetres and one metre in the space of 100 years.
- Other effects will include an increase in periods of hotter and drier climate, and the resultant increased flooding. Those countries that are the environmental losers of today will continue to be so in the future.
- Tens, maybe hundreds, of millions of people may have to live as environmental refugees and will be forced to leave communities and homes.

Industrialized countries took the threat so seriously that they decided to place restrictions on carbon dioxide emissions and other gases at the specially convened Rio Earth Summit in 1992. Two years later, after fifty countries had ratified a treaty that was negotiated in Rio De Janeiro it passed into international law. The fact that global warming takes place does not seem to be contended anymore but its significance is still hotly debated. As the Earth Summit treaty became law so the Institute of Economic Affairs published a pamphlet that urged governments to be wary of the 'cohorts of "ecodoomsters" to warn us that we are living on the edge of the abyss' (Bate and Morris, 1994). Perhaps all this arguing over predicting catastrophe is all hot air too, for observers know that wealth-creating man is damaging the environment. What use is wealth if it becomes progressively more difficult to live to enjoy it?

KEY TERMS

Global external influences
- STEP factors
- global factors

Borderless world
Pacific Rim
Global Triad

Global responses
Natural Environment
Greenhouse Effect
Wealth creation and pollution

1.6   Summary

Wealth creation has been of prime importance to Man for centuries, first, for subsistence, and secondly, as a springboard for him to increase his standard of living. The ebb and flow of history has shown Man that it is unwise to become complacent in the regard he pays to the external contextual factors that impact on wealth creation. As the century draws to a close the forces of change are gathering momentum and significantly altering the global wealth-creating environment.

QUESTIONS

1. Describe management skill.

2. What were the key developments in wealth creation activities that fuelled the development of the Industrial Revolution?

3. What lessons do you think that we can learn from the broad economic history of the West as the neoindustrial age approaches?

4. Wealth creation is clearly of vital importance to any society. What do you see as the main contributors to wealth creation in your country over the next ten years?

5. If creativity sparks new departures in wealth creation, why is it generally so badly understood in the West?

6. Outline the main external influences impacting on wealth creation in the world today. How do you think that managers should view them?

7. Environmental pollution can be regarded as the price we pay for rising standards of living. Discuss.

References

Bate, R. and Morris, J. (1994), *Global Warming : Apocalypse or hot air?*, International Economic Affairs Studies on the Environment, London.

Drucker, P. (1989), *The New Realities*, New York: Harper & Row.

Fortune (1992), Editorial, 23 March, 108.

Gazis, D. C. (1992), *Brief Time*. Long March, *Technology 2001*, Boston: MIT Press, 48.

Handy, C. (1994), *The Empty Raincoat*, London: Hutchinson, 15–19.

Ohmae, K. (1985), *Triad Power: The coming shape of global competition*, New York: Free Press.

Ohmae, K. (1990), *The Borderless World*, New York: Free Press.

Porter, M. P. (1990), *The Competitive Advantages of Nations*, New York: Free Press.

Reich, R. (1991), *The Work of Nations*, New York: Knopf, 81–6.

Taylor, F. W. (1911), *Principles of Scientific Management*, New York: Harper.

Toffler, A. (1990), *Powershift*, New York: Bantam Books.

Womack, J. P. and Roos, D. (1990) *Machine that Changed the World*, New York: Rawson Associates, 67–122.

Additional reading

A brief selection of useful material to broaden your understanding of the importance of the changing *contextual factors* impacting on wealth creating activity.

Drucker, P. (1991), 'Japan: new strategies for a new reality', *Wall Street Journal*, 2 October.

Handy, C. (1989), *The Age of Unreason*, London: Business Books.

Hout, T., Porter, M. E. and Rudden, E. (1982), 'How global companies win out', *Harvard Business Review*, Vol. 60, Sept.–Oct.

Johnson, P. (1983), *Modern Times*, New York: Harper & Row.

Kerr, C. (1983), *The Future of Industrial Societies*, Cambridge, Mass.: Harvard University Press.

Koch, J. V. (1989), 'An economic profile of the Pacific Rim', *Business Horizons*, Vol. 32, No. 2, March–April, 18–25.

Levitt, T. (1983), 'Globalization of markets', *Harvard Business Review*, Vol. 61, May–June.

Ohmae, K. (1987), *Beyond National Borders*, Homewood, Ill.: Dow Jones–Irwin.

van Loon, H. W. (1984), *The Story of Mankind*, New York: Liveright.

Wrege, C. D. and Greenwood, R. G. (1991), *Frederick W. Taylor*, Homewood, Ill.: Business One/Irwin.

Zeithaml, C. P. and Zeithaml, V. A. (1984), 'Environmental management: revising the marketing perspective', *Journal of Marketing*, Vol. 48, spring, 46–53.

The response to change

CONTENTS

2.1   Introduction   *37*

2.2   Backwards into the future   *37*

2.3   Forward into the future   *48*

2.4   Focusing intelligence   *50*

2.5   Organizational response patterns   *52*

2.6   Summary   *54*

Questions   *54*

References   *54*

Map: Chapter 2

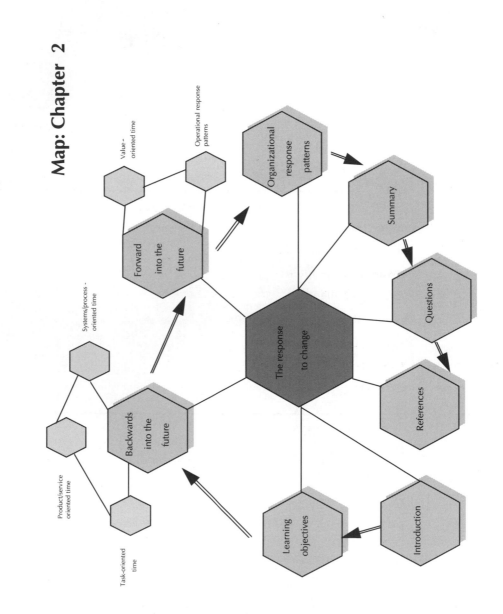

2.1   Introduction

The complex pattern of contextual stimuli that impact on the wealth-creating activity of individuals and organizations is constantly changing. Effective managers make sure that they are constantly aware of these variations. Sometimes they are dramatic and obvious and the price of complacency is abundantly clear. Or they can be gentler, almost un-detectable, building up over time to assume a devastating significance. The consequences of failing to respond to these changes is the classic fate of the myopic manager.

This chapter conducts an overview of the fifty years since the end of Second World War and outlines the general responses of management to the broad problems it faced. These years fall logically into two separate periods. The first entitled 'Backwards into the future (1945–1985)' is the story of the postwar supply gap problem and the growth conditions that followed. Three distinct response times are identified: task-oriented, product/service design-oriented, and systems/process-oriented. A fourth, the value-oriented time, ushers in the second period, 'Forwards into the Future (1985–2000)', and it is believed to mark the beginning of a new wealth-creating age – the neoindustrial age. The general management response to the stimuli of each of the four times identified is briefly analyzed in the light of the functional disciplines of marketing, production and people management.

The chapter closes with a brief discussion of the general management response patterns observed. A reflective summary of the key points raised in Part I is then presented in the form of an invitation to the reader to embark on a journey of discovery.

LEARNING OBJECTIVES

After reading this chapter the reader will:

- Realize the importance of the transition from production-oriented operations to people-oriented operations.
- Appreciate the market factors (from a suppliers' to a buyers' market) influencing the development of postwar Western economies from 1945 to the present.
- Be aware of the changing functional management response patterns (marketing, production and people) that occurred in response to changes in the contextual stimuli.

2.2   Backwards into the future (1945–1985)

2.2.1   Postwar problems and opportunities

Once the ink had dried on the treaties that ended the Second World War, so the work of reconstructing the economies of the war-torn nations began. Considerable aid was granted to the participants by the United States under the terms of the Marshall Plan to speed this process. Now that hostilities had ended, most of the parties were exhausted and keen to explore opportunities for a new beginning. The sheer relief of the declaration of peace stimulated a determined response to rebuild wealth-creating operations all

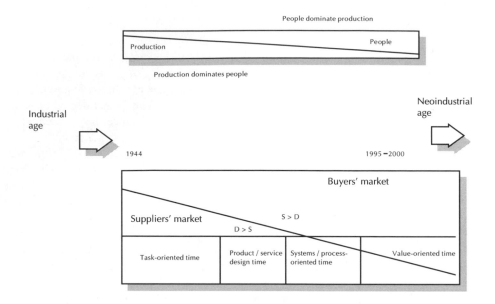

Figure 2.1   Market factors impacting on operations of Western organizations

around the world. The problems facing the economies of the wartime protagonists were of massive proportions but generally straightforward in nature. It was largely a matter of repairing the wartime damage to the economic infrastructure and of responding to the huge pent-up demand for basic goods and services.

The external stimuli impacting on economies were easy to read. Social expectations were high as people sought a better standard of living. A paradox associated with wars down the ages is that despite the destruction they inflict, they often act as a boost to technological development, which later finds peacetime applications. As damaged factories and plant were repaired and rebuilt, several organizations were able to benefit from the application of contemporary technology. The economic and political contextual influences also encouraged the recovery of wealth-creating activity. However, a serious constraint on activity was the heavy damage inflicted on the national economic infrastructures during hostilities.

Figure 2.1 illustrates the main contextual stimuli acting on Western organizations for the last fifty years. The dominant stimulus for a 40-year period was the *supply gap*. For the first two decades after the Second World War this presented a growth market to most industrialists as they sought to keep pace with demand.

2.2.2   Rebuilding the economic and social infrastructure

As a result of a nationally accepted desire to improve living standards after the deprivation of the war years, considerable investment was committed in the West to preserving the peace and to rebuilding the economic infrastructure. In the United Kingdom the education services were overhauled by the passage of the 1944 Education Act. The Health Service was reformulated to provide free accessible cover to all and the social services were reconstituted. Thus out of the ashes of war grew the modern welfare state.

Gradually at first, and then at an ever accelerating rate, this huge market potential began to give way to the demand gap or buyers' market of today. As this occurred, so increasing attention was focused on the cost of the welfare state. Whilst there always has been an argument in support of obtaining value for the taxpayer's money and in exposing these services to the forces that shape customer demand, they nonetheless formed an important part of the environmental stimuli that assisted wealth creation. As the ability of the country to pay its way in the world came in to question, so these services were progressively contracted and constrained and eventually committed for privatization. It is undoubtedly true that many of these services needed to be run with greater efficiency. However, it is important to consider how much their perceived poor showing was due to constant shifting of the goalposts by successive government administrations and to budget shortages. Over more than four decades they did make a massive contribution to the wellbeing of the country. Furthermore these services tend to be characterized by lengthy time cycles before their contribution to the economy is clearly evident. For example, it can take over fifteen years for an individual to pass through the educational system from entry to graduation from university. Sustained cuts in these services for short-term advantage may run the risk of inflicting critical long-term damage to the country's infrastructure that will impair its ability to compete in the future.

2.2.3   Wealth creation – changing times

With the benefit of hindsight over the last 50 years, three distinct times can be identified in the West that have dominated wealth creation (see Figure 2.1):

1. Task-oriented time.
2. Product/service design-oriented time.
3. Systems/process-oriented time.

A fourth, the value-oriented time, is contemporary and heralds the beginning of the neo-industrial age.

The initial task facing organizations was to get going and produce. Production capacity was stretched to the limit to satisfy the level of domestic demand and to rebuild export business. The pace of recovery was very slow and it took a long time for many Western nations to recover. The United Kingdom, for example, took nearly 40 years before it regained its prewar standing as a trading nation. This long uphill challenge was, at first, accepted patriotically by organizations recharged with officers and men discharged from military service. However, as the war years faded into memory management difficulties began to surface.

Figure 2.2 identifies three broad stream (marketing, production and people) organizational responses to the dominant stimuli of the period.

Figure 2.2   Key organizational responses in the United Kingdom 1994–95

Key organizational responses	Task-oriented time	Product/service design time	Systems/process-oriented time	Value-oriented time
Marketing	Seller's market. Focus on increasing sales.	Development of market segments. Positioning and targeting. *Niche marketing*	Strategic marketing. Increasing importance of single customer focus.	Relationship marketing. Value-added marketing.
Production	Supplying volume. Reducing costs.	Automation. Work study.	SPC. Quality/service chain. JIT.	Lean systems. Information management. Autonomous units. Improving response times. Networking.
People	Compliance. Work study. Problems caused by *growth* and *functionalisms*.	Manpower. Planning. Human resources. Management. Team working.	Quality (systems). *Kaizen.* Problem solving.	Task/project focused teams. Cross-functional teams. Information management. Proliferation of *messy* problems.

2.2.4   Task-oriented time

Sales and marketing

Faced with a strong unsatisfied demand, most organizations readily sold all that they could produce. Sales were not a problem. However, as competition developed from both domestic and overseas suppliers, so it became increasingly difficult to secure volume sales. Frequently, relatively small falls in sales resulted in severe pressure on bottom-line results. The new management function of *marketing*, following the publication of Theodore Levitt's (1960) famous article, 'Marketing myopia', soon caught the eye of many Western organizations. As volume production methods improved, so more and more emphasis was placed on generating additional sales. In many fast-moving consumer goods (FMCG) and consumer durable goods industries, attention began to be given to sustained programmes to build up brand loyalty in order to secure customer demand.

Production . . . maximizing supply

The production response was primarily directed at achieving volume output on a limited range of products. *Fordism* was the order of the day and comparatively little attention was given to quality and to the maintenance of high after-sales service standards. In many respects quality and service problems were condoned as inevitable difficulties of being in business. However, sample inspections after manufacture were conducted, with failures being returned for rework. To meet the pressure of demand there was a tendency to build large stocks 'just in case' (JIC) there should be any risk of delay in meeting customer's orders.

Managing people . . . toils and sweat

People were managed by the established 'old timers' of the business and demobbed officers, who broadly speaking, favoured a highly structured command hierarchy and sought worker compliance. This time was increasingly characterized by a drive for efficiency and exhibited many aspects of Taylorism (see Chapter 1, p. 20), particularly the 'one best way' approach.

2.2.5   Product/service design-oriented time

Increasing interest in marketing

As the economy started to pick up, the overall supply gap began to close. Under the combined effects of increased domestic and overseas competition the rate of market growth for many organizations' standard products began to slow down. So they responded by seeking to differentiate their products through paying increasing attention to product design. As traditional market sectors became crowded, so organizations began to show more and more interest in the latest marketing techniques that were crossing the Atlantic. For example, new segmentation techniques helped to identify market sectors that could be reached with traditional or newly designed goods and to discover small, relatively untapped market sectors. Increasing awareness that many small market sectors existed for customized product packages led some managers to begin to question the continued dominance of the mass production mind-set. This search for small but characteristic market opportunities later became known as *niche marketing*, as organizations discovered that volume supply was not the only route to earning profits.

Production . . . reducing costs

Meanwhile production management sought to reduce costs by progressively replacing people with new technology and capital (*automation*). This led to rapid productivity gains and further stimulated management to look for further savings in process engineering. A noteworthy development at this time was the introduction of *flexible manufacturing systems* (FMS), defined as a 'computer controlled manufacturing system using semi-independent numerically controlled (NC) machines linked together by means of a material handling network' (Maleki, 1991).

Human relations

Discontent progressively soured industrial relations. The causes of such unrest were complex. Continued substitution of labour for capital bred fear and resentment that was often amplified if the residual workforce failed to secure what they considered to be their share of the gains in productivity. Increasing standards of living and accompanying inflation led unions to press for larger and larger wage rises. Sometimes labour resented the residual power of managers and the imposition of, real or imaginary, 'us and them' cultures. Many managers just failed to adjust their style responses to suit the times.

On the management side this was the heyday of manpower planning. Seemingly permanent growth markets at home and or abroad stimulated an interest in management development and succession planning. Suddenly Western ears heard about the dramatic production successes of the Japanese. Organizations in the West had been steadily shedding people from production in the belief that the answer lay in modern technology and huge spends on automated lines. The Japanese approach appeared to place a great deal of emphasis on people contributions through their *kaizen* concept. *Kaizen* means ongoing improvement involving everyone – top management, managers, and workers. The Japanese author Masaaki Imai (1986) believed that *kaizen* was the single most important concept in Japanese management – the key to Japanese competitive success. In Japan many systems had been developed to make management and workers *kaizen* conscious. *Kaizen* coupled with the work of Deming (Walton, 1986) and Juran (1988) (SPC quality improvement through teams) became a powerful brew as it enabled productivity to steadily increase through sustained improvements in production processes and promoted product innovation. Western organizations soon realized the potential of this, for it demonstrated a powerful blending of technology and people involvement to secure quality products that achieved market recognition.

2.2.6   Systems/process-oriented time

Marketing . . . growing importance of customers

The 1970s and 1980s saw significant developments in some of the external contextual influences affecting wealth creation. Social expectations were changing rapidly under the combined influences of an ageing population, rising levels of disposable income and relatively low inflation. As the supply gap got narrower and narrower, so customers began to lose interest in being offered standard products of questionable quality with more and more technical features but fewer and fewer *real benefits*. They simply became *buy bored* and demanded better quality and service standards. Meanwhile the Japanese were combining innovation with technology to offer new and exciting quality products

such as cars, VCRs, televisions, motor cycles, pianos and machine tools at very competitive prices. This inflicted heavy damage on many domestic industries in both the United Kingdom and the United States. Some, like motor cycles in the United Kingdom and several electronics sectors in the United States were virtually wiped out. This was all clear evidence that times were changing – people at both the supply and demand ends of business were becoming more important.

As markets began to get tighter and sales more difficult to achieve, organizations drifted away from the traditional mass marketing techniques and turned toward *strategic marketing*. This blanket term incorporated a number of action responses including sophisticated market segmentation, product and organizational positioning, database marketing, media saturation, inflated claims and event marketing. This supply-driven marketing approach relied heavily on hard-sell techniques that frequently alienated customers. Oversupplied markets produced a buyers' paradise. In the light of this situation customers assumed a new importance, for in future they would have to be wooed.

Production . . . reducing costs and improving quality

Production responses in the Europe and the United States still contrasted markedly with those of Japan during this time. If prices were competitive, costs often were not, which resulted in reduced margins and, in turn, less money to invest in search of growth. Whilst the West tended primarily to look to technology to deliver process innovations the Japanese sought both people and process-oriented solutions. Innovations such as *computer integrated manufacturing* (CIM), designed to reduce production costs, often turned out to be inflexible when faced with shortening product life cycles and the demands of customer-focused marketing. Thus the computer systems that were intended to eliminate the human interface were often modified to incorporate it giving rise to the *human integrated manufacturing* (HIM) systems. It also started to become apparent that if the best performances were to be achieved with CIM/HIM systems, it was necessary to build in the soft flexibility advantages of just in time (JIT), total quality management (TQM) and *kaizen*. As the systems/process-oriented time developed, so Japanese organizations started to look beyond quality that is taken for granted (*atarimae hinshitsu*) and quality that fascinates (*miryokuteki hinshitsu*) to the production of value products that positively differentiate their producers.

Ironically, emphasizing quality as a production methodology was an American idea (Walton, 1986; Juran, 1988). It was the Japanese who adopted it and in the process gained a 'market edge' in quality. TQM shifted much of the responsibility for achieving quality from staff operations to those on the shop-floor. Juran (1988) was reluctant to advance a universal definition of quality, but he did identify two critically important factors to guide organizations in their search for improved quality standards, as follows:

1. The features of a product that customers saw as benefits.
2. Those features and performance standards that customers were unhappy with and lead to complaints, returns and repairs.

The key to TQM is to involve all the organization's personnel and to encourage the use of process control systems by suppliers. After experiencing better value (price and quality) from Japanese manufacturers, Western consumers demanded the same standards. Initially organizations reacted by adding more inspection stages to the 'just in case' model described above. This pushed up costs and made them uncompetitive compared with their Japanese rivals. They responded by seeking the assistance of gurus to provide them with a prescription that would give them the competitive edge they desired. Thus Philip Crosby (1984) listed his four commandments of product quality:

1. Definition: quality is the performance to requirements.
2. System: the prevention of defects.
3. Performance standard: zero defects.
4. The price of nonconformance to perfect quality.

As the astonishing, sustained, quality success of the Japanese manufacturers permeated world markets, many Western organizations set out to travel the road from JIC to JIT. Unlearning old ways and overcoming old mind-sets about quality became of prime importance. Whilst organizations knew *what* they had to do, many were uncertain as to *how* to proceed. Thus they sought inspiration from the successes of other organizations and started to become interested in *benchmarking*.

Some had opted to tackle the problem by setting quality standards, accepting few excuses for noncompliance. For example, Motorola set stringent quality goals for its products only accepting a performance of three defects per million parts. All over the world determined organizations realized that the emerging buyers' markets called for innovative products with excellent standards of service. Stalk and Hout (1990) of the Boston Consultancy Group carried out a comprehensive customer response survey and found 'demanding executives at aggressive companies are altering their measures of performance from competitive costs and quality to competitive costs, quality, and responsiveness'. Cutting the time it takes from design to tooling, together with the flexibility to make short product runs with a vastly shorter plant downtime, produced shorter product cycle times. This enabled organizations to react more quickly to changing customer requirements.

EXAMPLE 2.1

Saving time . . . cutting costs

The Ford Motor Corporation began to design V-8 and V-6 engines around a basic building block – in this case, a combustion chamber designed for maximum fuel economy. Then they equipped factories with machinery flexible enough to build several different models. This enabled Ford to contemplate bringing out a whole new range of engines in record time. As many as six new V-8 and V-6s are planned for the 1990s – everything from cast-iron workhorses to high-performance aluminium thoroughbreds.   (Stalk and Hout, 1990)

Having done their homework, organizations improved their process engineering and reduced their customer response times. It was now necessary to do something about the delays frequently experienced as a result of poor supplies delivery. A search for 'best practice' led many organizations to Taiichi Ohno's (1988) account of how Toyota had developed the *kanban* system to meet the challenge of delivering goods when they were needed.

EXAMPLE 2.2

Kanban

Kanban [is] an idea I got from American supermarkets . . . Following World War II, American products flowed into Japan – chewing gum and Coca-Cola, even the jeep. The first US style supermarket appeared in the mid-1950s. And, as more and more Japanese people visited the United States, they saw the intimate relationship between the supermarket and the style of daily life in America. Consequently, this type of store became the rage in Japan due to Japanese curiosity and fondness for imitations.

In 1956, I toured the US production plants at General Motors, Ford and other machinery companies. But my strongest impression was the extent of the supermarkets' prevalence in America. The reason for this was that by the late 1940s, at Toyota's machine shop that I managed, we were already studying the US supermarket and applying its methods to our work . . . We made a connection between supermarkets and the just-in-time system . . . A supermarket is where a customer can get (1) what is needed, (2) at the time needed, (3) in the amount needed . . . From the supermarket we got the idea of viewing the earlier processes in the production line as a kind of store. The later process (customer) goes to the earlier process (supermarket) to acquire the required parts (commodities) at the time and in the quantity needed. The earlier process immediately produces the quantity just taken (restocking the shelves). We hoped that this would help us approach our just-in-time goal and, in 1953, we actually applied the system in our machine shop at the main plant.   (Ohno, 1988: 25–6)

Kanban is Japanese for visible record and it describes an instant inventory check and replenishment system that can be used by manufacturers and their suppliers. When suppliers respond and deliver high quality in response to *kanban* cards, many of the overhead charges associated with mass production vanish. Accordingly there is no need for inspection, or to hold vast raw material stocks, or to work sophisticated invoicing, ordering, transporting and receiving procedures. Production becomes *lean* on the factory floor and paperwork is reduced in the offices.

For some time JIT was seen as some sort of Japanese magic until texts became available in the West that explained its mysteries. Schonberger (1982) defined its users as those who 'produce and deliver finished goods just in time to be sold, subassemblies just in time to be assembled into finished goods, fabricated parts just in time to be fabricated into fabricated parts'. Whilst Monden (1983) saw JIT as: 'the idea of producing the necessary units in the necessary quantities at the necessary time'.

The combined effects of lean production systems, JIT and TQC were staggering for organizations and delivered high-value packages in a competitive market. In the United States, Harley-Davidson reduced manufacturing cycle times for motorcycle frames from 72 days to 2 days and managed to increase final product quality from 50 per cent to 99 per cent. Digital Equipment reduced stock levels from 16 weeks' cover to 3 weeks at its computer workstation pilot line in Albuquerque and, in the process, reduced the defect rate from 17 per cent to 3 per cent. 3M, at their Columbia, Missouri plant, experienced a massive 70-fold reduction in critical defects, appearance, and packaging problems (Crosby, 1984).

The human touch

The growing awareness of the importance of the contribution of human talent to business led many organizations to increase their interest in quality and problem-solving training. As business problems became more and more people-oriented (supplier–employee–customer), so the conventional, technical and quantitative responses of organizations needed to be examined. Significant revisions to traditional management practice were required. Could the conventional management competencies adapt to cope with the new forces of competition? New problems continued to surface. Faith in old ways started to crumble. Uncertainty and fear abounded. Rapidly changing contextual conditions were forcing more and more organizations to take a long hard look at their standard operating procedures. Increasingly organizations began to realize that radical changes were called for in their management processes in order to respond to market pressures.

The underlying contextual stimuli were dramatically changing for most modern organizations. The gathering forces were triggering a period of change similar to that of the Industrial Revolution that ushered in a new wealth-creating age – the industrial age. Steadily, organizations began to realize that real and permanent changes were occurring. The twilight of the industrial age was giving way to the dawn of the neoindustrial age.

2.2.7 Management responses

The period 1945 to 1985 saw the United Kingdom economy recover slowly from a state of disarray after the Second World War to its present position of being, in the words of Anatole Kaletsky (1994), the economics editor of *The Times*, 'a good place in which to do business'. The basic stimulus of shortage has given way to the more complex stimuli of a buyers' market. Changing stimuli should theoretically evoke changing responses. Sometimes organizations get it right, sometimes wrong. Usually the response patterns are not as clear cut as this implies. Management can achieve a range of results from the totally disastrous to the miraculous. The task-oriented management responses of the postwar years achieved a lot. To speculate now on whether the management of the time might have done better had they adopted a different set of responses is probably mischievous, however interesting it might be. The contextual influences of that time have passed into recorded history, as opposed to the dynamic time of the present. Still it is fair to attempt to draw some lessons from the perspective of these years. What lessons did management learn? How was the future predicted? What kind of success rate did management generally achieve? Or did it all just happen?

As the task-oriented time gained impetus, management in many organizations appear to have depended increasingly on the use of quantitative techniques to manage their affairs. This is appropriate for all those inputs that are easily measurable at the plant level such as machine downtime, output, rework, productivity gains, and so forth. It becomes less so if it is abused to predict the future purely on the basis of what has happened in the past. In a sense the country went backwards into the future, as many people do each morning when they edge their cars out of their drives into the rush-hour traffic. Curiously, when the conventional, accepted, indicators register bad news there is a tendency to manipulate the measuring systems to produce the good news that is wanted. This brings the temporary comfort of 'fool's gold'. It is a myopic and dangerous tactic if adopted too frequently. A European colleague of ours, who is a true Anglophile, was nevertheless amazed to see that the United Kingdom had changed the basis on which it collected its unemployment statistics over 30 times since 1979. In such cases, what you measure is what you get! Supply pressure creates its own busyness as organizations struggle to keep up deliveries. Management processes can then so easily cause organizations to spend too much time looking inward and so miss, or only partially see, looming contextual dangers. Of course many organizations do keep close to developments and prosper. Sadly, many others are too busy and so fall on hard times.

Despite many contextual frights, such as numerous local wars and the oil crisis of the early 1970s, organizations broadly prospered in the growth times. However, increasing contextual pressures, as markets became more and more difficult to penetrate, started to change the playing field. Basically volume-oriented responses, whether of the task, product design or systems/process kind, found it more and more difficult to cope with the demand pressures associated with buyers' markets. This called for an increasingly qualitative approach to wealth-creation activities. The basic problems were now soft and not easily handled by conventional, often predominantly linear, models. Suddenly the traditional responses failed to deliver. Sales were getting harder and harder to secure at profitable prices.

The advent of the value-oriented time detectable from the late 1980s onwards posed many leading questions. In future organizations would have to abandon supply-based management responses and adopt demand-based ones. This meant getting to grips with the fads and foibles of customers and tapping the talents of people in order to add as much value as possible within acceptable cost limits. Now organizations had to acquire skills to produce marketable products. This meant that the old days of supply and guaranteed buy had gone. Organizations were faced with the difficulties of dealing with messy, nonlinear problems that are associated with people, in order to build up customer relationships.

KEY TERMS

Supply gap
Economic infrastructure
Demand gap (buyer's market)
Task-oriented time
■ Fordism
■ Taylorism
Product/service design time
■ niche marketing
■ automation
■ *kaizen*

Systems/process-oriented time
Supply gap narrows
Strategic marketing
Quality/TQM
■ bench marking
■ *kanban*
Management responses
■ supply-based
■ demand-based
■ use of key information

2.3 Forward into the future (1985–2000)

2.3.1. The value-oriented time

Wooing customers

Faced with severe competition, oversupplied markets and high stocks of finished goods the organizations turned to relationship marketing to secure sales. As Stalk and Hout (1990) have commented:

> The complex product markets of the twenty-first century will demand the ability to quickly and globally deliver a high variety of customized products. These products will be differentiated not only by form and function, but also by the services provided with the product, including the ability for the customer to be involved in the design of the product . . . A manufacturing company will not be an isolated facility of production, but rather a node in the complex network of suppliers, customers, engineering, and other 'service' functions.

To profitably supply such product packages, anytime, any place and in any variety, presents a totally new challenge to management. The starting point is to identify what the potential customer expects and then to exceed it. Put another way, organizations need to be constantly improving customers' perceived value for money. According to T. H. Nilson (1992) this is the role of marketing in the future. It requires much complex information and a sustained determination by organizations to discover and monitor customer requirements.

As product package life cycles shorten, as the pace of competition accelerates in the value-oriented time, organizations will be under constant pressure to introduce new product offerings. Customers' value expectations will increase, putting greater and greater pressure on organizations' innovative performance. Thus organizations will have to assign and sustain considerable resources to the development of new product value packages. Failure to do so will put at risk their previous efforts to build strong customer relationships. This is the route to securing long-term advantage (positive market/product differentiation) or a sustainable 'market edge'.

If securing a regular flow of value packages is *what* organizations should do in modern times the crucial question to be addressed by organizations is *how* this can be achieved. This is not the formal functional *how* described in numerous marketing texts – the conventional steps of new product development – but a broader process question that relates to *how* organizations' thinking can be developed to secure *real* market advantage. This relates to all the processes involved in the creation, channelling and communication of value packages. The basic or descriptor component of such value packages – for example, manufacturing cars or marketing holidays – is likely to feel the full force of competition as it can be copied relatively easily. However, the added value of the other components, such as management process skills (innovative production and supply techniques, quality, relationship marketing, and so on), in the value package are more difficult to copy. Conventional new product development relies heavily on a flow of customer information and ideas. The pace of competition will necessitate more and more information and ideas as product/market life cycles shorten. Similarly, the other components of value packages will need to sustain innovative development.

Production . . . leaner and leaner

On the supply side, production will continue to get leaner and more responsive to customer demand. *Lean production* appears to do the impossible. It delivers the great product variety once associated only with craft production at costs that are often less than those associated with mass production Furthermore these benefits are provided together with products of high quality by sophisticated networking processes.

Human aspect . . . the importance of brain power

The role of people in wealth creation is undergoing a revolution with the growing acceptance that the economies of the West, such as the United Kingdom and the United States, can no longer be so heavily reliant on mass production processes. Ideas are now increasingly regarded as an important component of modern product and service value packages, as organizations seek positively to differentiate their operations. *Brain power* has become a key contributor to wealth creation. Suddenly, the affairs of knowledge-based organizations, such as the Microsoft corporation, solicit greater interest than those of the heavy survivors of the mass production period, as typified by General Motors. As people assume an ever greater importance in the process of wealth creation – both in terms of their influence as choosy customers in buyer's markets and as the prime source of innovative ideas – so the orientation of organizational operations will have to change.

Machines and processes do not have ideas but people do when brain power is focused on identifying and solving complex problems. The successful product value packages of the future will result from the exposure of creativity to complex, curvilinear, messy, fuzzy logic-type problems. As demand grows for such value packages, so individuals will respond by having ingenious ideas. This will challenge organizations, with their liking for structure and order, as intensive creativity usually arises out of chaos and disorder conditions. It is a valuable force that needs to be encouraged by being given space. Traditional organizations tend to close down such space in their efforts to secure corporate uniformity. Thus old mind-sets and rule books will have to give way to new organizational patterns that continuously encourage individuals to have ideas. It is happening already. Cross-functional teams exist. There is increasing interest in new management processes, as less trust for our future is placed in machines and systems and more in human brains. Selecting the winners is always going to be difficult. Past experience has shown that it is necessary to generate several ideas for every one that eventually reaches the marketplace. The surge in innovative activity – the creative spark – that marked the transition from the agricultural to the industrial age will characterize the value-oriented age and in all likelihood power drive the emerging neoindustrial age.

2.4 Focusing intelligence

2.4.1 Recognizing reality

The agricultural and industrial ages were characterized by the purposeful application of the classical factors of production – land, labour and capital – to create wealth. In the value-oriented time there is a need to purposefully apply a fourth factor of production that Charles Handy (1994) refers to as 'focused intelligence, the ability to acquire and apply knowledge and know-how'. This factor describes a prime characteristic of man that enables him to apply the conventional factors of production to create wealth. It is a process skill that lies within the compass of free minds and is of virtually limitless potential. This is exciting. However, the problem many of us face is that we tend to spend much of our lives within the compass of a complex system of mind-sets and so fail to access much of our thinking potential. Focusing intelligence means stepping out from behind mind- and rule-sets and freely exploring contextual stimuli. This is the essence and the joy of creative thought.

Scientists view nature as a complex system of disordered parts that somehow combine to form an apparent order that we see every day. There is a basic contextual order to life but it is constantly changing, sometimes so slowly that we are largely unaware that it is happening and so fail to adapt our responses to life. Over long periods and ages of time man has adapted his responses massively to cope with environmental changes. Life in Ice-age Britain was very different to life in Britain now. In the same way, travelling down the timescale, life in Britain just after the Second World War was a lot different to life today. When confronted with sudden massive changes in his environment Man has to suspend the comfort of living in an ordered world enshrined in his mind-sets and innovate or die. This is the law of the jungle, as so vividly first popularized by the controversy that surrounded the publication of the work of Charles Darwin. In such conditions Man searches deep into his mind.

If really faced with a set of serious changes to the basic contextual stimuli that order his life, Man will attempt to think his way out of the problem and will sacrifice hitherto firmly practised mind-sets. The key word in the previous sentence is *really*. Man's inherent conservatism will inwardly debate this word and the thought paths it exposes. How real is the threat? Where is the threat? Is it happening now? How does it affect wealth creation? When will it happen? Will it be sustained or go away tomorrow? The perception of the threat is often clouded by poor information and closed thinking. If the threat is real but there is only a partial recognition of the incidence and seriousness of this instability, then individual and organized man will continue operating within established mind-sets but will probably remain inwardly worried. The longer the partial recognition continues, so the concern will continue but will not trigger a significant response unless the threat assumes an obvious and immediate challenge.

Scientists have long been aware that nature is a complex system and that significant changes that affect its contextual design are preceded by a period of turbulence. This is the edge of chaos out of which a new order will eventually emerge. This is the essence of the continuous development of creation. It may, to Man, be drawn out and adaptive as climatic changes are, or it may be born out of sudden violence, as in the case of an earthquake or volcanic eruption. Such change to the immediate contextual environment will cause Man to adopt adaptive responses. If the threat is sustained, serious and outside previous experience, it will result in man adopting an innovative response that will set a precedent pattern for future such disturbances.

2.4.2 Coping with reality

Reality, then, is the current set of stable contextual stimuli that influence our lives. This set of stimuli triggers a set of individual responses. If continuous but incremental change impacts on these responses, then behaviour patterns will only gradually adapt. Dramatic and sustained change will alter thinking and, if long lasting, will trigger significant changes in the prevailing rule-sets that govern behaviour. In the case of organizations they often tend to be resilient to change that would cause a response shift in individuals. The rule sets are more deeply enshrined and resistant. For this reason organizations often require a sustained and determined intent on the part of management to introduce new thinking. Short-term stimuli, even when quite violent, can just impact temporarily on the *force majeure*. It can be like impacting on a blanket that for a short while is disturbed and then recovers to its previous shape. Real change in organizations demands the commitment of management to alter current structures and procedures to encourage ideas. This calls for a new type of management skill that feels comfortable with looser, flatter organizational architecture. The conventional order is familiar and comfortable. Organizational man is thus faced with a paradox. The future demands a different approach that can be personally uncomfortable. Thus it can be no surprise that many managers resist change and try to preserve the status quo. Determined managements empower change by demonstrating their will to both encourage and enable different, creative procedures to evolve.

Buyers' markets and commercial reality require organizations to differentiate the value packages that they place on offer. This implies a need to innovate. To stimulate innovation it is useful for managers to provoke a significant disturbance to the status quo in organizations. This seems, in most cases, to be contrary to practice. Organizations usually impact on managers. As competitive pressures mount in the value-oriented age, both individuals and their organizations will experience increasing difficulties in their attempts to create wealth. This is basically as a result of substantial and permanent changes to the contextual stimuli impacting on wealth creation and will invoke a period of turbulence. The subsequent chaos will pose both threats and opportunities. To those, individual and corporate, who remain complacent, the future will bring disappointment and possibly extinction. This is the dodo response. Those who steel themselves, first, to introduce and then to persevere with change will survive to enjoy the coming of the neoindustrial age. This is the thinking response. Man possesses the ability to focus his intelligence and so successfully exploit a new factor of wealth creation. The choice is open to both individual and organizational man. As to deciding which is the better course, perhaps the unsure should ask a dodo – if they can find one!

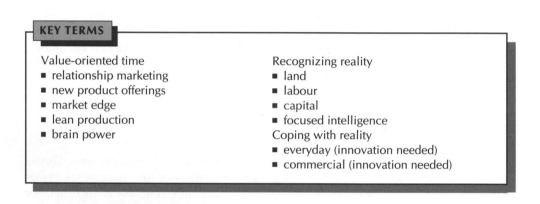

KEY TERMS

Value-oriented time
- relationship marketing
- new product offerings
- market edge
- lean production
- brain power

Recognizing reality
- land
- labour
- capital
- focused intelligence

Coping with reality
- everyday (innovation needed)
- commercial (innovation needed)

2.5   Organizational response patterns

2.5.1   The changing face of wealth creation

The 50-year period since the end of the Second World War has witnessed a dramatic change in the focus of wealth-creation operations of organizations in both Europe and the United States. There has been a clear movement from a concentration on production to an increasing operational focus on people. On both sides of the Atlantic the stimuli impacting on wealth creation have caused significant changes to occur in the ways in which organizations respond. The amazing technological advances achieved in the period have heightened customer expectations as more and more has been possible for less and less. Nowadays quality standards that were merely dreams a few years back can be met at almost ridiculous prices. These developments have stimulated fundamental change in the response patterns displayed by organizations.

As markets became tougher and customers looked for more and more value in their purchases, so pressure was placed on the traditional set of general management responses. Broadly speaking these can be grouped as follows:

- Managing people to achieve results.
- Applying management methods.
- Increasing management effectiveness.

Responding under pressure

As the pace of change accelerated so the response times of organizations came under increasing pressure. Suddenly the traditional general management models and rules of the mature industrial age failed to deliver on time and to the right quality standards. This caused organizations, with varying degrees of success, to view the *unidimensional* traditional management competencies in a mobile *second dimension of change*. As response times quickened and product life cycles became shorter and shorter, organizations found that the management courses and guide books were constantly being revised. In the United Kingdom it is possible to identify four distinct times that chart the response of organizations to these changing stimuli: task-oriented; product/service-oriented; systems/process-oriented; value-oriented (see Figure 2.2).

As unidimensional management has been superseded by two-dimensional management, so the pressures on organizations have increased by phenomenal proportions. Traditional adaptive responses to perceived change have been replaced by the need to respond proactively to changing market stimuli. Furthermore, as customers started to expect better and better value, so organizations were forced to face up to the problems associated with its provision. Unlike the basically linear functional problems of old, many of the process skills required to deliver value are often messy, fuzzy and difficult to resolve. This increasingly highlighted the need for a new management process technology. The traditional management approaches generally failed to cope. When re-interpreted to cater for accelerating change, organizations were still struggling to compete in marketplaces that had for many assumed global proportions. The net result was that the West started to become poorer as export trade became harder and harder to achieve. Over the years this placed a considerable strain on their resources and was one of the key factors involved in decisions to privatize public sector assets.

KEY TERMS

Change in wealth creation
- from production focus to people focus

Traditional management

Competencies (TDC)
- managing people
- applying management methods
- increasing management effectiveness

Changing conditions
- need for more than TDC
- need for a new approach

Quest for a new approach

2.6 Summary

The complicated and very serious set of stimuli explored in Part 1 have provoked organizations to seek miracle cures for these difficult times. Unfortunately there are no quick fixes and these difficult contextual stimuli will not suddenly go away. This is bad news for all who hold dear to the *coherence theory of truth*. According to this theory, it is the rest of the world, rather than a particular organization, that is out of step. All will be well tomorrow as the first green shoots of recovery are there for all to see. The British motorcycle and much of the American and European motor industry once thought along these lines. This is dodo logic and fatal thinking. The old ploys, such as increasing corporate and product-line advertising are unlikely to resolve the problem – that is, falling sales volumes. This is because in times of difficult trading conditions competitors, often right across the world, just follow suite. The result is that things simply settle down at a higher cost of sales level. Perhaps painful cost cutting will reduce costs – probably, up to a point, but overzealous cost cutting in the short term might be the cure that kills the patient.

The quest of this text is to offer an alternative response process that can be adopted and used effectively by individuals and organizations. It is not a quick solution. It requires a new approach to management that is possible to learn, though at first sight it may seem daunting. So, too, is driving, but most learner drivers progress to become competent drivers. The rest of this text describes this new approach and invites the reader to embark on a journey of discovery.

QUESTIONS

1. Outline the main 'times' experienced by the UK since 1945. Describe their distinguishing features. In terms of its management outlook, in which 'time' would you place the organization you interface with every day (e.g. university, business)?

2. Explain what is meant in the text by the phrase 'backwards into the future'.

3. How can we go 'forward into the future'?

4. What is the 'coherence theory of truth'? Is it a suitable solution for contemporary organizational difficulties? Discuss.

References

Crosby, P. B. (1984), *Quality Without Tears*, New York: McGraw-Hill.
Handy, C. (1994), *The Empty Raincoat*, London: Hutchinson.
Imai, M. (1986), *Kaizen*, New York: Random House.
Juran, J. M. (1988), *Juran on Planning for Quality*, New York: Free Press, 4–5.

Kaletsky, A. (1994), 'Britain's Great Economy' in *The World of 1994*, London: The Economist Publications, 28.

Levitt, T. (1960), 'Marketing myopia', *Harvard Business Review*, 48, July–Aug. 45–56.

Maleki, R. A. (1991), *Flexible Manufacturing Systems*, New York: Prentice Hall, 8.

Monden, Y. (1983), *Toyota's Production System*, Cambridge, Mass.: Industrial Engineering and Management Press, 4.

Nilson, T. H. (1992), *Value Added Marketing: The concept*, Maidenhead: McGraw-Hill.

Ohno, T. (1988), *Toyota's Production System*, Cambridge, Mass.: Productivity Press.

Schonberger, R. J. (1982), *Japanese Manufacturing Techniques*, New York: Free Press, 16.

Stalk, G. and Hout, T. (1990), *Competing Against Time*, New York: Free Press.

Walton, M. (1986), *The Deming Management Method*, New York: Perigree.

Additional reading

Contextual issues

Drucker, P. (1993), *Post-Capitalist Society*, Oxford: Butterworth-Heinemann.

Fukuyama, F. (1992), *The End of History and the Last Man*, London: Hamish Hamilton.

Management response issues

Baden-Fuller, C. and Stopford, J. (1992), *Rejuvenating the Mature Corporation*, London: Routledge.

Brown, M. (1971), 'Management's set solution', *Management Today*, April 1979.

Chandler, A. D. Jr. (1977), *The Visible Hand*, Belknap, Ia.: Harvard University Press.

Crosby, P. B. (1979), *Quality Is Free*, Cambridge, Mass.: McGraw-Hill.

Kennedy, P. (1993), *Preparing for the Twenty-First Century*, New York: Random House.

O'Neil, J. R. (1993), *The Paradox of Success*, New York: Putnam.

Peters, T. (1987), *Thriving on Chaos*, New York: Knopf.

Reflective summary

As discussed in the Prologue the main purpose of this text is not to insult readers but to awaken them to the importance of the fundamental changes that are occurring in the factors which influence wealth-creating activity. The contextual stimuli described in Part I are of fundamental importance to all managers. The relatively friendly growth markets experienced by many organizations up to the mid-1980s have changed dramatically. The swing from a broad suppliers' market to a broad buyers' market has brought a severe challenge to organizations. Fifteen years ago the Boeing Corporation had a long order book and could demand attractive contract prices. Today the biggest growth market for long-distance jet aircraft – China – can negotiate powerfully and successfully to achieve bargain contracts.

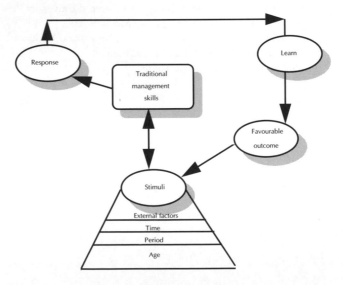

Figure 2.3 Management responses to contextual stimuli – I

So *what* has happened? Modern business trends reflect, on the one hand, growing competition from globalized operations seeking market opportunities and an acceleration in the rate and magnitude of change amongst the main contextual stimuli. On the other hand, this has encouraged many organizations to review their conventional management responses. Topics such as re-engineering, devolution, delayering and downsizing have suddenly become popular. As organizations have found it tougher and tougher to achieve desirable sales levels so they have started to evaluate the conventional management responses and to search for a new comprehensive response formula. Emphasis is moving away from the *what* of management to *how* to act in real time.

This text presents an alternative approach to management that has the capability of generating results in chaotic and turbulent conditions. Such times demand active as opposed to armchair management. So this book is a *how to* one and actively invites the participation of readers to try something new. This is the best road to discovering a new *how*. This text hopes to convince that a willing spirit *to have a go* will produce its own delights.

Figure 2.3 summarizes the argument so far. In the model the stimuli (macro and contextual) call forth a response that is triggered by the traditional approach to management. In good times the outcome is positive and the organization learns (by reflective practice) to improve. Failure to detect and/or fully appreciate the importance of fundamental changes in the pattern of external stimuli that affect wealth-creating activity can lead to varying degrees of myopia. If no serious attempts are made to revise the *how* of management, then the process cycle is actioned as of old and generates disappointing outcomes.

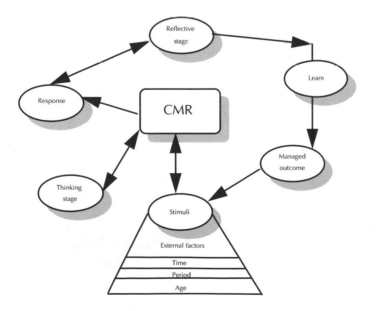

Figure 2.4   Management responses to contextual stimuli – II

This text introduces a process cycle that is illustrated in Figure 2.4. Here the changed set of stimuli impact on a new model of management that is sensitive to contextual factors to produce a *contextual management response* (CMR). This then triggers a thinking stage – as the individual or organization now has genuine real-time problems. In turn, this generates a suitable process solution that is then used creatively by the CMR to action a response. As CMR responses are sensitive to real-time problems a reflective stage is introduced to test the selected action. Learning is achieved by traditional *reflective practice* and by *process networking*. The outcome is usually positive. As the total management action (functional action – the *what* (e.g. manufacture a product) – plus process action – the *how*) is fine tuned to deliver quality for contemporary value-oriented markets.

The CMR process inevitably relies heavily on people skills. These are usually messy, nonlinear skills that demand a qualitative as opposed to the more traditional quantitative approach. To find buyers in overcrowded markets these solutions have to secure a positive differentiation. So the management solutions must be effective to produce and supply, and also novel to potential customers. This calls for the creative spark of man's genius – the same spark that triggered the end of the agricultural age and the beginning of the industrial age. This is the spark that is ushering in the neoindustrial age. Thus the sufficient response for contemporary conditions, which are likely to persist for some time, possibly indefinitely, is a contextual management response or CMR. The secret of *how* to

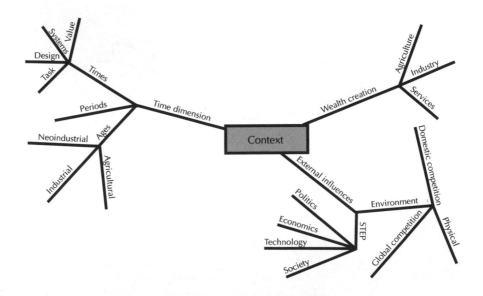

Figure 2.5   Contextual factors impacting on the creative management response

invoke this response lies within a factual and practical understanding of *creativity*. Thus a contextual management response (CMR) is in reality *a creative response*. So a CMR can now be viewed as a *creative management response*.

The main contextual factors influencing the CMR that have been explored in Part I are summarized in the mind map in Figure 2.5.

The only way to discover the practical power (and joy) of creative thought is to experience it. Part II takes you on a journey of discovery and will powerfully equip you to approach even the messiest of problems from a new and satisfying perspective. Creativity is not dancing around to the strains of Mozart whilst dressed in lime green leotards! It's a natural phenomenon that can come to the aid of all. Read on, discover it for yourself, and see how *creative management* can enhance your existing management skills.

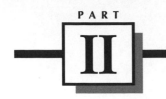

Journey in search of a new management approach

Approaching creative management – Part II

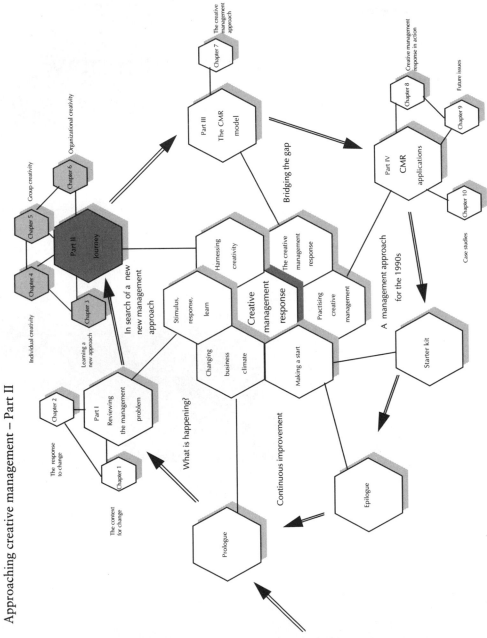

Introduction

Change is the natural result of the complex interaction between the stimuli that Man is exposed to and his wealth-creation intentions set in a time dimension. These stimuli vary in type and frequency. As Man is a thinking/learning being, so his ability to cope with these stimuli improves over time. The environment facing him never has been totally stable, but from time to time the rate of variation has been more predictable than in other times. In the West we live in an unstable period where man the hunter–gatherer will have to rely on his brain power to protect his ability to feed himself and to maintain his standard of living. As the complex stimuli impacting on human wealth-creating activity grows increasingly more complex and violent, Man, the thinker, will have to journey in search of a new way of managing wealth creation.

Part II

The journey begins by continuing the review of traditional management responses begun in Part I and concludes that the codified practice is necessary (or rather the best of it is) for present and future wealth-creating activity, but not sufficient (Chapter 3). Having identified a promising route, the rest of Part II explores the theoretical and practical implications at the individual, group and organizational levels (Chapters 4, 5 and 6.) At times the progress may appear to be a little unconventional, but so once were the first experiences of new concepts, ideas and responses that came, over time, to be regarded as conventional practice.

Readers are exhorted to join in, reserve judgement to the end of the line, roll up their sleeves, and have a go. All expeditions are by their nature risky to some extent but nonetheless throughout history have provided a contextual freedom and challenge that has furthered human material wellbeing. Explorers need constant encouragement if they are to succeed – especially those who set out to find new and better responses to managed activity. Old habits and old practices sometimes die hard and much distress is evident when this happens. However, the nations of the West must continue the journey or risk becoming demoralized lands littered with industrial museums.

Whilst this might at first sound a little depressing, in truth it is exciting – not the excitement of danger, but rather the enthusiasm that heralds an exceptional break-through in thinking. This text is offered as a contribution to the quest in the West to find a new management way.

Read on. Enjoy, but do also join in the fun and experiment. It is hoped that you will discover a new management thinker in your own mind by the end of this section of the journey.

3

Learning a new approach

CONTENTS

3.1 Introduction *67*

3.2 The evolution of management thought *67*

3.3 Traditional management competencies *71*

3.4 Process of management *75*

3.5 Time for a new management response *77*

3.6 Creative management response *78*

3.7 Summary *79*

Questions *80*

References *80*

Map: Chapter 3

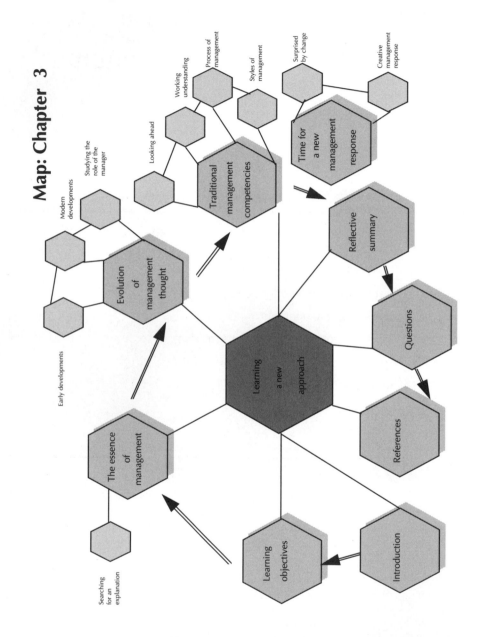

3.1   Introduction

The contextual stimuli impacting on wealth creation in the last decade of the century look as though they are here to stay. In fact the pace of change is likely to speed up as the new millennium approaches. The way that Western organizations respond to this escalating instability will ultimately determine the standard of living that the West is able to enjoy. As the wealth-creation activity or game changes, so it is becoming clear that serious players need to revise their game skills. This chapter takes a reflective look at how the traditional management game has evolved over the centuries and echoes the trumpet call at the close of Part I that the time is right for management to learn a new approach.

LEARNING OBJECTIVES

This chapter is intended to give the reader:

- A brief introduction to the evolution of management thought – the traditional game moves.
- An insight into the game style managers adopt.
- An exposition of the traditional management competencies.
- An appreciation of the importance of innovation and the quintessential role of creativity.
- A definition of *creative management* and an early view of the CMR model.

3.2   The evolution of management thought

3.2.1   Searching for a new explanation

For a noun that is in common parlance, 'management' is surprisingly difficult to explain. Several people who we come across in our lives call themselves managers. So what is a manager? Some would say that a manager is a manager. Or perhaps a manager is someone who is in a management position. Then some regard management as a rank or badge and dream about rising in an organization through the management hierarchy to achieve high corporate office. Perhaps some light can be shed on the matter by considering what managers do. The verb 'managing' suggests coping or perhaps contriving to accomplish something by the thoughtful choice of certain responses. If this is the case, then any individual can be a manager, as we all have a personal responsibility to cope with the problems of everyday life. The key words here are *thoughtful, choice, problems* and *responsibility*.

The ideal individual manager then assumes *responsibility* for coping with his or her own *problems* by a process (*management*) that includes *thinking*, understanding and the deliberate selection (*choice*) of appropriate responses. Managers think and managers act but as we all know our thinking and our choice of response may not always be strictly rational, for we often exercise our *judgement* largely on intuitive grounds or through

Figure 3.1   Management key words – I

Attributes	Skills	Focus	Performance
thoughtful	leadership	context	individual
choice	motivation	task	group
problems		people	organization
responsibility		resources	
judgement			
organized			
interacting			

habitual responses. At the same time we are not always well *organized* and so may adopt a reactive rather than proactive individual management style.

However, we are social beings and much of our lives involves *interacting* with other people. Few individuals are an island. Managing our individual affairs frequently involves a responsibility to manage others – for example, parents assume the responsibility for managing the early lives of their offspring. When we are at work we are all individual managers, in the sense described above, but usually find ourselves in some positions where we are expected to manage others.

3.2.2   Basic understanding of management

Management is an individual and a group activity in which we are responsible for thinking about the contextual stimuli (the facts bearing on the matter), clearly stating the problem, and then choosing an appropriate course of action. It is essentially a group activity that requires interactive skills such as leadership and motivation, as the purpose of management is to achieve a satisfactory result or outcome. This would appear to be similar to the role of the leader. Now sports teams (for example golf, soccer, tennis, and so on) all have leaders or captains but they also have managers. So here the role of manager is different from that of the team leader. Figure 3.1 presents a summary of the basic key words that describe a manager's role.

The main difference between the role of leader and that of manager in this case would appear to have something to do with *resources*. A leader has an acknowledged position of authority over his or her team or group and in a sporting context is expected to win. The manager, on the other hand, is vested with the business authority. In some cases the two roles can be combined, as in the case of a soccer player-manager who could also be the captain or leader.

3.2.3   Early developments

The search for a codification of management principles or precepts that could be applied to any situation has been pursued relentlessly since the dawn of civilization. Early

Egyptian writings indicate that the builders of the pyramids were well acquainted with the management principles of *authority, responsibility* and *specialization.* The Babylonian Code of Hammurabi set out the principles of *control* and *responsibility* and Moses did some invaluable work to advance the development of *organization theory* when he led the tribes of Israel into the Promised Land. Later on, writing in China in 500 BC Mencius emphasized the importance of the *systematic application of management principles.* Across the globe in Greece, Plato sketched the concept of *specialization* in his celebrated *Republic* and Socrates stressed the *universal nature of management.*

Examples of early management concepts appear in the writings of the great military strategists – the *staff principle*, for example, first appeared during the reign of Alexander the Great (336–323 BC). By the time of the sixteenth century, when Europe was in the midst of the agricultural age, Machiavelli developed *four key principles of management* to explain the workings of government organizations:

1. a reliance on mass consent;
2. cohesiveness;
3. leadership; and
4. the will to survive.

3.2.4   Modern developments

The modern development of management thought coincided with the introduction of the factory system during the Industrial Revolution which saw the introduction of:

- financial control systems;
- performance related pay;
- planning models; and
- investment appraisal methods.

The *rational–analytical* approach to management emerged in the nineteenth century. Tools and techniques were developed to advance the practice of *functional skills* such as product forecasting and production planning. Early attempts at work study were pioneered at the Boulton, Watt Company Engineering Works in England in the early nineteenth century. Meanwhile in the United States Eli Whitney was developing cost accounting, quality control and the concept of interchangeable parts. In contrast to these, essentially hard, management skills, a Welshman, Robert Owen espoused the foundations of modern *soft systems theory* at the New Lanark Mill where he demonstrated that a purposeful concern for employee welfare and the provision of good working conditions boosted productivity and profits. In Germany the economist and sociologist Max Weber (1947) studied management behaviour in relation to his *hard systems concept of bureaucracy.* He saw that the large organizations of his day were characterized by appointments that reflected a specialized division of labour and that were linked together in a hierarchical pyramid. He saw the need to have specialized people (managers) to interpret and apply the rules of the organization. Later organizational sociologists criticized

Figure 3.2   Fayol's management principles (Source: Fayol, 1949)

1.	Division of work and specialization.
2.	Authority must match responsibility.
3.	Discipline.
4.	Unity of command (one man, one boss).
5.	Unity of direction.
6.	Subordination of individual interest in favour of the general interest.
7.	Relation of remuneration to effort.
8.	Centralization.
9.	Hierarchical principle of line authority.
10.	Principal of order (place for everyone and everyone in their place).
11.	Equity.
12.	Stability of job tenure.
13.	Importance of initiative.
14.	Importance of *esprit de corps*.

Weber's rigid model for its failure to take into account some of the important features of the emerging modern organizations. They pointed out that it failed to acknowledge the processes of change and was too reliant on a hard hierarchy of authority.

The next important landmark was the publication of Frederick Winslow Taylor's (1911) *Principles of Scientific Management*, in which he developed earlier ideas of specialization and work study into hard management systems that fitted the organizations of the time. In the interwar years the development of management science was dramatically boosted by the work of the Frenchman Henri Fayol, the Americans Berle and Means, Elton Mayo, Mary Parker Follett and Chester Barnard, and Englishman Lyndall Urwick.

French mining engineer Henri Fayol (1916) published a work in France in which he described five basic principles of management: planning; organizing; directing; co-ordinating; and controlling. Whilst influential in France his work remained unappreciated elsewhere in the West until it was translated by Pitman and published by them as *General and Industrial Management* (Fayol, 1949). In addition to his five management precepts he identified a further fourteen principles (see Figure 3.2).

It was not until the publication of *The Modern Corporation and Private Property* by Berle and Means (1933) that attention began to be given seriously to studying the role of the manager. Berle and Means' work revealed a widespread divorce between ownership and control of corporations in the United States. Many of the managers running organizations held very small stockholdings. So the role of the manager deserved separate attention to that of the entrepreneur.

Harvard professor, Elton Mayo's (1933) research at the Hawthorn Works of the Western Electric Company in the United States confirmed the early findings of Robert Owen. Employee motivation and hence productivity was closely linked with the provision of a favourable work environment. Mary Parker Follett (1949) confirmed this finding. Chester Barnard (1938) provided a codification of the best of modern management thinking when he linked employee motivation, the role of the manager and the nature of organizations.

The modern concept of the manager evolved from the teaching of the American business schools who applied their interpretation of Weberism to the functional specializations of organizations. So managers were taught to understand such functional subjects as finance, marketing and production. Gradually academics and practitioners began to see that the role of management was greater than that of its parts. This resulted in managers being seen as generalists charged with achieving pre-set outcomes and being held accountable for their performance to some higher authority. This phase of the evolution of management thought was completed by Lyndall Urwick (1944) when he successfully synthesized the work of Taylor, Fayol and Follett in his text *Elements of Administration.*

The post Second World War period has seen a tremendous increase in the amount of management literature. One of the earliest writers to address the changing wealth creation environment has been Drucker (1971), whose writings have stood the test of time. Three American psychologists, Hertzberg, McClelland and Maslow have made especially significant contributions to management theory and practice. Hertzberg (1959) is well known for his work on motivation and the important influence of good working conditions he terms 'hygiene factors', whilst McClelland's work demonstrated the power of employees' motivation to perform well (McClelland and Winter, 1969). Maslow (1954) demonstrated a hierarchical ordering of human needs ranging from subsistence needs to higher-order needs such as esteem, achievement and self-actualization.

Traditionally managers have been seen as people who organize their people to achieve results. Writers such as Mintzberg (1973) and Stewart (1967) have studied management behaviour. Bass (1960) and Fiedler (1971) have thrown considerable light on the relationship between leadership and management style. March and Simon (1958) and Stafford Beer (1972) have sought to explore the application of the principles of cybernetics to management science. Latterly Majaro (1992), Morgan (1993) and Rickards (1988) have explored the interface of creativity and management.

KEY TERMS

Management process
Management – basic definition
Machiavelli's principles

Modern developments
Noteworthy approaches
- rational–analytical
- Taylor's principles
Emerging role of the manager

3.3 Traditional management competencies

3.3.1 Looking ahead

A key task of managers is to look ahead and to select and *plan* a course of action to achieve economically their required outcomes. Forward planning is a key skill that

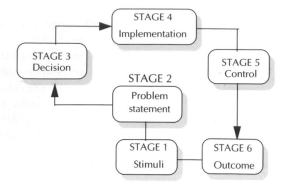

Figure 3.3 Management planning cycle

increases in complexity as a manager rises through an organization. The individual manager plans his or her own weekly and monthly tasks. A junior group manager, for example, plans for his or her charges over a month. A middle manager, such as a personnel manager, might organize his or her work over a year; a senior manager, perhaps over three years, a finance director over five years and a chief executive over seven years. The planning task is common to all managers at all levels at all times. There are six distinct stages to the planning as shown Figure 3.3. The planning-cycle stages are:

1. The manager, sensitive to the situation, becomes aware that a problem is about to break.
2. He or she produces a *problem statement* that defines the problem.
3. A particular course of action is selected and a *realization plan* is made.
4. Available resources are organized to realize the plan.
5. Resources are directed to implement the plan and control is exercised to record deviations from target outcomes and if necessary to trigger corrective action.
6. The final outcome is measured and compared against forecast.

3.3.2 Working understanding of management

The discussion in this section has revealed that managers do many things in support of their objectives and that it is very difficult, perhaps impossible, to come up with an all-embracing definition of the management process. However, managers, whether managing themselves or others, all act in a time frame or context and are held responsible for the effective use of scarce resources. Their behavioural responses are selectable and their achievements are assessed by individuals and groups. In short:

1. Management is the art of getting things done using available resources either as an individual or by co-ordinating the work of others in groups and organizations.
2. In their actions managers display a wide range of multifocused attributes and skills.

Figure 3.4   Management key words – II

Attributes	Skills	Focus	Performance
thoughtful	leadership	context	individual
choice	motivation	task	group
problems	functional	people	organization
responsibility	co-ordinating	resources	style
judgement		consent	
organized		universal	
interacting		environment	
authority		creative	
specialization			
control/			
cybernetics			
will to survive			

Managers are servants. Servants to themselves, their staff, peers, organizations and publics. Their role is multifaceted and subject to a constant stream of events and pressures. Managers live the life of the suffering servant. To be organized makes sense but to be a prisoner of tight administrative procedures will probably damage inter-personal relations. Generally speaking, procedures should serve managers rather than run them. Behavioural skills are of great importance. The views and perceptions of the managed, as voiced at the critical interfaces of organizations, are the true measure of these skills:

- Individual – personal organization.
- Individual/group – regard for all individuals.
- Group – promotes loyalty to individuals, groups and the organization.
- Group/organization – cultivates sound relationships between groups and the organization.
- Organization – seeks to develop sound relations between the organization and groups and individuals.

Managing themselves and other people successfully is a deft process skill that develops loyalty and trust in individuals at all levels in an organization. The management role is hard to describe comprehensively. Figure 3.4 builds on the basic set of key words listed in Figure 3.1. If you are a manager how would you describe your role?

KEY TERMS

Management planning cycle   Management role/function
Management working definition   - key words II (Figure 3.4)

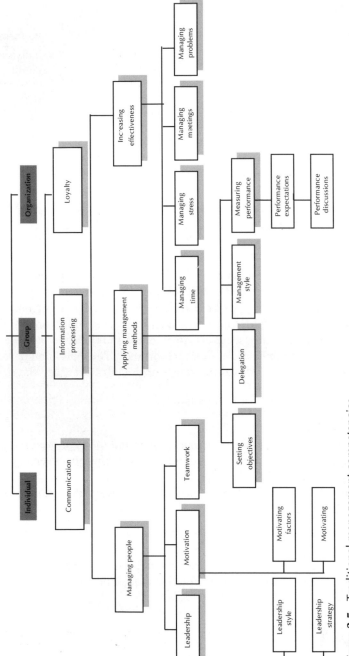

Figure 3.5 Traditional management competencies

3.4 Process of management

3.4.1 Traditional management competencies

The traditional management competencies are illustrated in Figure 3.5. Managers must be concerned to see that they are continually aware of the complex stimuli that directly affect their personal, group, departmental and organizational responsibilities. Communication skills are essential and need to be exercised as broadly and deeply as possible. Broadly to keep people in the know and deeply to build trust and to harness individual knowledge and skills. *Managing people, applying management methods* and striving to *increase effectiveness* all require high loyalty regard (trust) and good communication skills.

3.4.2 Styles of management

The way in which managers behave determines the way in which individuals and groups will behave towards them. So much of a manager's job is concerned with acquiring and fine tuning a sound set of interactive skills. Basically there are two broad styles open to a manager: the *autocratic* style; and the *democratic* style.

Autocratic style

The *autocratic* style is characterized by behaviour choices that are designed to force people to do what they are told. Sometimes this style is necessary – for example, in an emergency when people are shocked or there is no time for argument and debate. Exercised constantly this hard, authoritarian behaviour usually upsets people and backfires on the caring manager who is surprised as individuals desert his or her department. Practised by the uncaring manager this management *modus operandi* can be a cynical power game that damages individuals and groups, and inflicts untold harm on organizational receptivity.

Democratic style

The *democratic* style fosters staff participation and can empower an organization by encouraging staff to apply their knowledge and expertise. Practised by a caring manager this style can do much to release the soft skills of employees and associates. Exercised cynically, where the intent is to turn on the 'false charm' in order to manipulate people, this style tends to promote low trust and loyalty.

Is there one correct style? It is difficult to answer this question purely in terms of these opposing style categorizations. Different contextual stimuli will favour different responses. In practice these two styles describe opposite poles and there are many 'styles' between them. As they choose their responses to different stimuli over time managers will be 'unofficially classified' by their peers and staff. Their management style will be interpreted as OK or not OK – trustworthy or essentially political. Managers serve several individuals, including subordinate staff, peers, senior management, high-ranking company

Figure 3.6 Common management roles

Management role	Description
Guerrilla	Tough mercenary who fights on behalf of colleagues and staff.
Group leader	Team captain role, accepting responsibility for enthusing and holding the team together.
Diplomatic	Representing the interests of captive individuals and groups to other individuals and groups both within and without the organization.
Trainer	Seeing that immediate staff receive the education and training they need.
Arbitration	Seeking to resolve conflict and disputes.
Negotiation	Advocate for own staff.
Officer	Always seen to deal fairly with people.
Bureaucratic	A stickler for forms, order and procedures.
Pastoral	The caring manager.
Political	Seen to be in pursuit of personal power and quite prepared to sacrifice the interests of staff to secure a personal advantage.
Charismatic	High-profile, popular, well-regarded manager.

officers and, frequently, external publics or customers. Each of these individuals and groups will form their own judgement based on *what they see* as consistent responses.

The advent of the *value time*, with its dependence on people values, places a strong emphasis on *soft management skills* that promote team and group working. The old traditional view that managers were either *autocratic* or *democratic* has long since given way to other schools of thought. In the 1970s the *task* or *people* orientation continuum attracted much interest, as popularized by such writers as Blake and Mouton (1978) and Tannenbaum and Schmidt (1973). Today the *hard* or *soft* continuum seems to be gaining in popularity as individuals, groups and organizations face the challenges of the value time.

Meanwhile others have sought to understand management behaviour by describing the roles that managers are required to perform. Figure 3.6 lists some common management roles. Can you think of any others?

KEY TERMS

Traditional management competencies
Management style
- autocratic
- democratic
- task
- people

Manager's publics
- staff and other manager's staff
- own manager and other managers
- customers
- suppliers
- other publics
Soft management skills

3.5 Time for a new management response

3.5.1 Surprised by change

The previous chapter introduced a variant of the *Kolb learning cycle* to study organizational response patterns in the postwar period. As change gathers pace and increases in complexity, so traditional response patterns are increasingly unable to generate acceptable outcomes (see Figure 2.3). As the underlying contextual factors impacting on the West's ability to create wealth intensify it is becoming increasingly necessary for organizations to face up to the fact that their previously privileged position is under a serious and sustained threat. If this is *what* is happening in the 'borderless world', then Western management must give serious attention to reviewing the appropriateness of its typical responses. These vary from organization to organization and from manager to manager. Some organizations are alert and are seeking to alter the responses of their managers. Others are trapped in a mind-set that leads them to believe that they have seen it all before and that current difficulties, while they might be real, are essentially short-term. The good old days are bound to return – as long as managers keep their nerve. The contention of this text is that the 'You've never had it so good' (a remark made famous by the British Prime Minister Harold Macmillan) years are over for good and that management had better change its traditional practices before it is too late.

The realization that permanent changes to our wealth-creating environment are escalating, forces us to take stock of the situation. The choices are starkly simple. We can ignore what is happening and carry on regardless. This is potentially a dangerous option which will cause us to slip further and further behind in the global wealth-creation league. We can pursue a policy of adaptation and 'go with the flow'. The danger here is that the contextual changes that are impacting on wealth creation as we approach the next millennium demand a total overhaul of our traditional management approach. *Supply gap styles* (production and sales orientation), whilst relevant in the immediate postwar period, need to give way to *demand gap styles* (customer and value orientation) to enable the West to redeploy its main assets. As the rate of technological development quickens, the real asset of the West is its brains. Western education standards are still the envy of the world, as evidenced by the increasing numbers of students and managers wishing to attend Western educational establishments. The comparative strength of Western-style education over the years has led to an astonishing array of innovative achievements in wealth creation. With the rest of the world fast catching up (particularly the Pacific Rim countries) the West must deliberately set out to harness its brains to encourage innovation. This requires a firm determination based on a real, as opposed to partial or myopic, assessment of the strength of the contextual factors impacting on wealth creation.

Innovation requires sufficient funds to support it and a mind-set that encourages creativity. However, classical supply gap management breeds a collection of mind-sets (hard systems thinking, short-term payback periods, and hierarchical management structures, and so on) that tend to constrain and often snuff out creativity. A new approach to management is needed in the West to respond to the global stimuli affecting wealth creation. The reflective summary at the end of Part I introduced the concept of the *contextual management response* (CMR). Western wealth-creating activity must adopt a realistic as opposed to complacent view of its position. Reality is often more painful than imagined or virtual reality but is the springboard to lasting success. A contextual management response plots our current position. A *creative management response* (CMR) puts us on the road to recovery for *creativity begets innovation which entrepreneurs can convert to a positive market differentiation (marketing edge) on modern global markets.*

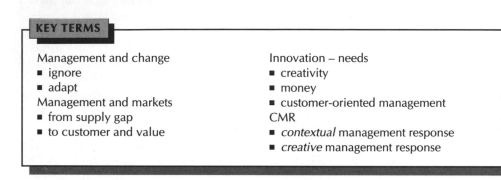

> **KEY TERMS**
>
> Management and change   Innovation – needs
> - ignore   - creativity
> - adapt   - money
> Management and markets   - customer-oriented management
> - from supply gap   CMR
> - to customer and value   - *contextual* management response
>   - *creative* management response

3.6   Creative management response

Creative management is a three-dimensional approach to managing wealth-creation activities (see Figure 3.7). It incorporates the best of the traditional management competencies (first dimension), practised in a full realization of the contextual factors that affect wealth creation (second dimension) and energized by creativity (third dimension) to generate innovative effort to secure a positive product/service/market differentiation. Creative management can be practised by individuals, groups and organizations.

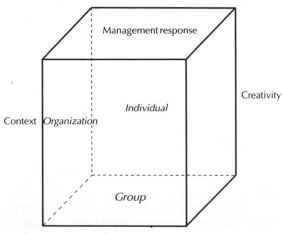

Figure 3.7   The creative management response

Chapters 4, 5 and 6 explore the enabling dimension (creativity) and show how it can be discovered, experienced and harnessed to the conduct of business affairs in turbulent times for wealth-creating activity.

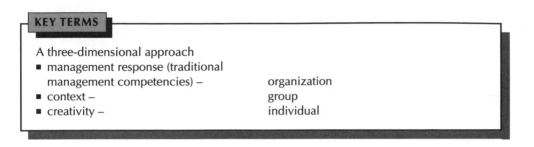

KEY TERMS

A three-dimensional approach
- management response (traditional management competencies) – organization
- context – group
- creativity – individual

3.7 Summary

Traditionally managers have sought to be proactive and organize their people to achieve results: to look ahead and plan a course of action rather than continuously to be caught on the hop and forced to be reactive. As time moves on and a new millennium beckons,

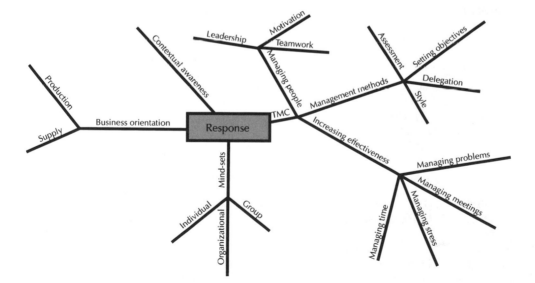

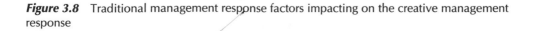

Figure 3.8 Traditional management response factors impacting on the creative management response

many managers are finding that they are increasingly snatching at problems as the contextual influences on global wealth-creation devastate their game. It is time to awake to the real contextual threat and to explore alternative ways of management. What is needed is a *creative management response*.

The mind map featured in Figure 3.8 summarizes the main component factors of the traditional management response. Chapters 4, 5 and 6 constitute a journey that will explore the remaining faces of the CMR cube featured in Figure 3.7. Chapter 7 will present an overview of the journey to the *creative management response approach* and present four views of the full CMR model.

QUESTIONS

1. What is a manager? Describe the role that they are required to play in the late 1990s.
2. Why are the *traditional management competencies* necessary but not sufficient for modern managers?
3. Describe the main styles of management. How do think that they will develop as we approach the year 2000?

References

Barnard, C. (1938), *The Functions of the Executive*, Cambridge, Mass.: Harvard University Press.
Bass, B. M. (1960), *Leadership, Psychology and Organisational Behaviour*, New York: Harper.
Beer, S. (1972), *Brain of the Firm*, London: Penguin.
Berle, A. and Means, G. (1933), *The Modern Corporation and Private Property*.
Blake, R. R. and Mouton, J. S. (1978), *The New Managerial Grid*, Houston, Tex.: Gulf Publishing.
Drucker, P. (1971), *Drucker on Management*, London: Management Publications Ltd. for the British Institute of Management.
Fayol, H. (1916), *Administration Industrielle et Général*, Paris: Pitman.
Fayol, H. (1949), *General and Industrial Administration*, London: Pitman.
Fiedler, F. (1971), *Leadership*, New York: General Learning Press.
Follett, M. P. (1949), *Freedom and Co-ordination*, London: Management Publications Trust.
Hertzberg, F. J. (1959), *The Motivation to Work*, New York: Wiley.
McClelland, D. C. and Winter, D. G. (1969), *Motivating Economic Achievement*, New York: Free Press.
Majaro, S. (1992), *Managing Ideas for Profit*, Maidenhead: McGraw-Hill.
March, J. G. and Simon, H. A. (1958), *Organizations*, New York: Wiley.
Maslow, A. (1954), *Motivation and Personality*, New York: Harper & Row.
Mayo, G. E. (1933), *The Human Problems of an Industrial Civilization*, Harvard Business School.
Mintzberg, H. (1973), *The Nature of Managerial Work*, New York: Harper & Row.
Morgan, G. (1993), *Imaginization*, London: Sage.
Rickards, T. (1988), *Creativity at Work*, Aldershot: Gower.

Stewart, R. (1967), *Managers and Their Jobs*, London: Macmillan.
Tannenbaum, R. and Schmidt, W. H. (1973), 'How to choose a leadership pattern', *Harvard Business Review*, May–June.
Taylor, F. W. (1911), *Principles of Scientific Management*, New York: Harper.
Urwick, L. (1944), *Elements of Administration*, New York: Harper.
Weber, M. (1947), *Theory of Social and Economic Organisation*, English trans. in *Encyclopaedia Britannica*, vol. xv.

Additional reading

Evolution of management thought

George, C. S. (1968), *The History of Management Thought*, Englewood Cliffs, NJ: Prentice Hall.

Traditional management competencies

Bass, B. M. (1985), *Leadership and Performance Beyond Expectations*, New York: Free Press.
Bennis, W. and Nanus, B. (1985), *Leaders*, New York: Harper & Row.
Cavalerii, S. and DeCormier, R. (1987), 'The microskill system for high-speed leadership', *Leadership and Organization Development Journal*, 12 (4).
Hamel, G. and Prahalad, C. K. (1989), 'Strategic intent', *Harvard Business Review*, 67, May–June.
Kotter, J. P. (1990), 'What leaders really do', *Harvard Business Review*, 68, May–June.
Nadler, D. A. and Tushman, M. L. (1990), 'Beyond the charasmatic leader: leadership and organisational change', *California Management Review*, 32 (2).

A new perspective

Belasco, J. A. (1990), *Teaching The Elephant to Dance*, London: Century Business.
Harvey-Jones, J. (1988), *Making It Happen*, London: Fontana.
Harvey-Jones, J. (1993), *Managing To Survive*, London: Mandarin.
Kanter, R. M. (1983), *The Change Masters*, New York: Simon & Schuster.
Parkinson, C. N. (1957), *Parkinson's Law*, London: John Murray.
Simonton, D. K. (1984), *Genius, Creativity, and Leadership*, Cambridge, Mass.: Harvard University Press.

The individual: discovering, experiencing and using creativity

───── CONTENTS ─────

4.1 Introduction   *85*

4.2 What is creativity?   *86*

4.3 Encouraging creativity   *90*

4.4 Capturing creativity   *93*

4.5 The incredible machine   *101*

4.6 Discovering creative personal problem solving   *114*

4.7 Getting to grips with creative personal problem solving   *116*

4.8 The toymaker: from lone apprentice to master craftsperson   *121*

4.9 Obstacles to personal creativity   *125*

4.10 Summary   *130*

Questions   *130*

References   *131*

Appendix 4.1   Management styles questionnaire   *133*

Appendix 4.2   Personal creativity audit   *133*

Appendix 4.3   The Peking Express   *136*

Appendix 4.4   Exercises   *137*

Map: Chapter 4

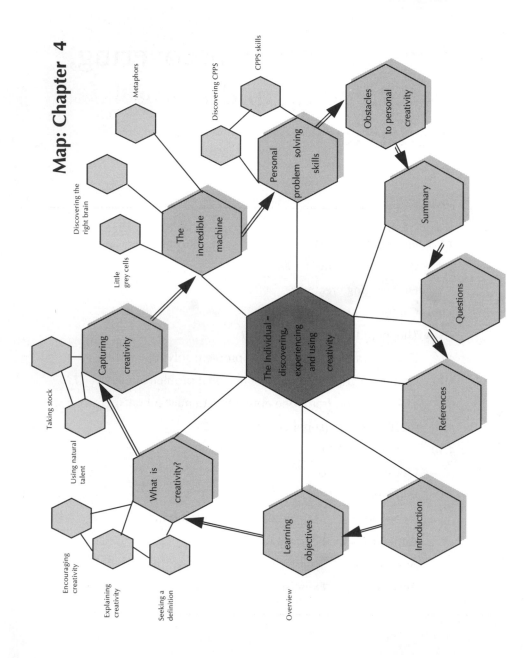

The Individual – discovering, experiencing and using creativity

Capturing creativity

The incredible machine

Personal problem solving skills

Obstacles to personal creativity

Summary

Questions

References

Learning objectives

Introduction

What is creativity?

Metaphors

Discovering CPPS

CPPS skills

Discovering the right brain

Little grey cells

Taking stock

Using natural talent

Encouraging creativity

Explaining creativity

Seeking a definition

Overview

4.1 Introduction

Most acknowledge that creativity exists. Many can name a creative person, live or dead, though it is amazing how many people seem to think that creativity and the after life go together! This chapter asserts that all individuals are naturally creative and that this is by design and not an accident of birth. Of course, some are more creative than others. However, we all have tremendous potential. The curious thing is that many of us keep our creativity under wraps. Perhaps this is because many of us find it easier this way. Many individuals and groups seem to radiate a latent hostility toward creative people. This makes about as much sense as the author of this text trying to convince you that you do not exist! Curiously, when Western wealth-creation activities were primarily facing a supply gap, the pearl of great price was not creativity or innovation but compliance. The pursuit of order portends a strong attraction to many – usually those doing the ordering – and is necessary for some of the adventures of life. If it becomes the norm – the way things are done at all times – it restricts the *creative force*. Practised to excess it can sometimes lead to a dangerous myopic condition. As the forces of change are 'neutralized' or managed for administrative convenience and short-term advantage so the real, long-term cost becomes staggering. Suddenly in a series of unstoppable shifts the contextual factors impacting on wealth creation undeniably enter a period of explosive change. The result is a dangerous crisis that frequently does not play the game by the rules. As instability is met by complacency, living standards are threatened. What is needed is a new management approach that is contextually aware.

In such a predicament we can place our trust in man's ingenuity, but only if it is given sufficient space. All over the West there are many potentially like Richard Branson, Sir John Hall and Anita Roddick. Ordinary individuals just need to believe that it can happen. A vital first step is for an individual to rediscover their own creativity. It is hoped that many honest enquirers will be helped by this chapter.

EXAMPLE 4.1

It can't be done!

This has been the cry that has greeted the publication of many good ideas. However, a creative idea is like a cork – no matter how hard people try to make it sink, it keeps floating back to the surface. Ask Richard Branson whose successful business operations include airline and cola interests as well as a radio station. Or Sir John Hall who built the Metro Centre shopping mall in the North East of England as well as developing Newcastle United Football Club. Or Anita Roddick who pioneered her dream of marketing cosmetics that have not been tested on animals. Then there was those who said that the Japanese would never successfully market cars in Europe or America!

LEARNING OBJECTIVES

After a reflective read through this chapter individuals should be able to appreciate, experience and realize that:

- They are creative.
- They possess considerable latent creativity that just needs to be re-awakened and released.
- The hardware of the brain has amazing possibilities.
- Total thinking makes sense and everyone can do it.
- Problems are not nearly so daunting when exposed to creative thinking.
- The basic tools and techniques are easy to master.

4.2   What is creativity?

4.2.1   Seeking a definition

Creativity is the application of imaginative thought which results in innovative solutions to many problems. Or creativity is the reorganisation of experience (Maier *et al.*, 1967). These solutions usually emerge either through the synthesis of a large amount of material (akin to expertise) or by searching for and finding connections and patterns that others fail to see. *Actively creative people* are unconstrained by rules, regulations, procedures and definitions that surround the problem in question. When faced with a puzzle, such as how to resolve a messy work problem (for example, one involving complex human elements), get a good idea accepted or generate alternative courses of action, *actively creative individuals* respond differently to the rest of us. So to us they seem unconventional, magical, amazing and gifted people that can achieve success in the midst of chaos.

Many of us, if we are honest, find such people strange and perhaps a little odd but do appreciate their achievements. They just operate on another wave length. In terms of the *stimulus–response–learning* model adopted at the close of Part I, they respond differently to challenges than the average person. They are naturally unique. Given man's constant search for order in the balanced disorder that is nature, man has sought throughout history to place rules round his environment in a systematic attempt to control it. In this light, *actively creative individuals* tend be seen as rebels who forever seem to be seeking to escape the boundaries laid down by the rule-sets of the average person. They have often, even when tolerated, been regarded as people who threaten the *status quo* and so need policing. Whilst their ideas are often valued their *modus operandi* are unconventional and, to many, misunderstood.

Throughout the centuries we have sought to box the stimuli that impact on our lives. Short-term successes convince us that we have indeed conquered nature. We can build dykes to control river and sea levels. We can place people in space. We can track and report on weather conditions. We can do much to reduce the uncertainty that natural events evoke. However, we cannot control, except within narrow limits, river and sea levels. We cannot change the weather or climate. These things seem to lie at a higher level of determination –

that of *creation*. Similarly, we can harness the ideas of *actively creative* individuals, as sailors down the ages have harnessed wind power. We cannot stop the wind. The wind is a force that we choose to use, to deflect or to resist. Creativity is like the wind.

The wind is everywhere. Creativity is everywhere. Creativity is in all people – it is a key force, part of creation itself, that distinguishes the highest form of life from other species. It is as real and potentially as useful as our eyes. If we choose to close our eyes then we can still exist but would inevitably condemn ourselves to a substantially reduced experience of life. Eyes are eyes and open eyes are better than closed eyes. Creativity is creativity and *active creativity* is better than frustrated or policed creativity. Creativity is not a theory – it is an ability that we all possess. We can choose to use it, or to constrain it in pursuit of the conformity exhibited by our average person.

This chapter will help you to rediscover creativity for yourself and help you to express it, as long as you keep an open mind. An instant rejection on the basis of 'this is not for me' is disappointing and self-satisfied. In a world that is rapidly changing, such complacency is bound to result in frustration and inner tension. It is denying the very existence of change. It is a fool's paradise. It is lemminglike. It is the philosophy of the dodo. It's unnatural. Like King Canute we cannot control the tides but we have learnt to harness their energy to produce power. Similarly we should not seek to control creativity by attempting to deny it or fence it in but instead encourage all to express their natural creativity. In short, we need to summon up our native inspiration to cope with today's problems (see Part I) not depend on perspiration to advance our causes. King Canute's courtiers soon realized the impossibility of trying to blow back the incoming tide! In reality our concept of the *average person* has been self-induced. We should not fear creativity, for it is a real part of life. What is needed is not a destructive revolution in the way we habitually approach our problems, but a positive revolution (de Bono, 1991) that builds on our existing thinking skills.

4.2.2   Explaining creativity

Many have sought to explain creativity. It is certainly about imaginative thinking that can lead to the discovery of hitherto undiscovered solutions. This it achieves by divergent, as opposed to conventional convergent thinking that seeks to find a predetermined correct solution. (*Encyclopaedia Britannica*, 1991, vol. xxviii). So where does this ability come from? This text will argue that creativity is an inherent characteristic of all peoples. So the question is not so much *how* did it happen but rather one of *how* is it used? It is not a chance happening, a piece of sheer serendipity, although it can sometimes appear as such. It originates from natural expression unrepressed by conventional rules or social norms. It is a manifestation that is usually accompanied by sheer joy. Section 4.5 explores the workings of the mind and describes how creative thought is often preceded by so-called 'right-brain activity' as sound and image suddenly stimulate a connection by association. Most of us have heard the tale of how Sir Isaac Newton discovered gravity from watching apples fall out of a tree. The associationist argument has been made powerfully in modern times by Koestler (1969) and by de Bono (1984) in his exploration of lateral thinking. However, in the end does it really matter how it happens? Why not just rejoice in the fact that it does!

However, is it really important to know *what* causes creativity? Does knowing *what* causes the wind help us? The key issue is surely *how* can we harness the power of the wind. Similarly *how* can we use creativity to benefit our lives? This is a question that directs our attention to discovering, experiencing and harnessing the power of creativity. Given that we are all capable of making a creative response, a useful starting point is to identify the characteristics of *actively creative people*.

4.2.3   Characteristics of actively creative people

Leading qualities that are identified in the literature (e.g. Garnham and Oakhill, 1994; Hellriegel and Slocum, 1975; Kreitner, 1980) include:

1. An ability to find the right problems to address.
2. An ability to defer judgement on possible solutions.
3. A desire for originality.
4. A tendency to resist social forces to conform.
5. A tolerance of ambiguity.
6. An ability to adopt a positive attitude.
7. A strong belief in their personal creativity.

Actively creative people have a talent for getting to the heart of a problem. They are not confused by detail and by the need to invoke standard approaches. They resist the 'quick fix' approach and ponder on the problem, letting their minds find space to express their creativity. They enjoy experimenting with ideas and whilst the answer sometimes comes to them in a flash they are also prepared to toy with a challenge for long periods of time. They are keen to discover new solutions and willing to innovate even if this means having to resist social paradigms and mind-sets – the way we do things here. Another distinguishing trait is their ability to cope with ambiguity in their thinking process – to evaluate several different options at the same time. *Actively creative people*, though often characterized by sudden changes in mood, are predominantly positive and have a strong belief in their own creative ability. A fascinating account of creative people can be found in Sternberg's (1988) *The Nature of Creativity*. To summarize, Goman (1989) defines creative people as people who do not suppress their innate creativity and who use their creative ability in various aspects of life and Maier, Julius and Thurber (1967) as people who can reorganize their experiences.

Theoretically individuals can exhibit creative qualities at any time and so be creative in a number of different fields, as staggeringly exemplified by the achievements of Leonardo da Vinci. There is also evidence to suggest that notable creative responses are often strongly contextual. In this case creative responses emerge from a great deal of work in one field, as typified in Edison's famous remark that 'invention is one per cent inspiration and ninety-nine per cent perspiration' and Louis Pasteur's comment that 'chance favours the prepared mind'. In contrast there are the creative BGOs (blinding glimpses of the obvious) that most people have experienced at some time or another which can often happen right out of the blue! The good news is that all of us have the ability to be creative; we simply need to believe it.

4.2.4   Studying actively creative people

Research into creative people has tended to adopt either a psychometric or an auto-biographical/biographical approach.

Psychometric research

This set out to discover what creative people are like with a view to designing, running and validating psychometric tests that can measure personal creativity potential. The work of such writers as Tardif and Sternberg (1988) identified a variety of cognitive traits that distinguished highly creative people. Sternberg argued that creative thinkers are distinguished by their form of mental self-government. They prefer a legislative (rule creating), rather than an executive (rule following) or judicial (rule assessing) style. Perhaps the most significant discoveries to emerge came out of the work of Getzels and Csikszentmihalyi (1976), who found that highly creative people seemed to posses the ability to pick the right problem to investigate, and that of MacKinnon (1962), who discovered that highly creative people possessed a marked ability to defer judgement on possible solutions.

When the Russians achieved a propaganda coup by beating the Americans into space with their Sputnik programme the Americans reacted by launching an initiative to find their creative brains. This gave a great fillip to the psychometric study of creativity. The most valuable research, in terms of its long-term durability, was undertaken by J. P. Guilford (1956, 1967, 1986), who studied conventional convergent thinking (one answer) and the unconventional divergent thinking (many answers).

Autobiographical/biographical research

Autobiographical and biographical studies have attempted to discover if actively creative people display a characteristic set of behaviour responses. The evidence of the literature suggests that creativity is very difficult to pin down. It is seemingly impossible to bottle, perhaps because it is the genie in the bottle. One thing that can be said with a degree of confidence is that there appears to be no close connection between creativity and intelligence (Hudson, 1987). For example, Einstein was a late reader and only achieved a mediocre performance at school! One of the most interesting things to emerge from the biographical studies was the four-stage account of creative thinking put forward by Wallas (1926) in his *The Art of Thought*:

1. *Preparation stage*, in which a great deal of information is absorbed prior to a problem being developed.
2. *Incubation stage*, where the problem is set aside and the mind diverts on a number of excursive activities.
3. *Inspiration stage*, where the solution appears either suddenly or by means of a sign-posted intimation.
4. *Verification stage*, where the solution is tested for its aptness and practicality.

Wallas found that these stages were not always separate. Several of the biographical accounts that he studied revealed considerable degrees of overlap. In general, creativity appears to flourish when possible solutions are not narrowed down too soon. This is related to the idea of tolerance of ambiguity that was a feature of the psychometric studies.

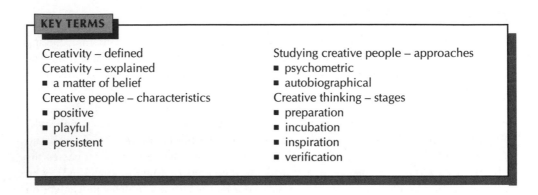

KEY TERMS

Creativity – defined
Creativity – explained
■ a matter of belief
Creative people – characteristics
■ positive
■ playful
■ persistent

Studying creative people – approaches
■ psychometric
■ autobiographical
Creative thinking – stages
■ preparation
■ incubation
■ inspiration
■ verification

4.3   Encouraging creativity

4.3.1   Contextual factors

Anyone is capable of responding creatively. The issue is to what end and how often. Of course some will be naturally more creative than others. Figure 4.1 illustrates some of the ways that ordinary everyday people exhibit creativity. The degree to which personal creativity occurs depends on a complex set of environmental or contextual factors. Social pressures, such as the pressure to conform to group norms, can either encourage or discourage creativity depending on the value placed on such activity by the dominant social rules. Technology can trigger creativity when a new and accepted (wanted) application suddenly appears. A useful example of this is provided by the development of the electric toothbrush that took off after the technology behind rechargeable batteries was perfected. Economic factors too can play their part, as many on low budgets know when they 'make a penny do the work of a pound'. Finally, political factors can influence creative responses. Examples of this include a variety of novel ways of 'getting round' – legally and otherwise – existing and proposed legislation. Take some time out and think of a handful of examples!

Whilst creativity will occur, to some degree, even when it is discouraged and opposed by organizations in society, its incidence increases if it is actively encouraged. This coaxing has to occur at two distinct levels: that of the individual and that of the social groups/organizations to which the individual belongs. An adult, like a child, needs to feel safe if he or she is to play creatively. Heightened tension and emotional pressure are bad for creativity. The individual has to experience a satisfactory level of safety and to trust the personnel around him or her. No trust, little creativity.

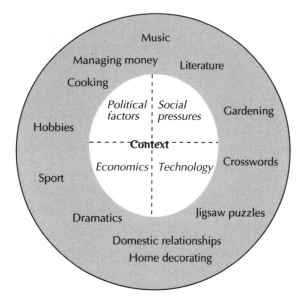

Figure 4.1 Activities that entail personal creativity

Organizations and creativity

Organizations cannot respond creatively. What they can do, though, is to actively encourage their individuals. Thus the incidence of creative activity is contextually governed
by the degree of group and/or organizational support. At the individual level the vibes
that are in the air have to be convincing. Corporate motherhood statements and other
forms of 'chin music' are to no avail unless the 'place feels right'. When this is the case
then the people will invoke the processes and creative responses will occur.

Managers and creativity

Thus managers have to make a real commitment, openly welcome creative responses and
then champion them. They need to adopt a new approach and develop individual personal relationships with their staff. The 'one manager, several staff members, one corporate relationship for all' strategy needs to become a process of the past. Whilst there
always has been a body of very good managers in organizational life, many have chosen
to play the detached corporate game. Not all car dealers are untrustworthy. The ones
who are ruin things for those who are not. If individual members of staff are to open up
and invoke creative responses they will need to *trust* their managers.

Figure 4.2 Management styles

Behaviour trait	High	High/medium	Medium/low	Low
Approachable				
Honest				
Supportive				
Fair				
Open dealing				
Communicative				
Total				

This will depend not on the individual manager's perception of him- or herself but rather the staff's collective perception of the manager. Food for thought! If you are a manager respond, on a separate sheet of paper, to the brief questionnaire in Figure 4.2 by ticking the appropriate column. Now turn to Appendix 4.1 and score your responses. Would you be happy for your staff to complete this questionnaire? Do you think that they would broadly agree with your perceptions?

Figure 4.3 presents a matrix that looks at individual staff and managers' interests. The ideal situation is when the interest of the manager and the individual is high. This is the high-trust quadrant and will enable the manager to cultivate creative responses and excellence. The quadrant below, high/medium trust, is when the individual is convinced of the manager's personal support but doubts if the manager really values the support of the individual. The quadrant to the left is where the interests of both are low. This produces mutual indifference. Finally, the quadrant above this is where the manager's interest is high and the individual member of staff's is low. This results in low trust, if any, as the individual assumes the worst.

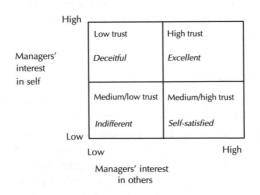

Figure 4.3 The perceived interests of managers

KEY TERMS

Creative/contextual responses
- social pressures
- technological factors
- economic factors
- political factors

Encouraging creativity
- individual aspects
- organizational aspects
- management aspects

Importance of trust

4.4 Capturing creativity

4.4.1 Using the what comes naturally

Whilst it is true that all individuals possess creativity – it's a gift of nature – most of us fail to make the most of it. As creativity is a dynamic phenomenon, a force, we cannot learn to improve effectively our use of it by only studying the literature. If we realistically wish to develop our creativity skills then we must be prepared *to have a go*. The first crucial challenge facing many individuals is to overcome their shyness and apprehension and let the genie out of the bottle. Starting with the knowledge that all individuals are creative is both reassuring and challenging. It provides comfort in that most of us are aware of our creative achievements, no matter what private beliefs we may harbour about their frequency, strength or durability. It presents a challenge because most will readily accept that any skill can be developed by sustained exercise.

Car drivers have to overcome inhibitions and agree to take their first driving lesson. Then, despite the possibility of a few shocks and surprises, they need the resolution to see a driving tuition programme through and subsequently to present themselves for examination. If successful most drivers then cease to put a lot of sustained effort into improving their general driving skills. Experience on the open road does develop their driving skills in some respects but also leaves them prey to developing bad habits. Most, for example, fail to continuously update their knowledge of the Highway Code. In short, many of us become lazy. We are easily satisfied with a relatively low level of achievement. Some of us later rue this, when a sudden challenge to our skill response leaves us wanting. As the environment on the roads is constantly changing we would be wise to keep our relative skill level high. Frequently the problems we face are the result of someone else's failings. Thus to survive on today's roads we need to be both continuously updating our own driving skills and learning how to cope with the mistakes of others. Passing the driving test and just driving is not sufficient. Likewise, making do with our natural creativity skill level is not enough.

4.4.2 Taking stock

If we are intent on discovering what we can do to improve our creativity, then it is helpful to start by getting a measure as to *where* we are now. This can be achieved, to some extent, by recourse to an appropriate audit or inventory. An improvement programme can then build on this apparent skill level. It is important to realize that such 'tests' are not infallible measures of our creative performance. They merely confirm that we are creative and provide some indicative evidence of the use to which we consciously put creative skills. A subsequent running of the selected audit should then provide evidence of development.

There are a number of tests widely available that can help us to get a picture of our present level of creative activity. However, few were designed exclusively to reflect creative responses. Most are intended to reveal other personal characteristics such as psychological type (Briggs and McCaulley, 1988), personality (16PF), learning style (Kolb, 1984b; Honey and Mumford, 1985) or team working attributes (Belbin, 1981). One (Kirton, 1987) was developed to measure creative style.

4.4.3 Personal creativity audit (PCA)

The *personal creativity audit* (PCA) was developed to provide evidence that individuals are creative and to give an indication of an individual's tendency to use creativity skills in daily situations. Appendix 4.2 contains our PCA together with response and scoring instructions. For any such inventory to be useful it has to be capable of measuring *what* it is intended to measure and to be reliable in the responses that it elicits from respondents. However, some people will inevitably try to read the algorithm to deliberately register high scores rather than complete the inventory with a view to seeing what it says about them. Despite these reservations such inventories can provide a snapshot that can be illuminating.

4.4.4 The release of group activity

Belbin's team roles

In a study first published in the mid 1970s that addressed the subject of successful teams (the release of creativity in the group situation to provide a winning outcome), Dr Belbin suggested that there were a number of finite and limited roles 'adopted naturally by the various personality-types found among managers' (Adair, 1987). These team roles included a Chairman, Plant, Monitor/Evaluator, Company Worker, Team Worker, Resource Investigator and Completer. An additional role of Chairperson was added later to the profile inventory (Table 4.1).

This inventory produces well-balanced teams and looks to the people-oriented Chairperson to keep the group together and moving in the right direction, the task-oriented Shaper to see that the job is achieved and the Plant to provide the creative spark. The other five roles are supportive ones once the people, task and ideas inputs have been addressed.

Table 4.1 **The Belbin Roles**

Role	Description
Chairperson (CH)	Good with people
Shaper (SH)	Good at getting things done
Plant (PL)	Good at generating ideas
Resource Investigator (RI)	Good at finding out what is needed
Monitor/Evaluator	Good at measuring progress and performance
Team Worker (TW)	Good at supporting and helping the group
Implementor (IMP)	Good at working for the organization
Completer/Finisher (CF)	Good at attending to detail to get the job done

4.4.5 The MBTI inventory

Jung's personality typologies

The Swiss psychiatrist Carl Gustav Jung, though an early follower of Freud, advocated that behaviour was influenced by drives other than purely sexual ones. He studied the differences between people and developed a set of typologies that reflected whether individual personalities were characterized by a tendency toward introversion or extroversion. He described four basic preference scales (see Figure 4.4).

Extroverts (E) tend to look outward and focus on an outer world of people and things. Thus they prefer to communicate verbally rather than in writing and tend to prefer action and variety. *Introverts (I)*, on the other hand, prefer to focus more on their inner world and they can appear to be timid and shy. *Sensing (S)* types prefer to work with what is given and so appear as practical people that have an eye for detail and prefer proven methods. Lastly, *Intuitive (N)* individuals can look beyond their senses and harness their imagination in order to see new possibilities and are not too bothered with points of detail.

For each of the four preference scales Jung identified two opposite preferences. *Thinking* types rely heavily on their powers of reason and are good at sizing up situations. *Feeling* types, on the other hand, pay an especial regard to the impact of their behaviour on others. *Judgers* have a strong liking for order, control and organization. Lastly, *Perceivers* prefer to react and adapt to the moment and thus appear more flexible (see Myers-Briggs, 1987).

The sixteen types described are not intended to be predictive but to assist individuals to recognize their own and other's gifts. The assessment procedure selects the highest score on each of the four scales as being the dominant characteristic of the individual. So, for example, a person who scores 10 for extroversion and 13 for introversion would be classified by the MBTI inventory as being introverted. As with the KAI inventory, environmental factors can distort the results.

Figure 4.4   Jung's personality typologies

1. *Extroversion* (E), looking outward.	*Introversion* (I), looking inward.
2. *Sensing* (S), manipulating facts according to established procedures.	*Intuition* (N), using imagination and refusing to be submerged by detail.
3. *Thinking* (T), application of logic and analysis in decision-making.	*Feeling* (F), reacting to personal preferences (own and others) and value sets.
4. *Judging* (J), tendency to be organized and controlled.	*Perceiving* (P), tendency to be spontaneous and flexible.

4.4.6   The KAI inventory

Kirton's KAI Inventory (Kirton, 1987) seeks to assess individual's response styles in terms of their characteristic approaches to decision making. His *adaption-innovation theory* places individuals on a continuum from highly adaptive to highly innovative. Adaptive individuals are seen as those who like to do things better within the same personal, group and organizational standard practices or mind-sets. They prefer not to rock the boat. They are less radical in their approach than innovators and so their failures tend to be less damaging to their reputation. They quite easily work with others. Innovators, on the other hand, approach problems from an entirely different perspective. They tend to escape from the mind-sets that surround the problem, the organizational environment, and look for inspiration by exploring the problem in another environmental setting. They reconstruct the problem and tend to produce less conventional solutions. They often find it difficult to work with others and many see them as being abrasive and insensitive.

The KAI continuum ranges from 32 (extreme adaptor) to 160 (extreme innovator) with a mean of 95. A difference of ten points between individuals can lead to communication difficulties. The inventory seeks to measure an individual's response to three sub-scales:

O *Originality* which has a range from 13 to 65 and a mean of 39. Innovators with a high score tend to produce a proliferation of ideas, whether needed or not and tend to adopt a radical style.

E *Efficiency* which has a range from 7 to 35 and a mean of 21.

R *Conformity* which has a range from 12 to 60.

The question remains what is it measuring? The way individuals respond to the KAI inventory is influenced by the key stimulants that they experience in their total living environment (domestic and professional). As much of Kirton's work was researched within an organizational context the organization itself will significantly affect the KAI score. Individuals will be more inclined to work within the accepted mind-sets in tight cultures than they will be in freer environments. Whilst it is undeniable that the KAI inventory does reveal some interesting information about individuals it also says quite a lot about the organizations in which they work. High-trust managers, groups and organizations are more likely to encourage what Kirton terms 'innovative' responses than restrictive cultures. It can therefore be difficult to determine what is the characteristic style. Is it that of the individual? That of the organization? There is a danger with the KAI inventory that organizations may see it as a way of classifying individuals according to their perceived level of creativity. Despite Kirton's efforts to prevent this – as he does argue that creativity can be exhibited at both ends of his continuum – many users or his inventory probably do associate *active creativity* with a high KAI score.

4.4.7 Multiple dimensions

Testing for creativity – the pitfalls

Both our Personal Creativity Audit (PCA) and Kirton's KAI inventory can only detect evidence of the level of creative activity at the time that an individual responded to the test questionnaire. Neither of these inventories should be taken as evidence of an individual's permanent creative attainment level. This is influenced by a complex set of factors that reflect their personal awareness of the potential of creative thinking, their ability to exercise left- and right-brain thinking skills and their current creative problem solving (CPS) ability. In addition, external stimuli such as social and organizational cultures strongly affect the level of personal creativity. If these inventories are completed at work the level of recorded personal creativity is likely to be heavily influenced by cultural factors and thus may tell us more about the host organization than about the individual.

Personal inventories, such as the MBTI and 16PF, do include some questions that can detect evidence or otherwise of creative output. As with the PCA and KAI inventories, their results are to be evaluated with caution. They are not prescriptive but if administered correctly may well be indicative. Much research has gone into the evaluation of psychometric testing in recent years and it would appear that the results must indeed be treated very carefully. As might be expected, it is possible to obtain some correlation between creativity and personality inventory scores. This has been identified in studies that have looked at data generated by the KAI and MBTI scores. As Jung's typologies heavily influenced the work of Kolb, as well as that of Briggs-Meyer, it is not surprising to find some relation between the Kolb Learning Systems Inventory and MBTI data.

As few individuals work totally alone it is pertinent to include a reference to a well-known group audit. Belbin's research (Belbin, 1981) indicated that eight key functions needed to be present in a balanced mix for teams to perform effectively (See Table 4.1). Whilst one of these is very much concerned with generating creative thinking (Plant) it should not be forgotten that this is primarily to spark the creativity of the others in the team.

Stimulating creative thinking

To think creatively individuals have to really believe that they enjoy the freedom to think in ways different from the accepted norms (the ways in which things are normally done). For this to happen regularly individuals should be given a succession of positive challenges and be constantly encouraged to perform to the best of their abilities. 'Carrot and stick', excessively autocratic management styles tend to cause creative output to die away to residual levels. This reductionist approach in the management of creativity is the opposite of what is needed when organizations are battling for business in crowded markets. To achieve a consistent market edge creative thinking must be released and continuously supported.

Creativity and intelligence

Many people strongly associate creative thinking with intelligence. Like many things in life, this is both true and untrue. Research into this question has not as far as is known come up with any conclusive proof that intelligent people *per se* are generally more creative than individuals who would not see themselves as being intelligent. Then what is meant by intelligence? There is a body of evidence that suggests that creative people tend to have high IQs, but not all people with high IQs are creative. Many of the psychometric profiles that have been constructed have often been built from data that has been recorded from tests that were originally intended to measure IQ levels. Several, notably Getzels and Jackson (1962), Torrance (1988) and Baron (1988), have tried to devise and validate tests that can accurately detect and measure the presence or otherwise of creativity. At present the hypothesis that intelligent people are *per se* also creative remains unproved. Creativity can flourish in all people and it is usualy just a question of letting the genie out of the bottle.

Personal creativity in action

How do you think that you can help yourself to release more of your natural creativity? Take a short break and try to jot down at least five ideas.

Here are a few exercises and ideas to help you develop your own creative thinking.

1. How many potential uses can you think of for an ordinary paper clip?

2. Irrespective of how good an artist you judge yourself to be, grab a piece of paper (A4 size is ideal) and try and draw a quick head and shoulders sketch of yourself. Now choose a hat from the options below.

   Mexican hat
   Top hat

Cloth cap
Deerstalker
Chef's hat

Now draw your chosen hat on your head and shoulders sketch.

Why did you choose the hat that you did? Express your reasons in a short sentence.

Would you have preferred to have chosen one of the other hats? If so, which one and why did you pass it by? If it was because you had doubts as to whether you could draw it . . . have a go right now.

3. How many uses can you think of for an ordinary builder's brick?

4. Ponder on these quotations:

   'According to all the laws of aerodynamics, a bumble bee cannot possibly fly. The bumble bee does not know this, so it goes ahead and flies anyway.' (Anonymous)

   'When in doubt, make a fool of yourself. There is a microscopically thin line between being brilliantly creative and acting like the most gigantic idiot on earth. So what the hell, leap.' (Cynthia Heimal, Lower Manhattan Survival Tactics, *Village Voice*, 1983)

5. Play a track of your favourite music. How would you:

   i.   Briefly describe it with words?
   ii. With pictures?
   iii. Can you hum it unaccompanied?

6. Look out of the window and focus for half a minute on an object.

   Now close your eyes. Think of something that has been troubling you today.

   Think about the object . . . make any connections? Get any good ideas?

   If not, try again, and you too can experience the *Eureka* effect!

Work environment and performance

No matter how we look at individual responses there is little doubt that the organizational work environment has a direct effect on the performance. The role models, paradigms, reward systems, management culture, peer pressures, official, unofficial and psychological contracts all act to encourage some responses and to discourage others. Capturing creativity in organizations places – as will be explored in Chapters 5 and 6 – a considerable responsibility on individuals who seek to work in teams. Figure 4.5 summarizes four response sets that we have discovered in our own research work in England. If an individual is working in an environment where the management are highly concerned about their own interests and render a poor regard to the individual's interest, then this is likely to result in programmed, robotic responses from the

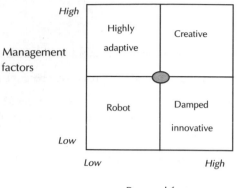

Figure 4.5 Individual response patterns resulting from interpreted management responses

member of staff. This situation is typified by people going through the motions to earn their corn and is unlikely to encourage a creative attitude to the job. Where the management are concerned with the personal wishes of their staff this will trigger a reciprocal response from the individuals and will provide the opportunity for highly creative responses. However, if these responses are not continuously encouraged and action is not seen to result, then this can lead, sadly, to situations where the individual becomes disenchanted. If this occurs, then initiative and interest are effectively lost and the individual will slip into the damped innovation quartile and possibly to the robot quartile.

Indicative information only

Whilst there is merit in an individual taking stock and seeking to discover a position on an audit such as KAI, MBTI or LSI, it must be remembered that these inventories only provide, at best, some indicative information. This information must be closely vetted for its contextual relevance – most people appear to be different at home than they are at work. Most psychometric tests carry error propensities resulting from a variety of factors such as environmental/contextual issues, test procedures and classification typologies, and so on. Furthermore some individuals may be discouraged by the results of such inventories and so withdraw into themselves, especially if they perceive that management are not very interested in them. Others may, unless carefully advised, believe that core behaviours and responses cannot be changed. Whilst this is true for the broad personality characteristics that tend to be set in the first twenty years of life, it is not true for several learnt behavioural responses that can be changed. Individuals can choose to change many of their behavioural responses such as learning and skill styles.

Creativity – a natural gift

Creativity is part of the whole (*gestalt*) of every individual. It is a natural gift that can and should be encouraged. This offers the individual the opportunity to derive more satisfaction out of life. Understanding creativity is difficult if we strive to define it in rules and try to put it in a box. By its very nature it is unpredictable, unique, infectious and real. Most, excepting those with closed minds, can quickly appreciate it when they see it. True creativity has a beauty of its own that often defies logical explanation. So are civilizations all over the world in danger of losing their way by attempting to justify creativity? Can it be bottled, or concentrated in a pill and swallowed? Is it possible to control it by logic alone? Or is it a mysterious force that seems to bless us in puzzling, usually joyful, ways?

Creativity is a unique force that distinguishes the higher orders of fauna, such as *Homo sapiens* from the rest of creation. Other creatures are capable of expressing creativity and creative thought. Squirrels, for example, can do amazing things in pursuit of food. Humans, however, are generally accepted to be the most advanced form of created life. So the way in which humans think would seem to hold promise if we are fully to appreciate human creativity and fully achieve our individual potential to express it. The next section explains how the human brain works. Prepare to be surprised by joy.

KEY TERMS

Creative force	Audit comparisons
Creativity audits	Audits – indicative not prescriptive
▪ PCA	Gestalt
▪ KAI	A life force
▪ MBTI	

4.5 The incredible machine

4.5.1 Physiology of the brain

Organic computer

By any account the human brain is an incredible machine. It controls all the activities and reactions of the body and is the centre of emotion, memory, and personality. Whereas the heart is the functional centre, the pump that circulates our blood, it is the brain, the organic computer, that is the true expression of life. Whereas the heart enables us to be, the brain enables us to live. It is made up of millions of very small cells called *neurons*. The average individual has over ten thousand million of them (*Encyclopaedia Britannica*, 1991). There are two categories of cells: those that carry information to and from the body via the spinal cord and those that cross-connect the constituent parts of the brain.

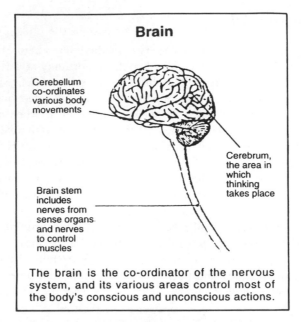

Brain

Cerebellum co-ordinates various body movements

Cerebrum, the area in which thinking takes place

Brain stem includes nerves from sense organs and nerves to control muscles

The brain is the co-ordinator of the nervous system, and its various areas control most of the body's conscious and unconscious actions.

Figure 4.6 Lateral view of cerebrum, cerebellum

Basically there are three key parts to the brain: the *cerebrum*, the *cerebellum* and *brain stem* or *medulla oblongata*, as shown in Figure 4.6.

The *cerebrum* is the largest and most highly developed part of the brain and on inspection looks a little like a walnut. It consists of two approximately equal halves or lobes called the *cerebral hemispheres*. In humans this part of the brain is so large that it has had to be wrinkled, like a walnut, to fit into our shells or skulls. The surface of the *cerebrum* is referred to as the *cerebral cortex* or grey matter. Below the *cerebral cortex* is the white matter that is a mass of nerve fibres connecting the *cortex* with the body and other parts of the brain. Information flows into the brain from the body by a process known as *sensation*. Messages come from the skin, the muscles, the eyes, the ears, nose and other sense organs by the sensory nerves. The brain processes the information and then sends out responses along the *motor nerves* to the muscles of the body that control all the body movements. Different areas of the *cortex* control different parts of the body. Curiously the left side of the brain controls the right side of the body and vice versa, with the centre brain somehow co-ordinating this activity.

The *cortex* is the place that determines our awareness of the environment around us. The eyes look at the world and the ears listen but it is the cortex that sees, hears and understands. It decides what responses to trigger having evaluated the external stimuli. This is where trust or suspicion are determined and it is the centre of our creativity.

The *cerebellum* is below the *cerebrum* (see Figure 4.6) and assists the cerebral cortex by providing fine control of intricate movements, such as walking, writing and driving.

The *medulla oblongata*, or brain stem, connects the cerebrum and cerebellum to the spinal cord and so to the rest of the body. This part of the brain provides a largely automatic control of the body's internal organs.

The working brain – a synaptic wonder

Each brain cell or *neuron* is structurally independent. In other words, they do not come into contact with each other. They communicate with other cells by a subtle interchange of complex electrochemical signals between the gaps between the cells. This process is known as *contiguity* and was first advanced by the Spanish scientist Ramon y Cajal in 1889. Each neuron has three distinct components: the cell body or *soma*; the main nerve fibre or *axon*, which is the main exit of information transmitted by the cell; and a number of receiving branches or *dendrites*. Dendrites and axons range in size from a millimetre to one and a half metres in length. All along their length are little acorn like shapes called *dendritic spines* or *synaptic buttons* that contain chemical material which provide the means for connections to be made between brain cells. This occurs when an electrical impulse travels through the liquid-filled space between two adjacent cells and connects their synaptic buttons.

The amount of activity going on in the brain is incredible. It can usefully be likened to the amount of traffic through a busy telephone exchange. Incoming messages are automatically connected to a multitude of cells as the brain processes the input stimuli to produce a suitable response or outcome. This is the product of a complex evaluation procedure that co-ordinates the contributions of thousands of individual brain cells and produces a distinct electro-magnetic routing or pathway that is known as a *memory trace*. If the same or similar stimuli or enquiry is repeated, then the brain automatically energizes the memory traces it formed, thus speeding up the response time. This is the essence of *learning*. As each brain cell is capable of directing information to as many as 10,000 other brain cells in the same instant, the problem-solving potential at the individual's disposal is virtually infinite.

4.5.2 Right- and left-brain thinking

Seats of learning

Having briefly described the workings of the brain it is time to return to the *cerebral cortex* to see how it handles the key intellectual components of thinking. The American psychologist, Professor R. W. Sperry posed that the two hemispheres of the cortex appeared to control separate, distinct intellectual enquiries (see Figure 4.7).

The right hemisphere appeared to be active in the processing of the following addresses:

- rhythm;
- spatial awareness;
- gestalt (wholeness);
- imagination;
- colour; and
- dimension;

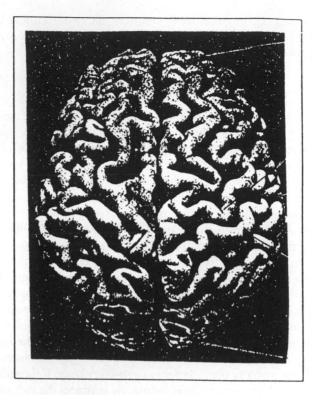

Figure 4.7 Contextual hemispheres

whilst the left hemisphere seemed to process an equally important but different pattern of memory traces covering a variety of learned skills including:

- language;
- logic;
- quantitative ability;
- sequential ability;
- linear ability; and
- analytical ability.

Learning skills

When the range of skills – the ability to cut, develop and maintain complex memory trace sets – of both cortextual hemispheres are combined, the individual has a dazzling potential to develop his or her thinking. The equipment is there for us to generate an amazing array of responses. The degree to which we are able to do this is a function of our thinking skills and our determination to improve them.

Many of us regard thinking as a natural skill and tend to get lazy in our approaches to information processing and problem solving. Effective thinkers take care of their grey matter as an athlete takes care of his physical skills. To do our best we need to look after our brains. If we look at the incredible human machine in computer terms, as a unit of hardware, then we can work towards getting the maximum from it by paying attention to how we put it to use. Thinking can be likened to the sustained development of software. The quality of output produced by computers is directly related to the quality of the input (in terms of clarity – the *what*); the method of processing it (software – the *how*); and the performance specification of the machine (individual ability). Whilst it is true that each individual has a different potential in terms of *what* can be achieved, as some are just cleverer than others, many of us can improve our thinking performance by making the best use of our potential. This can be achieved by thinking about thinking in order to select the most appropriate approach to solving a particular problem. Many of us try to get our brains to give us an instant answer or quick fix. We turn on our hardware and use the software already installed. If this can find the required collection of memory traces then this represents our thinking. Whilst this is probably in order for familiar problems this rather mechanistic or programmed approach will not serve us too well with rather more complex and or infrequent problems. This requires *total* as opposed to *partial thinking*.

4.5.3   Total thinking

Total thinking, it is posited, occurs when we seek to focus the full power of our brain that we can activate on a problem. This means using the potential of both hemispheres of the cortex described above. Strange as it may seem, many peoples around the world choose to develop the skills in the left hemisphere to a higher level than those of the right hemisphere. This produces an overdependence on logic as a key response to stimuli and the associated tendency to try to think in terms of programmed patterns. Overdependence on such *partial thinking* can result from personal choice or from a perception that the intuitive, emotive and 'arty' skills such as colour, design, imagination, movement, and sound are in general not the way to behave in public. This is curious as many of us actually take part in activities that utilize these skills in public as well as paying to view other people performing! Obviously there has been some sustained conditioning here that over time has resulted in the development of certain traditions or paradigms that preclude the regular adoption in our public lives of many right brain-skills.

Half-brained thinkers!

Both hemispheres of the cortex provide potentially powerful problem-solving power. In reality all individuals will display a degree of *total thinking* in their private and professional lives. The issue is the degree. In most cases it is small, as individuals tend to select a thinking style that is usually highly biased to the left hemisphere, and so in terms of degree are predominantly *partial thinkers*. Gifted artistic individuals can exhibit the reverse pattern. Both will fail to achieve the benefits that flow from a better-balanced use of total thinking. In many respects such people could, with tongue in cheek, be accused of half-brained thinking! Perfection, defined as a completely balanced total thinking approach to life, is very difficult to achieve. However, as the positive benefits from minor gains in our use of both left- and right-brained thinking are so immense all are capable of developing their problem-solving performance. The question is whether we choose to do so.

4.5.4 Limbering up

The next section sets out some ideas and routines designed to appeal to all those who genuinely wish – recognizing that they will need to put some work into it – to develop their thinking performance. See if you can solve the problem in Exercise 4.1 in five minutes – time yourself. If you think that you are happy with your answer after the five minutes are up, then turn to Appendix 4.3 to see if you have got the correct solution. If you are still puzzled, then have another go.

EXERCISE 4.1   Peking Express

1. Four spies in trench coats sat in four facing seats.
2. They travelled the Peking Express.
3. With two by the window and two by the aisle.
4. The arrangement was strange as you've guessed.
5. The British spy sat on Mr B's left.
6. Mr A had a tan-coloured coat.
7. The Spy dressed in olive was on the German's right.
8. Mr C was the only cigar-smoking man.
9. Mr D was across from the American spy.
10. The Russian, in khaki, had a scarf around his throat.
11. The British spy stared out of the window on his left.
12. *So who was the spy in the rust coloured coat?*

4.5.5 Problems . . . problems . . . problems!

What is a problem?

All over the world individuals have problems, but what is a problem? Think for a moment. A problem must be contextual – relevant to a particular time and situation. How did it occur? How important is it? Is there any potential for resolving the problem? Problems occur when we are in danger of selecting the wrong or only partially satisfactory response to stimuli and or events that confront us. This can result from uncertainty as to *how* to deal with the challenge. For example, finishing this text is a problem when the computer breaks down. Getting to work can be a problem when the car breaks down. Achieving at work can be a problem if the organization is tearing itself apart with politics rather than consolidating and co-ordinating its talents to serve its clientele. Poor communication is a problem as it generally restricts the performance of an organization. A problem is a problem when people sense that something is wrong but do not know what it is. Ranking problems in order of importance is a problem.

In short, a problem arises when an individual needs to achieve something and is faced with difficulties. These often arise from a poorly focused appreciation of the real problem, poor problem-solving ability, and the presence of real or imaginary obstacles.

Programmed responses to most stimuli?

As we deal with familiar problems we progressively develop a complex of memory traces that enable us to respond constructively. If the stimuli that produced the problem alter slightly, many are in danger of invoking the standard thinking response and so may fail to completely solve the problem. Many problems in life do not call for a single spot-on solution. If the stimuli now change significantly there is a danger that many individuals will still adopt the default problem-solving sequence and progressively accept weaker and weaker solutions. This often happens in rule-bound mechanistic organizations that are judgemental about both what has to be done and how it is to be done. The discussion in Part I of this text revealed how organizations can be stranded as they seek to preserve their inner world order as the outer world order is changing. This, sadly, unless addressed in time will result in myopic behaviour in a fantasy world.

Context, creativity and commitment

It is important to determine fully the true context of every problem. This is a basic thinking task for every individual. Failure to do so, whether born of ignorance or lazy thinking, will inevitably result in poor decision making. The key to making progress, as argued in this text, is to improve our *total thinking* in *real time* by consciously seeking to develop our natural creativity. This is not a quick push-button solution. It requires a personal commitment, first, to embark on an experiential journey, and then to finish the trip. Perhaps the first big step is to explore the right-brain domain.

4.5.6 Discovering the other side of the brain

Source of creativity

When Christopher Columbus left the known world and set sail in search of a new route to the Indies he discovered the American continent. Or rather he found it because it was already there. Furthermore some positive effects of this huge land mass, such as the Gulf Stream had been impacting on the known European world for ages. When individuals

1 Just dots?

Figure 4.8   Mystery face
Source: *Pentagram.*

2 The hexacube

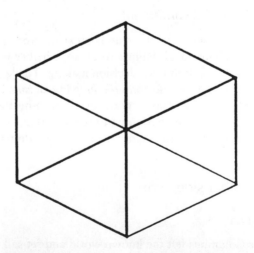

Figure 4.9   Hexagon or cube?
Source: *Pentagram.*

Here is an old lady. Here is also a young girl. If you can't see them both, try making the young girl's chin the nose of the old lady. This was first published by W. E. Hill in 1915.

Figure 4.10   Two faces in one
Source: *Pentagram.*

At first it seems just a jumble of shapes. Try turning the page anticlockwise through ninety degrees – then you should see something.

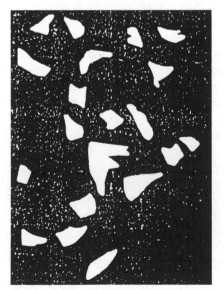

Figure 4.11   Horse sense?
Source: *Pentagram.*

Figure 4.12   Seeing is believing
Source: *Pentagram.*

discover something it provides the opportunity to explore its properties. Whereas vivid photographs and intricate medical sketches can logically convince us that there are two sides to the brain, the will to explore the unfamiliar side can be discouraged by personal and social convention. The reality is that both the right and left hemispheres work in a mysterious yet incredible manner to generate *true creativity*. This is a magical fusing of inspiration with perspiration. Whilst individuals can learn to think more creatively through learning (Thomson, 1959), few of us are sufficiently talented to be able to do everything. For example, Mozart was a brilliant musician but, according to numerous biographers, was not too successful at managing his business affairs. Closer to our own times there are many tales of inventors who have had brilliant ideas but have failed to exploit them successfully. Sir Clive Sinclair provides a classic example. Why this should be the case is not clear. Perhaps fertile minds grow bored with matters of detail that fail to interest them. Fortunately, other men and women are talented at converting ideas and inventions into products and services that others can appreciate. This is the role of the innovator. However, appreciation, though important, is not possession. To move a product or service innovation into the market place requires the especial gifts of the entrepreneur, as typified in the achievements of people such as Anita Roddick (Bodyshop), Richard Branson (Virgin Group) and Sir John Hall. The crowded markets of today place a high premium on a constant supply of new products and services. If *total thinking* unites the hemispheres of the brain then *effective creativity* represents the sustained partnership of idea generators, innovators and entrepreneurs.

Right-brain activity is happening all the time but is the average individual aware of this? Is such activity personally censored owing to a mistaken belief such as that captured in the oft heard retort, 'I'm basically not a creative sort of person'. Or its organizational equivalent, 'That's not the way we do things here'. To discover your potential have a go at the exercises in Figures 4.8–4.12. What do you see in those five graphics? You may like to photocopy them first. The point of these exercises is to reinforce the indication given in your personal creativity audit that you are creative and that you do use right-brained skills in expressing it. If you had trouble with Exercise 4.1 above, try it again and this time translate the problem into graphical images. You should find that this helps you to solve the problem easily.

Graphical images, movement, sound and imagination are powerful ways of expressing some truths which are not always easily presented in words. We all use right-brain thinking to check the sincerity of verbal messages. We are all capable of fantastic flights of imagination and can dream during the day as well as the night. Incidentally, do you dream? How do you remember your dreams?

4.5.7 Developing total thinking

If we focus our minds on a particular problem that is vexing us then we will, eventually, harness both left- and right-brain thinking and achieve a degree of total thinking. This, in whatever strength we can attain, carries a real inner peace however we are led to respond. Nevertheless, on many occasions we go for the quick solution, the instant action route which often is a well-worn track to disappointment. All individuals can improve their problem-solving abilities if they invest a little time and energy in developing both left- and right-brain skills.

Metaphor – bridging the gap

When individuals get bogged down in traditional left-brain thinking they often unconsciously attempt to tap into right-brain skills by resorting to the use of metaphors.

Table 4.5 **Some individual metaphors**

Individual metaphor	Meaning
Nature	
Iron horse	Determined progress
Lion	Brave, fierce character
Lamb	Meek person
Butterfly	Flits from problem to problem
Sport	
First passed the post	Winner

Table 4.6   **Jensen's categories of metaphors**

Major category	Subcategory	Examples
Restoration	Medical	Ills, rash, cancer
	Theft	Stolen, robbed
	Repairman	Repair, broken down
	Cleansing	Clean up, dirty
Journey	On land	Barriers, maze
	On water	Blocked channels
Unification	Family	Home, offspring
	Shepherd	Flock
	Sports	Team, out of bounds
Creational	Edifice	Foundation, planks
	Weaver	Fabric, weaving
	Musical composer	Disharmony, symphony
Nature	Light–dark	Sheds light, eclipse, dull, bright
	Physical phenomena	Whirlwind, oasis
	Biology	Cobra, monster

Source: Jensen, 1978.

A metaphor is a figure of speech that applies a name or description to an objective, subjective or abstract idea to which it is not really applicable. Metaphors are often subtle, and many authorities regard the construction of metaphors as a system antedating or bypassing logic or left-brain skills. Sometimes logical and analytical skills just cause the brain to go into a spin. When this happens, despite a probable explosion of synaptic activity going on in the brain it suddenly and often very powerfully switches into metaphoric mode. Metaphors are graphical images that trigger creative thought which can then be related back to the issue in question. Table 4.5 lists a few common, but powerful metaphors. Can you add five more that have been a great help to you?

Jensen (1978) has categorized five general types of metaphors that he intended to be used to redefine *Problem Statements* but they can be used at any stage in a creative problem-solving session (see Table 4.6).

Metaphors act as bridge between the left and right hemispheres of the cortex. They enable us to escape the domination of logical and analytical thought and to enable our imaginative skills to gain a different perspective on the problem. The impressive order of nature, paradoxically born out of a mass of chaotic events, has for long provided a fruitful stimulus for creative people. Powered flight, for example, was heavily influenced by the activity of birds. The development of radar was inspired by the echo-ranging system used by bats. The military use of smoke screens was suggested by the behaviour of threatened squids and octopuses. The famous American physician and medical researcher, Jonas Salk, who developed a vaccine for poliomyelitis, used to advise his students to 'Think like nature and ask how would nature solve this problem?' Edison's invention of the incandescent light bulb was accompanied by his invention of a suitable distribution system for electrical power. Apparently he was influenced by the maple tree in his garden: 'Nature doesn't just make leaves . . . it makes branches and trees and roots to go with them.'

Steve Jobs astounded some of his colleagues at the Apple Computer company when he told them that he wanted the company's personal computer to be like a refrigerator. Asked to explain himself he said, 'When you buy a refrigerator, you don't add anything to it. You just take it home and plug it in.' Later, when the company was developing the MacIntosh computer, Steve Jobs surprised his staff again when he insisted that the new machines should be as easy to use as a telephone. His machine was going to be user friendly and would avoid the need to consult complicated manuals.

Word pictures (metaphors) and stories (anecdotes, parables) are powerful ways of progressing problems as they facilitate right brain-thinking. Somehow they encapsulate the truth of a situation in a way that speaks directly to us. Our incredible machines (brains) do naturally attune to right-brain codes, yet so much of our lives seems to be directed by man-made codes such as rule-bounded speech and quantitative analysis. Have we become prisoners of our own paradigms? The two hemispheres of our brain cortex will naturally and miraculously combine to process our thoughts. So every day every individual exhibits *total thinking*.

Playing in tune and playing together

However, many of us appear to be distrustful of our intuitive selves whilst at work and, perhaps, prone to be too dependent on them whilst at home. Trust is a big issue here, for we feel safer at home than in the hurly-burly of organizational life. In left-brain terms it makes sense to harness the special abilities of the right brain if they can be demonstrated to improve our thinking performance. As research seems to indicate that intuition has a lot to offer it is illogical to ignore it, though some of us may think that fashionable. Similarly, freely intuitive people may get a host of brilliant ideas but may not possess the necessary left-brain skills to progress the problem in a practical way. The perfect individual can practise left- and right-brain thinking in the optimum proportions at all times. The problem is that such an individual does not exist. However, individuals in harmony can approach this state of perfection. Life is a symphony rather than a trumpet solo. That we need each other is a fact readily accepted at home but not always at work. Chapter 5 examines the greater order of creativity open to most of us if we opt to play in the orchestra. Comparatively few individuals can really do it *all* on their own.

However, we can do *some*, and it can be a very big *some*. We all have problems, so we can gain by harnessing left- and right-brain skills (total thinking) as individuals. Now that we have been introduced to the reality of total thinking, let's explore how it can be applied to personal tasks such as note taking, for example.

KEY TERMS

Brain – physiology
Brain – workings
Brain – usage
■ partial thinking
■ total thinking

Problems
■ definition
■ responses
Discovering creativity

4.6   Discovering creative personal problem solving

4.6.1   Note-taking skills

A problem that many of us face, whether at home or at work, is how to study efficiently. The student who has to summarize key information from articles and texts in a form that is user-friendly for memorizing and understanding. The individual at work who has to write a brief summary report for management on a complex subject. In both cases *creative problem solving* (CPS) has a lot to offer. Note taking can be a long and painstaking exercise which can easily become frustrating when an individual later returns to his or her notes only to find that the passage of time has made them difficult to use.

Note-taking styles

In common with Buzan and Buzan (1993) years of observing students reveals that there would appear to be three main styles of note taking:

1. *Narrative* – writing all selected information in narrative form.
2. *Listing* – recording interesting ideas as they occur.
3. *Outline* – seeking to arrange the material in a hierarchical sequence.

The *narrative* style demands a lot of writing and may be useful for those who are anxious to convince themselves that they really understand some taxing argument or theory. Generally speaking this style demands much recording effort and can be difficult to summarize for the purpose of revision or to write an essay or report. The *listing* style certainly saves on paper and time but may just produce copious columns of material that become difficult to handle later. The *outline* style is better, as the use of main and subheadings provides both order and visual variety for the brain.

However, such predominantly left-brain presentation, even if all three styles are combined, often results in the brain having to work hard to understand the key points. Many individuals find it hard going to make sense of such notes and may well have to devote a lot of time in getting to grips with the material. This is because the brain basically gets bored, as these styles of note-making only effectively stimulate the left brain and almost ignore the right brain. For efficient brain activity – learning and thinking – to occur, the missing stimuli are essential, especially for recall and argument. Sadly, many individuals make notes in a format that is almost guaranteed to bore the brain into wandering off in an effort to find something interesting to do.

Memory friendly information

To study effectively it is necessary to input information in the correct format for the brain to process. This means using both left- and right-brain stimuli. For example, we can produce better notes if we seek to:

- Use as few words as possible.
- Use analogies, metaphors.
- Use diagrams, sketches.
- Use colour for picking out key words and in marking key sections of diagrams.
- Summarize notes, once prepared, in a predominantly right-brain style such as a mind map or rich picture.

4.6.2 Learning skills

For learning, as opposed to note taking, try using the sound capabilities of the right brain by the following measures:

- Converting important pieces of factual information into ghost lyrics to well-known tunes and then do some humming. For example, if you were trying to remember Ohm's law consider setting it to the tune of the 'Rain in Spain' from Lerner and Lowe's *My Fair Lady*. (The unit of resistance is the Ohm!) Record it, play it back, listen for the rhythm.
- Selecting words that have a rhythmic flow rather than formal language. This is a technique that is often used by schoolchildren when they are swotting for exams. Here are a couple of examples:

Remembering trigonometry formulae

tan = opp/adj or 'toads over act'

sin = opp/hyp or 'snakes only hiss'

cos = adj/hyp or 'cats always howl'

Remembering the names and order of the planets

'My vet Eric munched jam sandwiches usually near Paris.'

Mercury
   Venus
      Earth
         Mars

> Jupiter
> Saturn
> Uranus
> Neptune
> Pluto

- Playing music, to your taste, in the background as you study. This text was written to a mixture of classical, light and pop background music.

You can also seek to produce material that appeals to the visual skills of the brain. For example:

- summary charts;
- mind maps;
- picture books;
- picture charts;
- broadsheets; and
- designs.

Put them up on the walls of your study. The brain works best when it is well stimulated. This incredible machine is a true multimedia device. Try to provide sufficient stimuli to keep your brain interested and entertained. Then even the most potentially boring of tasks assumes a different hue. Escape from the grey world of predominantly left-brain note-taking styles.

KEY TERMS

CPS   Learning skills
Note taking   - music
                                 - rhythm
                                 - visual stimulation

4.7 Getting to grips with creative personal problem solving

This section is based on an adaptation of the Nominal Group Technique first expounded by Delbecq *et al.* (1975) and is included to help you get started (Rikards, 1990; Van-Gundy, 1988).

4.7.1 Demonstration exercise: organizing a perfect wedding

To illustrate how CPS can assist in *personal problem solving* (PPS), imagine that you wish to formulate some ideas for discussion with your family to plan for the big day.

A useful CPS template to adopt to begin with is a simple, but powerful, three-stage approach (after Kolb, 1984a and Kreitner, 1980):

1. *Problem evaluation* – what is the problem?
2. *Idea generation* – process for generating and selecting apt ideas.
3. *Realization* – converting thinking into action.

Now the Nominal Group technique involves six basic steps:

(i)   private brainstorming
(ii)   round robin collection of ideas
(iii) consideration of each idea
(iv)   preliminary selection of ideas
(v)   consideration of chosen ideas
(vi)   final choice

In this case the problem is known, but it is good practice to state it, in as few words as possible, in a formal *problem statement*: **Planning the perfect wedding.**

4.7.2   Idea generation stage

Now generate some ideas using an adaptation of the Nominal Group Technique.

Private brainstorming (after Stevens, 1988)

This is a widespread and popular process for generating ideas and the rules are widely known:

- Write down spontaneous thoughts – do not exercise any judgement.
- Write down everything, however trivial it may seem at first.
- Aim to record as many ideas as possible.
- Use ideas you have written down to stimulate other ideas.

A period of about five minutes is usually enough for this step. (See Figure 4.13.)

Round robin

Transfer your ideas to Post-it note pad slips. Write out a separate Post-it slip for each idea.

Figure 4.13   The perfect wedding exercise: private brainstorm

The perfect wedding		
Place	Choir	Best man
Reception	Music	Ring
Guest list	Bridesmaids	
Seating plan	Pageboys	
Organ	Cost	

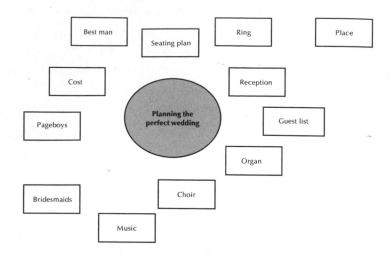

Figure 4.14   Planning the perfect wedding: mind map I

Mind mapping (Buzan and Buzan, 1993)

Now place your Post-it note slips on a convenient surface, such as a wall or broad table top (see Figure 4.14).

Consider each idea and cluster

Once your Post-it notes are in place examine them closely and look for ideas that appear to you to belong together. This process is known as *Clustering* and involves rearranging the Post-it notes into groups that appear to make sense (see Figure 4.15). The Post-its are particularly useful as they provide the facility to move ideas around and to experiment.

Analogy (Rikards, 1974)

Now if you should need to generate some more ideas select a tangible item at random, such as a picture, the view from the window, an outside tree (remember Edison's maple tree). You may like to keep a pack of picture post cards of famous paintings, views or steam engines! Or, perhaps, you may find that listening to your favourite music helps. Explore your multimedia brain! Often you can jump straight from this stimulus and think of new ideas. For example, looking out of the window, you may notice that it is raining and then get the idea of making sure that a supply of umbrellas are available for the wedding day! (See expanded mind map in Figure 4.16).

How would you use this analogy if you were charged with designing user-friendly software manuals for Northern Electric staff? (See Figure 4.17.)

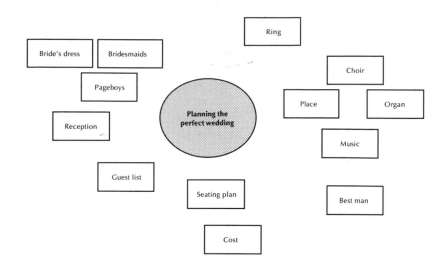

Figure 4.15   Planning the perfect wedding: mind map II

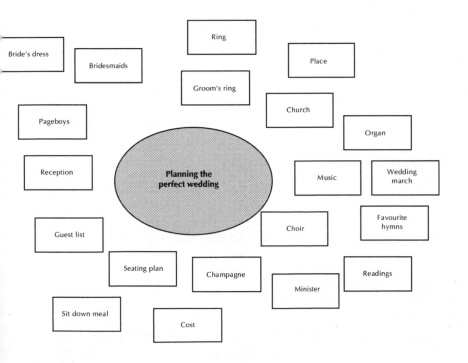

Figure 4.16   Planning the perfect wedding: mind map III

Figure 4.17   Personal problem solving exercise at Northern Electric plc

Problem owner:	Employee in IT Department
Problem statement:	Produce user-friendly computer software manuals for use within the company
Analogy:	Look out of the window

Provoked these thoughts:

Clear – broken – open – closed – opaque

Microsoft Windows – multiple views

Font – size – colour

Tree – branch – root – leaves – twigs – filters – chickens – wire netting – cells – nodes – route map

Large fonts – pictures – interesting

Children – small – concise – straight to the point

Reversal (Rikards, 1990)

Selecting ideas and inverting them often suggests additional useful ideas. Imagine the worst possible wedding. For example, best man fails to turn up, bride's car breaks down, one of the bridemaids is sick over her dress. Now simply invert and place on a Post-it note, and add to the mind map. It is a simple recipe but it works!

Shaping

Now study the Post-it slips on your wall or table top and do some further clustering if necessary. Spend some time looking at the complete pattern that has evolved. Look at the problem statement again. Is there anything else that you would like to add?

Preliminary selection and consideration of ideas

At this stage choose the most important matters and mark them with a red dot. For example, booking the church, settling on a venue for the reception. Now spend a few minutes writing out some brief guideline notes on your preliminary selection. For example, list some possible places in which to hold the reception, who you need to invite.

Time-out (Goman, 1989; Stevens, 1988)

Comparatively few problems really have to be 'solved' on the spot. Try to take time out to think about your notes. Many things that worry us are processed by the subconscious mind overnight when hopefully the conscious, worrying, mind is resting. Often gentle messages to our conscious minds, first thing in the morning, contain real pearls of wisdom.

Personal brainstorming	Mind mapping	Clustering
Analogy Reversal	Shaping	Time-out
Round robin	Notebook	Selection

Figure 4.18 Basic CPS tool kit

Notebook (Goman, 1989)

You may like to try keeping a summary notebook on your bedside table to capture these gentle promptings before you lose them in the hustle and bustle of the day's activities.

Final choice

As the prime purpose of applying creative problem solving (CPS) methods to personal problem solving (PPS) is to realize something, it is important to end the idea-generating stage by exercising personal judgement and selecting the most relevant issues. In this case select the five most important matters and bring them to the attention of close family or friends.

CPS tools used to generate ideas

Have a go at using these tools (see Figure 4.18) to progress one of your own problems. Follow the instructions in the text.

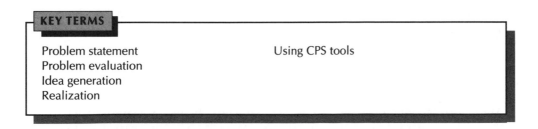

KEY TERMS

Problem statement   Using CPS tools
Problem evaluation
Idea generation
Realization

4.8 The Toymaker: from lone apprentice to master craftsperson

The planning a perfect wedding example presented a basic set of CPS tools. CPPS, like carpentry, is a craft that combines tools (*the necessary to*) with techniques (*the how to*). A DIY enthusiast usually possesses a basic skill level in handling some of the simple tools of the trade but is probably relatively unskilled in terms of technique. The skilled practitioner possesses *know-how* on the experiential synthesis of tools and techniques.

Individuals have the potential to perfect their CPPS performance into *know-how* provided that they are willing to learn experientially.

4.8.1   From what to . . . help!

We invite you to picture a doting father who wants to give his daughter an extra special birthday present. However, he is of modest means and cannot afford to go to the local toy shop and purchase something nice. Faced with this problem he thinks of giving up his intention to buy a special present. This leaves him inwardly unhappy and ill at ease. He knows that this is not a solution that he can accept and so decides to dwell on the problem overnight. As the morning light streams into his room he wakes with a jolt and *knows that* he wants to build a doll's house for his daughter. Excited, he begins to think about such a project and experiences difficulty in picturing the finished article. Driven by a force he cannot understand he gets up, sighs and feels a strong urge to open the bedroom curtains. As the full glory of the morning sun is revealed he blinks his eyes and looks over the garden below. The first thing that he notices is that his lawn is twice as high as his neighbour's; he shrugs his shoulders and commits himself to wrestling once more with the elderly and rather moody hover mower. To avoid the sun's rays, he looks sideways across his garden and suddenly realizes that his eyes have come to rest on the new house that has just been built down the road. In a flash he is convinced that he wants to build a model of this house. Happy in his discovery of what he will build, he goes downstairs for his breakfast. As he leaves the bright light in his bedroom and enters the relative darkness of the hall he becomes depressed. He is worried as to how he is going to build the doll's house in time.

Aware of a very strong inner motivation, he looks for inspiration in his cornflake bowl. A few soggy flakes stare back at him from the bottom of the bowl and, intrigued, he stares back and is suddenly aware tht his daughter would really like a doll's house with a thatched roof.

4.8.2   Getting started

After breakfast our man rushes out, gets into his car and reverses into the world. 'Backwards into the future' again he sighs as he speeds off down the road to buy a set of carpentry tools. A short while later he is back and proudly unpacks his new toolbox and tools. Picking up each tool, he imagines just what he could do if he could handle them as professionally as an expert. This is both exciting and almost immediately depressing. He feels nervous and exposed and now somewhat out of pocket but firmly decides to banish all self-doubt and go for it. Mastering a new skill set may be difficult but then so was learning to play the piano and how to drive. A cold shiver runs down his spine as he recalls that it took him ten years to learn to play the piano! Oh, well, wrong example for he passed his driving test after ten lessons. Mmm, he thought, just 15 days to go.

That evening the garage light shines late into the night as he tries out his new tools. Some are easy to handle but others claim bits of his fingers as he struggles to come to terms with them. Spurred on by his determination to build the doll's house he enthusiastically assaults a piece of plywood only to find that it bends one way then the other and then jumps off his work bench and clouts him over the head. Cross at this unreasonable behaviour and in a crazy attempt to release his fretsaw blade from the offending plywood board he bashes it with his hammer. The board takes off again and smashes into his lamp, knocking it off the bench to the sound of shattering glass. Suddenly he is in the dark again. As his eyes refocus to the subdued light from the street lamp he realizes that he will have to stop rushing at things and work within his capabilities. Imagination, top marks; tools, pretty good; technical profficiency with the tools, pretty basic. The thought of giving up once more flashes across his mind. No way, he thinks, for this was a task that he was going to complete and on time!

4.8.3 Assessing the situation

'In a word, depressing', he thinks, as he feels the pain from his bleeding and bruised fingers. There is something strangely informative about the semi-darkness in his garage. It seems to describe how he feels – a pale shade of grey instead of light, bright and active. So he decides to lighten up the garage with a can or two of white emulsion and to fix up a couple of fluorescent lights. That will lighten up the environment, he thinks. However, it would cost money and he knows he would have to plead his case with his wife for some extra cash for, as luck would have it, the current month was one when all the bills seemed to come in. He remains quietly determined to argue the case for some of the scarce household disposable income; he knows that this is going to challenge the existing order of things.

In the half light of his garage he begins to think about the whole business of combining ideas, tools and rather basic technique and is pleased to discover that he can build a doll's house as long as he works within the constraints of his limitations. Abandoning the idea of making a scaled down replica of the house down the road, he resolves to design a simpler structure that would be within his capability. Hearing the chink of glass bottles on the milkman's van he resolves to leave things for the time being, take some time out and have a cup of coffee.

Staring into his cup as he stirs his coffee he searches for inspiration. Soggy cornflakes had given him an idea yesterday morning; perhaps his coffee would now. After a minute with nothing of any note happening he begins to be discouraged. Perhaps he should give it up. After all, one night working in the garage had resulted in very little to show for his pains except of course his injured fingers. Finding himself thinking about the story of Archimedes in his bath, he suddenly shouts *eureka* followed by *aha*. The circular movement of his coffee had led him to see that he would go round and round and make little progress unless he learnt from the lessons of the night. He pondered on this for awhile. Well, the tools were up to the job. His revised task seemed sensible but his technical ability was still suspect. However, if he learnt from his mistakes in handling the tools: rushing ahead before reading the instructions in the DIY carpentry book he had purchased with his tool set but which lay on his workbench. Keen to follow this line of thought he opens his diary and starts to list the lessons that he had learnt that night.

4.8.4   A Creative Workshop

Two days later our father returned to the task of making a doll's house, having successfully obtained sufficient resources to brighten up his garage and install some effective lighting. As he settled down to work he disciplined himself into starting with a brief quiet time and resolved not to charge into his work. He remembered his childhood days when grand projects always seemed fun when they were tackled in a relaxed playful spirit rather than as a chore. Play was fun. Chores were boring. To add to the new environment in the garage he had brought in a portable disc player with a handful of his favourite music. Now to work . . . no, just a minute. What did I learn from my experiences in the garage earlier in the week. Mmm!

Three hours later much had been accomplished. The tools seemed more friendly. The structure, though simple, was starting to emerge and he felt at peace with himself. So he decided to take time out and go to bed. He fell asleep almost as soon as his head hit the pillow but he could see the finished article in full colour and was sure that his daughter would be very pleased.

4.8.5   Master class

Ten years later our father had become a master toymaker and had achieved considerable fame throughout the country for his one-off and low volume designs. It seems amazing but it was true. He had acquired a reputation for both his quality build and his designs, had left his old job in a solicitor's office and was now running his own business. Abigail, a keen, young reporter, stopped by, determined to find out how such creative people functioned. Content in his sense of fulfilment he was quite happy to talk to her.

He explained how he had started and described a couple of nights in his garage a decade ago. As the conversation developed, the reporter could see clearly that his first doll's house had been a significant event in his life. (The creative techniques that fired his imagination were described and then summarized in a picture of a doll's house with a thatched roof.) The master's main guides were:

1. A determination to prevent himself from restricting the flow of his and his staff's creative energies by the provision of a stimulating environment in which to work that served rather than strangled creative work.
2. A fascination in learning new skills and the patience to master them.
3. The ability to stop and quickly select the best tools for a job rather than be trapped in the repetitive boredom of always using the same techniques.
4. A determination to regularly think about the quality of *how* he and his staff worked as well as *what* they worked on. He was concerned to ensure that working practices were

adapted to suit the needs of his markets rather than become enshrined in company mind-sets.

5. Valuing the work of all his staff, encouraging them to work to the best of their capabilities when under pressure and to learn to develop their creative skills when time permitted.

6. Encouraging his staff to adopt a free rein in their design work. To practice total thinking (See pp. 105–6) unashamedly.

7. To build a climate of security and trust so that all felt free at all times to question the *status quo* in a positive way.

8. To seek inspiration from the natural world.

KEY TERMS

Encouraging creativity	Value staff
Willingness to learn	Practice total thinking
Selecting 'right' tools	Building climate of trust
Improve techniques	Seeking 'natural' inspiration

4.9 Obstacles to personal creativity

4.9.1 Practical difficulties

After a creativity workshop in Durham, delegates were asked to brainstorm the main obstacles, as they saw them, to introducing creative personal problem solving (CPPS) into the lives of their colleagues at work. They were also asked to suggest ways that these obstacles might be overcome. Figure 4.19 summarizes the results.

Figure 4.19 Personal creativity blockages

Obstacle	Antidote
1. Tiredness	Get a good night's sleep.
2. Anxiety	Relax.
3. Negativity	Be positive.
4. Fear of failure	Trust your intuition.
5. Fear of standing out from the crowd	Stand your ground.
6. Fear of challenging the rules	Rules should help, not hinder.
7. Fear of emotional things	Realize that total thinking makes sense.
8. Myopia	Wake up!
9. Distrust	Trust in the force!
10. Lack of personal confidence	Because you don't trust in the force.

Tiredness

Many exhibited a reluctance to put in the necessary time to learn a new skill. Home was seen as a place to relax and that did not include thinking about being creative! Work was identified with pressure, paper and politics that made people tire quickly and reduced their enthusiasm to attempt anything new. Invariably the workplace was seen as a mechanistic culture where some pulled the levers and the others 'did their bit'.

Anxiety

Experienced at work, anxiety was often transferred after working hours to home life. Many found it difficult to relax away from work and free their minds to attempt anything new.

Negativity

The harsh economic climate of the north-east of England led many to adopt a pessimistic outlook on life. Often frustration with the performance of 'the management' or the euphemistic 'they' seemed to produce a pronounced negative culture.

Fear of failure

This fear occurred frequently and was cited by individuals working in both large and small organizations. Many in this group did not realize that it was possible to practise creativity at home in a safe environment.

4.9.2 Blockages to personal problem solving (PPS) commonly identified in the literature

The key six blockages (see Figure 4.20) to personal creativity commonly identified in the literature are as follows (e.g. Osborn, 1963; Kreitner, 1980; Stevens, 1988):

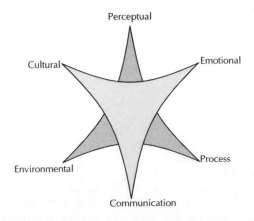

Figure 4.20 Common personal problem solving blockages

Perceptual

These blockages arise from the way that we have learnt (instruction and experience) to adapt to the stimuli that surround us in the world as we see it. Habitual responses can lead us to miss other, perhaps contextually more suitable, responses. For example:

- Seeing only what we expect to see, failure to really understand contextual stimuli – driving in fog!
- Stereotyping, tendency to jump to conclusions too quickly.
- Eyes down – propensity to tunnel vision.
- Mistaking cause and effect – if there turns out not to be hotel room for an invited guest and we assume that it is the hotel's fault when in reality our secretary forgot to make a reservation, then our search for solutions will be misdirected. The fact that there is no room at the inn for our guest is an effect of the problem not the cause.

Emotional

These blockages are evident when we deliberately suppress an idea or course of action because we perceive that it will be unpopular with our peer group and do not want to risk their scorn. Or, perhaps, when we come up with an idea that is different (such as, for example, an Imagineering approach) and we do not want to look silly in the eyes of our fellows. For instance:

- Fear of making mistakes or looking silly.
- Racing away – rushing in too quickly may result in the wrong problem being solved or the right problem but with the wrong CPS approach.
- Playing it safe and avoiding anxiety – a common response in individuals who are uncertain of how much support they will receive from the group or organization.
- Awaiting instruction – related to the above cause, and tends to be found in rule-bound organizations.
- Sloppy response – tends to be found in situations where the problem is routine and the overall motivation of the staff is low.

Process skills

These blockages are caused by a basic lack of technique. This can all too easily arise when we have been used to existing in fairly stable operational conditions where real problems and challenges are few and far between. For example:

- Lack of knowledge in problem-solving process.
- Lack of creative thinking – a reluctance to use the *creative force* rather than its lack of evidence.
- Too heavy a reliance on left-brain skills – wanting to write the proof before the problem is solved.
- Snatching at the problem – failure to apply methodical convergent/divergent tracking points.
- Lack of sufficient contextual information, poor or the wrong *problem statement* and poor CPS ability.
- Lack of understanding of the facts – shooting in the dark.

Communication

These blockages occur when we are unable to communicate in a suitable style for our voice to be heard and understood by those charged with tackling the problem in question. Examples are as follows:

- Failure to couch the problem and its proposed solution in suitable terms. General management will not understand functional jargon. Not all concerned outside publics will understand the organizational 'speak'.
- Difficulty in explaining position to others is sometimes unconsciously cloaked in jargon and/or organizational 'speak'. The safe default in such situations is to explain the things in a style appropriate to an educated third party.
- Failure to justify recommendations.
- Failure to capture the attention of vital parties owing to weak presentation skills.
- Autocratic, argumentative styles easily put people's backs up.

Environmental

These blockages often crop up to distract us from getting to grips with a problem and frequently result from unexpected or seasonal increases in our workload. For example:

- Management culture – the impact of the organizational mind-sets.
- Comfort factors – poor facilities (everything from loos to coffee and tea provision) can dampen enthusiasm and quality of response.
- Ambivalent attitude of key contact in the organization.
- Stress factors – the too frequent imposition of tight deadlines.
- Monotony – need-to-know management causes people to get bored.
- Absence of *kaizen* – people are more responsive if they know that they are expected to look continually for better ways of doing things.

Cultural

This set of blockages impacts on us through the impact of personal, group, organizational and national cultures. For example, some managers feel that the creative management style is too open and risky and may harbour the latent opinion that staff are to be instructed and not consulted! Instances are as follows:

- religious acceptance of the status quo
- resistance to major change
- distrust of right-brain skills
- belief that humour is for private life only
- prejuced suspicion that anything to do with *Imagineering* is definitely not management!
- reluctance to work in teams – everyone for himself mentality does not foster co-operative effort.

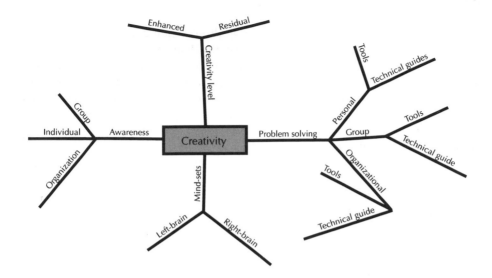

Figure 4.21   Important factors influencing the release of creativity

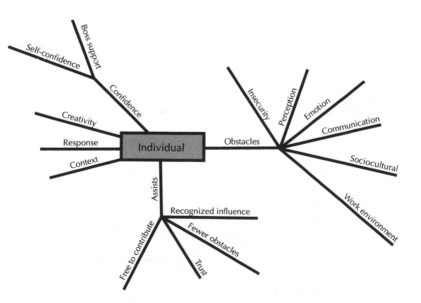

Figure 4.22   Leading factors affecting the individual creative management response

4.10 Summary

Having reviewed the contextual influences on wealth creation and briefly revisited the traditional management competencies, the task of this chapter has been to introduce the key driver of our model – *creativity*. It is evident from consultancy work that there is much misunderstanding abroad concerning creativity. All individuals are creative and most know it. The real issue is how much of our creativity we choose to make public. This is determined by how much we allow mind-sets to dictate our responses. A good way of exploring the creative problem-solving tool kit introduced in this chapter is to privately explore your own mind-sets.

The key factors affecting creativity are summarized in the mind map depicted in Figure 4.21. Given that an individual has accepted the contextual arguments advanced in this text and is prepared to explore the CMR approach, it is important to be persistent. There will be obstacles, real and imagined, but also many triumphs for those who are prepared to be surprised by joy. Figure 4.22 maps the main influences affecting the personal exploration of the *creative management response*.

QUESTIONS

1. How would you explain what *creativity* is to a person who has not read this text?

2. Name five living creative people and state why you think that they are creative.

3. If you have not already done so, turn to Appendix 4.2 and fill in the *personal creativity audit*. Following the instructions, score the result and see where you are on the *creativity spectrum*. Now respond to Exercise 4.2 in Appendix 4.4.

4. List five ways that you might use to encourage creativity in others.

5. Complete Exercise 4.3 in Appendix 4.4.

6. Be brave, try Exercise 4.4 in Appendix 4.4.

7. Briefly describe and then critique the main inventories that have been used to explore behavioural responses. To what extent do they pick up any useful information on personal creativity?

8. List three metaphors that you believe help you think about business organizations. Ask a friend to do the same independently, then meet and then discuss all six metaphors and by common consent select the top two.

9. Complete exercise 4.5 in Appendix 4.4.

10. Complete exercise 4.6 in Appendix 4.4.

11. Study the ten Master Guides described in Chapter 4. Select a problem, issue or challenge of your own. Plan a brief, personal, creative problem-solving session using the tool kit used in the wedding illustration in the text and the Master Guides.

12. What do you consider to be the main obstacles to the free expression of your creativity at home? What inhibits you in your work environment? How might you address these blockages?

References

Adair, J. (1987), *Effective Team Building*, London: Pan.

Baron, J. (1988), *Thinking and Deciding*, Cambridge: Cambridge University Press.

Belbin, M. (1981), *Management Teams: Why they succeed or fail*, Oxford: Heinemann.

Buzan, T. (1986), *Use Your Memory*, London: BBC Books.

Buzan, T. and Buzan, B. (1993), *The Mind-Map Book*, London: BBC Books.

de Bono, E. (1984), *Lateral Thinking for Management*, London: Pelican.

de Bono, E. (1991), *Handbook for the Positive Revolution*, London: Penguin.

Encyclopaedia Britannica (1991), 15th edn, vol. xxiv, 779.

Delbecq, A. L., Van de Ven, A. H. and Gustafson, D.H. (1975), *Group techniques for Program Planning*, Glenview, IL: Scott, Foresman.

Garnham, A. and Oakhill, J. (1994), *Thinking and Reasoning*, Oxford: Blackwell.

Getzels, J. W. and Csikszentmihalyi, M. (1976), *The Creative Vision*, New York: Wiley.

Getzels, J. P. and Jackson, P. W. (1962), *Creativity and Intelligence*, New York: Wiley.

Goman, C. K. (1989), *Creative Thinking In Business*, London: Kogan Page.

Guilford, J. P. (1956), 'Structure of intellect', *Psychological Bulletin*, 53, 267–93.

Guilford, J. (1967), *The Nature of Human Intelligence*, New York: McGraw-Hill.

Guilford, J. (1986), *Creative Talents: Their nature, uses and development*, Buffalo, NY: Bearly.

Hellriegel, D. and Slocum, J. W. (1975), 'Managerial problem-solving styles', *Business Horizons*, Dec., p. 33.

Honey, P. and Mumford, A. (1985), *The Manual of Learning Styles*, Maidenhead: Peter Honey.

Hudson, L. (1987), ' Creativity', in R. L. Gregory (ed.), *The Oxford Companion to the Mind*, Oxford: Oxford University Press, 171–2.

Jensen J. V. (1978), 'A heuristic for the analysis of the nature and extent of a problem', *Journal of Creative Behaviour*, 12, 168–80.

Kirton, M. J. (1987), *Adaption-Innovation Inventory Theory (KAI) – Manual*, 2nd edn, Hatfield: Occupational Research Centre.

Kirton, M. J. (1989), *Adaptors and Innovators: Styles of creativity and problem solving*, London: Routledge.

Koestler, A. (1969), *The Act of Creation*, London: UK.

Kolb, D. (1984a), *Experiential Learning*, Englewood Cliffs, NJ.: Prentice Hall.

Kolb, D. (1984b), 'Problem management: learning from experience', Ch. 5 in Suresh Srvastra and Associates (ed.), *The Executive Mind*, London: Jossey Bass.

Kolb, D., Cublin, S., Spoth, J. and Baker, R. (1991), 'Strategic management development and managerial competencies', in J. Henry (ed.), *Creative Management*, Chapter 17. London: Sage.

Kreitner, R. (1980), *Management: A problem-solving process*, Boston, Mass.: Houghton Mifflin.

Maier, N. R. F., Julius, M. and Thurber, J. (1967), 'Studies in creativity: individual differences in the storing and utilization of information', *American Journal of Psychology*, Dec., 492–519.

MacKinnon, D. W. (1962), 'The nature and nurture of creative talent', *American Psychologist*, 17, 484–95.

Morgan, G. (1993), *Imaginization*, London: Sage.

Myers-Briggs, 1987, *Type Indicator Report Form*, Palo Alto, Calif: Consulting Psychologists Press.

Myers, Briggs and McCaulley, M. H. (1988), *Manual: A guide to the development and use of the Myers–Briggs type indicator*, Palo Alto, Calif.: Consulting Psychologists Press.

Osborn, A. E. (1963), *Applied Imagination*, New York: Scribner.

Pentagram (1992), *Phantasmagrams*, London: Ebury Press. A collection of visual and optical illusions.

Rikards, T. (1974), *Problem Solving Through Creative Analysis*, Epping: Gower.

Rikards, T. (1990), *Creativity and Problem Solving at Work*, Aldershot: Gower.

Sperry, R. W. (1968), 'Hemispheric deconnection and unity in conscious awarness', *Scientific American*, 23, 723–33.

Sternberg, R. J. (1988), *The Nature of Creativity: Contemporary psychological perspectives*, Cambridge: Cambridge University Press.

Tardiff, T. Z. and Sternberg, R. J. (1988), *The Nature of Creativity; Contemporary psychological perspectives*, in R. J. Sternberg (ed.), Cambridge: Cambridge University Press.

Thomson, R. (1972), *The Psychology of Thinking*, London: Pelican Books.

Torrance, E. P. (1988), 'The nature of creativity as manifest in its testing', in R. J. Sternberg (ed.), *The Nature of Creativity: Contemporary psychological perspectives*, Cambridge: Cambridge University Press, pp. 43–75.

VanGundy, A. B. (1988), *Techniques of Structured Problem Solving*, Second edition, New York: Van Nostrand Reinhold.

Wallas, G. (1926), *The Art of Thought*, London: Cape.

Additional reading

There are many texts around. Here are some I have found helpful.

Armstrong, M. (1983), *How To Be An Even Better Manager*, London: Kogan Page.

Boden, M. A. (1990), *The Creative Mind: Myths and mechanisms*, London: Weidenfeld & Nicolson.

Buzan, T. and Buzan, B. (1993), *The Mind-Map Book*, London: BBC Books.

de Bono, E. (1968), *The Five-Day Course in Thinking*, London: Allen Lane.

Garnhâm, A. and Oakhill, J. (1994), *Thinking and Reasoning*, Oxford: Blackwell.

Goman, C. K. (1989), *Creative Thinking In Business*, London: Kogan Page.

McKenney, J. L. and Keen, P. G. W. (1974), 'How managers minds work', *Harvard Business Review*, May–June, 83.

Perkins, D. N. (1981), *The Mind's Best Work*, Cambridge, Mass.: Harvard University Press.

Spooner, P. (1992), *Museum of the Mind*, York: The Museum of Automata.

Stevens, M. S. (1988), *Practical Problem Solving for Managers*, London: Kogan Page.

VanGundy, A. B. (1988), *Techniques of Structured Problem Solving*, Second edition, New York: Van Nostrand Reinhold.

Weisburg, R. W. (1988), 'Problem solving and creativity', in R. J. Sternberg (ed.), *The Nature of Creativity: Contemporary psychological perspectives*, Cambridge: Cambridge University Press, pp. 148–76.

Management styles questionnaire

Behaviour trait	High 4	High/medium 3	Medium/low 2	Low 1	Total
Approachable	. . .	. . .	. . .	. . .	. . .
Honest					
Supportive					
Fair					
Open dealing					
Communicative					
Total					

The higher your *total* score the better! Do ponder on your individual behaviour trait scores.

Personal creativity audit

Instructions

Questionnaire

1. It is suggested that you copy the questionnaire and assessment forms before attempting the audit.
2. Put the assessment form to one side.
3. Turn to the questionnaire and answer the questions honestly and as quickly as you can.
4. Please do not confer with others whist you or they are completing the questionnaire.

Assessment

1. Turn to the assessment form.
2. Transfer the score for the box that you ticked in the questionnaire and record it beside your tick.
3. When you have scored each of your responses, run a quick check to see that you have recorded the right values for each question.
4. Add up your scores and plot the sum value on the creativity spectrum diagram.

Interpretation

1. If you wish to improve your score, work through the exercises suggested in Chapter 4.

2. Record your initial score and try the audit again in three months' time. If you have studied the text and experimented with creative thinking you should achieve a higher rating.

Questionnaire

Please tick the appropriate box

	Never	Occa-sionally	Fairly often	Regularly
1. Do you remember your dreams as images?	. . .	. . .	. . .	. . .
2. How often do you devote time to hobbies?				
3. How often do you read?				
4. Do you like to stick to the rules?				
5. Do you listen to other people's ideas?				
6. Do you inspire others?				
7. How often do you exhibit a sense of humour?				
8. Do you take part in outdoor sports?				
9. Are you a perfectionist?				
10. Are you an optimist?				
11. Do you have any ideas of your own?				
12. Are you usually courteous?				
13. How often do you hum and sing?				
14. Are you predictable?				
15. Do you like exercising administrative (rank) authority?				
16. Are you a good listener?				
17. Are you a resourceful person?				
18. Do you tend to work on one idea at a time?				
19. Do you welcome change?				
20. Do you have many original ideas?				
21. Do you enthusiastically promote your own ideas?				
22. Are you a loner?				
23. Do you like organizations with lots of rules and identified procedures?				
24. Are you self-motivated?				
25. Are you a good problem solver?				
26. Are you a good improviser/fixer?				
27. Do you prefer to adapt the ideas of others?				
28. Do you challenge existing rules if you honestly think that they are silly?				
29. If you meet with opposition to an idea of yours do you easily give up trying to promote it?				
30. Do you use a lot of metaphors when seeking to make points?				

Assessment form

	Never	Occa-sionally	Fairly often	Regularly
1. Do you remember your dreams as images?	1	2	3	4
2. How often do you devote time to hobbies?	1	2	3	4
3. How often do you read?	1	2	3	4
4. Do you like to stick to the rules?	2	4	3	1
5. Do you listen to other people's ideas?	1	2	3	4
6. Do you inspire others?	1	2	3	4
7. How often do you exhibit a sense of humour?	1	2	3	4
8. Do you take part in outdoor sports?	1	2	3	4
9. Are you a perfectionist?	1	2	3	4
10. Are you an optimist?	1	2	3	4
11. Do you have any ideas of your own?	1	2	3	4
12. Are you usually courteous?	1	2	3	4
13. How often do you hum and sing?	1	2	3	4
14. Are you predictable?	4	3	2	1
15. Do you like exercising administrative (rank) authority?	4	3	2	1
16. Are you a good listener?	1	2	3	4
17. Are you a resourceful person?	1	2	3	4
18. Do you tend to work on one idea at a time?	4	3	2	1
19. Do you welcome change?	1	2	3	4
20. Do you have many original ideas?	1	2	3	4
21. Do you enthusiastically promote your own ideas?	1	2	3	4
22. Are you a loner?	4	3	2	1
23. Do you like organizations with lots of rules and identified procedures?	4	3	2	1
24. Are you self-motivated?	1	2	3	4
25. Are you a good problem solver?	1	2	3	4
26. Are you a good improviser/fixer?	1	2	3	4
27. Do you prefer to adapt the ideas of others?	4	3	2	1
28. Do you challenge existing rules if you honestly think that they are silly?	1	2	3	4
29. If you meet with opposition to an idea of yours do you easily give up trying to promote it?	4	3	2	1
30. Do you use a lot of metaphors when seeking to make points?	1	2	3	4

Creativity spectrum

	68	80	95	
40				120

Basic creativity   Average creativity   High creativity
zone   zone   zone

APPENDIX 4.3

The Peking Express

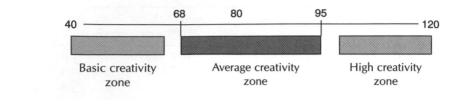

Problem

Who was the spy in the rust-coloured coat (see p. 106)?

Suggested approach

1. Draw a diagram of the train compartment.

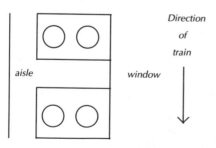

aisle   Direction of train   window

2. Place two by the aisle and two by the window.

3. Now place Mr B in the top left hand seat (Clue 5).

4. Which puts the British spy in the top right hand corner.

Mr B   British

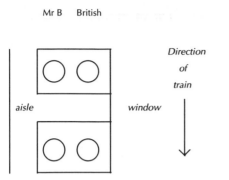

Direction
of
train

aisle   window

5. From Clue 7 the German and the spy dressed in olive must be opposite Mr B and the British spy.

6. Mr D is either in the top right-hand seat (the British spy) or in the lower left-hand seat (the German spy) from Clue 6 (Mr A has a tan-coloured coat) so Mr D must be seated in the top right-hand seat. (If he were in the lower left-hand seat he would be opposite the Russian.)

7. So the spy in the rust-coloured coat must be the British spy.

Mr B   Mr D
Russian   British
Khaki

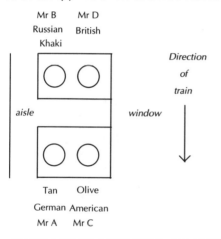

Direction
of
train

aisle   window

Tan   Olive
German American
Mr A   Mr C

EXERCISE 4.4   Write it, see it and believe it

Ask a close friend or someone at work seriously to list your five main talents.

1.

2.

3.

4.

5.

APPENDIX 4.4

Exercises 4.3 and 4.4

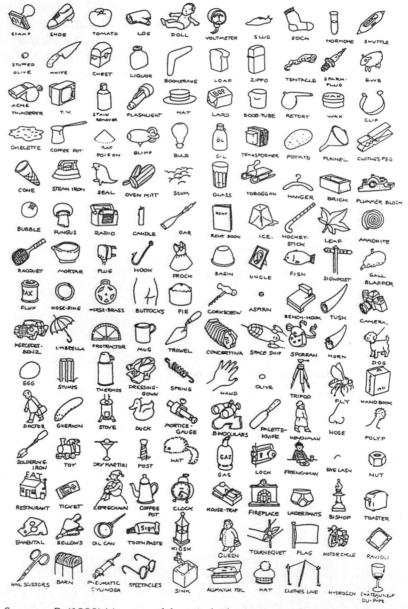

Source: Spooner, P. (1992) Museum of the Mind, The Museum of Automata, York, UK.

EXERCISE 4.3   Pictures tell more than words – I

Look at the icons in appendix 4.4 and select five that you feel best describe a member of your immediate family.

EXERCISE 4.4   Pictures tell more than words – II

Look at the icons in appendix 4.4 and select five that you feel best describe a colleague of yours at work.

5

Creative groups

CONTENTS

5.1   Introduction   *143*

5.2   Group behaviour   *143*

5.3   Helping others to experience creativity   *150*

5.4   Establishing a creative climate   *155*

5.5   Building up a creative problem-solving tool kit   *158*

5.6   Creative problem-solving tools   *164*

5.7   Creative group problem solving: Master Guides   *182*

5.8   Obstacles to group creativity   *185*

5.9   Group creativity audit   *186*

5.10 Summary   *187*

Questions   *188*

References   *189*

Note   *190*

Appendix 5.1   Group creativity audit   *190*

Appendix 5.2   Introductory CPS tool kit   *193*

Appendix 5.3   Practical creative problem solving   *195*

Map: Chapter 5

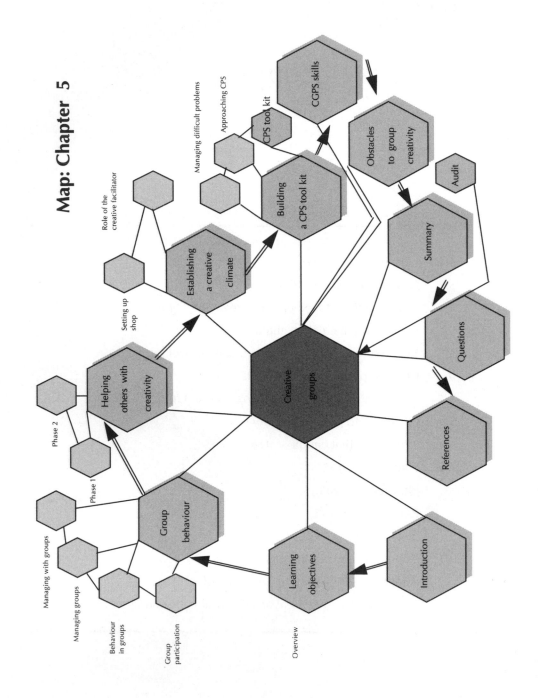

5.1 Introduction

Having experienced the personal joy of creativity, many shudder at the thought of 'giving it a go' at work. It involves some initiative and there is some risk involved. Our experience has shown that a *soft* rather than a *hard* sell generally gets results. The chapter opens with a brief review of group dynamics before moving on to introduce creative problem solving (CPS) to groups by direct involvement rather than instruction. Resist the temptation to explain to everyone in minute detail just how you are going to use individual CPS tools. This is not common practice when you are driving. At the same time, do not underrate the power of autosuggestion. So refrain from any discourse with colleagues about 'degrees of weirdness' of various tools and methods. Just get on with it, go with the flow, and accomplish.

Best results are obtained when individuals network with others who are experimenting with CPS tools and techniques. So try and set up a small cell of honest pioneers and try to see that they are not regarded as elitist. Pick relatively simple tasks to begin with as this should enable you to demonstrate some undeniable early successes.

The CPS tool kit introduced in the previous chapter is expanded and two further techniques are included to facilitate group CPS. Lastly – and deliberately right at the close of the chapter – one or two things about obstacles to group CPS. It is important that you adopt a positive attitude and get going rather than dwell too much on what could go wrong. Good luck.

LEARNING OBJECTIVES

This chapter is intended to help individuals share their rediscovery of *creativity* with colleagues at work. Reflective reading will:

- Provide a brief refresher on group behaviour.
- Show you how to help others to experience creativity.
- Suggest ways of 'getting going'.
- Continue the build up of your CPS tool kit.
- Provide some advice on common group CPS problems.

5.2 Group behaviour

5.2.1 Group participation

Man is a social animal and thus most of what we do as individuals has an effect on other people. Similarly what other individuals and groups do has an effect on us, either consciously or unconsciously. We are all prone to modify our behaviour, whether we are in the company of a single individual or a group of individuals. The degree to which we modify our responses is directly related to what we believe the expected behaviour pattern is (the group *norm*) and the magnitude of the threat that we perceive in the

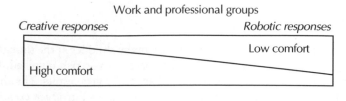

Work and professional groups

Figure 5.1   Group responses

social transaction. In the company of some people we are at ease, whilst the company of others leaves us fidgety and nervous. Generally speaking, behaviour breeds behaviour – how other people behave towards us determines the way that we behave towards them.

In the course of our everyday lives most of us belong to several different groups. Each of these groups assumes a collective individuality and personality and it is this to which we choose whether or not to adapt our behaviour. In our private lives we tune our responses very finely toward domestic stimuli and often feel quite at home in the social groups we choose. Social groups tend to be regarded as extensions of our family life and for most carry little perceived anxiety. Traditional professional groups, on the other hand, are usually regarded as being different, as many are deeply suspicious of the culture of the 'rat race'. Thus our responses tend to be carefully considered and can become programmed to fit into the observed habits of the group. In other words the further we move from home or our close circle of friends into the world of the workplace the more conditioned our behaviour becomes. This can and does place a damper on individual creativity as people seek the noncontroversial comfort of the group viewpoint. Figure 5.1 shows how our individual responses change from unchecked spontaneity (high tendency for creativity) to controlled norms (low tendency for creativity) depending on the degree of 'ease' or comfort the group culture provides.

High Comfort vs. Low Comfort *(Gemeinschaft vs.* Gesellschaft*)*

Gemeinschaft and *Gessellschaft* were ideal types of social or group organizations that were systematically elaborated by the German sociologist Ferdinand Tonnies in his influential work *Gemeinschaft* (community) *und Gesellschaft* (society), published in Leipzig in 1887. Tonnies' conception of the nature of social systems is based on his distinction between the *Gemeinschaft* (communal society) and the *Gesellschaft* (associational society). In social organizations that typify the *Gemeinschaft* personal relationships are defined and regulated on the basis of traditional social rules. People have simple and direct face-to-face relations with each other that are determined by *Wesenwille* (natural will), i.e. natural and spontaneously arising emotions and expressions of sentiment. In contrast the *Gesellschaft* is the creation of *Kurwille* (rational will) and is typified by modern societies, with their large government bureaucracies and organizations. In the

Gesellschaft rational self-interest and calculating conduct act to weaken the natural bonds and synergy of the *Gemeinschaft*.

Movement from *high comfort* individual behaviour to conditioned *low comfort* group behaviour is critically dependent on the level of trust expectations of individuals. If this is appreciably and consistently high, then individuals will tend to adopt common behaviour patterns and the group will function as a cohesive and united team. Everyone will pull together and the collective purpose (vision) of all will boost performance. The difference between a united and highly tuned crew and an ill at-ease-one is obvious to all standing on the river bank. Close identity with a group or team generates a collective loyalty or supraindividuality that in the right context can be highly creative. If this is missing in groups, then the collective individuality loses its dynamism and simply becomes a label – individuals go through the motions. They play the notes but the tune is flat.

Loyalty and group participation

Individuals choose the degree to which they are prepared to relax in a group culture (i.e. within a set of recognized and accepted norms or behaviour patterns).

When loyalty is high and the degree of participative membership (see Figure 5.2) is low individuals can be said to be displaying *dutiful adherence*. In this case the vision or the purpose of the group is accepted but there is little enthusiasm for joining in to further the cause. This appears to be the behaviour pattern adopted by many towards such groups as local churches, charities, and so forth. If both loyalty and degree of membership is low then individuals are practising *nominal adherence*. Such 'take it or leave it' attitudes rarely result in much creative output. This response is neatly captured by the words of President Kennedy who invited Americans in his inaugural speech to 'ask not what your country can do for you but rather what you can do for your country'. When

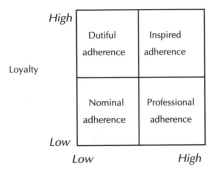

Figure 5.2 Degrees of group participation

group loyalty is low and group membership high, individuals will tend to see their inputs as being merely *professional adherence*. This behaviour pattern produces prescribed results characterized by a tendency to do just enough to meet expected job requirements but is often rule-bound and robotic. When the 'going gets tough, the tough get going'. When the contextual stimuli are both complex and fast changing, professional groups need to display both a high degree of loyalty and participative membership. This we term *inspired adherence* and can be seen in the daily work of many teachers, preachers, researchers and health and social workers whose loyalty to their clientele is often stronger than their loyalty to the organization.

Now complete the questionnaire and assessment form in Appendix 5.1. It is suggested that you photocopy the forms to avoid writing in the text.

5.2.2 Behaviour in groups

Basic group dynamics

Individuals are managers in the sense that every day they have to take a host of decisions relating to what behavioural actions they are going to select in response to contextual stimuli. Managing group responses is a totally different matter. As most training films point out, individuals need to learn how to manage themselves before they seek to manage groups. Individuals who are poorly focused and confused will only confuse themselves. If they are exposed to groups their confusion will be compounded. This inevitably leads to them becoming isolated in the group and often regarded with disrespect and scorn. Primitive attempts to pull rank to get their own way just result in inadequate and poorly supported group responses.

Every aspiring group manager should be aware of the basics of group dynamics before practising. Naive managers who just blunder in will cause severe damage to professional group relationships. They are like overhasty drivers who attempt to change gear without first depressing the clutch. Similarly, power managers who attempt to get their own way by hoodwinking groups will soon be found out and then found lacking. The resultant damage this cowboy approach does to groups can be devastating and long lasting. Responsible group managers should pay heed to: establishing group beliefs; empowering groups to perform; encouraging group members to interact; and attempting to understand interactions and group belief systems.

Establishing group beliefs

The group must have a constructive purpose or vision. This needs to be effectively communicated to all group members. When groups are formed to look at problems that are complex and messy, wise managers invite group members to discuss the initial brief to achieve a consensus understanding of *what* is involved and *what progress options* can be explored.

Empowering groups to perform

Avoid threatening individuals or deliberately forming subgroups under the manager's control to check or thwart progress. Divide-and-rule policies are sometimes legitimate ploys but only in exceptional circumstances. Everyday use of such tactics is a trait of the guerrilla manager – a person who is easily recognized by a tendency to have an exaggerated opinion of his or her own talents that is not validated by the rank and file in the group.

Encouraging group members to interact with themselves and the manager

Interaction is the mechanism that builds and sustains the belief system of a group. Interactions involve the mutual sharing of a situation between two or more people, so that each of them benefits from the experience and has his or her belief system strengthened by the encounter. Sensitive managers will be aware that interactions need not necessarily mean the same to all those who are involved. People are individuals and will have differing perceptions of the real meaning of what happened. Recognize this as a human trait and remember to summarize deliberations at regular intervals – in any case a good convergent creative problem-solving technique. As evidence of this, try asking individual members of a group one by one what they thought of their group meeting! You can expect a variety of answers.

Attempting to understand interactions and belief systems of groups

Responsible managers should endeavour to discover why one group clearly works more effectively than another that is apparently equally resourced. Why are the individuals who work in one section off-putting and difficult to talk to, while those in another section are happy and willing to help? Often it is because of the influence of one individual or a small subgroup of people who exert a strong influence on the rest of the group. This common occurrence is caused by the nature of the interaction within the group. Individuals who interact frequently tend to be the ones who influence the development of the group.

5.2.3   Organizing groups

Leadership role

Much has been written about the leadership role of the manager (Adair, 1983, 1985). If the intention is to focus the *total thinking* potential of the group in the expectation of finding a suitable agreed solution to a messy problem, the role of leader assumes a special significance. In this instance the traditional military task-oriented command approach needs to give way to a softer, more subtle, steering role that enables the group to perform to high standards. This is a highly skilled function that facilitates rather than dictates a response from the group. It is an enabling role that we describe as *creative facilitation*.

Group rewards

Man does not necessarily live by bread alone. Whilst the level of remuneration will always remain important to an individual it is not the only reward that most individuals expect. If an individual can be afforded respect by group peers this acts as a powerful motivator. If managers join groups as team members and not as members of the corporate aristocracy this will generate *high comfort* behaviour in the group and is likely to encourage creative responses. Most individuals will warm to this 'all for one and one for all' approach (as it is often in marked contrast to the residual expected behaviour pattern of 'all for one and one for one'), and will gain a great deal of satisfaction from participating in the group. Soon the group will become a pseudo-private gathering that displays high levels of trust and appreciation of the contributions of its members. If managers can achieve this, and it may take some sustained action, then a real corporate family culture will develop and individual group members will positively identify with the group. The resultant mutual appreciation and respect is, for many, a highly valued experience. This high level of mutual internal support will soon attract external attention and further enhance the kudos of group membership within the organization.

Group selection and initial briefing

To minimize the potentially stultifying effect of deeply entrenched mind-sets, *creative facilitators* should, wherever possible, assemble unstructured groups. The choice of individual group members is itself a subtle task that balances technical expertise with cross-functional objectivity. Nominated individuals should then be invited to attend a briefing meeting that is designed to:

- Inform them why they have been chosen for the exercise in question.
- Assure them that they are all equally valued. The creative facilitator could, perhaps, achieve this by adopting the slogan of Dumas's musketeers, 'one for all and all for one'.
- Tell them how the creative facilitator will operate.
- Tell them what they can expect to get out of the process.

5.2.4 Managing groups

Advantages

Every individual is a manager and regularly accepts and accomplishes a variety of tasks all on their own. Many may legitimately feel that they are the best person for an important job and opening up the matter to *group problem solving* (GPS) is not a very attractive option as it will lead to a lower performance standard and introduce the additional complexity of managing others. So does it always make sense to use groups?

   If a group is defined as consisting of more than one person, then clearly more than one mind can be focused on the problem, which should lead to a greater concentration of *total thinking*. This has real advantages if the problem is a messy one. In any case, even under traditional management practice, groups can potentially offer the following advantages to the lone manager:

- The mix of skills and experiences contained within a group.
- The potential to generate more ideas than a lone individual.
- A division of task responsibility.
- Members can *bulletproof* each other's arguments, thus cutting down the risk of the adoption of faulty or suspect solutions.
- The stimulation that results from personal interaction.

Disadvantages

Whilst there are obvious benefits to be obtained from working in groups it is interesting to note that even the smallest of groups – basic partnerships – often seem to generate operational difficulties. How many such difficult partnerships can you recall? Start your train of thought with Gilbert and Sullivan, Tim Rice and Sir Andrew Lloyd Webber, etc. On the other hand, some groups have been found to be disastrous for the following reasons:

- Members were too similar in character and functional speciality.
- Ill-managed group discussion which failed to harness the potential strengths of the group.
- Too many members – ten to twelve is probably the optimum number.
- The tendency to develop what Janis (1982) referred to as group think – 'a determination of mental efficiency, reality testing and moral judgement that results from in-group pressures'.
- A tendency for certain members to dominate group discussion.
- Too great a tendency to wander off the point.
- Poor use of GPS skills.
- An overhasty desire to find a solution at any cost.
- Failure to identify expertise lying within the group.
- Deliberate restriction of key information.

All these disadvantages can be directly addressed by a skilled *creative facilitator* as long as the organizational management are supportive. However, when pressed to achieve something quickly, especially if it involves a superior, many individuals seriously consider doing the job themselves. Over the years many have acquired the belief that in a crisis it is better to do the job themselves. This can become such a strong personal behavioural norm that it can potentially threaten the acceptance of the group manager by his staff. A suspicion arises that their manager does not trust them with important tasks and assignments. As behaviour breeds behaviour this inevitably dampens enthusiasm and the standard of group performance.

Solo or team run?

Clearly it is impossible for group managers under pressure to do everything. Delegating authority for important tasks remains a difficult challenge for many managers. If the contextual stimuli are well known the solution to the problem is often straightforward and may simply entail a subordinate following a clearly defined problem-solving sequence. However, if the contextual stimuli are complex and changing rapidly, the problem under examination may be better addressed by a group. The decision to go it alone or to take the problem to a group is one of the most taxing that managers have to make. The key element here is mutual trust. If this is not evident, then interactions will be severely limited in what they can accomplish. The interactive process of management becomes more difficult when the contextual stimuli are messy. This is often the time when managers need to open up to their staff. If their style in more stable times has been autocratic and characterized by their staff as mainly 'one for one' they will need to set about securing a 'one for all and all for one style'. As individuals take some convincing, this will take time. The problem is that time is just is not available. This text argues that managers should seriously consider and then experiment with creative management responses (CMRs). If the underlying contextual stimuli are changing rapidly, managing successfully may mean abandoning traditional mind-sets and intricate management models and risking real-time action. Theory often lags behind practice. Indeed it often manifests itself as the codification of previous practice. Rapidly changing stimuli call for a new style of practice. We believe that this is the *creative management response*.

KEY TERMS

Group responses
- high comfort
- low comfort

Loyalty and participation
- nominal adherence
- dutiful adherence
- inspired adherence
- professional adherence

Group dynamics
- beliefs
- empowerment
- interaction
- belief sytems

Organizing groups
- leadership
- rewards
- selection

Managing groups

5.3   Helping others to experience creativity

5.3.1   One to one (primary networking) – Phase 1

The previous chapter was designed to help the individual discover and experience creativity. Whilst native curiosity, persistence and a willingness to persevere will bring its reward at the individual level it can, nonetheless, be difficult for individuals to share their discovery and experiences with others. This is a result of a complex set of factors including a degree of self-consciousness – not wanting to look silly to colleagues – and the personal approaches that all of us have to make in order to find and appreciate the *creative force* (Goman, 1989). Unfortunately there is no common, foolproof, detailed map or set of procedures that all can follow. Whilst it is a matter of going from A to B – from a theoretical and *abstract regard* (most of us, even the most cynical, admit that creativity exists) to an a individual *experienced regard* (feeling the *creative force*) – the journey is different for all individuals. Whilst carefully trained facilitators can render assistance the ultimate discovery is truly a personal one.

Thus one individual cannot lead another by reason alone to a realization of the potential of the creative *force majeure*. However, if a curious individual can temporarily suspend his or her personal prejudices and adopt an open, *inquiring regard*, then a successful outcome will result. Creativity passes many individuals by as it is very hard to describe in words. It is a natural force that convinces doubters at a deeply personal level – that of inner trust and conviction. Sharing creativity cannot be achieved through words alone and it is a disservice to the cause for individuals to attempt this. Pious false charm turns people off as there is no argument to be won. The *force* exists; the issue is how to assist others to find it for themselves.

Research has clearly shown that the best way to assist inquirers is to facilitate their self-discovery by guiding them over a series of simple stepping stones. If the will is present for inquiring individuals to open up to the possibility of discovering something meaningful, then progress can be made. If the approach mentality is heavily tinged with doubt and obduracy the process of discovery will be long, possibly personally painful, and may never happen. The discovery you can make for yourself is free, exciting, quite natural, and very much of the real world. It cannot be explained by logical thought. It is the free gift of creation to all mankind.

5.3.2   Stepping out

Demonstration exercise (adapted from Idea Tracking sequence developed by Armstrong (VanGundy, 1988))

Now follow the creative group problem-solving (CGPS) track in Figure 5.3. The hexagonal slabs represent stepping stones and the conical shapes difficulties that will tax you if you stray off the stepping stones. Imagine that you are acting in the role of a *creative facilitator* as well as being a fully fledged member of the group. Knowing when to progress from one stepping stone to the next is a skill that you will soon master, so do not be put off by any early wobbles. Aim to keep on the stepping stones.

Step 1   *Finding your feet (Assessing the situation)*

- Select a matter of personal concern such as where to go on holiday, how to reorganize the front garden, or where to go out for an evening meal.

Step 2   *Preparing to make a start*
Materials instructions:

- You will need approximately six separate sheets of A4 paper.

Figure 5.3 Creative group problem-solving track

- Two well-sharpened pencils.
- Two separate firm surfaces on which to rest the sheets of paper.
- A supply of *Blu-Tack*.

People:
- Yourself and spouse or close friend.
- Now sit down somewhere quiet where you will be undisturbed by interruptions such as telephone calls and tradesmen ringing the doorbell and relax for two or three minutes before you begin.

Step 3   Getting going (Defining the problem; idea producing)

- Hand your partner one of the sheets of A4 paper.
- Next agree a *problem statement* between you and write it on another sheet of A4 paper and place this (*Blu-Tack* may help) where you can both see it easily.
- Now each person, with no conferring, should *privately brainstorm* the *problem statement* and write down everything that comes to mind on a sheet of A4 paper.

Step 4   Setting things out

- Conduct a *round robin* and list each new idea on a *Post-it* slip.
- Once all such new ideas have been transferred to the *Post-it* slips collect up all the slips and arrange them on a suitable surface. A large table, or better still a wall, is ideal.

Step 5   Taking a look

- Now ask your partner to join you and study the *Post-it* slips that you have arranged on the table or wall. Now that several salient ideas have been *mind mapped* it permits problem owners to achieve an overview of the problem and often affords the opportunity easily to distinguish the wood from the trees and obtain significant insights into the matter under study.

Step 6   Developing the picture (Idea producing; use of subconscious in creativity)

- The *mind map* of *Post-it* notes usually makes it easy for problem solvers to add detail to the picture by resorting to creative problem-solving (CPS) tools such as *analogy* and *reversals*.
- Look out of the window and select the first thing that you see (for example, a garden path, driveway, hedge, tree). Now forget the original problem and *privately brainstorm* the object that has been chosen.
- Then conduct a *round robin* and collect what you and your partner have written on a summary sheet of A4 paper. Now select an idea and relate it back to the original problem (*force-fit*) (VanGundy, 1988).
- Repeat until you sense that you are losing momentum.
- Alternatively you could actually stop formally exploring the original problem and go for a walk (*excursion*) round the garden or round the block. As your minds switch off

the issue under study and relax, you should find that you and your partner will notice things in the environment and then, as it were, 'back project' these into the original problem. The process is quite natural – as, say, avoiding on-coming traffic and other hazards when you first learn to drive.

- Return to the room where you began the CPS exercise, discuss the stimuli and *force-fit* into the original problem.

Step 7   Shaping

- Return to the table top or to the wall where you and your partner have arranged your collection of *Post-it* notes, look at them together, and make any adjustments to them that you consider necessary.

Step 8   Time out (Use of subconscious in creativity)

- Unless the problem that you have chosen is really urgent leave the *Post-it* slips on the table or wall overnight. If you look at them first thing in the morning you may find that you wish to adjust the pattern of the mind map and/or add extra slips.

Step 9   Selection (Use of judgement to select best idea)

- If you have more than one option, you and your partner will now have to select one in order to realize a solution. There are many ways of accomplishing this, ranging from simple straightforward techniques to sophisticated quantitative techniques. How about each of you ranking the ideas on a *colour code*, say a red dot for really good ideas and a yellow one for very promising ideas. The winning idea is the one that attracts the most red dots.

Step 10   Reflection

- How do you feel after following the stepping stones?
- How does your partner feel?
- CGPS is usually fun . . . why not have another go with a different problem?

5.3.3   Maintaining momentum

If you reckon that your partner has enjoyed this short CGPS exercise it is quite common for them to ask you what was behind each step. This will provide you with an opportunity to talk about the stepping stones and to describe the CPS tools that you used (marked in italics). Demonstrating the techniques live is a powerful way of introducing CPS tools. Something, often spectacular, happens fairly quickly, which stimulates curiosity. Depending on circumstances, it may well be a good idea now for you to take your partner through Chapter 4 and encourage them to do the exercises.

5.3.4   One to a group (secondary networking) – Phase 2

Following the CGPS stepping stones with a private partner should give you some confidence to try the exercise with one or more colleagues at work.

- To begin with choose problems that have a low risk or sensitivity rating to avoid taking on more than you can handle.
- Prepare carefully before you start (Step 2). Be sure to check that you have sufficient raw materials to get the exercise underway.
- Keep things simple – do not resort to 'chalk and talk' methods to introduce what you are going to do. As quickly as possible get on with the action!
- Start things moving with a warm-up session – why not try a variant of the wedding exercise (outlined in Chapter 4) that you feel would be acceptable to your colleagues. For example, the ideal domestic garage, the ideal holiday, and so forth.
- If you want to make rapid progress through the warm-up you will, of course, have to shorten Step 8. As an overall guide, a complete warm-up run should only take about 5 minutes!

Then introduce the work problem that you want to progress. It is usually best to begin with a well-defined problem to avoid losing any early momentum in the early days of CPS. Later you may well choose to invoke CPS tools and techniques to determine useful problem statements. This is because many contemporary professional problems are complex, messy (not easily addressed by the traditional management competencies), and with several possible solution options.

At first, until you gain in confidence, experiment with a small kit of tools. Change the order of applying the tools but stay within the same stepping stone order as described above until you are ready to design your own CGPS paths or, in the language of the brain, your own *memory traces*.

KEY TERMS

Primary networking	Secondary networking
■ personally discovering creativity	■ helping others to experience creativity
Demonstrating to others	

5.4   Establishing a creative climate

5.4.1   Setting up shop

First task of a creative facilitator

As Chapter 4 has set out to demonstrate, individuals need to step off the familiar stepping stones (memory traces) of their everyday lives and express a willingness to try a different path. The first task of a *creative facilitator* is to stimulate individuals to become curious about creative thinking. The *creative force* is omnipresent but not always obviously active in the behaviour of individuals. As individuals can choose their behaviour, then they can choose to harness their natural creativity to any challenge in life. So it is a matter of choice to get going with the *force*, rather than specific *know-how*, and this choice factor is heavily dependent on dominant contextual factors such as climate or environment.

To foster creative thinking the championing individual needs to create a local climate in the work organization that, first, upholds the favourable psychological dimensions, as, for example, described in the research of Professor Goran Ekvall (1983) of the Swedish Council for Management and Work Life Issues in Stockholm:

- The need to issue a challenge to employees.
- To grant employees the freedom, at least at regular intervals, to exercise their own initiative on problems – to do their own thing. This is a powerful motivator (see Amabile, 1983).
- To support CPS as a bona fide workplace activity.
- To trust individuals to deliver an answer or set of options to the *what* problem without feeling that the method (the *how*) has to be proven beforehand. A purely cognitive explanation of creativity is not possible as its presence is critically dependent on contextual stimuli (see Garnham, A. & Oakhill, J. 1994). Thus it cannot be modelled and repeated repetitively. It may, and usually does, throw light on complex issues, but it cannot be switched on and off as a lamp-post. It is not a standard single solution to a problem. A lamp-post is a static object with a single intensity light. Creativity is a spontaneous flash that can be regular or intermittent in frequency and can also vary in its illuminescence (obviousness) to others.
- To acknowledge that real-life stimuli are dynamic and so, therefore, should be the response patterns of individuals, groups and organizations. The construction of individual and organizational patterns, rules and mind-sets that are too tight, in a bid to capture the cognitive understanding of control, is always a dangerous practice – particularly so in times of rapidly changing stimuli.
- The acceptance that playfulness is a legitimate creative trait and not a childish, gimmick activity.
- The openness both to permit and then debate the effectiveness of various CPS tools and techniques.
- The recognition that conflicts will occur in groups, will need to be sensitively managed, and can also be a powerful stimulant to creative activity.
- The realization that quickly changing stimuli cannot always be accommodated by low-risk responses. New challenges always will put pressure on precedent. New memory traces have to be fashioned.
- The realization that teams can only function well in crises if there is mutual respect.

Second task of a creative facilitator

Secondly, the aspiring creative facilitator needs to give careful attention to the visual climate or environment. This entails:

- Taking a positive lead – in the creation of a new climate.
- Getting self and others trained as *creative facilitators*.
- Seeing that a suitable room, light and airy, with uncluttered walls, informal physical layout (chairs in circles rather than rows), good table tops, preferably brightly painted with some carefully chosen right-brain stimulants placed on shelves and walls (e.g. plants, interesting shapes, pictures, audio/visual facility, and so on).
- Seeing that the room is well stocked with vital materials, such as *Blu-Tack*, paper (A4, and it is useful to have a supply of A3 sheets too), marker pens, flipchart/s, *Post-it* slips, clipboards and notebooks), thus encouraging individuals and groups to use the room.

Third task of a creative facilitator

Thirdly, it is important for *would-be* creative managers to take the plunge themselves and lead by example, as follows:

1. Perhaps the first task here is to generate a supportive atmosphere in the established physical setting by purposefully signalling to your work groups that you really mean business. Convey that you have a genuine desire for the group to solve real problems and expect to see some action.
2. Being prepared to give it a sustained go for at least a year and to meet and manage any carping criticism from other parts of the organization.
3. By encouraging the formation of small groups (seven, is about right) and balancing the group members in terms of functional and general skill and length of service. Resist any early temptation to invite senior executives to attend. Wait until you have sorted out early teething troubles and the group is ready to include senior management.
4. By encouraging all group members to contribute, affirming right at the beginning that your philosophy is 'all for one and one for all'. Discourage any tendency for any one individual to assert too great an influence on the group. Keep the group together and resist the formation of splinter groups.
5. By informing the group that you are looking for the interplay of three main roles in the meetings of the CGPS Group:
   (a) a *problem owner*;
   (b) up to five additional assists or helpers; and
   (c) a *creative facilitator* – a responsibility you should be prepared to take on initially yourself – who is responsible for keeping the group on a *creativity* path and for introducing suitable CPS tools.

5.4.2 The creative facilitator

Key process skills

The role of *creative facilitator* is a vital one and calls for a sound understanding of the basics of group dynamics and a familiarity with simple CPS tools and techniques. It is important to:

- Sustain the oscillations between divergent and convergent thinking modes (see Section 5.5.3 CPS tracking). This is a subtle task that is necessary to activate both left- and right-brain thinking modes in order to achieve the potential benefits of the total thinking mode. If the group gets bogged down or gets stuck, then it is the responsibility of the creative facilitator to prompt some right-brained excursions to get the group back on track.
- Mix periods of heavy disciplined thinking with periods of light and zany thinking.
- Watch the quality of the group's performance. Be flexible. It is better to have several short bursts of energetic activity than persevere with long sluggish sessions. With all the will in the world most people's performance starts to wane when they get tired and hungry.
- After each session ask each group member to write down on a *Post-it* slip what they liked about the session and one thing that could be improved.
- End each session by thanking people for the involvement and announce the date and time of the next session.

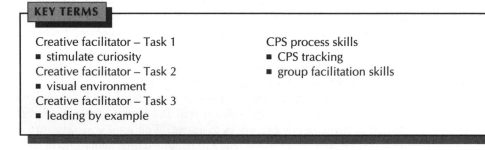

KEY TERMS

Creative facilitator – Task 1
- stimulate curiosity

Creative facilitator – Task 2
- visual environment

Creative facilitator – Task 3
- leading by example

CPS process skills
- CPS tracking
- group facilitation skills

5.5 Building up a creative problem-solving tool kit

5.5.1 Managing difficult problems

Focused thinking

Creative problem solving is a potent management activity that coaxes the best out of individuals and groups. It co-ordinates both left- and right-brain thinking. Both reasoned argument and intuition are powerful contributors to any problem-solving activity. The art, science or know-how is developing the expertise to co-ordinate *left-* and *right-brain thinking modes* into the practice of *total thinking*. Once this is applied to *real-time* events and concerns then the total thinking activity can incisively focus on the true problem.

Problems and problem types

A *problem* can be regarded as an event or concern that becomes known to individuals or organizations and which threatens to impair significantly the ability of the individual or organization to perform to expected standards.

Such problems can be viewed as being simple or messy. A *simple problem* is one that lends itself easily to a logical solution which is based on predetermined models, logic and previous experience. Such 'I have seen it before' or 'consult the organization manual' problems are important in daily life. However, the furious energy of the contextual changes that are impacting on wealth creation today are generating messy problems and these cannot usually be progressed by 'wiring diagram management'! A *messy problem* is one that is characterized by lack of information, contradictory information, complex people issues, uncertainty as to the true nature of the problem, novelty and lack of obvious solutions. This can be imagined as an increasing incidence of seismic activity. The basic ground of the individuals is dangerously unstable. This will be immediately obvious to individuals, who may try all they know to manage the situation. However, all honest endeavour born of the traditional management competencies will sooner or later lead to failure. As contextual change accelerates, the seismic shocks occur more and more frequently and more and more violently. The inevitable result is confusion heaped upon confusion, and, in severe instances, catastrophe.

If individuals and groups are suddenly faced with a rapid growth in the number of messy problems when they have been used, most of the time, to dealing with straightforward simple problems, this will cause a severe performance challenge. What is needed in such challenging times is a new way of solving problems – a way that concentrates the thinking power of individuals and helps them to come to terms with *reality* (true context). Unfortunately, many people in difficult times tend to assume that the instabilities are purely temporary and all will be well tomorrow. Or the day after. Or the month after. Or the year after. Isn't recovery just around the corner? It is human nature in times of instability to hang on to what is familiar for as long as possible. This is the *big problem* we face in the West at present. As explained in Part I, we believe that the contextual changes impacting on wealth creation are going to be turbulent for some time. It is time to look for a new path on firmer ground. This is the way to real management advantage – just follow the signs to the CMR centre.

Facing the future – options

A CMR centre is an outpost, a staging post, that affords the opportunity of acquiring new insights which will equip you to face the new future. There is a semantic problem here. The future by definition must be new and it will be real. However, several of us have been prepared to face the future by a programme of instruction and set of experiences related strongly to a very different past. This is unreal. The realities are:

- There is strong and continuous contextual change underway.
- This change already threatens our livelihood (wealth-creating ability) and will continue to do so – probably more and more severely.

Our options would appear to be:

1. Ignore it – the dodo's reaction. Remember what happened to this happy bird?
2. Stop it – the armchair manager's reaction. Too far away from the action – pure fantasy?

3. Adapt to it – the logical reaction. This is the opposite of trying to adapt it to us!
4. How to adapt? Drop in at the CMR centre. Take your seats. A *creative manager* is addressing his or her staff on the *big problem*:
   (a) 'Face up to the coming of the new age (neoindustrial).'
   (b) 'We will have to change the way we do things now – alter our operational norms (climates).'
   (c) 'We will have to develop a new house style – develop a new operational house style (culture).'
   (d) 'We will have to adapt our wealth-creating behaviour – concentrating on using our brain power (total thinking).'

5.5.2 Approaching creative problem solving (CPS)

The previous chapter introduced creativity to the individual and, in the process of its discourse, described a few basic CPS tools. This was done deliberately in order to demonstrate some CPS tools in action before raising some important basic principles in the Technical Guides (pp. 122–6). If a potential learner-driver watches someone driving a car before their first lesson it normally provides strong motivation to have a go! It is now time to take a look at the process dynamics of CPS and a selection of CPS tools to consolidate your understanding so far and to equip you with a good basic CPS tool kit.

CPS stages

Most authorities (e.g. Kolb, 1984; Kreitner, 1980, etc.) agree that there are three main phases of CPS:

1. problem evaluation;
2. idea generation and development; and
3. realization.

And a fourth – reflection – is advisable if you wish to master the approach.

However, is there really a problem in the first place? If there is, does it lie within our sphere of influence? Do we have the resources to tackle it? Before launching into a CPS session it is essential to get a firm enough view of the problem in order to express it cogently (see Figure 5.4).

Problem evaluation

The first phase, *problem evaluation* (VanGundy, 1988), is an initial inquiry into the nature of the problem requiring a creative management response (CMR). This is not always immediately obvious. Many busy managers spend considerable time trying to identify the real problems. Operational intuition often tells them that something is wrong or needs attending to, but not always *what* needs to be solved. Airing the problem at a CPS session often results in a reformulation of the original *problem statement*. Many heads are usually better than one in solving a problem and that goes for defining the real

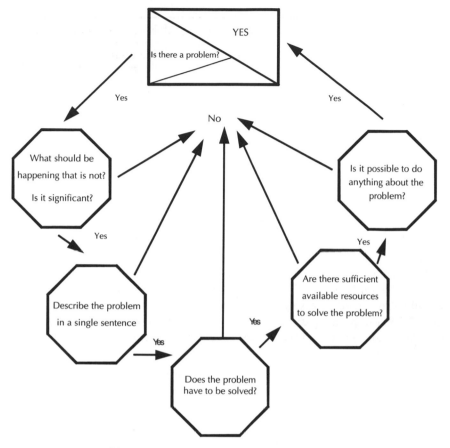

Figure 5.4   Does a problem exist?

problem in the first place. It is amazing how much of our consultancy starts with assisting clients to tackle the real problem.

Idea generation and development
The second phase, *idea generation and development*, is concerned to find the best method of solving the problem in the circumstances – a matter of great concern to individuals and organizations experiencing competition on, say, cost and quality grounds. VanGundy (1988) proposes that the selection of a CPS tool should match the problem characteristics:

- the more complex the problem, the more complex a tool is justified;
- the greater the need to solve the problem, the greater the justification for selecting tools that have high training needs;
- if consensus decisions are required, seriously consider the use of group CPS tools;

and that idea generation tools can be categorized as follows:

Problem relevance	Free association	Forced relationship
Related	Brainstorm	Reversal
Unrelated	Analogy	Force-fit

Realization stage

Finally, the *Realization* includes all the actions necessary to implement a selected *creative management response* (CMR).

5.5.3   CPS tracking

Finding the right line

CPS exercises follow a clear-cut tracking pattern that is similar to the tracks followed by Grand Prix racing drivers who are looking for the shortest route round the circuit. Whilst the racing car driver is essentially concerned with speed and economy the creative manager usually wants to add a strong variation option.

Figure 5.5 illustrates a typical CPS tracking pattern for the *problem evaluation stage*. Track Point 1 maps the start of the CPS exercise. The problem is unclear and needs to be

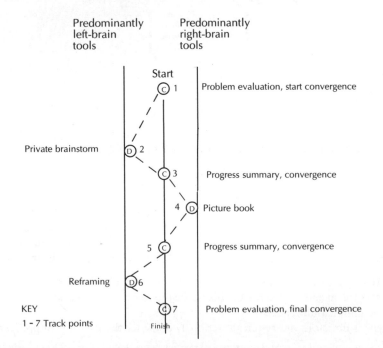

Figure 5.5   CPS tracking – sample problem evaluation stage

explored. Track Point 2 represents a left-brain divergence (*private brainstorm*). This is followed by a convergent process summary (Track Point 3) which triggers a right-brain divergence (*picture book* – Track Point 4). This is followed by a process convergence (Track Point 5); a further left-brain divergence (*selection* -Track Point 6) and a final problem evaluation convergence (Track Point 7). A similar pattern would follow the process tracks of the *idea generation and development* and the *realization stages*.

Of course, as in the case of a racing car driver, a CPS manager may take a looser or tighter track according to the requirements he or she sees as best suited to the task. The centre line down the track represents the most efficient routing (the total thinking position). The amount of deviation from this will depend on the difficulty, complexity and messiness of the problem. A clean problem (a familiar challenge) may have almost a straight-line tracking pattern – depending on just how straightforward it really is. An unfamiliar or messy problem would probably display a very divergent track.

An attractive feature of the CPS approach to managerial problem solving is that it offers the opportunity to explore a number of different process tracks. Left-brain rule-dominated ones at one extreme, right-brain 'imagineering' ones at the other, whilst in between, an almost infinite opportunity to combine the two approaches. From time to time, and more often with tricky messy problems, a CPS facilitator will get stuck. This is most likely to occur if the individual or group has spent some considerable time exploring left-brain tools or is perhaps getting tired or hungry. In either case a break is probably in order. If you decide to take a formal break in the middle of a CPS exercise it is important to agree your current position with all participants and to document it. Try to complete your CPS activity on a topic in one session. If too long a break is scheduled between sessions that are addressing the same problem, it will become increasingly difficult to keep the *creative force* going. Refreshment breaks are fine. Breaks lasting several days, say, owing to diary complications of attendees, are usually disruptive to the CPS process.

After your break you can return to the position on the process track where you decided to take your break. If you intend to learn how best to apply CPS tools it is advisable to keep a record of your CPS tool track selections. This will help participants immensely during the *reflection stage*. All you need is a pad of graph paper and a willing scribe.

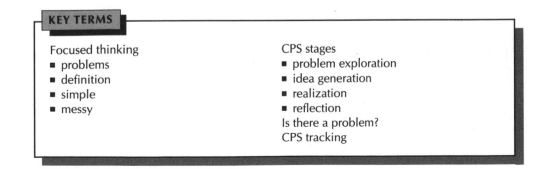

KEY TERMS

Focused thinking
- problems
- definition
- simple
- messy

CPS stages
- problem exploration
- idea generation
- realization
- reflection

Is there a problem?

CPS tracking

5.6   Creative Problem Solving (CPS) tools

This section expands the collection of idea generation and selection tools introduced in Chapter 4 and adds others that are particularly useful for the problem evaluation stage of CPS exercises. As the section progresses the shape of our *introductory* CPS tool kit for personal and group creative problem solving emerges.

5.6.1   CPS Phase 1   Problem evaluation

Explore the problem statement

Having decided to call a CPS session, a creative facilitator should ensure that the problem to be addressed is clear and concise to all session attendees before initiating the second phase of a CPS exercise. A skilled facilitator will explore the original problem statement using tools such as *'Why?'*, *Kipling's Questions* and *Stakeholder analysis*. After a brief creative personal problem solving (CPPS) exercise the original problem statement usually gets revised. Our experience shows quite dramatically that it pays to address the real problem!

Problem evaluation tools

Below are four basic tools for you to try plus a couple from the *Synectics* collection[1] (Gordon, 1961; Rikards, 1974). Try them out. In a subsequent CPS session use them in a different sequence.

1. 'Why?' (VanGundy, 1988)
2. Five W's and H or Kipling's Questions (Rikards, 1990; VanGundy, 1988)
3. Stakeholder analysis (Stevens, 1988)
4. Wishful thinking (Rikards, 1974)
5. 'How to . . . ?'
6. 'In how many ways can we . . . ?'

'Why?'

This is a simple but surprisingly powerful tool that enables creative problem solving groups to define a problem at several levels of abstraction. The tool has five cycle steps:

1. Read the problem as originally defined.
2. Question why you want to do what is in the problem statement.
3. Answer the question asked in 2.
4. Redefine the answer in the form of a new problem question.
5. Repeat questions 2 and 3 to achieve another level of abstraction.

Then repeat as many times as is sensible. Then agree a new problem statement.
    Here is an example:

Question:	Why do we want to go on holiday?	
Answer:	To get a break from work.	
Redefine:	In what ways might (IWWM) we get a break from work?	

Question:	Why do we want to get a break from work?
Answer:	To relax, and recover from the strains of everyday work.
Redefine:	IWWM we relax and recover?

Question:	Why do we want to relax and recover?
Answer:	To charge up our batteries to face the rest of the year at work.
Redefine:	IWWM we charge up our batteries, etc.

Five W's and H

This is a powerful tool as it uses the main interrogatives of the English language: *Who? What? When? Why?* and *Where?* rounded off with a *How?* question (VanGundy, 1988). Each member of the problem solving group is asked to write down the six questions and then asked privately to answer them briefly:

- Who is involved in this matter? Who is interested in this issue? etc.
- What is it all about? What is the matter? etc.
- When did this occur? When must it be solved? etc.
- Why did this happen?
- Where did this happen? etc.
- How did this come about? etc.

Stakeholder analysis

With both personal and group CPS exercises, both the problem and the potential outcomes are often of interest to other parties. Most *problem evaluation* sessions benefit by the inclusion of an analysis of the key publics involved. This can be achieved in a variety of ways, so feel free to experiment. You might like to try the following sequence:

1. *Problem owner* states problem.
2. Individual or group carry out a *personal brainstorm*.
3. *Problem owner* or *facilitator* conducts a *round robin* and gathers in ideas.
4. *Problem owner* or *facilitator* collects information on a mind map or *force-field* diagram (see p. 181).

Wishful thinking

This is a useful technique to assist groups to break out of the constraints imposed by conventional approaches to problem solving and work practices. There are five steps involved:

1. State the problem.
2. Now tell the group to imagine that anything is possible.
3. Ask them to state what they would like to happen.
4. Get them to relate this back to the problem statement.
5. If you need to, repeat steps 3 and 4.

When asked by the Engineering Department at the University of Durham to teach creative problem solving to undergraduates studying engineering we were perplexed as to how we were going to explain right- and left-brain thinking. So we asked the question:

What do we need to do to get inside their heads?

Relating this back to the problem triggered the idea of using a working model of a head to illustrate different ways of thinking. This led us to adapt a mechanical joke designed by Spooner (1992). So wishful thinking led us to a pneumatic visual aid that fascinated the students and helped them to understand right- and left-brain thinking!

Synectics collection

'Synectics' is a registered trade mark. It is the brand name of an American firm of consultants who have developed their own style of CGPS out of the original work on brainstorming carried out by Osborn (1957) in the 1930s (e.g. Stevens, 1988).

'How to . . .

The advantage of the format of this question and the way in which it is used is that it welcomes all suggestions irrespective of whether the group intends to adopt the suggested solution. Thus practical constraints do not deter thinking. Suppose that the group was faced with the problem of a 'cracked furnace'; then they might ask:

'How can we get the furnace going?'
'How can we stop it from causing so much trouble to our operations?'
'How can we get it properly relined?'
'How can we best project manage the job?'
'How can we get this done quickly?'
'How can we get X to be more careful in the future?'

Facilitate the group to generate at least twenty questions and try for thirty! Possible answers to these are generated by asking the group to respond to the prompt:

'In how many ways can we . . .'

'Get the furnace going?'
'Stop it from causing so much trouble to our operations?'
'Get is properly relined?'
'Get it project managed?'
'Get it done quickly?'
'Get X to be more careful in the future?'

Try these questions on your problem statement and see what happens, but be careful to keep up the pace. The facilitator then gathers up their replies and assists the group to redraft the problem statement. Then try 'Why?', *Kipling's Questions* and maybe *Stakeholder*.

5.6.2   CPS Phase 2   Idea generation and development

Stuck in a rut?

Sometimes it is hard to think of ways to generate ideas for progressing problems when groups find that tools such conventional brainstorming, checklists, etc., do not seem to produce any good results. When this occurs it can cause a facilitator to panic. To all intents and purposes the group is stuck in a rut. Fortunately, there are a group of CPS tools that can deal with this situation. They are the so-called right-brain tools.

Ask the group to look out of the window or round the room and then ask them to focus on a particular object. This often provides individuals with new insight by simply unblocking their right-brain thinking channels (see pp. 103–6). Suitable tools to try here include *analogies, metaphors* and *reversal* to cut thought paths (which then become memory traces) in your mind. The ideas generated are then related/forced back to the problem definition. An interesting and frequently successful option is to take time out (an *excursion* in the Synectics terminology) from the problem situation and give your attention to something else. A short break or a brisk walk usually works wonders as they provide a means of breaking through the paralysis of analysis and set the mind free to look and connect. It is amazing how easily such new ideas and approaches can occur. On returning to the group room or after an *in situ* look and connect exercise it is often a good thing to conduct a round robin, to collect participants' selected images and then to transfer them as graphics to a new pictorial mind map. Then ask individuals to state what new ideas came from the forced fit part of the exercise, collect them up and place them on a conventional mind map. Then ask the group to study both mind maps and see what happens!

Wildest Idea (Rikards, 1974)

This is another useful tool to use when groups get bogged down. It simply involves the facilitator introducing a new idea totally at random. For example, in a recent workshop in Durham, a group were looking at ways of introducing a creative management training programme to a local borough council. Faced with the seemingly impenetrable problem of how to sell it to the executive, the group found themselves stuck in a rut. At this point the facilitator responded by asking the group to brainstorm sausages! To show that he was serious he drew a picture of a string of sausages on a flip chart. The group laughed, but to their amazement soon 'connected' sausages with a 'fry-up' and then with Elizabeth Fry the local Investors in People executive! Later the organization signed up on a scheme with their local Training and Enterprise Council delighted to find both the expertise and to discover that they could obtain some financial support.

Should one wild idea not work then the facilitator can suggest another or call for some suggestions from the group.

A variation on this tool that we have used successfully is to keep an odds and ends box. Produce this when the going gets tough and pull an item out at random and get one of the group to say to the rest 'Look what I've got!'

Analogies (Rikards, 1974)

An alternative option to taking an *excursion* on the move is to take one from an armchair. Try to imagine the problem being explored in a different scenario:

- Place a writing pad (A4 ideally) and a sharp pencil to hand.
- Relax, breathe in and out slowly for a few seconds, then close your eyes for a minute or so.
- Now think of your favourite hobby (e.g. fishing, gardening), or sport (e.g. cricket, golf, rugby, soccer, tennis), or your last summer holiday, or your last trip to London, or a recent long-distance drive. Concentrate on your experience and attempt to picture the scene in as much detail as you can. Picture the sky, the background and the foreground, listen for any sound, see if you can detect any movement.
- Now open your eyes and summarize what you have 'seen' on your A4 pad, trying to use drawings, sketches and symbols as much as you can.
- Then relate the material summarized back to the original problem.

Cut and Connect!

Try this one! Get a couple of old magazines and a pair of scissors and select five pictures to cut out. Then relate back to the group's problem statement.

Checklists

The main attraction of the right-brain family of CPS tools is that they encourage you to see one set of stimuli you have experienced by means of another that you have experienced. It is an interactive process and will often inspire you. If you experience difficulties in using this group of tools you may like to try some *checklists*. They can be useful for personal problem solving (PPS) but can easily tend to become monotonous if used in group sessions. Essentially they are stepping stones that can prove useful to define a path to approach a problem. It is *what* you do on each stepping stone that is important. However, they can be useful in the same way that a motorist, for example, may use a road atlas to find the way. Coping with what happens on the way is entirely a different proposition.

Attribute listing (Majaro, 1992; Rikards, 1990; Stevens, 1988)

This reductionist approach entails reducing the problem statement to its prime components and auditing the characteristics of each identified part. This can be extended through a number of sub-component rounds if required. The ultimate objective is to discover what is really needed to do the job and whether the existing components can be put together in another, more efficient, way that directly addresses the original problem. Experimenting with this tool, we built a wooden caterpillar at Durham and a wooden mechanical wave machine that provide useful creative divertimento for our CPS sessions. A more complex version of this technique, morphological analysis, is often used in the development of new products, services and systems. It is a powerful, though time-consuming, tool, but has resulted in some spectacular successes in high-technology industries (see Majaro, 1992; Rickards, 1974).

SCAMPER

This is a variation of Osborn's (1957) checklist rearranged by Eberle (1973) after Stevens (1988).

S *Substitute*
Who else? What else? Alternative inputs/outputs, people, places, and so forth.

C *Combine*
Blend different approaches, ideas, use, cross-functional teams units, cost centres, plants.

A *Adapt*
What else is similar to this? What other ideas seem to fit this problem? What precedents are there? Who else had this problem recently?

M *Magnify/minify*
What needs to be added? Time, resources, product/service features, promotional messages, and so on. What needs to be reduced, saved, omitted, simplified, and so forth.

P *Put to other uses*
How else could this product/service be used? Who else may want it? Where else might it be used?

E *Eliminate/elaborate*
What needs to be scrapped? How can this be made more user-friendly? How can things be simplified? What savings can be made? What delays can be eliminated? What needs to be stressed? What needs to be developed? Can we manage with existing supply/distribution arrangements? Is something more elaborate required?

R *Rearrange/reverse*
What other ways can we find/develop to do this? How can we reverse known consequences? A good recent example of this was the development by the inventor Clive Sinclair of a suitable rechargeable electric motor to assist cyclists to cope with hills.

5W's and H or Kipling's Questions

Some of us first heard this on our mother's knee as we listened to her reading Kipling's famous children's poem:

> I keep six honest serving men
> (They taught me all I knew);
> Their names are *What* and *Why* and *When*
> And *How* and *Where* and *Who*.

This tool features the leading interrogative adverbs and pronouns in the English language. It is useful as it opens up a number of different aspects of a problem and ensures that CPS activity pays due regard to material and people, resources, delivery and time implications. Try it next time you get stuck.

Software packages

For those who like computer-based packages, the *Think Thunder* and *Visual Outliner* programs deserve a place in an introductory CPS tool kit. *Think Thunder* is shareware and is a computer-aided brainstorming tool. However, as with most software packages, in the final analysis:

- It's someone else's CPS tracking.
- Each problem is unique therefore it requires an original selection of CPS tools.
- Computers cannot always go to the CPS session – not everyone has a laptop machine.
- Computers should serve in CPS sessions as a tool and should not be allowed to dominate the proceedings.
- Many people experience problems in correctly using software and these can easily take over a CPS session.

The *Visual Outliner* is a shareware package that runs under *Microsoft Windows* and is a useful mind mapping programme. Many have found it a helpful program to record and manipulate mind maps produced in CPS sessions.

Sometimes switching between manual and computer CPS modes can be advantageous. Other points worth mentioning here include the use of presentation packages, such as *Microsoft Powerpoint* or *Harvard Graphics* in slide-show mode to display random arrangements of computer graphics as a source of stimulation. Also, outline facilities on good quality word-processing packages.

5.6.3   Imagery – an alternative dimension

Focused total thinking

There is little doubt that we would be wise to use both left- and right-brain thinking (*total thinking*) to concentrate as much thinking power as we can on problems. However, in the West the learned way is traditionally seen as being left-brain oriented and right-brain thinking is often regarded as being odd. This is a pity, as in reality we are meant to use both means of thinking. It is hoped that this text may play a small part in correcting this strange practice.

The art of harnessing both modes of thinking enables individuals to see problems in their proper perspective (context) and to find and select a suitable problem-solving track. Truly creative thought is the result of a subtle synthesis between left- and right-brain modes (*total thinking*). Bright ideas on their own are fine but usually disappoint unless they can be practically applied to a real personal or group problem. As Fritz (1989) elegantly describes, there are three stages in the creative process:

1. Conceiving what it is that you want – knowing what you want.
2. Knowing what exists at present – developing an accurate contextual perception.
3. Doing something about it – by invention, learning and adjusting *usual* responses.

The *visualization* lobby argue vociferously that if you start out by visualizing the outcome you are more likely to end up closer to it than if you rely predominantly on the traditional left-brain tools.

Imagineering

The deliberate selection of imagery tools to stimulate ideas has assumed the title of 'Imagineering' (Morgan, 1993). For ease of explanation the eight imagery tools included in the introductory CPS tool kit have been divided into three categories: passive; bridging; and active; though, in practice, problem solvers often use all or a selection of the eight tools in combination.

Passive approaches I – Relaxation

All CPS exercises should begin with a quiet time of relaxation and gentle preparation. Too hasty an entry into either left- or right-brain thinking modes tends to result in an inharmonious (divergent) response to the *problem statement*. Good creative facilitators know that CPS takes time. Quick answers emanating from a codified rule-set are permissible if the conventional mind-sets fit the problem and the context in which the rule-set has occurred. In times of escalating change this is less and less likely to be the case. The whole mind needs to be focused on clearly defined problems, which calls for active participation and co-ordination of both thinking modes. This takes a little time and therefore, to avoid the onset of early bias, individuals need to be aware of the tendency for 'spur of the moment panic' to override sounder options that will emerge from disciplined total thinking.

To counter the 'quick solution' tendency, we begin all our CPS sessions with a brief period (two to three minutes) of gentle relaxation. This entails sitting comfortably in a chair (or if you prefer lying horizontally) and seeking to reduce stress levels in the body by:

- taking a few deep breaths – three or four is usually enough;
- relaxing all your muscles – easing the tension out of your face, arms, legs, neck and torso; and
- closing your eyes and trying to imagine the tension flowing out of your body.

There are a number of good, respectable audio tapes that will assist if you prefer to be precisely guided by a commentator. Others will find their peace by gently just relaxing in their favourite chair with some soothing music playing in the background.

Passive approaches II – Sounds inspirational

Sound is a powerful and emotive medium. So too is nature. Good recordings can capture the natural world in great clarity and depth. Many CPS sessions have been run with soothing music playing in the background. The following composers have been found to be particularly evocative:

- Beethoven – Symphony No 6 ('The Pastoral')
- Copland's 'EL Salon Mexico'
- Grofe's 'Grand Canyon Suite'
- Hadyn – Symphonies Nos. 6 ('Morning'), 7 ('Afternoon') and 8 ('Evening'); 'Creation'
- Handel – 'Water Music', 'Fireworks' and 'Messiah'
- Mozart – Piano Concerto No. 21 ('Elvira Madigan')
- Smetana – 'River Moldau'
- Vivaldi – 'The Four Seasons'
- and, surprisingly, most of the Beatles' recordings!

Compile your own list and share it with colleagues and friends.

If the creative facilitator is looking for some interesting CPS tracks it is useful from time to time to ask the group to record on paper (resorting to graphics and images wherever possible, but if the group finds this difficult, then word pictures are acceptable) what they hear in the background music. Then share this information with the group via tools such as *round robin, mind mapping*, and so forth.

Bridging approaches I – Group

These tools are particularly useful in jogging the mind – with right-brain stimuli – into cutting and then exploring new memory traces. The main tools in this category are *metaphors, analogies* and *puns*.

Bridging approaches II – Metaphors

Metaphors (VanGundy, 1988) are a fascinating source of inspiration for a creative manager. We hear them virtually every day as sports commentators, politicians and ordinary folk employ them to make powerful points about groups. (Personal metaphors were discussed in Chapter 4.) Such expressions as 'first past the post', 'I'd rather have him on the inside of the tent pissing out than on the outside of the tent pissing in' (President Lyndon Johnston), 'their moves always break down in the box', 'have we missed the boat?', and so on. List the metaphors that you habitually use when involved in group activity at work. If this is a difficult task, ask some of your work colleagues to help. Turn back to Appendix 4.4, Exercises 4.5 and 4.6. Take a photocopy before starting the exercise if you prefer not to write in the text.

The use of metaphors is closely entwined with the use of analogies. What do you think is the difference between a metaphor and an analogy?

Bridging approaches III – Analogy

Thinking through action sequences, such as catching a train, and then relating this back to the problem statement can provoke an array of useful ideas (see Figure 5.6).

Figure 5.6   Group creative problem-solving exercise: Northern Electric plc

Problem owner:	IT Department
Problem statement:	Produce user-friendly computer software manuals
Analogy:	Catching a train

Relating analogy to problem statement:

Event/issue	Software manual
Catch a train	Cut it down to one page
Get to station	Prioritize
Timetable	Five separate guides
Waiting	Question and answer page
Late train	Explore software enhancement
Frustration	Transparent pages
Easy, quick journey	Help sheets
Colour-coded timetable	Importance of spacing, layout, use of icons, and alphabetic listings.

Bridging approaches IV – The art of punning

Imagining an object and then punning for as long as you can keep it up can be a useful ice-breaker for a group CPS session. For example, show a picture of a tree and ask group members to talk about their day using 'tree puns'.

'I had to *bough* out of X's meeting to day'.
'I got to the *root* of a tricky problem'.
'Did your boss *leaf* you alone today?'
'How can I *branch* out in something else . . . I have got enough to do!'
'She expected me to do it all, *root* and *branch*.'

Whilst criticized by some – usually rather uncreative – people as a low form of wit, punning is good a warm-up exercise for creative managers as it lubricates the channels between left- and right-brain thinking modes. Have a go!

Active approaches I – Computer-based methods

1.   *Multimedia*   Now that modern technology has given us the opportunity to acquire relatively low-cost multimedia equipment, a modest investment will provide you with the opportunity to seek right-brain inspiration by *playing* with some suitable software. As the CD revolution gets underway it is truly amazing what is coming on to the open market. However, once again it is wise to consult a real expert (rather than a commercial one!) before parting with your money.

2.   *Virtual reality*   Alternate reality is nothing new. We have all imagined at some time or another – most of us more frequently than we think – that we are doing something impossibly exciting such as driving a racing car, piloting a plane, getting totally absorbed and involved in a good book, play or film. There seems to come a point in these experiences when fantasy takes over and we partially believe we have

leapt into a new contextual reality. We are a character in a film. We are on the track at Monte Carlo. *Virtual reality*, or 'cyberspace', takes alternate reality a step further by introducing a computer system as a mediator, or imagination enhancer. A typical system incorporates one or two input devices (such as a joy stick, a steering wheel, or a body harness), several forms of output (such as light, sound and pressure), and a powerful computer to process all the data. The net result is that many of your senses are duped into thinking that you are really in control as you grapple gainfully to keep a jet aircraft in the air and on course!

We have a selection of Virtual Reality software that we occasionally use in creative management courses to ring the changes and literally blow people into a new world, where they can shake off the shackles of the old and dream new dreams and dare to be creative! As the computer companies are working to perfect virtual reality systems, researchers in California are working on technologies that allow people to view their own virtual or subconscious reality – in other words, their dreams (Foremski, 1994).

Active approaches II – Drawing
This tool switches the traditional emphasis from verbal to graphical skills from left- to right-brain expression. Given a free hand to draw a problem on paper, individuals, either on their own or in groups, are presented with an entirely new perspective that avoids the tendency to get trapped in familiar verbal memory traces. Here is a small selection of some of the simpler tools that are particularly suitable for group CPS sessions.

1. *Picture* This is a neat and 'user-friendly' tool that brings out key issues in a very powerful way. It is especially helpful when produced in a meeting or CPS session on a flipchart and used by an individual to convey important information to a group. There are three stages:

> Stage 1   Declare problem statement.
> Stage 2   Draw picture on flipchart (mixing colour pens helps).
> Stage 3   Discuss.

Figure 5.7 illustrates the feelings of an undergraduate studying Engineering and Figure 5.8 is an example of this tool as used by a marketing manager at Northern Electric plc.
2. *Picture book* (VanGundy, 1988)   This is a tool that is suitable for either CPPS or CGPS exercises but is usually best when used in group sessions. There are five stages:

> Stage 1   Individuals or groups produce a conventional *problem statement* and convert into a simple picture format.
> Stage 2   Generate ideas to progress the problem and express them in picture format.
> Stage 3   Each individual chooses two or three ways to progress the problem (i.e. what needs to be done) and draws a picture illustrating each option, using colour to emphasize important issue or aspects.
> Stage 4   The individual (in the case of CPPS exercises) or group (with CGPS exercises) *select* the most suitable progress picture for the *problem statement*. This is straightforward in the case of individuals. Groups have a two-phased task to complete during this stage:

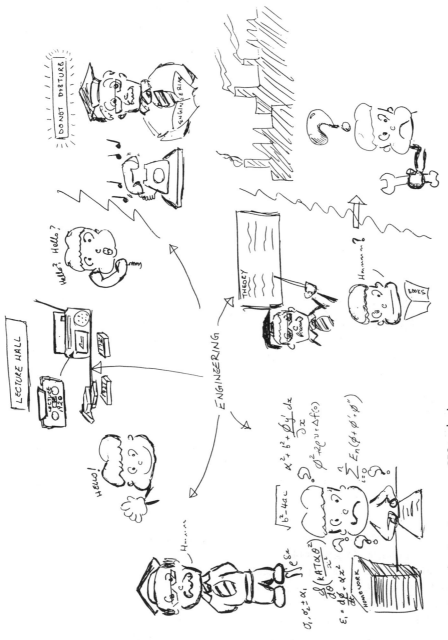

Figure 5.7 The picture as a CPS tool – I

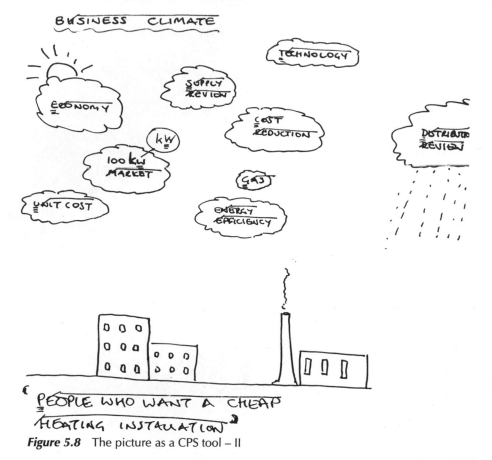

Figure 5.8 The picture as a CPS tool – II

(a) selection of suitable picture (after a 'showing' of all the efforts of each individual in the group); and

(b) revision of selected picture (partial or complete) after reviewing each individual picture.

Stage 5   Draw the final solution as individuals would like to see it.

You do not have to be to be a gifted artist to produce an acceptable *picture book*; you can use simple diagrams and stick-people. Do the best you can. With a bit of practice you will be pleasantly surprised by the results. It is advisable to complete Stages 1 and 2 sequentially. Then some prefer to complete Stage 5 before Stages 3 and 4. Alternatively you can complete Stage 5 after Stages 1 and 2 or you can opt to work progressively through the five stages. Experiment and see what suits you best. Some individuals, if they are bashful about the standard of their art, opt to revise their original drawings using standard computer-clip art. Figure 5.9 is an example of this tool as used by a manager at Newcastle College.

3. *Broadsheet*   This uses the same five stages as the *picture book* but presents the 'story' using a computer desktop package as a broadsheet that features pictures and

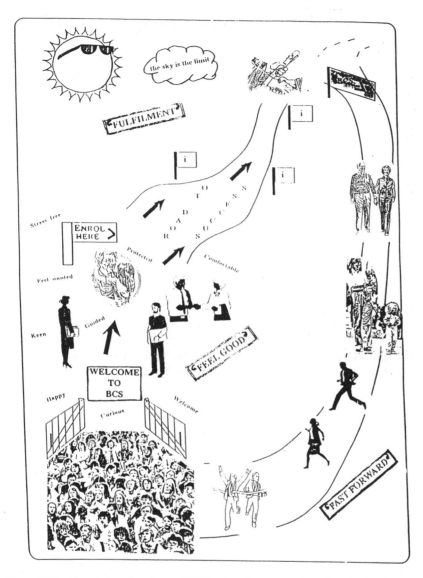

Figure 5.9 The picture book as a CPS tool, using computer-clip art

words. Best results are normally achieved if roughly three-quarters of a side of A4 is covered by graphics and one-quarter by words.

Active approaches III – Therapeutic activities

1. *Guided imagery* A number of well-regarded short scenarios are available that should be sensitively read by an expert. There is a rich audio tape library available for

sale. Do take expert advice before you spend your money either on commercial tapes or on the services of a guided imagery expert.

5.6.4 Selection

Generating a flow of ideas is an important process in any CPS exercise and quickly builds up creative momentum. To progress there comes a point, which is usually obvious to the individual or creative facilitator, when it is sensible to assess the ideas that have been generated in the light of the *problem statement* and to select the most promising ideas for adoption in the *realization* stage (p. 121). This reductionist stage can in complex exercises be a very lengthy phase of a CPS exercise. To help you to get started quickly the introductory CPS tool kit offers four good all purpose tools.

Colour code (VanGundy, 1988)

For quick and easy selections you can try colour code. This involves simply giving each individual a supply of red and yellow coloured stickers and asking them to select and then mark the best idea or ideas with a red sticker and the second best ideas with a yellow sticker. Then the idea with the most red stickers emerges as the winner. Discuss this with the group in the light of its practicality and acceptability. This is a rough-and-ready tool but can be useful to gain a quick measure of group opinion.

Creative Evaluation (VanGundy, 1988)

This is a straightforward ranking tool that can be used after *colour code* and assigns numbers to the leading ideas as follows:

1. represents a simple idea (requires little time and money)
2. represents a hard idea (requires more time and money)
3. represents a difficult idea (requires the most time and money)

The idea categories are then referred to management for further evaluation.

Advantage–disadvantage (VanGundy, 1988)

After using *colour code* issue all participants in the group with a selection matrix and ask them to privately evaluate all the red ideas in the light of the constraints declared on the matrix. Figure 5.10 presents an example of this tool in a group problem solving exercise concerned with finding a suitable hotel for a one-day creative management workshop.

Participants were simply invited to assess each of the 'red' ideas in the light of the criteria and to respond by placing a tick or star in the appropriate column.

Criteria	Advantages	Disadvantages
Location	*	
Ease of access	*	
Parking		*
Conference facilities	*	
Reputation of venue		*

Figure 5.10   Advantage–disadvantage matrix

Intuitive judgement or Gut feel (Rikards, 1990)

This simply relies on right-brain skills to sense a suitable solution and is particularly well suited to 'messy' or 'fuzzy' problems. A useful way to use this tool is to ask group members to privately think about the main options (say after running *colour code*) for 5 to 10 minutes and then for the facilitator to conduct a *round robin* to collect participant's choices. These can then be simply expressed in tabular form on a flip chart for all the group to see. If the result is indeterminate further discussion may reveal a winning idea. Failing this the facilitator will have to try another selection tool.

5.6.5   CPS Phase 3   Realization Planning

Once a CPS exercise has generated a realistic option (*What* can sensibly be done) it is important before too much of the momentum and inevitable enthusiasm is lost that some action is planned to achieve the implementation (*How* to respond) that its adoption assumes. In instances where more than one main option is generated it is often prudent to carry out a detailed *Realization Planning* exercise for each option before inviting executive evaluation. This is because both the *What* and *How* aspects of the proposed solutions or responses to the initial challenge, issue or problem may need to be presented to decision-making management. It is prudent to spend some time thinking about the arguments that may be raised in opposition to a suggested idea or set of options. Generally speaking, there are two broad factor sets to consider: those affecting the proposed problem solution and those surrounding the people who have an interest in the solution. There are many helpful tools but here are a couple to experiment with: *Advantage and disadvantage* (a variation of the selection tool outlined on pages 178–9) and *Comfort zones* which addresses the delicate subject of presenting to other people's mind-sets.

Advantage and disadvantage: revisited

This is a simple checklist approach to assist in the early identification of the likely support for and opposition to a proposal. The criteria adopted by individuals and groups are

Criteria	Advantages/support	Disadvantages/opposition
Who?		*
What?	*	
Why?	*	
Where?		*
When?		*
How?	*	

Figure 5.11 Advantage/support and disadvantage/opposition

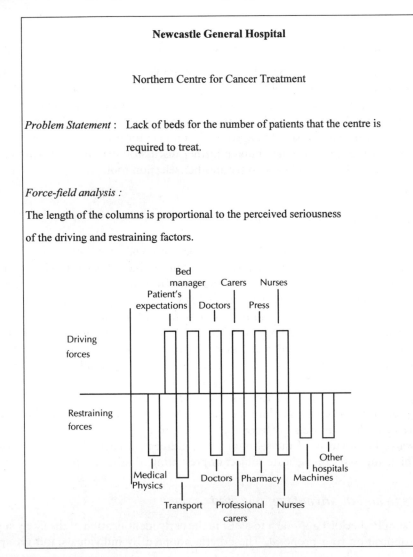

Figure 5.12 Force field analysis

usually contextual determined but progress can generally be made by adopting the six questions of *5 W's and H* (see figure 5.11).

Force-field analysis is a variation of this tool. Figure 5.12 presents an example of is use in a CPS session held in Newcastle General Hospital.

Comfort zones (Rikards, 1990)

All of us are influenced by both our own mind-sets and value systems as well as those of the organizations in which we operate. When proposals are being prepared for presentation to executive management, it is prudent to take into account the personal mind-sets of the individuals who are going to be vitally involved in the decision process. However, remember that not all mind-sets will be hostile. Some will be supportive, others tolerant and some possibly hostile. To be forewarned is to be forearmed.

5.6.6 CPS introductory starter kit

Appendix 5.2 includes the introductory creative problem-solving tool kit for personal and group creative problem-solving exercises. The tools in the kit cover a wide range of approaches and the hope is that you will experiment, enjoy and select those that suit you best. All the tools have their place but you will probably find that in most cases you can manage with a cut-down kit of between 20 and 25 tools.

KEY TERMS

Problem evaluation tools
 'Why?'
 Five W's and H
 Stakeholder analysis
 Wishful thinking
 Synectics

Right-brain tools
 Excursions
 Wildest idea
 Analogies
 Cut and connect!

Checklists
 Attribute listing
 SCAMPER

Software packages

Imagery I – Passive
 Relaxation
 Sounds inspirational

Imagery II – Bridging
 Metaphors
 Analogy
 Punning

Imagery III – Active
 Computer-based
 Drawing
 Therapeutic

Selection
 Colour code
 Creative evaluation
 Advantage–disadvantage

Realization
 Advantage–disadvantage
 Comfort zones

5.7   Creative group problem solving: Master Guides

5.7.1   The CPS tool kit

The previous section presented the introductory CPS tool kit and we hope that you will use it in CPPS and CGPS sessions. The tools themselves – with the exception of some of the imagineering ones – are all relatively user-friendly. Thus once you are familiar with the instructions you should be able to try the ones that are suitable for CPPS exercises (see Appendix 5.2) right away. Many of the CPPS tools are also suitable for use in CGPS sessions and we suggest that you find a friendly guinea pig or two to help you find your feet. The more complex CGPS tools (such as *synectics* and *imagineering*) are best experienced first under the guidance of a trained facilitator. All of these tools require some patience and perseverance if you wish to be able to use them as a creative craftsman or woman. Mastering how the tools work is one thing, but real know-how is characterized by demonstrable skill in applying the tools and techniques to real problems. This process can be accelerated if you attend a brief course of CPS lessons given by a qualified and experienced creative facilitator. Just like learning to drive!

If a tool or selection of tools does not have a positive impact on the problem you are facing, then you have either not used the tool/s properly or chosen the wrong one/s in the first place. A welding torch will remove the four studs on a car wheel so that you can remove the wheel. However, it is better to use a socket set. The difference between these two hypothetical situations is explained by expertise or *know-how*. This implies practice in the use of the tools in order to select the correct tool for the job and an appreciation of how to tackle the job at hand. This generally comes with reflective practice but it helps to network with someone who has real (i.e. contextual) experience.

After introducing the individual to creativity in Chapter 4 a simple CPPS exercise was described that outlined 10 basic CPS tools. This was followed by a brief discussion of 8 key PPS techniques or approaches. This section returns to this theme and adds a master guide that is particularly relevant to CGPS exercises.

5.7.2   Master Guide 9   Working with others

Most would agree that the potential output of several minds is greater than that of a single mind. Working with others obviously seems to make sense. However, in the often frantic activity of an average day, many managers probably attempt to progress far too many problems under their own steam. Opening problems up to others makes sense, but is there time to call the necessary meetings? Or might there be some latent reluctance to do so, since the organizational culture may take the view that it is the manager's job to solve problems?

When this occurs in organizations it tends to make individual managers reluctant to separate the *what* from the *how* in problem-solving activity. Some managers may even perceive working with others as a sign of weakness, preferring to take everything on themselves and working long and arduous hours. Such managerial supermen can find it very difficult to share problems with others, even though they may appreciate the logic of harnessing the talents of colleagues. Coping with pressure is a constant process for busy managers. As the problems come faster and faster and as the complexities increase, many managers must feel that they are running in order to stay in one spot. There inevitably comes a point when sheer workload convinces them actively to contemplate involving others.

Management problems can usually be viewed in the light of five key issues, as follows:

1. Functional/technical skills.
2. General management processing skills.
3. Cost constraints.
4. Time constraints.
5. Quality expectations.

Most managers have a sound perspective on their functional/technical ability and experience has equipped many with know-how in relation to cost and time constraints. As their operational environment becomes more and more chaotic in the current *value time* (see Chapter 2) so greater emphasis needs to be placed on the realization of the skill potential contained with groups and organizations. This contextual pressure is challenging many individual management styles and is promoting the cause for effective team working.

Whilst managers usually value talking to others about functional and technical skills, there is frequently a marked resistance to seek the thoughts of others on problem-processing matters. The management *how* is often seen as a very private affair. There are immense gains to be made by opening up problems to groups. As the pressures on managers to perform to high standards in difficult conditions intensify, so many, hitherto private, managers will steel themselves to explore the dynamics of team working. Apart from organizational mind-sets the most significant factor restraining many managers is probably a deep concern of losing control. There is no doubt that whilst opening up problems to others is beneficial and, if handled correctly, a creative joy, people can be difficult too. Individuals need regularly to take a check on their interpersonal skills as it is so easy to gradually slip back into an autocratic style in the heat of the moment. Then, as behaviour breeds behaviour, suspicions gain ground and the essential band of trust is damaged. Most team workers will allow the captain to have the occasional private moment and still respect his or her role. If this becomes the regular mode of behaviour, then teams will soon collapse in a regrettable climate of mutual suspicion and fear. Effective managers have to win through thick and thin. Team or group spirit is essential.

Fostering good group relations is not easy. It means giving people space to express themselves. It means not being too judgemental too early and carping in any criticism that you may make. It means being responsible to all your individuals, to groups and to the organization. It means promoting a 'one for all and all for one' climate in place of an 'all for one and one for one' approach. It means playing a considered and honourable political game when pressures threaten individual, group or organizational relationships. Politics was intended to be an honourable pursuit; it has only become an object of popular scorn because it has been conducted irresponsibly for private gain. Unfortunately private gain can be achieved both by irresponsible and responsible means. The former is unlikely to foster the growth of group creativity, but the latter will and, in the process, make a real hero of the manager.

So, many managers who are determined to have a go at becoming *creative managers* can expect to be apprehensive to begin with and bold enough to re-examine their interpersonal skills and their practical understanding of group dynamics. Apart from any individual contemplation that managers may care to make, a good way of embarking on a creative management experiment is to call a meeting of your key staff away from the workplace and explain to them just why it is sensible to try something new. This is the value of a strong contextual approach. Different conditions require a different approach. Every sportsperson knows that, and most others soon appreciate it too. Once the contextual argument has been put, concerned individuals should then open up to new problem-solving initiatives. Then, as soon as possible demonstrate some CPS action. Help from a fully trained creative facilitator is invaluable at this stage. Be careful of the temptation to do too much too soon on your own. Again, just like learning to drive!

Once underway, talk amongst your immediate involved colleagues about your experiences with various CPS tools and techniques. Find others who are also in the process of getting to grips with creative management and compare notes. Set up a real networking system to share knowledge and experience in the use of the CPS tools and techniques. This can be done using a variety of means including face-to-face meetings, the telephone, computerized mail systems, modem accessed bulletin boards, and conferences, fax machines, teleconferencing, and so on.

5.7.3 Putting it together

Creative management is essentially a proactive as opposed to a reactive process. So it is important to take time out to think about how you might manage it. Here are some general hints (see pp. 162–3):

- Always try to keep the momentum going with well-timed, tactful and skilled interventions.
- Be prepared to put in some time to practise different CPS tracking. This means trying different tools and techniques and, by implication, writing different CPS tracks. Do not expect one standard track to apply to all situations – an unsound contextual judgement!
- Stop from time to time when you feel that it is right to do so. Resist any dutiful temptation to keep on going and going in order to solve the problem. Regularly burning the midnight oil usually produces poor performances. It is generally much

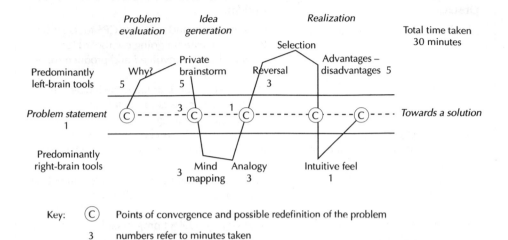

Key: (C) Points of convergence and possible redefinition of the problem

3 numbers refer to minutes taken

Figure 5.13 Example of CPS session schedule

better to break and return to the problem the following day. Sound performance is better than a satisfied (because you have put the hours in) conscience. Creative management is all about generating apt creative responses and not the implementation of tired solutions.

- Be a purposeful custodian of time. With a little practice a complete CPS session can be achieved in 40 to 45 minutes (see Figure 5.13).
- Do not introduce too many tools and techniques all at once
- Do not give up too easily – give CPS a chance. Commit to a least a six-month trial period.

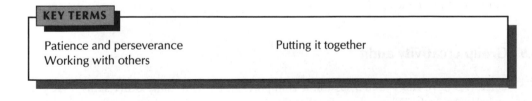

KEY TERMS

Patience and perseverance   Putting it together
Working with others

5.8 Obstacles to group creativity

Some weeks after delegates on a creativity workshop in Durham were requested to report what they saw as the main barriers to introducing CPPS to individuals in their organization,

Figure 5.14 CGPS difficulties: an empirical sounding

Obstacle	Antidote
1. Negative attitudes.	Quietly get on and try some CPS tools and techniques without going overboard to explain the *how* involved and produce some good results.
2. Politics.	Stand your ground, argue to be judged on results – seeing, rather than telling, encourages believing.
3. Fear of exposing poor teamwork of other groups in the organization.	Operate tactfully. Tackle problems – resist any temptation to evangelize the CPS cause.
4. Myopia.	Tactfully explain contextual factors affecting the problem situation to all group participants.
5. Concern over choosing the right problem to obtain a recognized success.	Start simply – select progressable issues.
6. Low creativity.	Need for instruction and guidance of a creative facilitator.
7. Lack of trust.	Do your best to earn it.
8. Poor problem-solving ability.	Introduce and demonstrate some basic tools.
9. Unclear aims.	Try to clarify.
10. Reward structure viewed as unfair.	Show your appreciation and seek to influence the system.

another set of delegates on a creativity workshop were asked to indicate what they saw as the main blockages to introducing CGPS successfully. Figure 5.14 summarizes the results. On the other hand, blockages commonly identified in the literature on CGPS – basically stemming from a poor understanding of how to manage groups – are summarized in Figure 5.15.

5.9 Group creativity audit

Once you have run a CGPS session it is important, as with many other skills, that you practise regularly. When you judge that the time is appropriate, perhaps after one or two sessions, you may like to ask your group to complete our *group creativity audit* to take stock of the active creativity level of the group. If the audit is given to the same group in say three months, you should be able to see a visual improvement in creative thinking. The audit form plus scoring sheet and score graph are available for easy photocopying in Appendix 5.1.

Figure 5.15 CGPS difficulties: identified in the literature

Obstacle	Antidote
1. Lack of vision	Inform group of what is involved and seek their collective ownership of it.
2. Poor participation	Encourage individuals to contribute – provide a safe environment. Avoid power-driving the group.
3. Poor interaction	Get the group to talk amongst themselves as well as to you. Promote a 'one for all and all for one' philosophy.
4. Lack of trust	Up to the creative facilitator to dispel.
5. Poor reward	Up to the creative facilitator to use imagination – successful group behaviour has to be recognized in some way. Remember that man does not live by bread alone.
6. Starting too soon	Need for the creative facilitator to impose restraint and ensure that the group do not rush in too quickly.
7. Confused operation	The creative facilitator needs to ensure that the members of the group converge and diverge at suitable intervals.
8. Tendency to argue preconceived solutions	The creative facilitator needs to resist the formation of group blindness – a preference to operate in a predictable form irrespective of the problem and contextual environment.
9. Failure to harness the expertise of the group	Creative facilitation skills needed.

5.10 Summary

Having personally experienced creativity, few deny that it is invigorating and exciting. Many, though, are at first apprehensive about taking their new-found creativity into the workplace. This chapter recognizes this problem and so has sought to provide some practical advice on *how* the *creative management response* (CMR) can be applied professionally. It is hoped that you will be excited by the potential benefits of CMR to run some CGPS sessions at work. Provided that you choose your group members carefully – avoiding, if possible (to begin with), the professional cynics – and the temptation to discuss every tool that you may like to use before you use it, you ought to be surprised by joy. Further practical advice can be found in Chapters 7, 8 and 9.

Lastly, Figure 5.16 summarizes the main factors that influence the expression of the creative management response in group situations.

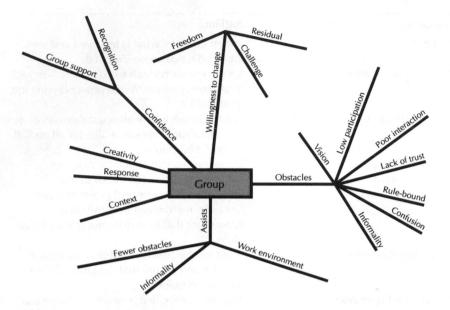

Figure 5.16   Leading factors influencing the creative management response of groups

1. Discuss the main ways in which group behaviour differs from individual behaviour. How can groups be organized and managed?

2. Describe how you would help others to achieve a personal and collective experience of creativity.

3. What is a *creative facilitator*? How might he or she assist in stimulating a group? Try and illustrate your response by reference to your own experience.

4. Describe a personal or group problem-solving session and illustrate your selection of CPS tools by plotting what happened on a CPS *tracking chart*. With the benefit of hindsight, what would you have done differently and why?

5. Use the *introductory tool kit,* selecting at least three right-brain tools to tackle a challenge issue, problem or issue of concern. Justify your choice of imagery tools and summarize what you learnt from the exercise.

6. Outline the main obstacles to group creative problem-solving activity. Discuss how you might manage them.

7. After a group creative problem-solving session of your choice complete the *group creativity audit.* Discuss the result with the group.

References

Adair, J. (1983), *Effective Leadership*, London: Pan.

Adair, J. (1985), *Effective Decision-Making*, London: Pan.

Amabile, T. M. (1983), *The Social Psychology of Creativity*, New York: Springer-Verlag.

Eberle, R. (1972), *Scamper: Games for Imagination Development*, Buffalo, NY: D. O. K. Press.

Ekvall, G., Arvonen, J. and Waldenstrom-Linblad, I. (1983), *Creating Organizational Climate: Construction and validation of a measuring instrument*, Stockholm: F. A. Rodet.

Foremski T. (1994), 'Waking up to dream control', *Financial Times*, 22 February, London.

Fritz, A. (1989), *The Path of Least Resistance: Learning how to become a creative force in your own life*, New York: Ballantine.

Garnham, A. and Oakhill, J. (1994), *Thinking and Reasoning*, Oxford: Blackwell.

Goman, C. K. (1989), *Creative Thinking In Business*, Los Altos, CA: Crisp Publications.

Gordon, W. (1961), *Synectics*, New York: Harper.

Janis, I. L. (1982), *Groupthink*, 2nd edn, Boston: Houghton Mifflin.

Kolb, D. (1984), 'Problem management: learning from experience', ch 5 in Suresh Srvastra and Associates, ed., *The Executive Mind*, London: Jossey Bass.

Kreitner, R. (1980), *Management: A problem-solving process*, Boston, Mass.: Houghton Mifflin.

Majaro, S. (1992), *Managing Ideas for Profit*, Maidenhead: McGraw-Hill.

Morgan, G. (1993), *Imaginization*, London: Sage.

Osborn, A. F. (1957), *Applied Imagination*, 3rd edn, New York: Scribners.

Rickards, T. (1974), *Problem Solving Through Creative Analysis*, Aldershot: Gower.

Rikards, T. (1990), *Creativity and Problem-Solving at Work*, Aldershot: Gower.

Simon, H. A. *et al.* (1977), *The New Science of Management Decision*, Englewood Cliffs, NJ: Prentice Hall.

Spooner, P. (1992), *Museum of the Mind*, York: Museum of Automata.

Stevens, M. S. (1988), *Practical Problem Solving for Managers*, London: Kogan Page.

VanGundy, A.B. (1988), *Techniques of Structured Problem Solving*, New York: Van Nostrand Reinhold.

Additional reading

Firestein, R. L. and Treffinger, D. J. (1983), 'Ownership and converging: essential ingredients of creative problem solving', *Journal of Creative Behaviour*, 17 (1), 32–8.

Gawain, S. (1982), *Creative Visualization*, New York: Bantam.

Glouberman, D. (1989), *Experiences with Imagery*, London: Unwin Hyman.

King, N. and Anderson, N. (1990), 'Innovation and creativity in working groups', in M. A. West and J. L. Farr (ed.), *Innovation and Creativity at Work*, Chichester: Wiley.

Maier, N. R. F. (1970), *Problem Solving and Creativity in Individuals and Groups*, Belmont, CA: Brooks/Cole.

West, M. A. (1990), 'The social psychology of innovation in groups', in M. A. West and J. L. Farr (ed.), *Innovation and Creativity at Work*, Chichester: Wiley.

Note

1. Synectics is a problem-solving process developed in 1944 by W. Gordon for Synectics Inc., Cambridge, Mass., and Hemel Hempstead, Herts, in the UK. (See Gordon, 1961).

APPENDIX 5.1

Group creativity audit

Instructions

Questionnaire

1. It is suggested that you the copy the questionnaire and assessment forms in the appendix before attempting the audit.
2. Put the assessment form to one side.
3. Turn to the questionnaire and answer the questions honestly and as quickly as you can.
4. Please do not confer with others whilst you or they are completing the questionnaire.

Assessment

1. Turn to the assessment form.
2. Transfer the score for the box that you ticked in the questionnaire and record it beside your tick.
3. When you have scored each of your responses, run a quick check to see that you have recorded the right values for each question.
4. Add up your scores and plot the sum value on the assessment zones diagram.

Interpretation

1. If you wish to improve your group working turn to the text (in particular, Chapters 4 and 5) for some pointers.
2. Record your initial score and try the audit again in three months' time – if you have studied the text and experimented you should record a higher rating.

Questionnaire

Please tick the appropriate box

	Never	Occa-sionally	Fairly often	Regularly
1. Are the group members at ease with one another?	. . .	. . .	. . .	. . .
2. Do individual members participate?				
3. Does the group always know what it is supposed to achieve?				
4. Is the group closely regulated?				
5. Is the group empowered to achieve?				
6. Do group members interact well with each other?				
7. Is their work acknowledged by a manager?				
8. Do group members get together socially after work?				
9. Are their efforts visibly rewarded?				
10. Are they optimistic?				
11. Does the group generate any ideas of its own?				
12. Is the group membership well balanced?				
13. Can team spirit be described as 'one for all and all for one'?				
14. Does the group tend to be predictable in what it achieves?				
15. Is the expertise within the group efficiently utilized?				
16. Is the work of the group appreciated by the organization?				
17. Has the group assumed an identity of its own?				
18. Does it use group problem-solving tools and techniques?				
19. Is change welcomed?				
20. Does the group like meeting?				
21. Do they use right-brain tools?				
22. Do group members work well together?				
23. Are they highly motivated?				
24. Reach consensus decisions?				
25. Effective in progressing problems?				
26. Does the group get easily distracted?				
27. Do you prefer to adapt the ideas of others?				
28. Does the group challenge existing procedural rules if it honestly thinks that they are silly?				
29. If the going gets tough do the group back off?				
30. Does the group wander off the point?				

Assessment form

	Never	Occa-sionally	Fairly often	Regularly
1. Are the group members at ease with one another?	1	2	3	4
2. Do individual members participate?	1	2	3	4
3. Does the group always know what it is supposed to achieve?	1	2	3	4
4. Is the group closely regulated?	4	3	2	1
5. Is the group empowered to achieve?	1	2	3	4
6. Do group members interact well with each other?	1	2	3	4
7. Is their work acknowledged by a manager?	1	2	3	4
8. Do group members get together socially after work?	1	2	3	4
9. Are their efforts visibly rewarded?	1	2	3	4
10. Are they optimistic?	1	2	3	4
11. Does the group generate any ideas of its own?	1	2	3	4
12. Is the group membership well balanced?	1	2	3	4
13. Can team spirit be described as 'one for all and all for one'?	1	2	3	4
14. Does the group tend to be predictable in what it achieves?	4	3	2	1
15. Is the expertise within the group efficiently utilized?	1	2	3	4
16. Is the work of the group appreciated by the organization?	1	2	3	4
17. Has the group assumed an identity of its own?	1	2	3	4
18. Does it use group problem-solving tools and techniques?	1	2	3	4
19. Is change welcomed?	1	2	3	4
20. Does the group like meeting?	1	2	3	4
21. Do they use right-brain tools?	1	2	3	4
22. Do group members work well together?	1	2	3	4
23. Are they highly motivated?	1	2	3	4
24. Reach consensus decisions?	1	2	3	4
25. Effective in progressing problems?	1	2	3	4
26. Does the group get easily distracted?	4	3	2	1
27. Do you prefer to adapt the ideas of others?	1	2	3	4
28. Does the group challenge existing procedural rules if it honestly thinks that they are silly?	1	2	3	4
29. If the going gets tough do the group back off?	4	3	2	1
30. Does the group wander off the point?	4	3	2	1

Assessment zones

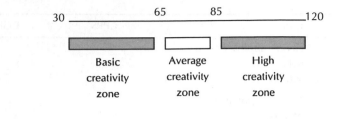

| Basic creativity zone | Average creativity zone | High creativity zone |

Introductory CPS tool kit

Introductory CPS tool kit – I

Function	Tool	CPPS	CGPS
Problem evaluation	Stakeholder analysis	x	x
	Synectics		x
	5 W's and H	x	
	'Why?'		x
	Wishful thinking	x	x
Idea generation	Notebook	x	x
	Private brainstorming	x	x
	Round robin	x	x
	Right-brain tools		
	Analogies	x	x
	Cut and connect	x	x
	Excursions	x	x
	Metaphors	x	x
	Mind mapping	x	x
	Reversal	x	x
	Wildest idea		x
	Checklists		
	Attribute listing	x	x
	SCAMPER	x	x
	5W's and H	x	x
	Software packages		
	Think Thunder	x	
	Visual outliner	x	
	Classification		
	Clustering	x	x
	Shaping	x	x

Introductory CPS tool kit – II

Function	Tool	CPPS	CGPS
Imagineering	*Passive approaches*		
	Relaxation	x	x
	Sounds inspirational	x	x
	Bridging approaches		
	Analogy	x	x
	Metaphor	x	x
	Puns	x	x
	Active approaches		
	Multimedia	x	x
	Virtual reality	x	x
	Drawing		
	Picture book	x	x
	Picture chart	x	x
	Broadsheet	x	x
	Therapeutic		
	Guided imagery	x	x
Selection	Advantage/ Disadvantage	x	x
	Colour code	x	x
	Creative evaluation	x	x
	Intuitive judgement	x	x
Realization	Advantage/ disadvantage	x	x
	Comfort zones	x	x
	Force-field analysis	x	x

Practical creative problem solving

Getting underway

As any teacher will know there is a world of difference between telling students *what* they need to know and helping them to use this *what* knowledge practically. This difference between education and training has become very obvious to us in our workshop and consultancy assignments. Many attendees 'caught the drift' of the individual and group CPS tools and master guides but experienced considerable difficulties in making their first forays into practical CPS activity.

CPS Tool kits

Chapters 4 and 5 present our Basic and Introductory CPS tool kits. Whilst there is good reason to progress from a Basic kit to the more complex Introductory kit experience has shown that many potential creative managers are 'dazzled' by the Introductory kit. We have termed this the 'Aladdin's cave effect' as many have been panicked by the array of tools on offer. To facilitate the entry path of new practitioners we have introduced a Starter tool kit. This is described in Chapter 8 (Section 8.4.1, on pages 315–16). Early feedback indicates that many find this easier to manage. No excuses now – go on 'have a go' and experience for yourself the joy of creative thinking!

6

Organizations and creativity

CONTENTS

6.1   Introduction   *199*

6.2   Management thinking   *199*

6.3   Harnessing systems thinking   *206*

6.4   Hard systems   *206*

6.5   Soft systems   *208*

6.6   Cybernetics   *218*

6.7   Organizational responses   *218*

6.8   Organizational tools   *226*

6.9   Creative organizational problem solving: Master Guides   *228*

6.10   Summary   *229*

6.11   Organizational creativity audit   *230*

Questions   *230*

References   *231*

Appendix 6.1   Organizational creativity audit   *233*

Map: Chapter 6

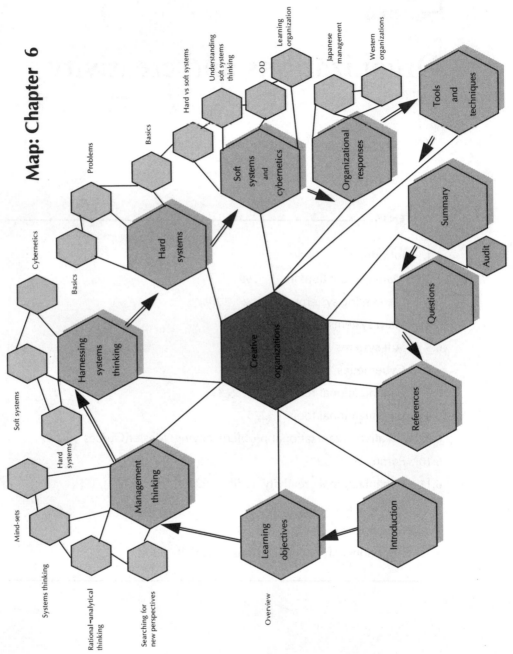

6.1 Introduction

Chapter 3 presented a broad overview of the evolution of management thought before taking a brief look at the traditional management competencies and arguing the case for a new management approach to meet the severe contextual challenges of the last half of the decade. Chapters 4 and 5 then followed the broad theme of creativity through individual and group discovery and practice. In similar vein this chapter looks at corporate or organizational thinking and then addresses some of the key issues that organizations will have to face if they wish to adopt the *creative management response* (CMR). Five more creative problem-solving (CPS) tools are introduced to complete the introductory CPS tool kit and the addition of three more Master Guides completes the introductory set of techniques. The chapter closes with an invitation to interested managers to undertake a *creativity audit* of their own organizations.

LEARNING OBJECTIVES

To provide the reader with:

- An introduction to the origins and evolution of management thinking.
- A broad overview of hard and soft systems thinking.
- An appreciation of the 'way the Japanese do things'.
- A brief selection from the best of Western management practice.
- Extra CPS tools and techniques to complete the basic CPS tool kit.

6.2 Management thinking

6.2.1 Searching for a new perspective

Rethinking the management response

The complex set of stimuli impacting on wealth creation that we explored in Part I have introduced a marked and accelerating instability into the environment that faces organizations in the 1990s. As the balance of economic power shifts to the Pacific Rim countries, so organizations in Europe and the United States have been forced to rethink their basic management approach. The 'borderless world' is not a temporary phenomenon that will disappear one sunny day, but a permanent one that demands a new managerial perspective.

The series of contextual changes and developments that triggered the Industrial Revolution in the West – such as the discovery of new forms of motive power, transport and the accompanying emergence of a new social milieu – changed the pattern of wealth creation. Gradually a new system, the *industrial* system replaced the traditional hunter–gatherer and agricultural economic system. As the horse gave way to steam and steam to the internal combustion engine, so individuals were forced to develop new skills in order to operate the new transportation systems effectively and safely. The quest to achieve control over these new systems boosted the evolution in eighteenth-century Europe of a new style of coping with the problems of the new industrial age. So what we now recognize as *rational-analytical thinking* emerged as individuals and groups sought to gain a scientific understanding and mastery over the wealth-creating engines and innovations of the industrial age.

Rational-analytical thinking

Rational-analytical thinking is a reductionist style. It seeks to understand complex situations by reducing them into their separate identifiable parts. This tended to reduce the complexity of problems and so made it easier to select and execute suitable responses. This problem-solving approach, first developed and perfected by scientists, was readily adopted by the new breed of business people and managers that fostered the Industrial Revolution. It was an attractive style as it was easy to learn and through reflective practice – learning by experience – could be readily adapted as a process systems control. For over 150 years this style provided the dominant thinking approach until by the mid- to late 1930s it began to falter as wealth-creating instruments and systems gained in sophistication and complexity.

The rational approach to problem solving is based on three sets of beliefs:

1. Reductionism.
2. Determinism.
3. Positivism.

As we have seen *reductionism* argues that the best way to understand something is to break it down into its component parts. *Determinism* assumes that the environment normally operates in a natural rhythm that is determined by universal influences which can be noted and measured. Thus most significant changes impacting on wealth creation can be anticipated, as the system is governed by the laws of nature. *Positivism* assumes that all stimuli affecting a given situation are known, easily analyzed and understood and thus measurable. If something cannot be measured, therefore, it cannot exist. This is an acceptable premise for many mechanical systems (such as the internal combustion engine) but is very limited in its ability to explain complex dynamic interactions such as those commonly experienced in rapidly changing organizations.

The complex organizational problems encountered during the prosecution of the Second World War led to the development of *systems thinking*. This is a style of thinking that attempts to understand the causal relationships between components of a system. The underlying assumption is that the forces which affect the way a complete system behaves are determined by the way in which the system is structured and the way that its constituent parts interact in circular patterns of cause and effect – relationships that are often referred to as *vicious circles* and *virtuous circles*. When an analyst harnesses both *rational-analytical* and *systems thinking* to a problem, he or she is able both to break up the problem into its constituent parts (study the trees) and have the advantage of helicopter vision (see the way that the whole wood is moving), say, in response to an environmental force such as wind or an environmental threat (acute and dangerous stimuli) such as a fire.

Systems thinking

Systems thinking helps managers to get to get to grips with complex problems by enabling them to jump out of their habitual *rational-analytical* mode and so see the problem from a different perspective. This usually stimulates additional ideas and ultimately provides response options that would escape the attention of conventional analytical managers. This is particularly important, as we have seen in Chapters 4 and 5, as it permits a manager to redefine or *reframe* the critical problem that needs to be addressed. *Systems thinking*, as with most other skills, improves with practice (Kim, 1990) and reflection. As the situational environment changes so managers need to view their operational world from a different vantage point. Fine-tuned default *rational-analytical thinking* in such circumstances merely leads to poor problem solving.

When the very ground on which people stand to think changes unexpectedly there is a tendency for many individuals to try and find a reason for what has happened in order to regain their confidence. Many find chaos uncomfortable and so search in a determined manner for a way to restore things to normal. At first they usually look for simple *cause-and-effect relationships*. Surely the new situation has been experienced before and so it should be possible to find comfort if only the previous response can be found and repeated. Such basic *linear causality* rarely assists if the underlying contextual stimuli are causing constant instability that challenges the manager's state of mind. In these situations a new way of thinking is required. *Systems thinking* posits that change often results from a cycle of patterned loops (*causal loops*). For example, should an organization's sales fall, then this will put pressure on its finances if no efforts are made to reduce costs. Reducing costs could result in redundancies (skill losses) and severe cutbacks in finished goods inventories. If sales prospects suddenly pick up the organization may not be able to respond quickly enough to demand. This leads to a loss of market share, which in turn may lead to a further round of cost reduction exercises and so on.

When times are good there is a tendency for managers to look for simple *linear causal* explanations. When the going gets tough managers are often faced with messy situations where the *causal loops* are far less obvious. The temptation to go for a 'quick solution' to please the City or to appease a corporate macho mind-set may lead to a range of responses, from problem avoidance (attempting to ride out the crisis by doing nothing) to dramatic but ill-considered action that inflicts massive damage to the trust perceptions of the subsystems (groups and individuals) which make up the organization. Repeated doses of the same old medicine whenever market conditions change for the worse (and in the contemporary *value time*, this will be the norm rather than the exception) will ultimately, for many organizations, be self-defeating. What is needed is to find a new understanding of these complex causal loops. The way forward lies in a willingness to overhaul our habitual thinking patterns.

6.2.2 Mind-sets

As managers are placed under sustained pressure to perform in the rapidly changing wealth-creating environment that characterizes the 1990s *how* they think in chaotic conditions is attracting increasing attention. This is determined by a complex pattern of mental input factors that include personal, group, and organizational influences. At the individual level thinking patterns that fashion behaviour are determined by four key *factor sets*: cultural; social; personal; and psychological.

Thinking-pattern factor sets

Cultural factor sets include the dominant cultural and social class factors that surround an individual from birth. *Social factor sets* encompass an array of influences such as preferred reference groups, family expectations, and so forth. *Personal factor sets* describe a complex collection of variables that shape individuals' thinking and value choices, such as age, lifestyle, economic status, personality, and so on. *Psychological factor sets* address the key variables that determine individuals' perceptions, learning patterns, and the way that they acquire beliefs and attitudes. These *factor sets* integrate to form a complex system (*personal mind-set*) that governs the general/habitual thinking patterns of individuals.

When individuals are viewed in group situations further complexity arises. *By definition a group is a collection of individuals all with their own unique collection of factor sets.* Harmonizing their behaviour is cognitively a highly complex task. The imposition of linear causality – for example, the belief that the way to get individuals to work together is to stick them together, give them something to do and then determine their reward on how much they accomplish in a given period of time – is a mechanistic approach to management that will inevitably constrain individual performance. At its most extreme this reduces individuals to units of input, and unless they have private reasons for accepting this (because there is little if any alternative employment), most individuals will tend to go through the motions and do the minimum that is necessary to earn their bread. Others, though severely repressed by insensitive management, will for their own satisfaction – perhaps to stay sane – put in some extra effort to innovate somehow.

Group mind-sets

A group of individuals is by definition a collection of individual mind-sets. These will be modified as the individuals get together. As we saw in Chapter 4, individuals change their behaviour patterns when they interact with others. Behaviour breeds behaviour. The degree to which behaviour choices are changed is governed by a complex set of factors that include perceived trust, motivation, and so on. (Individuals tend naturally to release more creative effort at home than in the workplace where the sensed group and/or organizational climate – contextual stimuli – makes them less at ease.) A new *group mind-set* emerges that is separate from and additional to each individual's *personal mind-set*. The nature of this is conditioned by the perceived level of trust in the group. In short, more personal trust produces more collective or group trust and potentially greater creativity.

Chapter 5 discussed the basics of group dynamics and the leading factors that commonly arrest group performance. Individuals can be encouraged to express themselves in groups and this is a key skill of an effective traditional manager. Sustained high group performance requires sensitive management skills that seek to enable or release it rather than impose it. If external stimuli make a group's task more and more difficult to achieve, then effective managers will know that they have a real problem. Months of sound management practice can dissipate into chaos, falling morale and disillusionment if a group manager is tempted to go for a quick (often linear) solution to appease some organizational authority. The credibility – and thus success – of an enabling manager can take months to achieve but can be lost in less than a minute. Group managers under pressure should be given open encouragement by their organizations to audit their skills personally, and should be afforded the opportunity to improve key competencies and to acquire new ones that are relevant to the prosecution of their responsibilities. They should not be required to perform in new and changing contextual situations using management tools and techniques that were designed for quite different days. Nor should they be hindered by beliefs and attitudes that were formed to serve the needs of former times.

Organizational mind-sets

So a manager who is responsible to his or her staff/group (is loyal) will have to find an approach that harmonizes all the constituent mind-sets. This is further complicated by his or her need to exercise responsibility to the organization, which will possess yet another collection of mind-sets. Managing effectively in a chaotic context will often place the manager where it is very difficult to win. The *organizational mind-sets* may insist that things are done in certain ways because that is how they have always been done. To suggest anything different smacks of disloyalty. Most of us at some time or another have been reprimanded for an unconventional approach to a problem by the sharp retort, 'We don't do things that way here'. Organizations like individuals are jealous guardians of

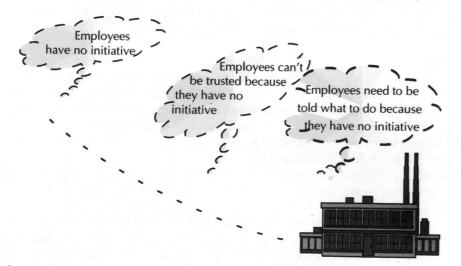

Figure 6.1   Assumptions becoming mind-sets

their beliefs and attitudes. Again individuals may dislike some organizational ways that perhaps owe their origin to sunnier days and which over the years have become enshrined in the corporate mind-sets. Frustration abounds when individuals realize that these organizational mind-sets are blocking their efforts to solve today's complex problems. Similarly, several thought for a long time after the publication of modern bible translations in the common idiom that these were blasphemous. Then there are the work groups. These often present real problems as they tend to be caught between the individual and corporate mind-sets.

To any manager, and especially a potential creative manager, warring mind-sets pose a really difficult challenge. To make matters worse, mind-sets are self-perpetuating and self-reinforcing mechanisms that are capable of flying high over and out of touch with current contexts whilst attempting to understand and manage those contexts with the tools and techniques that originated in the past (see Figure 6.1).

Challenging mind-sets

It is therefore quite understandable for managers to spend much time agonizing over how much they can challenge an organizational mind-set head on if they honestly believe that it is restraining problem-solving activity. Some managers, in the belief that most problems are temporary and that organizational mind-sets are permanent, become oblivious of the need to change their management approaches. In turbulent times this can severely damage individual and group morale and hence achievement levels.

Psychological factor sets

Some useful light can be thrown on understanding individual, group and organizational mind-sets by taking a brief look at the psychological factor sets whilst, for the time being, treating the cultural, social and personal factor sets as hygiene factors. The key psychological factors are: perception; learning; and beliefs and attitudes.

Perception

When individuals and groups are exposed to external contextual stimuli they either accept that the stimuli are real and so seek to respond positively to the challenges this brings, or they modify this reality (under the influence of heavy mind-sets). One modification is to distort the reality so that it becomes agreeable or comfortable. An alternative modification is to reject the current stimuli altogether and to retain older, more comfortable, perceptions. Once individuals and groups have made their respective selections they need to collect and collate information that will assist them to interpret fully the meaning of the contextual factors and so be in a position to think about their positions. As individuals and groups tend to be closer to contextual reality than organizations they are often aware earlier of the need to move away from the *virtual reality* that many organizations display. This means that they are often ready to think about alternative courses of action before their organizations. So why try and change organizations from the top down? In essence an organization is the shared view of its members and so can be seen as a single collective mind (Mitroff, 1984). The private response activities of individuals and groups will be characterized by changes in behaviour resulting from a careful consideration of the changing stimuli. This is the learning factor.

Learning

A willingness to modify and sometimes abandon old ways makes sense for private groups, for they are custodians of their own future. Stay in one place too long and the social world passes you by. Organizations, on the other hand, are frequently characterized by stronger mind-sets and so seek to maintain the comfort of their status quo when everything else around them is changing rapidly. This stiff-upper-lip approach can be quite valid if the change dynamics are purely temporary and confidence expects the good old times to return soon. If the change dynamics are not temporary this failure to acknowledge the real state of the environment can be suicidal.

Beliefs and attitudes

Organizations can so envelop themselves with mind-sets and paradigms that they effectively lose sight of their operating environment. Solid successes in previous times may well have led to the construction of immense bureaucracies whose job is often interpreted as being to maintain this status quo at all costs. Sometimes whole organizations can become the prisoner of myopic thinking and overzealous administrators. Forms, regulations, statistics and other measures are designed to keep the organization happy. If powerful cliques feel that the real news is just unacceptable, then some will attempt to blow it away by altering the measuring system so that it says what they want it to say. This is an acute version of *distorted perception*, but it is more common than many would like to admit.

Of course there are many fine organizations that capture the wind of change and use it to create wealth, but, sadly, many fail to perceive accurately the seriousness of their contextual positions until very late in the day. No overharsh criticism is intended to be levelled at administrators, for their services are required. However, they are needed to support management not to subsume it or to place it in chains. Administrators should serve organizations and not dominate them. Organizations that allow their administrations to escalate in the good times later discover that they are still employing large numbers of administrators when times become less prosperous. Some even continue to expand their administrative departments even when operating conditions are waning.

Consultancy work has given first-hand awareness of many vastly inflated administrative empires that in some cases outnumber the productive headcounts in organizations. As operating environments become harsher, most organizations are faced with more and more complex problems that require more than basic *rational-analytical thinking* and the common tendency to oversubscribe to *linear causality* models. Today's 'borderless world' is a complex place that is increasingly characterized by complex systems. To understand these systems, managers need to become acquainted with *systems thinking*. There is mounting evidence to suggest that *how* managers think about problems and their organizations is directly related to their ability to achieve responses (Senge, 1990). The next section provides an overview of *hard and soft systems thinking*.

> **KEY TERMS**
>
> | | |
> |---|---|
> | Management responses | Orchestrating mind-sets |
> | Rational analytical thinking | Challenging mind-sets |
> | Systems thinking | Psychology factor sets |
> | Mind-sets | ▪ perception |
> | ▪ factor sets | ▪ learning |
> | ▪ personal | ▪ beliefs and attitudes |
> | ▪ group | |
> | ▪ organizational | |

6.3 Harnessing systems thinking

Individuals, groups and organizations all have management problems. In each case the issues are complex and generally increase in difficulty as the task of management is extended to orchestrating more and more individuals and groups. Broadly speaking there are three broad approaches to *systems thinking* that can provide helpful insights which will assist us to understand the dynamics of management thinking: hard systems; soft systems; and cybernetics.

6.4 Hard systems

6.4.1 Basics

Hard system approaches are heavily dependent on the core beliefs of the *rational-analytical thinking* school of thought. They assume that manager's goals are both rational and well communicated, that problems can be identified easily and clearly and that organizations can be run successfully by management techniques. Cause and effect are mapped to provide management with 'fix it' models that can be realized easily. Best theory and practice seek:

- To reduce uncertainty by rationalization.
- To predict the future – to map the road ahead.
- To prepare for the future – to find and select optimum journey plans.
- To exercise control over the organization in order to keep it on track and to measure progress.

The amazing development of computer hardware and information technology (IT) over the last twenty years has seen a dramatic growth in the development of hard systems approaches. Similarly, at the macro level, hard system technology has been rigorously applied in an attempt to understand the factors that influence the performance of national economies. If this can be achieved, then in theory, it will be possible to find macro and micro policy mixes that will realize mathematically the desired results of individuals, groups and organizations as efficiently as possible.

6.4.2 Problems

Diagnosis

A tenet that is open to question, especially in times of accelerating change, is that individuals, groups and organizations are able to diagnose key problems correctly. Frequently it is organizations, rather than groups or individuals, that have the greatest difficulty in obtaining accurate problem diagnoses as their collective thinking can be confused and distorted by their corporate milieu of mind-sets. Some organizations like to believe that they never really have serious problems since such problems only confront other, and in their eyes usually badly run, organizations. This mind-set has variations, such as a strong confidence in the power of *rational-analytical thinking* to solve almost anything, and the belief that all problems have happened before and may therefore confidently be considered as temporary irritants that will soon be gone.

Belief in measurement

Another drawback in turbulent times is the tenet that all goals, decisions and important issues can be quantified and measured. This positivist contention has prompted many organizations to invest in sophisticated IT systems to produce vast wads of information. Whilst this has made many corporations 'feel good', it has also left many of them struggling to get to grips with all the data that their mainframe and networks provide. However, many organizational activities, such as operational and tactical matters (Boulding's (1956) *clockworks*) where the situations are clearly structured, can be capably handled by *hard systems thinking*.

Risk spots

Even in the best of times most organizations have *risk hot spots* in their operations that seem to continually resist the efforts of hard systems to control. Here chaos reigns and life is uncomfortable. In these cases reality is reality and attempts to rationalize and programme these *hot spots* inevitably lead to disappointment and frustration. Some organizations find that their mind-sets blind their vision, so causing them to function in an imagined or *virtual reality*. When this occurs frustration mounts, as the chaos continues and managers tend to apportion blame for poor performance levels on the contextual factors. In stable times, when most of the organization is functioning well (in equilibrium), the *hot spots*, though still irritating, can be carried along by the general positive momentum of the organization. As fundamental changes in contextual stimuli cause chaos in the base operations and as the hot spots become more and more unstable, many managers must feel that life is very unfair. In this situation *soft system thinking* may be the most appropriate course of action.

Faith in management techniques

Finally, the belief that organizations can be steered into the future by traditional management techniques alone is a critical assumption, especially in times of accelerating contextual change. Mechanistic planning is fine where the probability of being able to forecast the future accurately is high; when the reverse is the case, managers need to form a clear picture of what makes sense in the new context.

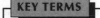

KEY TERMS

Hard systems	Problems
Heavily influenced by rational	■ diagnosis
analytical thinking	■ belief and measurement
	■ risk spots
	■ belief in management techniques

6.5   Soft systems

6.5.1   Basics

Systems for changing times

Hard systems are appropriate if the problem is clear, the systems are mechanistic, and the relationships between the component parts (elements) follow known paths and can be addressed independently of the rest of the system. However, many of the problems that face managers today are difficult to define, fuzzy and messy. As the underlying contextual factors are undergoing significant change, so the ordered, hard systems approaches, are losing their ability to deliver. The onset of the *value time*, as we have seen in Chapter 2, will place a heavy emphasis on people factors. The new, emerging scenario will require a different thinking approach.

Soft systems provide a good start. They are based on the assumption that perceptions are experiential. So there is a strong likelihood that different people viewing the same situation will generate a number of different approaches. There is no single optimum intervention path to follow to keep an organization on track – no single reality. Now if the favourable contextual influences of recent decades (in general terms, say, since 1945) suddenly lurch into chaos (say, since *circa* 1985), then the established management thinking finds itself confronted with a new reality. However, this reality is a global/universal reality and not the commonly *perceived reality* that has dominated much of management practice over the last 50 years. The immediate decades after the end of the Second World War presented the reality of a supply gap. Hence the contextual (relative to time and place) reality encouraged the adoption of rational-analytical and hard systems thinking. There was a job to be done and this could be accomplished efficiently by adopting military and scientific theory to management problems.

The crucial point is that this experienced *perceived reality* was only a component of a larger, in fact global, and some would argue *universal reality*. As the world recovered from the ravages of war and became economically a 'borderless world' or global village so *geographical reality* was subsumed by *global reality*. As the physical environment came under ever-increasing mistreatment by man in what appears to have been a single-minded quest for wealth creation, growing concern began to be voiced as fears mounted that the *natural reality* was being damaged by pollution and ill-considered exploitation of the earth's resources.

As Western wealth creators slowly awakened to this *global/universal reality* so they increasingly began to realize that change was a *global/universal reality*. For many, the previous *perceived reality* fostered a false sense of security that was cemented over the years by the evolution of organizational mind-sets and enshrined by corporate cultures. The rude awakening focused by falling sales has led to a concern amongst many managers to manage change. Such change is happening all the time but only becomes sharply focused when developments in the overall global economic system impact severely on the fortunes of geographical economies. In this context the geographical losers will have to develop geographically winning ways to increase their share of the world's wealth.

Change is a global/universal phenomenon. As living standards come under threat in the West, as the Pacific Rim territories acquire a larger and larger share of the world's wealth, it is natural to expect Western organizations to attempt to defend their corner. This can be achieved by two basic strategies: revitalize domestic operations, or invest in more promising territories. The latter is potentially dangerous for the living standards of the home countries. Both of these alternatives can, in a sense, be described as managing change. Whilst this appears rational at first glance, say, to Western eyes, there is potential for myopic thinking, for it would be safer to think in terms of change management! This involves a global/universal understanding of reality and a willingness to explore other methods of organizational problem solving.

New management response

The consequences of this are that problems cease to be regarded as 'one-off' irritants and are seen as part of a complex system that is continually changing and where there are no single solutions. *Soft systems* thinkers see the world in such dynamic terms, and acknowledge that perfection is probably not attainable and that everything is relevant to time and place. Rapidly changing contextual factors are accepted as inevitable. Problems therefore come and go but the underlying issues that cause them are perpetually changing. So the aim of management becomes not to eradicate problems but continually to improve their responses as the issues unfold. This is well expressed by Japanese management practices.

6.5.2 Hard vs soft systems: Western vs Japanese management

People orientation

Nothing speaks louder than success. As Western management experienced falling sales, rising costs and falling profits in the early 1980s, Japanese management were clearly doing demonstrably better. The undeniable evidence of the *what* led Western management to probe the *how*. Observers had long known that Japanese methods were different to those of the West but paid them scant regard until their accomplishments threatened their own.

Western managers typically adopt a hard management approach within a complex, regimented, bureaucratic organizational system. The Japanese, on the other hand, favour a people- rather than production-oriented system. To Western management they are seen to favour a soft management approach that for a time was explained away as the way the Japanese do things, the implication being that it is not the way we do things in the West. A classic paradigm.

Human capital valued

Japanese management clearly sees brain power as being a significant contributor to its success. Consequently it seeks to assist its human capital to achieve high levels of performance. This it achieves by the deliberate establishment of a climate of mutual support. Managers move to the other side of their desks and out into the working groups. They integrate with the workforce, eat in the same canteens, and wear the same uniforms. All work is highly valued and seen to be for the benefit of the firm. In contrast, the West has tended to adopt a different *modus operandi* that has been strongly influenced by Taylorism and Weberism. The former posits that workers are less efficient if given the opportunity to exercise their discretion, initiative or creativity, and so must be put in their place and subjected to detailed instruction. The latter emphasizes the bureaucratic approach to work whilst stressing the importance of efficiency and hierarchical control.

Kaizen vs Western management philosophy

Japanese management requires workers to undertake more than one job and so rotates the workforce from department to department and plant to plant. This both motivates the workers by giving them a regular set of new challenges, keeps the managers close to what is happening, and provides a climate that actively encourages continuous innovation or *kaizen*. In contrast the Western approach tends to make managers overconfident in hard systems and often deeply suspicious of soft ones.

6.5.3   Understanding soft systems thinking

Organic cells

Soft system thinking continuously searches for improvement in all aspects of an organization's affairs, which includes the shape and function of the organization itself. Sustained thinking effort is harnessed to discover the best way to use the organization's material and people resources. Organizations are seen as organic, rather than mechanistic, entities that are contextually aware and seek to prosper by a strong commitment to learning. An organization can be likened to a body that consists of a collection of live integrated cells (components) all working for a common purpose. Single cells (individuals) are as important as task cells (clusters or groups of individuals), generated to achieve certain tasks, and the complete body (organization), which is the sum of all the individual cells. All these components are regarded as important as they all perform functions that are vital for the success of the organization.

To be successful, most advanced organisms or animals are contextually aware – they can recognize danger and safety. Man is the most sophisticated collection of organic cells on the planet and is gifted with a highly developed potential both to exercise creativity and to think. Groups (small and large) of men (and women) working in harmony are capable of amazing achievements. To harness successfully the talents of individuals, organizations must recognize the importance of continuous learning. This incorporates both the acquisition of key information and the opportunity to put it into practice. All individuals should be encouraged to engage in learning for the benefit of both themselves and the organization.

Soft system approaches actively encourage such learning by stressing its importance, resourcing it, and making sure that it is continually happening. Individuals and groups are expected:

- To learn – functional (e.g. marketing) and process (e.g. thought processes, CPS skills).
- To practise the learning – turning mental knowledge into contextually applied skills.
- To reflect on their success (*reflective practitioning*).
- To discuss the *how* (putting learning into practice process – *process networking*) with other individuals.

Continuous improvement – learning organizations

Smart individuals recognize the importance of continuous learning as an essential component of the pursuit of excellence. Smart organizations are *learning organizations* and actively value their human capital, promote training, active experimentation (putting training into practice) and networking, and maintain open and clear communication channels. They are also deeply committed to continuous improvement (*kaizen*) in everything that they do.

Coping with change – continuous improvement vs single reality solutions

Soft systems view the organization and the system as being there to serve the needs of the people in the system. So that when important changes in external stimuli impact on an organization, that organization should then adapt its systemics to accommodate these changes. This adaptation should be *bottom up* as opposed to a hierarchical *top down* activity. According to this logic it is difficult – some would argue impossible – effectively to change (in terms of perceived performance gains) a complex organization from the outside. This is because outsiders, whilst they might possess objectivity, do not have a personal stake in the society of the organization. Real change has to come from within the organization. M. Weisbord (1991) proposes a four-stage sequence for organizations intent on change, as follows:

1. Experts address individual problems (Taylorism).
2. All address individual problems (participative management).
3. Experts improve complete systems (systems management).
4. All seek to improve the complete system.

Obstacles to improvement are deemed to come from inside the organization. This means that they lie with individuals and groups, and within the organizational milieu (Ackoff, 1974).

Most individuals have blind spots. Many of these can be identified and explored in effective group working. However, groups and organizations too have blind spots and these are more difficult to identify. This is because they are often masked by group and organizational mind-sets. A sympathetic and concerned outsider can perform an invaluable assist by helping to facilitate change. This enabling (as opposed to prescriptive) role is a the positive benefit that a *creative facilitator* can bring to an organization.

At the time of writing, it looks as though uncertainty is probably going to be a permanent factor of organizational life. Soft systems have much to offer contemporary management as they encourage individuals to reflect constantly on how they interact with their own system (organization) and its constituent subsystems (groups), and how all their systems interact with rapidly changing contextual stimuli. Coping with uncertainty and change in turbulent times, when most problems are messy, favours the adoption of soft system thinking to secure consensus-driven continuous improvement rather than the implementation of single reality solutions.

6.5.4 Achieving consensus

When organizations are continuously troubled by turbulent contextual conditions, management that oversubscribe to hard systems typically discover that their corporations are in process of being torn apart. A frequent observation in consultancy work is a scenario that can be termed the *three-way stretch*. Organizations afflicted with this phenomenon are dynamically unstable and characterized by poor information flows, lack of confidence, failing hard systems and low morale.

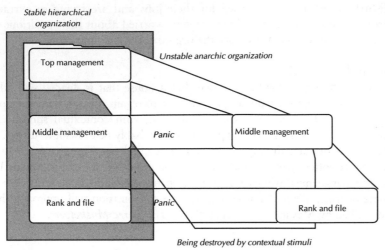

Stable hierarchical organization

Top management

Unstable anarchic organization

Middle management

Panic

Middle management

Rank and file

Panic

Rank and file

Being destroyed by contextual stimuli

Coping with contextual stimuli

Figure 6.2   The three-way stretch

The three-way stretch: a case study of despair

The scenario develops as follows. *Top management* (directors and senior managers) sense, in the face of falling sales and mounting costs, that business is difficult. If they judge this to be a temporary blip in the expected (i.e. familiar) course of events they may decide to keep a stiff upper lip and retreat to their board and meeting room. For fear of panicking the organization, they may resort to a policy of keeping mum (very restricted communication) and/or pressing familiar hard systems tools into action in order to be seen to be doing something. Meanwhile, *middle management* is trying to hold back the tide and making repeated entreaties for help to both senior and junior colleagues. In the worst cases, top management retreat and middle managers find that they are subject to considerable pressure by the *rank and file* below them to do something about it. This they may feel unable to do before receiving the active or tacit approval of their senior colleagues. If this response to mounting contextual change continues for long, huge fissures will start to open up in the organization that will send it hurtling out of control.

The top management will be locked in the board room, the middle management in their offices, and the rank and file (junior managers, supervisors, workers) will be calling mass meetings. This may seem a little far fetched to many readers, but let's look a little more closely at what is happening. Figure 6.2 illustrates the fundamental point. The onset of chaos has distorted the organization so that it is in the process of breaking into three suborganizations, each concerned about the dangers to the original organization. The original organization, represented by the shaded rectangle in the figure, has been pulled into the hatched polygon. Top management are conspicuous by their absence and communication with the middle management and rank and file is poor, if indeed it exists at all. Middle management are concerned for their jobs and are trying to extract some direction from the top. The rank and file are very worried about their positions and are getting increasingly frustrated as they see the organization disintegrating.

'All for one and one for all'

Since the dawn of history it has been known that a house that is divided will fall. If the organization is to survive, then top management have to regain control, unite the house and change their *modus operandi*. In unstable conditions, with contextual stimuli changing rapidly, a predominantly hard systems approach will probably be difficult to justify. What is needed is a new way of doing things. The old corporate mind-sets must give way to a new set that will emphasize softer systemics and acknowledge the value of human capital. To effect real change, top management will have to consult openly with individuals and begin to build a new climate of trust. When this is established the organization will approach that ideal consensus described by Alexander Dumas (1991) in *The Three Musketeers*.

6.5.5   The search for lasting change

Many have explored the problem of devising soft systems to bring about lasting change in organizations. The conceptual models of Churchman (1971), Ackoff (1974) and Checkland (1979) are worth a brief look as they contain much of the best soft systems development work in this area.

Keeping up with the times

Churchman (1971) believes that organizations should be constantly updating themselves to reflect changes in key external stimuli. His work emphasizes the importance of two main factors (elements) that are needed to introduce change effectively. The first he terms *the inquiring system* which is charged with the responsibility of gathering, interpreting and analyzing contextual data. The second element is what he calls *an individual's world view* that is highly selective. So to change a system it is necessary to discover a way to change the beliefs and mind-sets of all the individuals who make up the system. Sometimes this can be achieved by facilitating individuals to unite (reach a consensus) on a third party concern such as customer service or quality targets. A good example of this is quoted by Peters (1987) in *Thriving on Chaos* when he gives the example of Nordstrom's fervent belief in customer service. To emphasize the point, the corporation symbolized this by the inclusion of helping hands at every level on its organization chart.

In their best-selling book *In Search of Excellence* Peters and Waterman (1982) listed seven core beliefs that distinguish high-performing organizations:

1. A belief in being the best.
2. A belief in the importance of the details of execution, the nuts and bolts of doing a job well.
3. A belief in the importance of people as individuals.
4. A belief in superior quality and service.

5. A belief that most members of the organization should be innovators, and its corollary, the willingness to support failure.
6. A belief in the importance of unfamiliarity to boost communication.
7. An explicit belief in and recognition of the importance of economic growth and profits.

A shared vision

Ackoff (1974) maintains that a good focus for organizational consensus is achieved when individuals meet regularly to discuss their ideal vision for the future and how to bring it about. This he terms *interactive planning*. As all individuals are assumed to want the best for their organization, this approach encourages them to meet regularly (networking) to make continuous improvements.

Checkland's soft systems methodology (SSM)

Checkland (1979) has produced a comprehensive model for achieving change in social organizations that incorporates Churchman's *inquiring systems* and continuous learning elements. Managers are seen as organizational process operators who are aware and responsive to contextual changes. Problems are recognized as being subjective interpretations

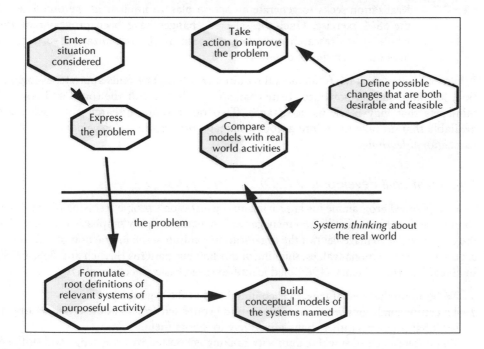

Figure 6.3 Seven-step soft systems methodology (Source: Rosenhead, 1989)

of events that are based on individual's *world view* and previous experience. So a manager can expect a single event in a dynamic system to trigger multiple issues that need to be aired, discussed and rationalized by consensus for progress to result. Also wise executives are aware that individual's *world views* are shaped by personal, group and organizational mind-sets.

Checkland's model has proved to be an outstanding contribution to soft system approaches and has undergone continuous development since it was first publicized in the early 1970s. Rosenhead (1989) presents a useful seven-step sequential model (see Figure 6.3), which further demonstrates SSM:

Steps 1/2	Generate an agreed *problem statement*, nominate a *problem owner* and describe the contextual factors affecting the situation.
Step 3	Describes the world views that influence decision making of all the key parties (individuals, groups and other organizations) that are important to the organization.
Step 4	Addresses the relationships that affect the interaction of subsystems within the organization and builds models to assist understanding and problem solving.
Step 5	Relates the model to the real situation and explores the divergences with a view to challenging assumptions and finding ways of applying the key ideas (selected) that have emerged to the *problem statement*.
Step 6	Looks at the results of the previous steps from the point of view of the problem owner.
Step 7	Realization seeks to generate an action plan to implement the outcomes of the SSM exercise. Once the selected changes have been programmed the whole action-research cycle begins again as the organization sustains its intent to improve continuously.

Whilst SSM does meet the fundamental requirements of soft systems approaches (regulation, learning, and the power to create change), it fails to tackle the social and political mind-sets that may block its acceptance. Two other action-research approaches are available that do take these into account, namely, *organizational development* and *organizational learning*.

Organizational development (OD)

OD is a planned programme for improving an organization's problem solving (OPS) that is championed and managed by top management. It places a heavy emphasis on improving the collaborative management of the organization's culture – the interaction of individual, group and organizational values, thinking and behaviour patterns (French and Bell, 1978). In an earlier article, French (1969) had identified seven basic objectives of OD:

1. To build up the level of trust in each individual in the organization.
2. To create conditions where individuals and groups felt free to address openly organizational problems rather than deliberately to ignore them.
3. To establish a climate where authority ranking is boosted by knowledge and skill, i.e. the label on the door plus what individual managers do.

4. To emphasize the importance of and to develop open horizontal, vertical and diagonal communication channels.
5. To boost morale in the organization – happy individuals are more highly motivated.
6. To encourage regular cross-functional problem-solving sessions to seek consensus and synergistic solutions.
7. To increase the responsibility of individuals and groups in planning and monitoring their work.

Experience has shown that OD programmes are usually better led by skilled external consultants in situations where top management is committed to the implementation of a programme of interventions to improve an organization's climate.

Organizational learning

Most people regard learning as primarily an individual or small group activity. For years responsible organizations have sponsored such learning in the belief that this benefits the organization, as individuals and groups will use what they have learnt in the daily course of their work. This osmotic process can be intensified and managed so as to secure the continuous improvement of the organization if top management openly champions the importance of learning at all levels within the organization. Argyris and Schon (1974) were amongst the first to identify the potential of organizational learning when they argued that learning was required at two levels within an organization for it to have confidence in its ability to sustain continuous improvement.

First, *single-loop learning* occurs when a simple system processes feedback after an event. For example, a room thermostat will adjust the temperature of a room once its programmed setting detects that it needs to intervene. *Double-loop learning* is more sophisticated, as individuals and groups (subsystems within the organization) actually alter their habitual operations to respond to contextual changes, thus assisting the organization to change. Other noteworthy work on learning organizations has been done by Senge (1990) and Kim (1990), who have experimented with learning laboratories in the United States, and Pedler, Burgoyne and Bodell (1991), who have pioneered the concept of the learning company in the United Kingdom.

KEY TERMS

Hard vs soft systems
- people orientation
- human capital values
- *kaizen*

Understanding soft systems
- organic cells
- *kaizen*

Consensus management
- inquiring systems
- continuous learning

SSM

OD

Organizational learning
- single-loop
- double-loop

6.6 Cybernetics

This is a branch of *systems thinking* which posits that control mechanisms such as feedback loops can be used to improve performance. The underlying reasoning is that every output must be the result of an input, and that this input will be more effective if it is adapted after studying the output of previous inputs. Basic cybernetics is a mechanical control process that helps managers to appreciate the importance of assessing the success of the *how* of problem solving as well as the *what* outcome. As response times become more demanding and resource allocations meaner, so the *how* or process aspects of management assume a greater relative importance.

6.7 Organizational responses

6.7.1 Japanese management approach

Japanese management success

As the contextual factors impacting on wealth creation in the West have gathered pace, many organizations, noting the success of the Japanese corporations in Europe and the United States, have investigated Japanese management ideas in a bid to discover the key common factors that explain their impressive achievements. Early benchmarking studies revealed the importance of culture and soft system general management practices. As there is mounting evidence that the Japanese approach is working in Western cultures, where real productivity gains are increasingly being reported (e.g. the Nissan plant in the UK and the Sony plant in San Diego in the United States), attention was directed to studying their general management practices. It is interesting to note that McGregor (1960) recognized that: 'effective performance results when conditions are such that the members of the organization can achieve their own goals best by directing their efforts towards the success of the enterprise.'

Research into the literature over the last twenty-five years presents a steady succession of academic articles chronicling the increasing interest in Japanese management practices. Peter Drucker (1971) published an article entitled 'What we can learn from Japanese management'. Then throughout the 1970s a host of articles appeared that extended Drucker's thought to Europe and the United States. The 1980s opened with Hayes and Abernathy (1980), in their article 'Managing our way to economic decline', bringing to public attention the lack of innovation in American business. As Japanese innovation continued to flourish, attention was increasingly directed to understanding the *how* of their operations.

Behavioural patterns

Three key factors seem to characterize Japanese good practice:

1. A special concern for people, a marked belief in human capital – *people approach*.
2. A different way of doing things, predominantly soft systems – *process approach*.

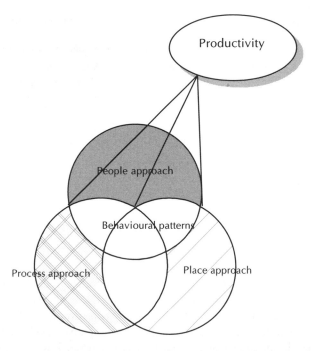

Figure 6.4   Japanese soft systems management practices

3. A realization that the working environment has an important influence on performance – *place approach*.

Increasingly it became apparent that much of the Japanese success lay in their skilled integration of these approaches in the behavioural patterns that they nurtured in their organizations (see Figure 6.4).

People approach

In common with Western management the Japanese agree that the key concern of management is to make the optimum use of an organization's assets. This calls for a subtle blending of financial, technological and human resources. However, the Japanese regard human resources as the key source of long-term profits.

The Japanese management mind-set has a high regard for human resources and devotes considerable attention to securing both sustained loyalty and high levels of motivation from employees by the skilled integration of three basic strategies (see Figure 6.5):

1. The provision of secure long-term employment.
2. The provision of a unique organizational philosophy.
3. The integration of individuals into groups and from there into the supra group of the organization.

Figure 6.5   Japanese management mind-set (Source: Hatvany and Pucik, 1981)

Mind-set	Strategies	Tools and techniques
Marked concern for human resources.	Long-term employment.	Slow promotion. Complex appraisal systems. Stress on work groups.
	Development and communication of unique organizational philosophy.	Open communication. Consultative decision making.
	Integration of all employees into the organizational family.	

Basic strategies

Secure employment

In contrast to the general practice in the West the Japanese prefer to provide secure employment for all their employees. They are prepared to accept a short-term price for this, which they believe is in the best interest of the organization in the longer term as it promotes good morale, limits the disruption of high staff turnover levels, reduces training costs, and promotes the organization's cohesiveness. So when business gets tough the Japanese will typically resort to such measures as the following:

- Placing a freeze on new recruitment.
- Offering voluntary early retirement to eligible staff.
- Asking full-time employees to undertake the work of temporary staff.
- Transferring their own staff to work that is currently subcontracted.
- If things get really bad, imposing across-the-board reductions in base salaries and bonuses for all staff (including managers).

By such means, adept organizations are often able to secure 10 to 15 per cent savings in labour costs.

Development and communication of organization philosophy

In the firm belief that employee commitment and productivity are interrelated, Japanese organizations actively develop and promote a strong positive culture that keeps both the goals and achievements of the organization constantly before employees (see Figure 6.6). This approach fosters a sense of belonging that provides unity, structure and control (Ouchi and Price, 1978). Typically the corporate philosophy stresses the importance of co-operation and teamwork within the organizational family.

Integration of employees into the organization

This organizationwide belief that all work is for the organization ('all for one and one for all') is sustained by effective communication with employees, promotion of group working

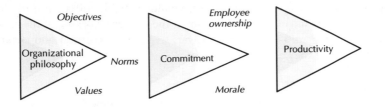

Figure 6.6   Japanese organizational philosophy

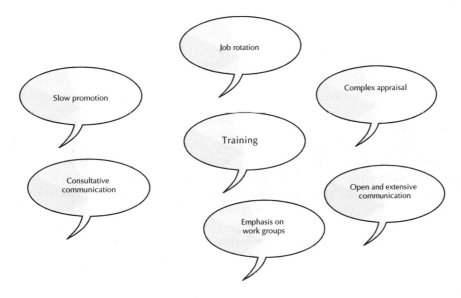

Figure 6.7   Japanese management techniques

practices and job rotation, and is validated by the observable behaviour of the management. This produces a high level of morale nurtured constantly by an appropriate organizational social programme including cultural, sporting and recreational activities.

Process approach

As the main focus of Japanese management is on people development it perhaps should come as no surprise that they favour soft systems thinking. Figure 6.7 summarizes the most significant techniques typically used to integrate and orchestrate the skills of their employees.

Slow promotion
Unlike many Western organizations the Japanese do not encourage a promotion race as they are concerned that in any such race they would have one winner but several losers.

Whilst the winner can bask in glory the losers would probably suffer a loss of morale, and as behaviour breeds behaviour this could impair the efficient working of the groups in the organization. So they tend to favour a slower, stepped progression and ensure that all employees know that they are valued.

Job rotation

Job rotation occurs in the West but tends to be less planned and structured than in Japanese organizations where it is not unusual for highly skilled blue-collar workers to have 10-year job rotation plans. This system is used in an imaginative and creative way to promote the formation of internal networks and to 'fire up' bored employees.

Training

Training employees at all levels is afforded a high priority and takes place both on and off the job. Career paths are flexible and senior posts are rarely filled with outside personnel (though there are some noteworthy exceptions such as Honda, who believe that the regular acquisition of staff from other organizations stimulates the evolution of their culture).

Complex appraisal

Whilst individual output may well be measured, the main source of output generally is seen to be the work groups. Attention is given to assessing individual employees on a wide range of personality and behavioural factors – such as emotional maturity, team working and creativity – to identify their potential. Occasional mistakes are regarded as part of the learning process. As employee rankings within the cohort are not generally disclosed, the climate encourages keen employees to put in unpaid overtime in order to make a good impression. As group performance is a critical focus for evaluation the organization is able to encourage inside training in the form of peer instruction.

Emphasis on work groups

The Japanese approach emphasizes the importance of groups and uses them to inculcate the norms and beliefs of the organization as well as to motivate employees. Tasks (the *what*) are delegated to groups who are often given considerable freedom as to *how* they process them. This promotes team spirit as groups vie with one another to produce quality responses. When problems arise, employees are encouraged to network and form *quality control circles* to seek solutions. Outsiders are only brought in to educate group members in key process skills, such as creative problem solving (CPS), or to provide specialized technical advice.

Open and extensive communication

All ranks are encouraged to integrate and so managers can be seen regularly on the shop floor or in the 'organizational kitchen' and frequently have their offices sited in the thick of activity. This promotes effective face-to-face vertical communication. Managers too are assessed in a similar pattern as their employees and are expected to demonstrate and sustain sound human management practices. In contrast, we have come across a number of organizations in the West that adopt a carefree attitude to human development and from time to time commission independent surveys of staff morale. When the results come back to top management they are often considered to be too contentious and are therefore sanitized before publication. This would be unthinkable as a Japanese management practice.

Consultative decision making

Most individuals like to feel that they have some say in decisions that affect them. Recognizing this, Japanese organizations adopt a far more open set of procedures than many of their Western counterparts. Whenever it is possible, peers and supervisors are afforded an opportunity to air their views, and many decisions are ultimately taken at *ringi* meetings where all present mark their agreement with the final proposal. However, many more decisions are taken laterally and generally accepted by everyone, in the firm belief that all work for the organization.

Place approaches

In addition to valuing human capital and seeking to develop it by soft systems management practices, the Japanese recognize that environment has a vital contribution to make as well. So they sanction expenditure to improve the working environment for all, as opposed to just some. This is reflected both in the provision of excellent hygiene standards and in sustained effort to improve the working environment.

6.7.2   Western organizations

Meanwhile in the West . . .

The above brief sketch of a typical Japanese management approach to organizational life is not intended to stand in judgement of Western management practices. As in most walks of life there are good and bad examples on both sides of the fence. Many organizations in the West have seen their staff as high-value assets for decades. IBM, Hewlett-Packard, Procter & Gamble, Cummins Engines in the United States and Berol, Bonas, Marks & Spencer, Volvo and Virgin Airways in Europe are all prime examples of the best in Western practice. The aim of this chapter is to point out the importance of human resources to all managers and management, to show that soft systems can and do deliver high levels of productivity, and to encourage them to draw inspiration from best practice. Many Western organizations are already operating and developing their own soft styles and this is applauded unreservedly. Others have yet to change their *modus operandi* effectively and hence their responses to the dynamic contextual changes that have been emphasized in this text.

As wealth creation in the West comes under pressure from the steady increase in the activities of the Pacific Rim territories, and as the *value time* develops, so added value will dominate organizational activity. What is more, such added value must be wanted by the market. People are instrumental in demanding higher and higher value products or services, and people will have to exercise their creativity in order to meet the expectations of the market through innovation. So the soft systems approach to management has much to offer, but to introduce it fully in an integrative way means a complete overhaul of many organizations' traditional ways of working. Many corporations have investigated soft management tools over the last 20 years or so and others have effectively been practising selected soft skills for longer than this – for example, Marks & Spencer in *supply chain management*.

The acknowledged success of Japanese management has stimulated many organizations to study their methods. A crucial factor at this point of the argument is the overall perception that the West retains of what business is all about. In the case of the United States this was given a loud blast by Hayes and Abernathy (1980) when they declared that the preferred response of American business was:

- To service existing markets rather than create new ones.
- To imitate rather than to innovate.
- To acquire existing companies rather than invest in research and development.
- To focus on short-term rather than long-term growth.

The increasing competitiveness associated with wealth creation in the West has led many organizations to take up *total quality management* (TQM) and to set out their stalls to score zero defects. Whilst many quality schemes are commendable they are far from instant solutions and require sustained commitment for them to become successful. After the first foray or two with the new quality wine many organizations have experienced difficulties in adapting the theory and cant to their organizations. Some have persevered and others have all but given up, perhaps because ultimately a hard systems culture has not given way enough to support a soft systems initiative.

Advances are also evident in Western organizations in the study and practical adoption of organizational learning programmes. Organizations are awakening to the potential that lies within their human resources. In the United States Motorola decided to train its workforce to enable them to successfully operate their new TQM programmes in the early 1980s. This action touched the top of a large iceberg and subsequently led them to review critically the basic human skills of their employees, whereupon they found that many were sorely lacking in many respects – some were hardly literate. The more the company sought to correct this problem, the more learning they found to be necessary. Ultimately they founded the Motorola University that was charged with the remit to cover the whole workforce – from top management to the rank and file in the offices and on the shop floor.

In the United Kingdom, Rover (now part of BMW) committed £30 million in 1990 when they established Rover Learning Business to develop the residual and potential talents of their workforce. This attracted quite a lot of attention at the time and Rob Meakin (1990) commented:

> You can try to gain competitive advantage through technology, but within six months everyone has caught up. You can try to achieve it through style, but it is very difficult these days to find a style which meets aerodynamic specifications and is still significantly different from everything else that is still on the market, and you can try to achieve it through fittings but nearly every car nowadays is a Christmas tree of goodies. We believe that we have a real chance of achieving it through our people.
>
> In Rover we have got 40,000 very good people, some of them extraordinary. If we could get to a situation where we had 40,000 people who were totally committed to us, multi-skilled, highly flexible , and with us all the way, we would have that competitive advantage.

Now half of Rover's workforce are engaged in learning programmes at a cost to the company every year of around £35 million. Unlike the leading Japanese organizations, Rover do not offer guaranteed secure employment. Nevertheless this initiative does make a powerful point – that individual and corporate destinies are critically linked to learning. Other organizations that have appreciated the importance of corporate learning programmes and responded in some style include ICL, who see it as 'part of the corporate glue' (Caulkin, 1994). In September 1993 Unipart, the Oxford-based car components group launched Unipart 'U' which in the words of its chairman John Neill, 'exists to train and inspire its stakeholders to achieve world class standards of performance'.

The good news is that such initiatives are starting to be seriously considered by many Western organizations. The sad and bad news is that active and purposeful initiatives are so few. Herein lies a paradox. If organizations think that learning is expensive what price do they put on ignorance? Whilst the learning cause is receiving a better reception these days, it is important to distinguish between education and training. Both are needed but they are not one and the same thing. Education should be primarily aimed at broadening individuals' horizons – for example, making them contextually aware, teaching them CPS skills. Training should provide the opportunity for people to acquire traditional job-related skills and be encouraged to experiment with new ones (new *hows*). Particularly impressive in this respect are the Problem Solving Centres run by Black & Decker.

The success of the Japanese approach has stimulated many organizations to show interest in developing group activity. Some are actively promoting job rotation schemes, reducing the 'inner court approach space' between the managed and the managers, adopting flatter management structures, and seeking to improve communication. The question is how committed are these organizations? To benefit from real teamwork and the creative problem-solving skills of multidisciplinary groups requires a full organizational commitment to the bonding that Dumas described in his novel *The Three Musketeers*, namely, 'all for one and one for all'. This should be both the rallying cry and the reality throughout truly liberated organizations. The others will still to all intents and purposes be managed by hard systems. The contextual factors affecting wealth creation in the West would seem to favour the adoption of soft system approaches. Surely they are worth evaluating seriously!

KEY TERMS

Japanese management
success
Behavioural patterns
- people approach
- process approach
- place approach

Western management
- Increased interest in Japanese model
- TQM
- learning organizations
- interest in group activity

6.8 Organizational tools

6.8.1 Creative organizational problem solving (COPS)

This text has sought to equip individuals and groups with a good basic collection of CPS tools, which were introduced in the previous two chapters (see Appendix 5.2). An organization is a composite group so all the tools making up our introductory tool kit should be useful at organizational level. However, there are a few additional tools that would appear to have a particular relevance to organizational rather than group thinking. These are: re-engineering management; benchmarking; creative facilitation training/learning organization; office of information; and quality initiatives.

Re-engineering management (Hammer, 1990)

In theory, re-engineering management is a good idea. Organizations should change, as this text has argued, to respond adequately to modern business conditions. However, change in this context means a total redesign. Altering the physical space in which business activity takes place, tearing down old process structures and instituting new leaner and sharper ones is fine too. Top management is in a position to insist that employees work in new ways and can install control systems to 'organize' the workplace. This amounts to re-engineering the organizational processes of employees. Nevertheless, unless real, visible and sustained efforts are made by senior management to change their management processes, such initiatives are likely to run into the sand.

Re-engineering exercises need to be managed from the top. Things need to be seen to be really changing. The re-engineering places and processes must be accompanied by the adoption of a new management response style by the senior executives. It is unwise for top management to assume that if they are seen to be moving, then the employees can just get on with it and manage the detail themselves. What is required to respond effectively to change is a complete rethink of management processes. Soft systems need to replace hard ones. Management need to become more approachable, to be seen in cross-functional teams, to come out of the executive suite. In fact, to tear down traditional, hierarchical, organizational charts and replace them either by inverting them (senior management at the centre fostering growth at the edges of the organization), or by substituting a 'flatarchy' system. The conversion from the old ways to the new ones that are contextually appropriate for the advent of the twenty-first century must be total. Senior managers, in a sense, need to be born again. They must accept new roles, styles and management systems, set their employees free to express creativity in their tasks, set realistic challenges, and encourage their staff all the time. It is not an easy task but it is possible, given the right approach attitudes and some true grit to see it through. The *creative management model* described in this text is not a toy or academic abstraction. However, to realize the potential benefits, managers have to adopt a new vision of organizational life. The potential reward is vast, but so too are the short-term costs to management pride. Sitting in the State Suite of the *Titanic* and waited on by polished servants is personally agreeable, in the short term. Being inspired by a new corporate ship, fitted with radar and modern gadgets and with a highly trained and creative crew, is much better than sailing in fog!

Benchmarking

In 1980 Xerox discovered that despite their efforts to achieve greater productivity they were falling further and further behind the Japanese. They sought consultancy help from McKinsey and sent a party of their engineers on a fact-finding trip to Japan. Benchmarking is a tool that identifies the organization's best competitors (in the eyes of the market) and seeks to discover their *how* (methods) and to improve on them at lower cost levels.

Creative facilitation training/learning organization

The success that has been achieved by the few organizations that have experimented with corporate learning programmes (see previous discussion) seems to be conclusive. Whilst problem solving probably appears on the learning menu of such organizations, this text stresses the importance of releasing creativity and CPS as they are key competencies for today's individual, group and organizational wealth creators. Creative facilitators are skilled process experts who progress CPS sessions (on virtually any subject) and are discussed further in Chapter 8.

Office of information/creativity centres

As competition for business intensifies, responsive organizations are continually looking for ways of shortening the time that it takes to bring a product to the marketplace. Generally speaking, smaller organizations seem to be more creative and entrepreneurial than larger ones. Aware of this problem, Eastman Kodak introduced a collection of tools known as the 'Office of Information' (OI). This has five basic stages:

1. Idea generation.
2. Initial screening.
3. Group review.
4. Seeking sponsorship.
5. Sponsorship.

Eastman Kodak report that roughly 60 per cent of ideas are abandoned in the first two stages and only about 20 per cent are ultimately championed. Other organizations that have used the OI include Amoco, Bell Canada and Union Carbide.

Organizations that have exposed themselves to creativity training are strongly recommended to set up internal creativity centres to act as a focus from which creativity can be diffused throughout the organization.

Quality initiatives

Quality control and the broader concept of total quality management (TQM) evolved from cybernetic principles in the United States. Quality management is a discipline that seeks to obtain continuous improvement in performance by relying on systems thinking. According to Juran (1988) quality is about 'product performance that results in customer satisfaction' and 'freedom from product deficiencies, which avoids customer dissatisfaction'. TQM is a management philosophy that is based on the work of Feigenbaum (1961) who argued that quality should be a key concern of everyone in an organization. He also maintained that faults should be identified and corrected at the point of origin.

Currently there are many quality management programmes available, with the best known being those proposed by Philip Crosby (1979, 1984), Edward Deming, Joseph Juran (1988), and Genichi Taguchi. Though all with their own distinguishing features, all three programmes concur that responsibility for quality begins at the design stage of a product.

6.9 Creative organizational problem solving: Master Guides

6.9.1 Master Guide 10   Managing innovation

Several organizations, aware of the need to innovate continuously, have fashioned their own techniques for obtaining and processing ideas into marketable products. 3M is famous for its ability to sustain innovation which it does by:

- keeping divisions small;
- tolerating failure;
- motivating innovators;
- staying close to the customer; and
- sponsoring employees to develop their own ideas (15 per cent of their time can be devoted to a project to help them prove that it is viable).

Many other companies, including such famous names as the Body Shop, Hewlett-Packard, Microsoft and Sony, all have comparable systems.

6.9.2 Master Guide 11   Structural change – downsizing

To meet the pressures of competition, several organizations are seeking to acquire sleeker and leaner structures and reduce the complexity of their administrative systems. Small has become beautiful as in most cases smaller organizations are quicker to respond than larger ones. In theory, smaller structures should help, but only if top management are prepared to introduce softer management systems. Small organizations run predominantly by hard systems miss out on the chance to build a new culture.

6.9.3 Master Guide 12   Supply chain management

This is a proven technique for reducing supplier lead times. The retailers Marks & Spencer have been practising this for years as they sought to ensure that only products of acceptable quality would be shipped to their warehouses. Supplier-chain management has a high profile in the automotive industry.

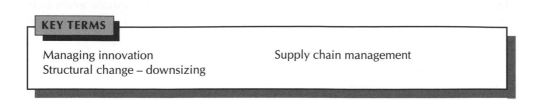

KEY TERMS

Managing innovation   Supply chain management
Structural change – downsizing

6.10 **Summary**

6.10.1 Last stop on the line

This chapter marks the last stop on the line on our journey through the component factors of the *creative management response*. We have briefly reviewed the history of management thinking and discussed the merits and demerits of hard and soft systems thinking. Much of the discussion has featured the soft systemics of the lauded Japanese style of management and has contrasted this with the harder styles of many Western organizations. It is important to realize that not all Japanese organizations are shining examples of 'best practice' in buyers' markets. At the same time there are some very good

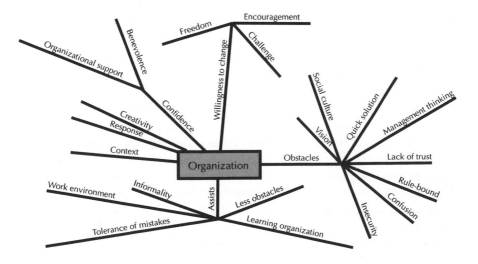

Figure 6.8 Main factors affecting the approaches of organizations to the CMR model

Western organizations that display excellent practice. The purpose of this chapter was to provide some interesting management process issues for you to think about, reflect on, and discuss (network) with colleagues. As you turned the pages of this (and the previous two chapters), the leading factors that influence the attitudes of organizations toward the *creative management response* emerged. They are now summarized in the mind map in Figure 6.8.

6.11 Organizational creativity audit

Organizational practitioners are invited to complete our *organizational creativity audit* before moving on to the practical material in Parts IV and V. Full details are to be found in Appendix 6.1

QUESTIONS

1. Some assert that the heyday of *rational-analytical thinking* has long since gone. Discuss, paying particular reference to the main relevant belief sets.

2. In what ways does systems thinking differ from that of *rational-analytical thinking*? Why is this significant to the Western world in the latter half of the 1990s?

3. Why are mind-sets so important to managers? Describe the factor sets that lie behind them. How do you manage individual, group and organizational mind-sets? How might you seek to change them?

4. Outline the main tenets of hard systems thinking. What do you think are their main drawbacks in managing in globally competitive markets?

5. 'What you measure is what you get.' Discuss.

6. Describe the main characteristics of hard and soft systems thinking. Select an example of a hard systems organization and an example of a soft systems organization known to you. Which do think is better managed and why?

7. How might you avoid what is referred to in this text as 'the three-way stretch'?

8. Select an issue or a problem of interest to you in your own organization. Apply the seven-step model (SSM) (after Rosenhead, 1989). Write a brief report to your manager summarizing your results.

9. 'Effective managers play with possibilities, tinker with systems, and use their resources to fund workable solutions.' (Nohria and Berkley, 1994). Discuss.

10. Imagine that you have been asked to prepare a short written piece for your local newspaper on the Japanese management approach. Draft a 1,200 word article that captures the most important points.

11. Describe the main barriers to introducing *creative management* to a traditional organization. Suggest ways in which they might be overcome.

12. Describe three *creative problem solving tools* that might be particularly helpful for an organization that wants to respond positively to change. Assuming that you are a consultant advising the CEO, what advice would you deem it necessary to impart?

References

Ackoff, R. L. (1974), *Redesigning the Future*, New York: Wiley.

Argyris, C. and Schon, D. (1974), *Theory in Practice*, San Francisco: Jossey-Bass.

Boulding, K. (1956), 'General systems theory: the skeleton of science', *Management Science*, 2.

Caulkin, S. (1994), 'Let my people profit', *Observer*, 6 March.

Checkland, P. (1979), 'Techniques in soft systems practice, part 1: some diagrams – some tentative guidelines', *Journal of Applied Systems Analysts*.

Churchman, C. W. (1971), *The Design of Inquiring Systems*, New York: Basic Books.

Crosby, P. B. (1979), *Quality is Free*, Cambridge, Mass.: McGraw-Hill.

Crosby, P. B. (1984), *Quality without Tears*, Cambridge, Mass.: McGraw-Hill.

Drucker, P. (1971), 'What can we learn from Japanese management?', *Harvard Business Review*, 49.

Dumas, A. (1991; first pub. 1844), *The Three Musketeers*, Oxford World Classics edition.

Feigenbaum, A. V. (1961), *Total Quality Control: Engineering and management*, New York: McGraw-Hill.

French, W. (1969), 'Organization development: objectives, assumptions and strategies,' *California Management Review*, 12, 23–4.

French, W. and Bell, C. (1978), *Organizational Development: Science interventions for organization improvement*, 2nd edn, Englewood Cliffs, NJ: Prentice Hall.

Hammer, M. (1990), 'Re-engineering work: don't automate, obliterate', *Harvard Business Review*, 68. July–Aug.

Hatvany and Pucik (1981), 'Japanese management practices and productivity', *Organizational Dynamics*, spring.

Hayes, R. and Abernathy, W. (1980), 'Managing our way to economic decline', *Harvard Business Review*, 58, July–Aug.

Juran, J. (1988), *Juran on Planning for Quality*, New York: Free Press.

Juran, J. (1988), *Planning for Quality*, New York: Free Press, 332.

Kim, D. (1990), 'Learning laboratories: designing a reflective learning environment,' Working Paper No. D–4026, Systems Dynamics Group, Sloan School of Management, Cambridge, Mass.: MIT.

McGregor, D. (1960), *The Human Side of Enterprise*, London: McGraw-Hill.

Meakin, R. (1990), 'Rover learning business', *Personnel Management*, April. 1990.

Mitroff, I. I. (1984), *Stakeholders of the Organisational Mind*, San Francisco: Jossey-Bass.

Nohria, N. and Berkley, J. D. (1994), 'Whatever happened to the take-charge manager', *Harvard Business Review*, 72, Jan.–Feb.

Ouchi, W. and Price, R. (1978), 'A new perspective on organizational development', *Organizational Dynamics*, autumn.

Pedler, M. J., Burgoyne, J. G. and Boydell, T. H. (1991), *The Learning Company: A strategy for sustainable development*, Maidenhead: McGraw-Hill.
Peters, T. (1987), *Thriving on Chaos*, New York: Knopf.
Peters, T. J. and Waterman, R. H. (1982), *In Search of Excellence*, New York: Harper & Row.
Rosenhead J. (1989), *Rational Analysis for a Problematical World*, Chichester: Wiley.
Senge, P. (1990), *The Fifth Discipline*, New York: Doubleday.
Weisbord, M. (1991), *Productive Workplaces*, San Francisco: Jossey-Bass, 262.

Additional reading

Management thinking

Barnard, C. (1938), *The Functions of the Executive*, Cambridge, Mass.: Harvard University Press.
Drucker, P. (1980), *Managing in Turbulent Times*, New York: Harper & Row.
Quinn, R. (1988), *Beyond Rational Management*, San Francisco: Jossey-Bass.

Hard systems

Kwak, N. and DeLurgio, S. (1980), *Quantitative Models for Business Decisions*, Belmont, Calif.: Duxbury Press.
Walton, M. (1986), *The Deming Management Method*, New York: Perigree.

Soft systems

Beer, S. (1959), *Cybernetics and Management*, London: English Universities Press.
De Geus, A. (1988), 'Planning as learning', *Harvard Business Review*, 66, March–April.
Flood, R. and Carson, E. (1988), *Dealing With Complexity*, New York: Plenum Press.
Schon, D. (1987), *Educating the Reflective Practitioner: Toward a new design for teaching and learning in the professions*, San Francisco: Jossey-Bass.
Senn, J. (1990), *Information Systems in Management*, 4th edn, Belmont, Calif.: Wadsworth.

Organizational responses

Clark, R. (1979), *The Japanese Company*, New Haven, Conn.: Yale University Press.
Kennedy, C. (1989; repr. 1991), 'Xerox charts a new strategic direction', *Long Range Planning*, 22 (1), 10–17. Reprinted in J. Henry and D. Walker (eds), *Managing Innovation Reader*, London: Sage.
Kilmann, R. (1984), *Beyond the Quick Fix*, San Francisco: Jossey-Bass.
Nonaka, I. (1990), 'Redundant, overlapping organization: a Japanese approach to innovation process', *California Management Review*, 32 (3).
Ouchi, W. G. (1981), *Theory Z*, Reading, Mass.: Addison-Wesley.
Pascale, R. and Athos, A. (1985), *The Art of Japanese Management*, New York: Simon & Schuster.

APPENDIX 6.1

Organizational creativity audit

Instructions

Statements

1. It is a good idea to copy the statements and assessment forms in this appendix before attempting the audit.

2. Put the assessment form to one side.

3. Turn to the statements and and respond as honestly and as quickly as you can.

4. Please do not confer with others whilst you or they are completing the audit.

Assessment

1. Turn to the assessment form.

2. Tick the boxes that match your response to the statements on the audit statement sheet. For example, if you felt that 'We are supply-oriented' (Statement 1) and you agreed strongly with this statement, you should place a tick at the intersection of the AS column and the Statement 1 row.

3. When you have ticked your responses in the six assessment boxes run a quick check to see that you have ticked the right boxes.

Interpretation

1. The six boxes carry information that assess your organization in the light of the six primary components of our CMR model (see chapter 7).

2. Study the picture that emerges and keep it for a while. Look through the text for ideas and information that best fits your audit result. For further information please contact the author at Durham University Business School, Mill Hill Lane, Durham, Co. Durham, UK (0191) 374 2211 or 374 3394, Fax (0191) 374 3748. Email M.R.V. Goodman@durham. ac.uk.

Statements

Agree strongly (AS); Agree (A); disagree (D); Disagree strongly (DS)

Please tick appropriate box

	AS	A	D	DS
1. We are supply oriented organization	. . .	. . .	. . .	. . .
2. We have standard training programmes				
3. We are aware of creativity				
4. We encourage individual creativity				
5. We support group working				
6. We value our staff				
7. We are service-oriented				
8. We believe in tailor-made training programmes for individuals				
9. We value creativity				
10. We practise open communication				
11. We provide suitable training				
12. We try to make the organization serve the staff rather than make staff serve the organization				
13. We are a domestic organization				
14. We use hard systems thinking				
15. We are prepared to evaluate new ways of management thinking				
16. We try to provide secure employment				
17. We provide time for creative group work				
18. We are acutely influenced by external factors				
19. We believe that customers are more important than our organizational architecture				
20. We provide space for CPS				
21. We cultivate a trust environment				
22. We use open channels of communication				
23. We are a learning organization				
24. We know what the market thinks of us				
25. We adopt an open management style				
26. We will resource a creativity centre				
27. We provide good working conditions				
28. We reward group creativity				
29. We tolerate mistakes				
30. We encourage loyalty upwards and downwards				

Assessment form

Context-related factors

Please tick appropriate box

Statement	AS	A	D	DS
1. We are supply-oriented	. . .	. . .	. . .	. . .
7. We are service-oriented				
13. We are a domestic organization				
18. We are acutely influenced by external factors				
24. We know what the market thinks of us				

Management response

Statement	AS	A	D	DS
2. We have standard training programmes				
8. We believe in tailor-made training programmes for individuals				
14. We use hard systems thinking				
19. We believe that customers are more important than our organizational architecture				
25. We adopt an open-management style				

Creative response

Statement	AS	A	D	DS
3. We are aware of creativity				
9. We value creativity				
15. We are prepared to evaluate new ways of management thinking				
20. We provide space for CPS				
26. We will resource a creativity centre				

Individuals

Statement	AS	A	D	DS
4. We encourage individual creativity				
10. We practise open communication				
16. We try to provide secure employment				
21. We cultivate a trust environment				
27. We provide good working conditions				

Groups

Statement	AS	A	D	DS
5. We support group working				
11. We provide suitable training				
17. We provide time for creative group work				
22. We use open channels of communication				
28. We reward group creativity				

Organizations

Statement	AS	A	D	DS
6. We value our staff				
12. We try to make the organization serve the staff rather than make staff serve the organization				
23. We are a learning organization				
29. We tolerate mistakes				
30. We encourage loyalty upwards and downwards				

From *what* toward *how*

This section completes Part II of the text and concludes the journey in search of the components for a new management approach (the *what*). After Chapter 3 surveyed the familiar ground, Chapters 4 and 5 explored the subject of individual and group creativity and offered readers the opportunity to try out some of the material for themselves. *Personal* and *group creativity audits* appear in the appendices to Chapters 4 and 5 and a fully-fledged *introductory CPS tool kit* is presented in Appendix 5.2. Chapter 6 completed the exploratory phase of the text by taking a look at management systems in search of an approach that would foster creativity. Part III presents an overview of the *creative management response* (CMR) *approach* (the *what*) and provides a full statement of the complete CMR model. Part IV addresses the *how* issues surrounding the introduction of CMR to organizations large and small.

The CMR model:
bridging the gap

Approaching creative management – Part III

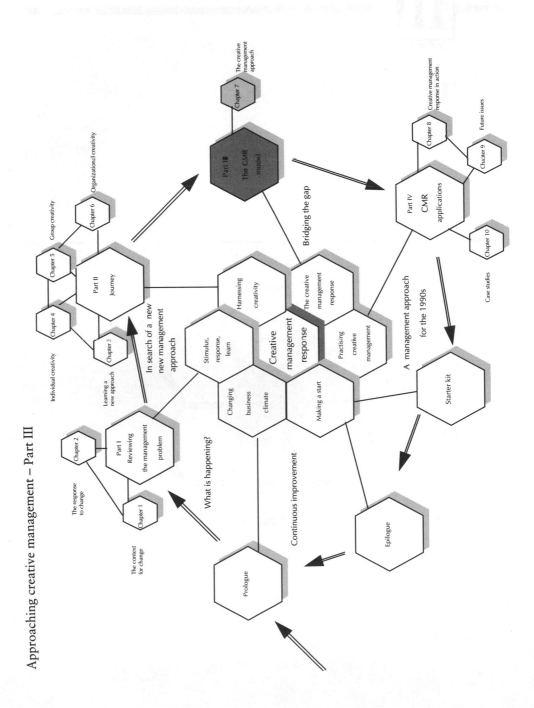

Introduction

Part III consists of a single chapter that summarizes the ground covered in Parts I and II, and then moves on to present four views of the fully developed *creative management response (CMR) model*. It acts as a bridge between the approach to the formation of the CMR model and its execution in real life situations. Only a fool would claim that he or she has stumbled on *the* answer to the pressing problems of Western organizations. It is believed that the CMR does represent a reasoned contribution to the search for a new *modus operandi* for the West's wealth creators. In practical applications the model has performed well and has been seen to work. At the end of the day it is what happens that counts rather than what is promised.

In Part IV, Chapters 8, 9 and 10 present material that is essentially concerned not with the derivation of the CMR model but with its execution in the minds and plans of individuals, groups and organizations.

7

The creative management approach

CONTENTS

7.1 Introduction *245*

7.2 Approaching creative management I – the diagnosis *246*

7.3 Approaching creative management II – the journey *250*

7.4 Creative management response model *252*

7.5 Top gear *261*

7.6 Summary *265*

Questions *266*

References *266*

Appendix 7.1 Creative management response model *266*

Appendix 7.2 Creative management response model – factor codes *274*

Appendix 7.3 CMR model – factor code cards *278*

Map: Chapter 7

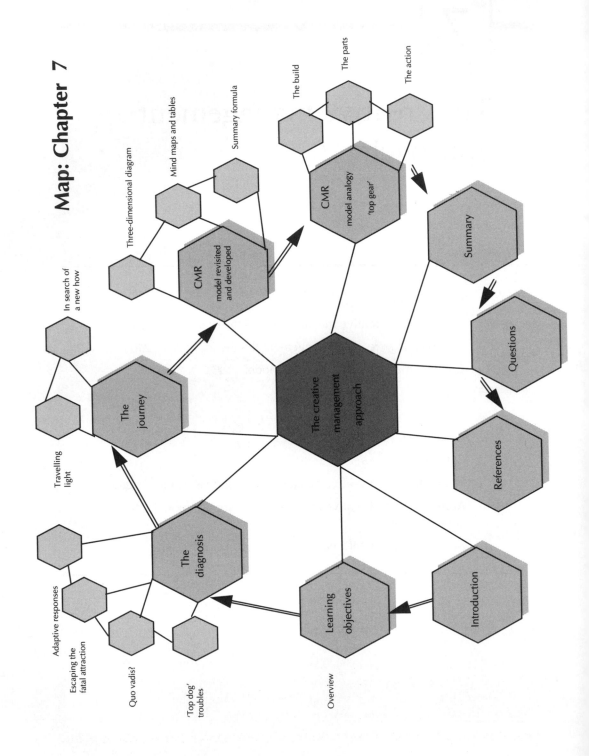

Three-dimensional diagram

Mind maps and tables

Summary formula

The build

The parts

The action

In search of a new how

CMR model revisited and developed

CMR model analogy 'top gear'

Travelling light

The journey

Summary

The creative management approach

Questions

References

Adaptive responses

Escaping the fatal attraction

The diagnosis

Quo vadis?

'Top dog' troubles

Learning objectives

Introduction

Overview

7.1 Introduction

7.1.1 A suitable case for treatment!

This chapter briefly reviews the argument so far and presents both a restatement and an exposition of the *creative management response (CMR) model* components. The CMR model is presented in four different ways:

1. By a three-dimensional diagram.
2. In a series of six mind maps and tables.
3. As a summary formula.
4. In the form of an analogy ('top gear').

Appendix 7.1 assigns unique descriptive factor codes to each component (primary, secondary and tertiary factors) of the model. Appendix 7.2 presents a classified listing of the factor codes. To assist readers who may like to experiment themselves by 'playing' with the model's components, Appendix 7.3 contains a full set of factor cards that can be photocopied, cut out and used for mind-mapping exercises.

EXAMPLE 7.1

A question of attitude – leadership or authority?

When managers are faced with rampant, external contextual change, they often find themselves hamstrung by the reluctance of their own organizations to change. Sometimes this is a situation when everybody blames everybody else. Top management blames front-line employees or middle management and they blame top management. Whose problem is it? Where does the buck stop?

If organizations are to become the servants of thriving wealth-creating (or distributing) activities, then they need to be overhauled to suit the requirements of the present. Thus they have to bow to contextual influences on wealth creation – from top to bottom. The hierarchical authority mind-set needs to be softened and real leadership strengthened. This means mobilizing the organizational troops to confront difficult problems themselves – to release many of them from the mind-set that expects straight-line answers to be handed down. *Creative-management* holds great promise but it needs to be championed by top management if it is to be accepted quickly in organizations. This requires talented leadership and a real willingness to change the traditional exercise of authority and power. Another powerful inhibiting factor is the question of *how* to cope with change. The *creative management response* provides an exciting morale-boosting opportunity if it can be introduced as an organizational team building exercise. (Source: Lorenz, 1994)

LEARNING OBJECTIVES

On completion of this chapter the reader should be well placed to progress to the case study material contained in Part IV of the text. An understanding is required of the following topics:

- The effect of the contextual influences on wealth creation.
- The need for a new management response.
- The power and potential of creativity.
- The worth of CPS tools and techniques.
- The CMR model and its components.

7.2 Approaching creative management I – the diagnosis

7.2.1 'Top dog' troubles

For over two hundred years the economies of the West have led the world in wealth creation and, as a result, have achieved a rising standard of living for their people. As economic performance and international political influence go hand in hand the West has played a prominent role in world affairs. However, in the last quarter of a century or so the forces of change have been altering the balance in favour of other countries – notably those of the Pacific Rim. To maintain their standard of living, let alone seek to improve it, the nations of the Western alliance will first have to acknowledge their situation fully and then be prepared to take serious action. After two centuries of leading from the front the West will not find it easy to run second. The declining performance of the Western wealth-creating effort has been evident for some time. However, national and corporate memories of supply opportunities go back many years. As corporations have grown to realize these opportunities, they have acquired elaborate administrative systems to protect their interests. When things suddenly change, and this seems to have occurred to a large number of corporations in the mid-1980s (e.g. IBM, ICI), corporate mind-sets enshrined in corporate bureaucracies can cloud the eyes. Chapter 1 argues that this decline in the economic fortunes of the West is likely to persist for some time into the next century.

7.2.2 Quo vadis?

Options

If this is *what* has been going on, *how* should the West respond? Sit back and do nothing and hope for better days? Take on the powerful emerging wealth-creating nations of the Pacific Rim? Accept a declining standard of living as our ability to generate wealth loses its impetus? This text argues that the West should believe the truth (the real context) and then think through a suitable response. This will mean a commitment to produce what

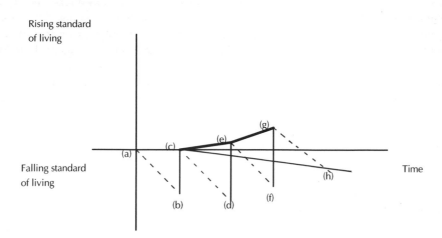

Figure 7.1 Falling standard of living and innovative effort (Source: R. Layton, Professor of Anthropology, University of Durham)

makes sense in today's markets rather than what we like offering for sale. In recent years many have sounded the trumpet in warning and many have sounded the Last Post. This text, it is hoped, will become notable for its optimism and belief in the potential achievements of creative minds.

It is in the nature of man to adapt continuously to change until the magnitude of the change becomes so great that he is forced to innovate in order to protect his basic social standards. These have been eloquently described in the work of Maslow who described a hierarchy of needs that are familiar to many a student of marketing. Figure 7.1 shows that as real living standards fall people swallow hard and adapt but there comes a point when adaptation becomes no longer acceptable and innovation is triggered – point (b). In the case illustrated in the diagram this restores the previous standard of living at point (c). Further pressure on living standards triggers innovative effort at points (d), (f) and (h). The standard of living regains a positive impetus as indicated by the curve (c), (e), (g). The situation facing the West today is probably more like the curve (c), (h) which is traced as a hairline.

As non-Western countries increasingly assume both technical know-how and the ability to sustain higher levels of productivity than those the West can achieve, the warning bells are already sounding. To stay ahead, or at the least to protect our standard of living, means that we will have to evaluate closely the following leading options:

1. Harness our brains and boost expenditure on research and development.
2. Find alternative means of wealth creation.
3. Accept falling living standards.

Many would regard the third option as the least desirable and it may already be the way things are going. Less wealth creation means less and less money to meet the costs of sustaining infrastructure and social services. For several decades governments of all political persuasions have intervened heavily in Western economies to control inflation. However, a low level of inflation is consistent with sustained real growth. At the same time there has been a tendency for wealth creators to chase short-term profits and for governments to woo the electorate with convenient pre-election booms and tax presents. This has created a mind-set that has become too focused on rigid cost control. Whilst cost management is necessary to any well-run business, if driven to extremes, the *lean and mean* mind-set can discourage adequate preparation for the future. The obvious signs of this are falling corporate investment, research and development and training spends in comparison to our main global competitors.

The first two options seem to be far more palatable. Both offer hope but both demand fundamental changes in our thinking. Searching for new ways of wealth creation seems obvious. The problem is the cost. Traditional supply (production)-oriented thinking tends to favour increased spending on research and development when times are good. The paradox is that such expenditure is most in need when wealth creation is under severe pressure. Whilst there always will be some organizations who will set their faces to the wind and ride out the rough times, many more succumb to traditional management remedies and trigger savage cost reduction programmes, thus running the danger of throwing the baby out with the bath water. In the same year that the *Financial Times* (1994) reported a clutch of encouraging 'Ingenuity' stories, a UK government-sponsored report (Buxton, Chapman and Temple, 1994) revealed that real expenditure on research and development was falling at an alarming rate. The report was compiled by a group of economists from the disbanded National Economic Development Office who found that the research and development record of British companies was pretty dismal. On average United Kingdom companies spend 2.5 per cent of their turnover on research and development – which is half the spend of the top 200 international companies.

For years the educational systems of the leading Western powers have been the envy of much of the rest of the world. Today both the United Kingdom and the United States appear to be placing their systems in dire peril. How can this be so? It is hard to escape the conclusion that the real cause is lack of money. More painful is the suspicion that the English-speaking West may be close to becoming bankrupt of ideas.

New forms of wealth creation require ideas. To generate a sufficient flow of ideas in modern times requires a sustained commitment to creative thinking. Sadly, declining fortunes indicate that much of the Western wealth-creating activity is too firmly influenced by the code of practice refined and enshrined by bureaucracies in the good times of the past. We are being administered backwards into the future. We need creative people, innovators and entrepreneurs. Yet our leading business schools offer the degree of Master of Business Administration! How about substituting Enterprise for Administration?

The pessimistic option strangely dulls the brain. Many may feel that they personally are OK – it's therefore somebody else's problem. Is this a natural consequence of the divorce of ownership from control? In reality, it's everybody's problem. We all need to create wealth (preferably the real kind, not that born of paper speculation) and we all possess the ability to be creative. So what is the real problem?

7.2.3 Escaping the fatal attraction

This text argues that it lies within the compass of our conventional thinking. We need to encourage more forward thinking instead of automatically triggering familiar pattern responses that hail from sunnier times. We need to adopt the concept of *total thinking* and expand the use that we make of our potential. We need to enable people to release their natural creativity rather than imprison them in hard systems born of yesterday's business world.

It is strange that at the individual and group levels there are many people involved in creative behaviours. Curiously, the organizations that we built to serve the needs of individuals and groups have assumed a special supra group-think all of their own. Sadly for many, they rarely provide committed and sustained support for creative thought.

7.2.4 Adaptive responses must give way to innovative responses

The strong postwar supplier markets encouraged a predominantly production-oriented approach to wealth creation that became strongly influenced by hard systems thinking. As the century draws to a close the contextual stimuli impacting on markets are increasingly tilting them in favour of buyers. Faced with tight market conditions, wealth creators are being forced to place an increasing emphasis on valuing customers. In contrast to the heady supply gap days, supply surplus times do not lend themselves quite so neatly to quantitative thinking. As organizations strive to retain existing customers and win new ones on the battlefields of business, the old production-oriented interpretation of the traditional management competencies are failing to deliver acceptable outcomes. Whilst the process of management has adapted to face the new challenges of the new market forces, as with the biblical 'new wine' it cannot be contained in the old bottles. What is needed is a new general model of management that fits the problems of the times. It is time for the adaptive to give way to the innovative.

The innovation offered by this text is a *contextual management response* (CMR) that recognizes the domination of contemporary buyers' markets, incorporates all that is best of the traditional management competencies (for there is no point in reinventing the wheel), and adds creativity. For a contextual management response to deliver in competitive markets it needs to be a *creative management response*.

KEY TERMS

Contextual awareness   Danger – subordinating context to process
Options   Need for innovative approach – CMR

7.3 Approaching creative management II – the journey

7.3.1 Travelling light

There must be a variety of concerns in the minds of men and women as they prepare to undertake long journeys. Is the journey necessary? Surely it is safer to stay put. Will there be a better place at the end of the road? How much baggage – trappings from the familiar – will be needed on the way? Seasoned travellers know that there is much to recommend travelling light. Wants and needs that the new contextual environments dictate can be acquired *en route*. Such innovation is usually a better bet than continually trying to adapt the old baggage to the new conditions. However, there is a comfort in being accompanied by the familiar, as long as this does not become an excessive concern. Some travels, by their very nature, require careful planning and meticulous attention to detail. Few would attempt to climb a high mountain with little or no instruction in the necessary skills and without an adequate concern for the correct safety standards.

The purpose of this text is to take the reader on a journey, as mapped in the Preface, to find and experience a new thinking skill. It is a journey through the mind in search of a new approach to the pressing problem surrounding wealth creation as the century draws to a close and a new one beckons. It is a personal journey that is best undertaken with a completely open mind. The mental baggage of our old lives (mind-sets) needs to be set aside. From time to time the mind traveller will slip into a dream.

In search of a new *How*

With the *what* clearly in focus (falling standards of living) and the present *how* (traditional management competencies) failing to deliver, it is tempting to blame the contextual factors impacting on wealth creation. The danger in this is that it is partially true and many regularly confuse cause with effect. The real issue is not the *what* (the contextual stimuli or reality) but our *how* (responses that seek to continue an old or virtual reality). In this sense the West is its own worst enemy.

Chapter 3 clears a path through the mental undergrowth of the past by exploring the essence of management. It traces the evolution of management thought, includes a set of conventional management tools, and stresses that management activity consists of a complex set of behaviours which interface with individuals and groups. The contextual factors that have been responsible for the rapid growth of buyers' markets are likely to continue unabated. Achieving success in these unstable conditions will place a premium on creativity.

Harnessing creativity is a very individual matter. It is present in all of us, yet few choose to release much of it in our professional lives. This is partly a matter of perception and partly conditioning. The personal discovery that creativity is common to all carries the potential to change many personal and professional lives. Chapter 4 is designed to assist individuals both to discover and to experience the potential power of creative thought. It follows an experiential track and introduces some simple creative personal problem solving (CPPS) tools and describes the key CPPS skills.

The theme is broadened to include groups in Chapter 5 which looks at how creative problem solving (CPS) can be introduced in team situations. The small collection of CPPS tools is expanded by the addition of several more tools to form an *introductory CPS tool kit* for individuals to use in creative group problem-solving (CGPS) sessions. Two extra skills to facilitate the introduction of CPS tools across the individual/group interface are included. Before tackling the steep, difficult, track towards organizations, individuals and groups are encouraged to practice CPS skills. It can be likened to learning how to ride a bicycle: the occasional early fall is soon replaced by a growing skill base that generates rapid progress over the ground. Provided of course that individuals and groups do not give up too easily!

Dreams and visions are an important source of inspiration. The rhythm of the ride causes the traveller to close his eyes and awakens his imagination . . . The last part of the journey is through difficult terrain. The well-worn organizational paths are walled on both sides by mind-sets. The light is murky and carping critics seem to be lying in wait round every bend . . . A strange paradox, for in the words of Mintzberg, quoted in Peters (1992): '"Professional management" is the great invention of this century, "an invention that produced gains in organisational *efficiency* so great that it eventually destroyed organisational *effectiveness*."' Organizations developed a will of their own and assumed an importance that was above that of their prime function – to serve the creation of wealth. Chapter 6 explores the development of organizational thinking before taking a look at how they are tackling the problems associated with the birth of the neoindustrial age (see Chapter 2). Four CPS tools that are particularly useful for creative organizational problem solving (COPS) are introduced to complete the introductory CPS tool kit introduced in Chapter 5 and three additional COPS skills are introduced to complete the CPS collection of core skills.

Creative thinking involves a sustained commitment to learning to think in a different way. It involves cutting new thought traces in the mind . . . that take the traveller onto the higher ground, above the mind-sets where vision is unimpaired. Progress can be difficult at times. Climbing up the steep mind-set paths presents many hazards. Individuals can lose their nerve and give in to real or imagined obstacles. Some organizational stormtroopers and officers may continually conduct guerrilla warfare. Groups may mutiny. Standing out from the crowd takes courage and persistence but time and place will favour the brave . . . and there may well be opposition to overcome, but gradually the senior staff of the organizations will see that it is easier to fight the real war (falling living standards) than resist new ways of thinking.

The journey ends when the mind traveller reaches the higher ground and directly experiences the potential of the force of creativity. As the traveller awakes and the imagery fades we hope that the creativity cause has been won. Worthwhile dreams or visions provide challenges that require some application of effort to achieve. They are not quick solutions. Creativity is potentially a powerful force that has much to offer the professional world of wealth creation. Its release is largely dependent on questions of perception: the individual's perception of custody; the organization's perception that it needs to be released in the workplace. Finally, a question of trust. The potential benefits of the creative management response (CMR) are vast. Introducing CMR to organizations will change not only their face but their very structure. The process involves creatively managing the interfaces:

- between change and context;
- between traditional management responses and creativity; and
- between individual, group and organizational conventional practice.

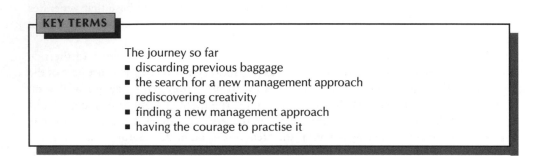

KEY TERMS

The journey so far
- discarding previous baggage
- the search for a new management approach
- rediscovering creativity
- finding a new management approach
- having the courage to practise it

7.4 Creative management response model

7.4.1 A restatement

This section provides a restatement of the *creative management response* (CMR) model in three forms:

1. A basic, three-dimensional illustration that summarizes the six *primary factors* of the model.
2. A series of mind maps and tables that explode the *primary factors* to reveal their respective components, *secondary* and *tertiary factors*.
3. A summary formula that assigns codes to the *primary factors*.

7.4.2 Three-dimensional illustration – primary factors revisited

The complete model is shown in three-dimensional form in Figure 7.2. The contextual component described by the face *hcdf*, is always dynamic but has become especially so in the last decade or so as the West moves into the global buyers' market of the *value time*. This component is now in an unstable condition and is not easily managed by the traditional management responses, described by the face *gedf*, that emerged in the heyday of suppliers' markets. As business becomes tight for the private sector, product/market

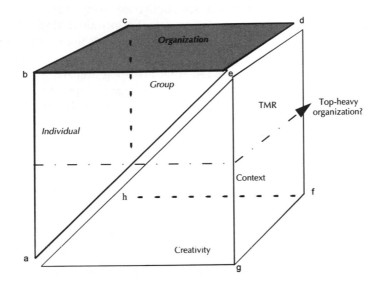

Figure 7.2   The creative management response (CMR) model

differentiation will assume a massive importance. To obtain a positive differentiation in the global marketplace organizations will have to generate and sustain a succession of innovative products and services. Creativity, described by the face *ahfg*, is the driving force behind innovation.

7.4.3   Organizational implications

Owing to years of conditioning, in sunnier contextual periods, much of Western management has a pronounced tendency to adopt a hard, production-oriented approach to wealth creation. So while *creativity* carries the promise of being able to generate a 'market edge', it is generally not well understood in many of the more traditional organizations. This is partly an awareness problem but more seriously an attitude problem. The mind-sets born of quieter contextual periods in the past can blind managers to the real issues of the present. Whilst the *what* of the problem facing the West is known (falling sales, increased difficulties in holding our own in the highly competitive world markets of the *value time*), the realization that coping with it may call for a different approach to management (the *how*) is not so widely appreciated.

This text argues the case for the adoption of the CMR model. It builds on the best of the traditional management competencies familiar to many managers and offers something new. However, there is a price to pay. To introduce CMR into a large organization can take up to three years of sustained effort. It is not a quick solution. It requires a new approach to management that places a high value on the potential creativity of individuals working in groups. It means being prepared to adopt a new management process (committing to an investment in human capital) in order to reap real advantages in the market in the future. Whilst the main benefits of the model mature in two to three years, most organizations will benefit from significant short-term benefits.

In the good times in the postwar period many organizations built up large bureaucracies to support their activities. At the time, this course of action, if not excessive, was useful. However, bureaucratic organizations often seem to have a habit of expanding and expanding until they eventually threaten the ability of the organization to respond to real contextual changes in the marketplace. Suddenly the *how* (and the wrong one for the real context) has become more important than the *what*. Organizations frequently react in traditional ways that often seem to strangle the *creative management approach*. Overweight organizations can flatten inspirational attempts to get to grips and manage the real (i.e. contextual) problem. Reference to Figure 7.2 shows that if the organization is 'too heavy' in this sense its organizational activity tends to assume most of the volume of the cube. The face *bcde* expands downwards and, as it does so, it can regard groups as being of secondary importance and individuals as a tertiary concern. As a result, creativity is severely constrained but not eradicated. Individuals just seek to release most of it outside the organization.

As creativity is a residual force in people, some creativity (*residual creativity*) is released in organizations at all times. Heavy hierarchical organizations run the risk of driving creativity output down to a minimum residual level. If *top management* choose to stimulate creative responses they will need to ensure that their bureaucracies do not restrict its growth. Given freedom, encouragement and a constructive challenge, individuals and groups will readily respond and the organization's creativity output will be enhanced. An organization's *enhanced creativity* is a powerful positive differentiating factor. At the same time, heavy bureaucracies (procedures plus the endemic attitudes) find that they cannot control the vibrant *context* interface (*abeg*). Attempting to manage change to contain it is impossible. It is better for top management to change the traditional management style to a creative management style (CMR) to relate to the new contextual reality.

7.4.4 Creative management response model mind maps

The following set of six mind maps (constructed on the *Visual Outline* software introduced in Chapter 5) and six tables explode the *primary factors* to reveal their subcomponents.

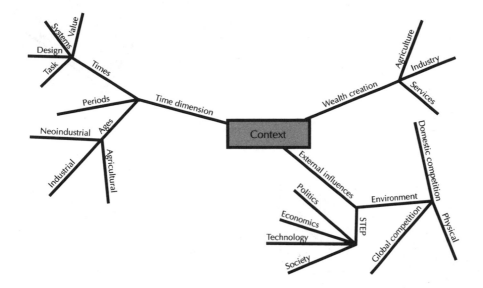

Figure 7.3   CMR model primary factor: context

Table 7.1   **CMR context subcomponent factors**

Primary component	Secondary component	Tertiary component
Context	Time dimension	Ages
		Periods
		Times
	Wealth creation	Agriculture
		Industry
		Service
	External factors	Sociocultural
		Technological
		Economics
		Politics
		Environment (physical)
		Competition (domestic)
		Competition (global)

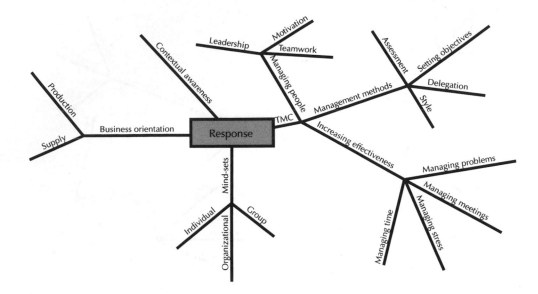

Figure 7.4   CMR model primary factor: management response

Table 7.2   **CMR management subcomponent factors**

Primary component	Secondary component	Tertiary component
Management response	Traditional management competencies	Managing people
		Leadership
		Motivation
		Teamwork
		Management methods
		Setting objectives
		Delegation
		Style
		Assessment
		Increasing efficiency
		Managing time
		Managing stress
		Managing meetings
		Managing problems
	Business orientation	Supply orientation
		Demand orientation
	Mind-sets	Individual
		Group
		Organizational

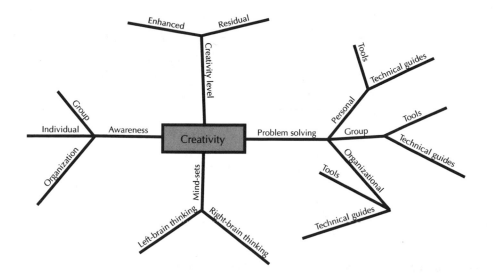

Figure 7.5   CMR model primary factor: creativity

Table 7.3   **CMR creativity subcomponent factors**

Primary component	Secondary component	Tertiary component
Creativity	Awareness	Individual
		Group
		Organizational
	Creativity	Residual
		Enhanced
	Total thinking	Left-brain
		Right-brain
	Creative problem solving	Personal
		Group
		Organizational

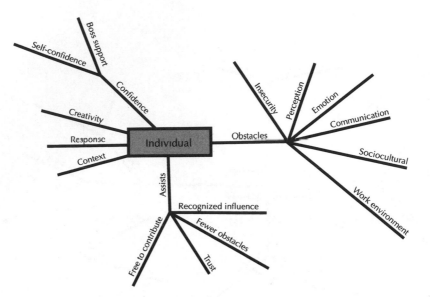

Figure 7.6   CMR model primary factor: individual approach

Table 7.4   **CMR individual approach subcomponent factors**

Primary component	Secondary component	Tertiary component
Individual approach	Context	
	Management response	
	Creativity	
	Confidence	Self-confidence
		Boss support
	Willingness to change	Freedom
		Challenge
		Encouragement
	Obstacles	Insecurity
		Perception
		Emotion
		Communication
		Sociocultural
		Work environment
	Assists	Freedom to contribute
		Recognized influence
		Less obstacles
		Trust

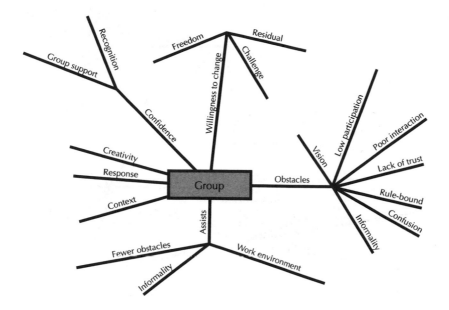

Figure 7.7   CMR model primary factor: group approach

Table 7.5   **CMR group approach subcomponent factors**

Primary component	Secondary component	Tertiary component
Group approach	Context	
	Management response	
	Creativity	
	Confidence	Group support
		Group recognition
	Willingness to change	Freedom
		Challenge
		Encouragement
	Obstacles	Vision
		Low participation
		Poor interaction
		Lack of trust
		Rule-bound
		Confusion
		Informality
	Assists	Work environment

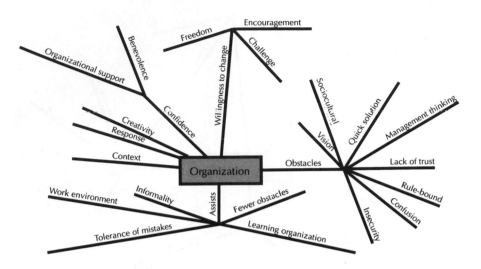

Figure 7.8   CMR model primary factor: organizational approach

Table 7.6   CMR organization approach subcomponent factors

Primary component	Secondary component	Tertiary component
Organization approach	Context	
	Management response	
	Creativity	
	Confidence	Organization support
		Benevolence
	Willingness to change	Freedom
		Challenge
		Encouragement
	Obstacles	Staff appreciation
		Vision
		Sociocultural
		Quick solution
		Management thinking
		Lack of trust
		Rule-bound
		Confusion
		Informality

Table 7.7 **CMR primary components**

Theory (the *what*)	Practice (the *how*)
1. Context (CX)	4. Creative individual response (CMRI)
2. Management response (MR)	5. Creative group response (CMRG)
3. Creativity (CR)	6. Creative organization response (CMRO)

7.4.5   CMR model components summary formula

The *primary factors* of the complete CMR model are restated again in the summary formula below. All the components of the model (primary factors and subcomponents) are assigned factor codes in Appendix 7.1. This is for readers who might like to experiment by using the factor code cards (in Appendix 7.3) to build mind maps. The fully assembled model is described by the formula:

$$CMR = f\{[CX + (MR + CR)] + [CMRI + CMRG + CMRO]\}$$

The six *primary components* are shown in Table 7.7. Each primary component is formed from a number of subcomponents or inputs, and these are referred to as *secondary components*. These, in turn, are formed from a further set of inputs that are termed *tertiary components*.

A fourth view of the CMR model is provided in the format of a metaphor in the final section to the chapter.

7.5   **Top gear**

7.5.1   Introduction

This chapter has presented our formal *creative management model*. This section is included as a divertimento before Part IV addresses some pressing matters of CMR general practice. We invite you to visualize your organization as a bicycle – a machine that is intended for movement. To get anywhere the machine needs a rider and is dynamically unstable unless that rider is providing power and direction. When the rider attempts to sit on the saddle it soon becomes obvious that it is not possible to balance if both feet are on the pedals.

New cyclists can receive instruction on how to ride their machines but in the end success is only achieved if the novice 'has a go'. Learning to ride is an experiential matter. The rider learns on the job or rather in the saddle and may well take the occasional tumble. The good news is that things usually progress quickly and the rider soon discovers how to control the machine. However, learning to ride in safe places (contexts) is quite different from learning to ride on the open road where critical decisions often have to be made in the light of events (*stimuli*). Other cyclists are trying to overtake. Some might be trying to knock our rider off the road. Mastering the gears is easy on flat ground

– it's just a matter of confidence and speed. The open road provides a continuous set of challenges – ups and downs, bends, cross winds, other cyclists, and so forth.

If our rider feels that it is right to break out of the pursuing pack and head for new ground, he or she would be wise to take stock of his or her skills as a rider and the condition and type of machine being ridden. Wise riders would also take a realistic look at the new ground before rushing in to explore. If it is new it may need to be mapped first and a suitable routing determined before generating top speed (innovation needs planning for successful realization). The first journey is likely to be an exploratory one and very real. Having discovered something interesting, our rider then has to decide how to cut a road through the terrain. A sensible evaluation may well determine that his or her present skills and the machine specification are ill equipped to function to a high enough standard. Also, other riders are coming into view. Our rider needs to move quickly.

So our rider must just risk it or *reframe* his or her problem. A wise rider would take the latter course and might then discover that he or she needed a new type of machine and some new skills to operate this machine in the new terrain. Lets take a look at the machine side of the problem.

7.5.2 The machine

The standard parts of a bicycle are illustrated in Figure 7.9. The primary components are: the frame; the saddle; the handlebars; the wheels; the tyres; and the power train.

To stand much chance of success the frame needs to be tough but not too heavy. A top-heavy frame will make it difficult for the rider to get the machine going and might make it difficult to steer. The power to weight ratio is important. The handlebars are critical for steering and must be comfortable for the rider to operate. As for the saddle – this is the interface between rider and machine! The wheel assemblies also need to be tough and light. The tyres – the part of the machine that is directly interfacing with the ground (context) – will need to be appropriate. If the ground presents challenges that have never been experienced before, the rider will have to face up to this and obtain suitable tyres. Risking the old ones could well result in disaster. The power train consists of a three-speed gear arrangement, a chain drive, crank and pedals. All need to work together to produce satisfactory movement when the power is applied by the rider. A low gear is useful to get the machine rolling and for tackling tough ground but is hard for the rider to power. The two higher gears provide some relief for the rider when faster speeds are sensible. The main secondary components are the light and reflectors so that the rider can see and be seen.

All components need to be designed for the job (contextually aware) and must be assembled with the right tools for the machine to work properly.

7.5.3 The rider

The traditional skills of the rider will most likely stand him or her in good stead in this new terrain but will not of themselves be sufficient to successfully find a route over the

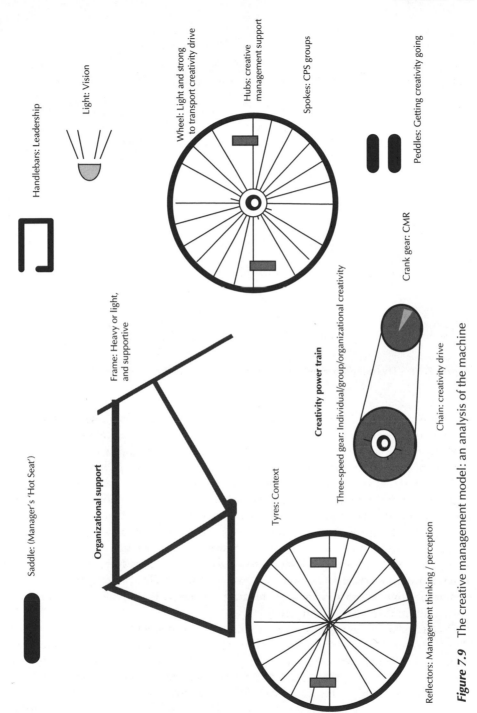

Saddle: (Manager's 'Hot Seat')

Organizational support

Frame: Heavy or light, and supportive

Handlebars: Leadership

Light: Vision

Wheel: Light and strong to transport creativity drive

Hubs: creative management support

Spokes: CPS groups

Peddles: Getting creativity going

Crank gear: CMR

Creativity power train

Three-speed gear: Individual/group/organizational creativity

Chain: creativity drive

Tyres: Context

Reflectors: Management thinking / perception

Figure 7.9   The creative management model: an analysis of the machine

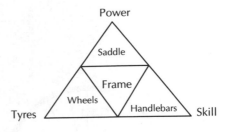

Figure 7.10 The machine badge

Figure 7.11 The rider's badge

ground. Some new skills will probably be necessary. Failure to acknowledge this could be disastrous. Now the rider cannot fully test both machine and motive skills unless he or she gets on the machine and pedals. Armchair theories and paper models are fine, but what happens in the rough? By its very nature much of the learning has to be experiential, but that does not mean to imply that the rider is managing reactively. Sometimes this is necessary to deal with sudden crises. However, if both machine and rider are carefully prepared this should lessen the incidence of reactive decisions. One temptation needs to be resisted. This is the belief that power always compensates for weight. Perhaps sometimes it does. At other times, too much power reduces reaction times (remember the Highway Code!). On other occasions, too heavy a machine is cumbersome and slow to react. Put both together and it may well produce a mess! The frame of the machine needs to suit the contemporary purpose of the machine. Yesterday's models will probably be a risky venture for today's conditions.

A wise rider will exercise due concern for all the components of the bicycle (see Figure 7.10). The machine is skilfully powered to bring the revolving tyres into contact with the context. The handlebars are for steering, the saddle is the seat of power and the wheels move the machine over the ground. The frame is the central support of the machine.

The rider takes his or her traditional skills and innovates in order to be able to manage the new conditions (context) (see Figure 7.11). The organization he or she works for provides direction whilst putting him or her in charge of the project. Colleagues in the

Figure 7.12 The action – putting machine and rider together

organization (group) co-operate to assist in getting the machine in motion. His or her main support comes from the creative management style operating in the organization.

The action: putting the two together

The machine and the rider can only function when the two are in harmony. A dynamic organization is like the bicycle and rider – a well-balanced synthesis between Man and machine, between hard and soft systems thinking (see Figure 7.12).

7.6 Summary

7.6.1 The journey so far

This chapter has summarized the argument of the text so far and presented the *creative management model*. The prime task of Parts I and II has been to warn readers of the significance of the contextual factors impacting on wealth creation for the foreseeable future and to argue that a new management response is needed. The text argues that creativity has much to contribute to the task of managing wealth creation and has sought to persuade you in Part II to drop any preformed prejudices that you may consciously or unconsciously harbour and 'have a go'.

Most participants should be able to record some early spectacular successes and this is very right and proper. However, the *creative management* response is not a novelty to be brought out periodically when the sun goes in on an organization, but a serious long-term management approach. Sustained commitment, or at least tolerance, is directly proportional to the success that can be gained.

QUESTIONS

1. Outline the options facing the Western economies that would help them to maintain their standard of living. How might the concept of *total thinking* help?
2. Illustrate the CMR model in three different ways. Which one do you prefer and why?
3. Select a sample of people in your *organizational creativity audit*. Analyze the result, discuss the findings and suggest ways in which your organization can respond to them.
4. Creatively play with the *model mind mapping cards* in Appendix 7.3 to aid your understanding of the CMR model.

References

Buxton, T., Chapman, P. and Temple, P. (1994), *Britain's Economic Performance*, London: Routledge.
Financial Times, 'Engineering Review', 23 March, 1994.
Lorenz, C. (1994), 'Top dogs bark up the wrong tree', *Financial Times*, 3 June.
Maslow, A. H. (1943), 'A theory of human motivation', *Psychological Review*, 50, 370–96.
Peters, T. (1992), *Liberation Management*, London: Pan.

APPENDIX 7.1

Creative management response model

Component/sort codes

To facilitate mind-mapping exercises, each of the *creative management* components has been given a unique descriptive code. For example, the address code for the primary component *Context* is CX. *Time dimension*, which is a secondary component of CX, is addressed as CX TD. *Ages*, a subcomponent of CX TD, is described as CX TD A. For the purpose of clarity the full address codes have not been included in the tables below but are used in the factor descriptions.

Primary component: Context

Summary factor component codes

Primary component	Secondary components	Factor code	Tertiary components	Factor code
Context (CX)				
	Time dimension	TD	Ages	A
			Periods	P
			Times	T
	Wealth creation	WC	Agriculture	AG
			Industry	I
			Brains	B
			Service	S
	External factors	EXT	Sociocultural	SOC
			Technological	TEC
			Economics	EC
			Politics	POL
			Environment (P*)	ENVP
			Competition (domestic)	CD
			Competition (global)	CG

Note: (P*) = Physical environment.

Factor descriptions

The primary component *Context* (CX) of wealth creation is a compound expression of the following secondary components:

Time dimension (CX TD) + Wealth creation (CX WC) + External influences (CX EXT)

Tertiary components

(a)   Where *time dimension* (CX TD) is a function of:

Ages (CX TD A), Periods (CX TD P) and Times (CX TD T)

(b)   Where *wealth creation* (CX WC) is a function of:

Agriculture (CX WC AG) + Industry (CX WC I) + Services (CX WC S) + Brains (CXWC B)

(c)   Where *external factors* (CX EXT) is a function of:

Society (CX EXT SOC) + Technology (CX EXT TEC) + Economics (CX EXT EC) + Politics (CX EXT POL) + Environment – physical (CX EXT ENVP) + Competition – domestic (CX EXT CD) + Competition – global (CX EXT CG)

Primary component: Management response

Summary factor component codes

Primary component	Secondary components	Factor code	Tertiary components	Factor code
Management response				
	Traditional management competencies	TMC	Managing people	MP
			Management methods	MM
			Increasing efficiency	IE
	Business orientation	BO	Supply-oriented	SO
			Demand-oriented	DO
	Mind-sets	MS	Mind-sets (ind.)	MSI
			Mind-sets (grp)	MSG
			Mind-sets (org.)	MSO

Factor descriptions

The primary component *Management Response* (MR) is a compound expression of the following secondary components:

Traditional management competencies (MR TMC) + Business orientation (MR BO) + Mind-sets (MR MS)

Tertiary components

(a)   Where *traditional management competency* (MR TMC) is a function of:

Managing people (MR TMC MP) + Management methods (MR TMC MM) + Increasing effectiveness (MR TMC IE)

(b)   Where *business orientation* (MR BO) is a function of:

Supply-oriented (MR BO SO) or Demand-oriented (MR BO DO)

(c)   Where *mind-set* (MR MS) is a function of:

Individual mind-sets (MR MS MSI) + Group mind-sets (MR MS MSG) + Organizational mind-sets (MR MS MSO)

Primary component: Creativity

Summary factor component codes

Primary component	Secondary components	Factor code	Tertiary components	Factor code
Creativity				
	Awareness	CA	Awareness (Ind.)	CAI
			Awareness (Grp)	CAG
			Awareness (Org.)	CAO
	Creativity level	CL	Residual level	CLR
			Enhanced level	CLE
	Total thinking	TT	Left-brain	LBT
			Right-brain	RBT
	Creative problem solving	CPS	Creative personal problem solving	CPPS
			Creative group problem solving	CGPS
			Creative organizational problem solving	COPS

Factor descriptions

The primary component *Creativity* (CR) is a compound expression of the following secondary components:

Awareness (CR CA) + Creativity level (CR CL) + Total thinking (CR TT) + Creative problem solving (CR CPS)

Tertiary components

(a)   Where *awareness* (CR CA) is a function of:

Individual awareness (CR CA CAI) + Group awareness (CR CA CAG) + Organizational awareness (CR CA COA)

(b)   Where *creativity level* (CR CL) is:

either Residual (CR CL CLR), or Enhanced (CR CL CLE)

(c)   Where *total thinking* (CR TT) is the sum of:

Left-brain thinking (CR TT LBT) + Right-brain thinking (CR TT RBT)

(d)   Where *creative problem solving* (CR CPS) is a function of:

Creative personal problem solving (CR CPS CPPS) + Creative group problem solving (CR CPS CGPS) + Creative organizational problem solving (CR CPS COPS)

Primary component: Individual approach

Summary factor component codes

Primary component	Secondary components	Factor code	Tertiary components	Factor code
Individual approach				
	Context	CX		
	Management response	MR		
	Creativity	CR		
	Confidence	CON	Self-confidence	SC
			Boss support	BS
	Willingness to change	WTC	Freedom	F
			Challenge	CH
			Encouragement	ENC
	Obstacles	OB	Insecurity	IN
			Perception	PER
			Emotion	EM
			Communication	COM
			Vision	VI
			Sociocultural	CUL
			Work environment	WE
	Assists	AS	Freedom to contribute	FC
			Recognized influence	RI
			(minus obstacles)	(OB)
			Trust	TR

Factor descriptions

The primary component *individual approach* (CMRI) performance is a function of the following primary and secondary components:

[CF + (MR + CR)] + CMRI CON + CMRI – CMRI OB + CMRI AS

Tertiary components

(a)   Where *individual confidence* (CMRI CON) is a function of:

Self-confidence (CMRI CON SC) + Boss support (CMRI CON BS)

(b)   Where *individual willingness to change* (CMRI WTC) is a function of:

Freedom (CMRI WTC F) + Challenge (CMRI WTC CH) + Encouragement (CMRI WTC ENC)

(c)   Where *individual obstacles* (CMRI OB) is a function of:

Insecurity (CMRI OB IN) + Perception (CMRI OB PER) + Emotion (CMRI OB EM) + Communication (CMRI OB COM) + Culture (CMRI OB CUL) + Individual visions (CMRI OB V)
+ Individual work environment (CMRI OB WE) + CPS skills (CMRI OB CPSS)

(d)   Where *individual assists* (CMRI AS) is a function of:

Freedom to contribute (CMRI AS FC) + Recognized influence over own and other's work
(CMRI AS RI) – CMRI OB + Trust (CMRI OB TR)

Primary component: Group approach

Summary factor component codes

Primary component	Secondary components	Factor code	Tertiary components	Factor code
Group approach				
	Context	CX		
	Management response	MR		
	Creativity	CR		
	Confidence	CON	Group support	GS
			Group recognition	GR
	Willingness to change	WTC	Freedom	F
			Encouragement	ENC
			Challenge	CH
	Obstacles	OB	Vision	V
			Low participation	LP
			Poor interaction	PI
			Lack of trust	LT
			Rule-bound	RB
			Confusion	CONF
			Informality	INF
	Assists	AS	Work environment	WE

Factor descriptions

The primary component *group approach* (CMRG) performance is a function of the primary and secondary components:

[CX + (MR + CR)] + CMRG CON – CMRG OB + CMRG AS

Tertiary components

(a)   Where *group confidence* (CMRG CON) is a function of:

Group support (CMRG CON GS) + Group recognition (CMRG CON GR)

(b)   Where *group willingness to change* (CMRG WTC) is a function of:

Freedom (CMRG WTC F) + Challenge (CMRG WTC CH) + Encouragement (CMRG WTC ENC)

(c)   Where *group obstacles* (CMRG OB) is a function of:

Vision (CMRG OB V) + Low participation (CMRG OB PL) + Poor interaction (CMRG OB IL) + Lack of trust (TR) + Rule-bound (CMRG OB RB) + Confusion (CMRG OB CONF) + Insecurity (CMRG OB IN) + Creative problem-solving skills (CMRG OB CPSS)

(d)   Where *group assist* (CMRG AS) is a function of:

Work environment (CMRG AS WE) – CMRG OB + Informality (CMRG AS INF)

Primary component: Organizational approach

Summary factor component codes

Primary component	Secondary components	Factor code	Tertiary components	Factor code
Organizational approach				
	Context	CX		
	Management response	MR		
	Creativity	CR		
	Confidence	CON	Organizational support	OS
			Benevolence	OBN
	Willingness to change	WTC	Freedom	F
			Encouragement	ENC
			Challenge	CH
	Obstacles	OB	Staff appreciation	SA

Primary component: Organizational approach continued

Primary component	Secondary components	Factor code	Tertiary components	Factor code
			Vision	V
			Sociocultural	CUL
			Quick solution	QS
			Management thinking	MT
			Lack of trust	LT
			Rule-bound	RB
			Confusion	CONF
			Insecurity	IN
	Assists	AS	Work environment	WE
			Informality	INF
			(minus obstacles)	(OB)
			Learning organization	LO
			Tolerance of mistakes	TM

Factor descriptions

The primary component *organizational approach* CMR (CMRO) is a function of the primary and secondary components:

[CX + (MR + CR)] + CMRO CON- CMRO OB + CMRG AS

Tertiary components

(a)   Where *organizational confidence* (CMRO CON) is a function of:

Organizational support (CMRO CON OS) + Benevolence (CMRO CON OBN)

(b)   Where *organizational willingness to change* (CMRO WTC) is a function of:

Freedom (CMRO WTC F) + Challenge (CMRO WTC CH) + Encouragement (CMRO WTC ENC)

(c)   Where *organizational obstacles* (CMRO OB) is a function of:

Staff appreciation (CMRO OB SA) + Vision (CMRO OB V) + Culture (CMRO OB CUL) + Quick solution (CMRO OB QS) + Management thinking (CMRO OB MT) + Trust (CMRO OB TR) + Rule-bound (CMRO OB RB) + Confusion (CMRO OB CONF) + Insecurity (CMRO OB IN) + Creative problem-solving skills (CMRO OB CPSS)

(d)   Where *organizational assists* (CMRO AS) is a function of:

Work environment (CMRO AS WE) + Informality (CMRO AS INF) – CMRO OB + Informality (CMRO OB INF) + Learning organization (CMR OB LO) + Tolerance of mistakes (CMRO OB TM)

Creative Management Response Model

Factor codes

Primary factor codes

Primary Factors	Description
CX	Context
MR	Management Response
CR	Creativity
CMRI	Creative Management Response – Individual
CMRG	Creative Management Response – Group
CMRO	Creative Management Response – Organization

Primary factor – Context (CX)

Secondary Factors	Description
CX TD	Time Dimension
CX WC	Wealth Creation
CX EXT	External Factors

Tertiary Factors

Time Dimension (CX TD)

CX TD A	Ages
CX TD P	Periods
CX TD T	Times

Wealth Creation (CX WC)

CX WC AG	Agriculture
CX WC I	Industry
CX WC S	Service
CX WC B	Brains

External Factors (CX EXT)

CX EXT SOC	Sociocultural
CX EXT TEC	Technological
CX EXT EC	Economics
CX EXT POL	Politics
CX EXT ENVP	Environment – Physical
CX EXT CD	Competition – Domestic
CX EXT CG	Competition – Global

Primary factor – Management Response (MR)

Secondary Factors Description
MR TMC	Traditional Management Competences
MR BO	Business Orientation
MR MS	Mind Sets

Tertiary Factors

*Traditional Management
Competencies (MR TMC)*
MR TMC MP	Managing People
MR TMC MM	Managing Methods
MR TMC IE	Increasing Effectiveness

Business Orientation (MR BO)
MR BO SO	Supply Oriented
MR BO DO	Demand Oriented

Mind Sets (MR MS)
MR MS MSI	Mind Sets – Individual
MR MS MSG	Mind Sets – Group
MR MS MSO	Mind Sets – Organizational

Primary factor – Creativity (CR)

Secondary Factors Description
CR CA	Creativity Awareness
CR CL	Creativity Level
CR TT	Total Thinking
CR CPS	Creative Problem Solving

Tertiary Factors

Creativity Awareness (CR CA)
CR CA CAI	Creativity Awareness – Individual
CR CA CAG	Creativity Awareness – Group
CR CA CAO	Creativity Awareness – Organization

Creativity Level (CR CL)
CR CL CLR	Creativity Level – Residual
CR CL CLE	Creativity Level – Enhanced

Total Thinking (CRTT)
CR TT LBT	Left Brain Thinking
CR TT RBT	Right Brain Thinking

Creative Problem Solving (CR CPS)

CR CPS CPPS	Creative Personal Problem Solving
CR CPS CGPS	Creative Group Problem Solving
CR CPS COPS	Creative Organizational Problem Solving

Primary factor – Individual Creative Management Response (CMRI)

Secondary Factors Description

CMRI CON	Confidence – Individual
CMRI WTC	Willingness to Change – Individual
CMRI OB	Obstacles – Individual
CMRI AS	Assists – Individual

Tertiary Factors

Confidence, Individual (CMRI CON)

CMRI CON SC	Self Confidence
CMRI CON BS	Boss Support

Willingness to Change, Individual (CMRI WTC)

CMRI WTC F	Freedom – Individual
CMRI WTC CH	Challenge – Individual
CMRI WTC ENC	Encouragement – Individual

Obstacles, Individual (CMRI OB)

CMRI OB IN	Insecurity
CMRI OB PER	Perception
CMRI OB EM	Emotion
CMRI OB COM	Communication
CMRI OB CUL	Culture
CMRI OB VI	Vision – Individual
CMRI OB WEI	Work Environment – Individual
CMRI OB CPSS	Creative Problem-Solving Skills

Assists, Individual (CMRI AS)

CMRI AS FC	Freedom to Contribute
CMRI AS RI	Recognized Influence over own and others' work
CMRI AS TR	Trust

Primary factor – Group Creative Management Response (CMRG)

Secondary Factors Description

CMRG CON	Confidence – Group
CMRG WTC	Willingness to Change – Group
CMRG OB	Obstacles – Group
CMRG AS	Assists – Group

Tertiary Factors

Confidence, Group (CMRG CON)

CMRG CON GS	Group Support
CMRG CON GR	Group Recognition

Willingness to Change, Group (CMRG WTC)

CMRG WTC F	Freedom – Group
CMRG WTC CH	Challenge – Group
CMRG WTC ENC	Encouragement – Group

Obstacles, Group (CMRG OB)

CMRG OB V	Vision – Group
CMRG OB PL	Participation Level
CMRG OB IL	Interaction Level
CMRG OB TR	Group Trust
CMRG OB RB	Rule Bound
CMRG OB CONF	Confusion
CMRG OB IN	Insecurity
CMRG OB CPSS	Creative Problem-Solving Skills

Assists, Group (CMRF AS)

CMRG AS WE	Work Environment
CMRG AS INF	Informality

Primary factor – Organizational Creative Management Response (CMRO)

Secondary Factors Description

CMRO CON	Confidence – Organizational
CMRO WTC	Willingness to Change – Organizational
CMRO OB	Obstacles – Organizational
CMRO AS	Assists – Organizational

Tertiary Factors

Confidence, Organizational (CMRO CON)

CMRO CON OS	Organizational Support
CMRO CON OB	Organizational Benevolence

Willingness to Change, Organizational (CMRO WTC)

CMRO WTC F	Freedom – Organizational
CMRO WTC CH	Challenge – Organizational
CMRO WTC ENC	Encouragement – Organizational

Obstacles, Organizational (CMRO OB)

CMRO OB SA	Staff Appreciation
CMRO OB VO	Vision-Organizational

CMRO OB CUL	Culture
CMRO OB QF	'Quick Fix'
CMRO OB MT	Management Thinking
CMRO OB TR	Organizational Trust
CMRO OB RB	Rule Bound
CMRO OB CONF	Confusion
CMRO OB INS	Insecurity

Assists, Organizational (CMRO AS)

CMRO AS WE	Work Environment – Organizational
CMRO AS INF	Informality
CMRO AS LO	Learning Organization
CMRO AS TM	Tolerance of Mistakes

APPENDIX 7.3

Creative management response model (CMR) model – factor code cards

Mind-mapping cards

Exercise 1   Where are we?

Introduction
This is an exercise that is designed to help you get to grips with the first three primary factors – the *what* factors – to form an accurate picture of where your organization is at present.

Instructions
1. Shuffle the cards.

2. Sort cards into primary factor sets.

3. Sort primary factor sets into secondary component sets.

4. With your own organization in mind, read the cards in each primary factor set and reflect on the secondary and tertiary components.

5. Now write a brief report to your organization describing what you think that they should do in the light of your findings.

Exercise 2   How me . . . ?

Introduction
This exercise is intended to help individuals to think about the core issues affecting their approach to the CMR model.

Instructions

1. Find the *individual approaches* (CMRI) primary factor cards and sort them by secondary components.
2. For each secondary code sort the cards (by tertiary component) into three separate piles:
   (a) OK;
   (b) acceptable;
   (c) not OK.
3. Gather the 'OK' cards and feel good about it.
4. Gather the 'acceptable' cards and jot down three ways that you could improve the situation (try a personal brainstorm).
5. Gather the 'not OK' cards and think through how you might change the situation using the CPS tools of your choice.

Exercise 3   How we . . . ?

Introduction

As for Exercise 2.

Instructions

1. Find the *group approaches* (CMRG) primary factor cards and sort them by secondary components.
2. Follow same steps as described for Exercise 2.

Exercise 4   How our organization . . . ?

Introduction

This exercise is intended to assist individuals and groups to understand the model and to view it from within their own organization.

Instructions

1. Find the *organization approaches* (CMRO) primary factor cards and sort them into their secondary components.
2. Now follow the same steps as described for Exercises 2 and 3.

Exercise 5   Look, think and act

Introduction

This exercise is designed to help you use the CMR Model cards to expose some critical issues for your organization.

Instructions

1. Look at the secondary components of the *what* primary factor sets (CMRI, CMRG and CMRO) and make separate piles of all the secondary factors that are common to all three primary factors (e.g. 'Willingness to change').

2. Now look for and collect in a separate pile all the common tertiary components within the secondary component piles (e.g. Willingness to change: freedom, challenge, encouragement).

3. Write a brief memo to your organization making whatever recommendations form in your mind after completing the exercise.

Context – CX		
Secondary *Component*	External Factors	Factor code EXT
Tertiary *Component*	Society	Factor code SOC

Context – CX		
Secondary *Component*	External Factors	Factor code EXT
Tertiary *Component*	Politics	Factor code POL

Context – CX		
Secondary *Component*	External Factors	Factor code EXT
Tertiary *Component*	Technology	Factor code TEC

Context – CX		
Secondary *Component*	External Factors	Factor code EXT
Tertiary *Component*	Environment – Physical	Factor code ENVP

Context – CX		
Secondary *Component*	External Factors	Factor code EXT
Tertiary *Component*	Economics	Factor code EC

Context – CX		
Secondary *Component*	External Factors	Factor code EXT
Tertiary *Component*	Competition – Domestic	Factor code CD

Context – CX		
Secondary Component	External Factors	Factor code EXT
Tertiary Component	Competition – Global	Factor code CG

Management Response – MR		
Secondary Component	Traditional Management Competency	Factor code TMC
Tertiary Component	Increasing Effectiveness	Factor code IE

Management Response – MR		
Secondary Component	Traditional Management Competency	Factor code TMC
Tertiary Component	Managing People	Factor code MP

Management Response – MR		
Secondary Component	Business Orientation	Factor code BO
Tertiary Component	Supply Oriented	Factor code SO

Management Response – MR		
Secondary Component	Traditional Management Competency	Factor code TMC
Tertiary Component	Management Methods	Factor code MM

Management Response – MR		
Secondary Component	Business Orientation	Factor code BO
Tertiary Component	Demand Oriented	Factor code DO

Context – CX		
Secondary Component	Time Dimension	Factor code TD
Tertiary Component	Ages	Factor code A

Context – CX		
Secondary Component	Wealth Creation	Factor code WC
Tertiary Component	Agriculture	Factor code AG

Context – CX		
Secondary Component	Time Dimension	Factor code TD
Tertiary Component	Periods	Factor code P

Context – CX		
Secondary Component	Wealth Creation	Factor code WC
Tertiary Component	Industry	Factor code I

Context – CX		
Secondary Component	Time Dimension	Factor code TD
Tertiary Component	Times	Factor code T

Context – CX		
Secondary Component	Wealth Creation	Factor code WC
Tertiary Component	Services	Factor code S

Context – CX		
Secondary Component	Wealth Creation	Factor code WC
Tertiary Component	Brains	Factor code B

Management Response – MR		
Secondary Component	Mind Set	Factor code MS
Tertiary Component	Individual Mind Sets	Factor code MSI

Creativity – CR		
Secondary Component	Creativity Awareness	Factor code CA
Tertiary Component	Individual Awareness	Factor code CAI

Management Response – MR		
Secondary Component	Mind Set	Factor code MS
Tertiary Component	Group Mind Set	Factor code MSG

Creativity – CR		
Secondary Component	Creativity Awareness	Factor code CA
Tertiary Component	Group Awareness	Factor code CAG

Management Response – MR		
Secondary Component	Mind Set	Factor code MS
Tertiary Component	Organizational Mind Set	Factor code MSO

Creativity – CR		
Secondary Component	Creativity Level	Factor code CL
Tertiary Component	Residual	Factor code CLR

Creativity – CR		
Secondary Component	Creativity Awareness	Factor code CA
Tertiary Component	Organizational Awareness	Factor code CAO

Creativity – CR		
Secondary *Component*	Creativity Level	Factor code CL
Tertiary *Component*	Enhanced	Factor code CLE

Creativity – CR		
Secondary *Component*	Creative Problem Solving	Factor code CPS
Tertiary *Component*	Creative Personal Problem Solving	Factor code CPPS

Creativity – CR		
Secondary *Component*	Total Thinking	Factor code IT
Tertiary *Component*	Left Brain Thinking	Factor code LBT

Creativity – CR		
Secondary *Component*	Creative Problem Solving	Factor code CPS
Tertiary *Component*	Creative Group Problem Solving	Factor code CGPS

Creativity – CR		
Secondary *Component*	Total Thinking	Factor code IT
Tertiary *Component*	Right Brain Thinking	Factor code RBT

Creativity – CR		
Secondary *Component*	Creative Problem Solving	Factor code CPS
Tertiary *Component*	Creative Organizational Problem Solving	Factor code COPS

Individual Approaches – CMRI CF + MR + CR		
Secondary Component	Willingness to Change	Factor code WTC
Tertiary Component	Individual Freedom	Factor code F

Individual Approaches – CMRI CX + MR + CR		
Secondary Component	Willingness to Change	Factor code WTC
Tertiary Component	Challenge	Factor code CH

Individual Approaches – CMRI CX + MR + CR		
Secondary Component	Confidence	Factor code CON
Tertiary Component	Self Confidence	Factor code SC

Individual Approaches – CMRI CX + MR + CR		
Secondary Component	Willingness to Change	Factor code WTC
Tertiary Component	Encouragement	Factor code ENC

Individual Approaches – CMRI CX + MR + CR		
Secondary Component	Confidence	Factor code CON
Tertiary Component	Boss Support	Factor code BS

Individual Approaches – CMRI CX + MR + CR		
Secondary Component	Obstacles	Factor code OB
Tertiary Component	Insecurity	Factor code IN

Individual Approaches – CMRI CX + MR + CR		
Secondary *Component* Obstacles		Factor code OB
Tertiary *Component* Perception		Factor code PER

Individual Approaches – CMRI CX + MR + CR		
Secondary *Component* Obstacles		Factor code OB
Tertiary *Component* Culture		Factor code CUL

Individual Approaches – CMRI CX + MR + CR		
Secondary *Component* Obstacles		Factor code OB
Tertiary *Component* Emotion		Factor code EM

Individual Approaches – CMRI CX + MR + CR		
Secondary *Component* Obstacles		Factor code OB
Tertiary *Component* Work Environment		Factor code WE

Individual Approaches – CMRI CX + MR + CR		
Secondary *Component* Obstacles		Factor code OB
Tertiary *Component* Communication		Factor code COM

Individual Approaches – CMRI CX + MR + CR		
Secondary *Component* Obstacles		Factor code OB
Tertiary *Component* CPS Skills		Factor code CPSS

Individual Approaches – CMRI CX + MR + CR		
Secondary Component	Assists	Factor code AS
Tertiary Component	Freedom to Contribute	Factor code FC

Group Approaches – CMRG CX + MR + CR		
Secondary Component	Confidence	Factor code CON
Tertiary Component	Group Support	Factor code GS

Individual Approaches – CMRI CX + MR + CR		
Secondary Component	Assists	Factor code ASI
Tertiary Component	Recognized influence over work	Factor code RI

Group Approaches – CMRG CX + MR + CR		
Secondary Component	Confidence	Factor code CON
Tertiary Component	Group Recognition	Factor code GR

Group Approaches – CMRG CX + MR + CR		
Secondary Component	Willingness to Change	Factor code WTC
Tertiary Component	Freedom	Factor code F

Group Approaches – CMRG CF + MR + CR		
Secondary *Component*	Willingness to Change	Factor code WTCG
Tertiary *Component*	Encouragement	Factor code ENCG

Group Approaches – CMRG CF + MR + CR		
Secondary *Component*	Obstacles	Factor code OB
Tertiary *Component*	Vision	Factor code V

Individual Approaches – CMRI CX + MR + CR		
Secondary *Component*	Assists	Factor code AS
Tertiary *Component*	Trust	Factor code TR

Group Approaches – CMRG CX + MR + CR		
Secondary *Component*	Obstacles	Factor code OB
Tertiary *Component*	Participation Level	Factor code PL

Group Approaches – CMRG CX + MR + CR		
Secondary *Component*	Willingness to Change	Factor code WTC
Tertiary *Component*	Challenge	Factor code CH

Group Approaches – CMRG CX + MR + CR		
Secondary *Component*	Obstacles	Factor code OB
Tertiary *Component*	Poor Interaction	Factor code PI

Individual Approaches – CMRI CX + MR + CR		
Secondary *Component*	Obstacles	Factor code OB
Tertiary *Component*	Vision	Factor code V

Group Approaches – CMRG CX + MR + CR	
Secondary Component Obstacles	Factor code OB
Tertiary Component Trust	Factor code TR

Group Approaches – CMRG CX + MR + CR	
Secondary Component Obstacles	Factor code OB
Tertiary Component Insecurity	Factor code INS

Individual Approaches – CMRI CX + MR + CR	
Secondary Component Obstacles	Factor code OB
Tertiary Component Rule Bound	Factor code RB

Group Approaches – CMRG CX + MR + CR	
Secondary Component Assists	Factor code AS
Tertiary Component Work Environment	Factor code WE

Group Approaches – CMRG CX + MR + CR	
Secondary Component Obstacles	Factor code OB
Tertiary Component Confusion	Factor code CONF

Group Approaches – CMRG CX + MR + CR	
Secondary Component Obstacles	Factor code OB
Tertiary Component Vision	Factor code V

Group Approaches – CMRG CX + MR + CR		
Secondary Component	Assists	Factor code AS
Tertiary Component	Informality	Factor code INF

Organizational Approaches – CMRO CX + MR + CR		
Secondary Component	Willingness to Change	Factor code WTC
Tertiary Component	Freedom	Factor code F

Organizational Approaches – CMRO CX + MR + CR		
Secondary Component	Confidence	Factor code CON
Tertiary Component	Organizational Support	Factor code OS

Organizational Approaches – CMRO CX + MR + CR		
Secondary Component	Willingness to Change	Factor code WTC
Tertiary Component	Encouragement	Factor code ENC

Organizational Approaches – CMRO CX + MR + CR		
Secondary Component	Confidence	Factor code OB
Tertiary Component	Organizational Benevolence	Factor code OBN

Organizational Approaches – CMRG CX + MR + CR		
Secondary Component	Obstacles	Factor code OB
Tertiary Component	Rule Bound	Factor code RB

Organizational Approaches – CMRO CX + MR + CR		
Secondary Component	Obstacles	Factor code OB
Tertiary Component	Staff Appreciation	Factor code SA

Organizational Approaches – CMRO CX + MR + CR		
Secondary Component	Obstacles	Factor code OB
Tertiary Component	'Quick Fix'	Factor code QF

Organizational Approaches – CMRO CX + MR + CR		
Secondary Component	Obstacles	Factor code OB
Tertiary Component	Vision	Factor code V

Organizational Approaches – CMRO CX + MR + CR		
Secondary Component	Obstacles	Factor code OB
Tertiary Component	Management Thinking	Factor code MT

Organizational Approaches – CMRO CX + MR + CR		
Secondary Component	Obstacles	Factor code OB
Tertiary Component	Culture	Factor code CUL

Organizational Approaches – CMRO CX + MR + CR		
Secondary Component	Obstacles	Factor code OB
Tertiary Component	Trust	Factor code TR

Organizational Approaches – CMRO CX + MR + CR		
Secondary *Component*	Assists	Factor code AS
Tertiary *Component*	Tolerance of Mistakes	Factor code TM

Organizational Approaches – CMRG CX + MR + CR		
Secondary *Component*	Obstacles	Factor code OB
Tertiary *Component*	Creative Problem Solving Skills	Factor code CPSS

Organizational Approaches – CMRO CX + MR + CR		
Secondary *Component* Obstacles		Factor code OB
Tertiary *Component* Rule Bound		Factor code RB

Organizational Approaches – CMRO CX + MR + CR		
Secondary *Component*	Assists	Factor code AS
Tertiary *Component*	Tolerance of Mistakes	Factor code TM

Organizational Approaches – CMRG CX + MR + CR		
Secondary *Component*	Obstacles	Factor code OB
Tertiary *Component*	Creative Problem Solving Skills	Factor code CPSS

The journey to come

Part IV is presented in a form designed to appeal to practitioners. However, the material presented must not be seen as prescriptive, but it is hoped that it will prove to be useful.

Chapter 8   Creative management response in action

This chapter addresses a number of important topics associated with the introduction of CMR, as follows:

- Managing the interfaces between individuals, groups and the organization.
- The link between traditional management competencies and creativity.
- The advantages of a *creativity centre*.
- The role of *creative facilitation*.
- Learning the tools and principles.

Chapter 9   Future issues

Chapter 9 presents a broad brush stroke of the issues that are most likely to impact on wealth-creation activities in the future. Topics featured include the following:

- The contextual factor (CF) secondary and tertiary components.
- Education issues.
- Training issues.

Chapter 10   Case studies

An assortment of case study material, featuring large and small organizations in both the private and public sectors, makes up this chapter. Included is a case where CMR failed to take off, because the senior management declined to really back it.

CMR applications:
a management approach
for the 1990s

Approaching creative management – Part IV

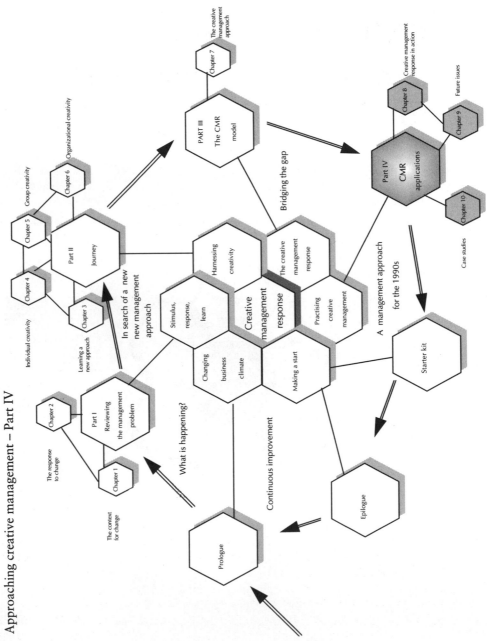

Introduction

The argument and material presented in Part IV addresses important contextual matters as well as material drawn from practical experience in applying the *creative management response (CMR) model*.

Chapter 8:   CMR in action

This chapter examines issues relating to managing the internal and external interfaces of an organization and includes analysis that draws on both primary and secondary CMR factor components. We then move on to describe briefly a selection of individual and group issues that have cropped up regularly during consulting and training sessions. Following is a selection of organizational issues, ranging from running CPS sessions to introducing change, that have come up during the course of practical work involving organizations.

Chapter 9:   Future issues

One of the principal themes running through the argument assembled in this text has been the increasing complexity and potency of rapidly developing contextual stimuli. The wealth creator's world is now global and the inexorable power of competition and environmental degradation have assumed a critical importance. In this chapter we present a small selection of issues that demand the attention of Western economies ahead of time. They are included at this point as it is right to approach the end of the text on a contextual note. Contextual influences will be of critical importance to managers as we enter the twenty-first century. How managers respond will ultimately determine whether the future will be characterized by rising or falling living standards. The choice facing the West is starkly simple – either shape up or decline. The issues raised in the chapter cannot be ignored if the West wishes to maintain, let alone increase, its standard of living.

Chapter 10: Case studies

Lastly, Chapter 10 contains a selection of case studies to enable readers to experiment with the 'nuts and bolts' of the *creative management response (CMR) model* and to relate their expertise to 'real-life' scenarios. The chapter opens with a brief analysis guide to help you on your way and then presents five cases for analysis and comment. The sixth is a worked example of the *'what'* stages of the learning process sequence illustrated in Figure 10.1. Of course whilst case study material is a valuable source of learning there is nothing to beat live applications of the CMR model. Pluck up courage and experiment with a live project. Complete the *'what'* stages of the featured learning process sequence. Then attempt the *'how'* stages. You should find more than enough material in the pages of the text to speed you on your way – but remember go carefully and resist the temptation to conduct the orchestra before you can play an instrument!

8

The creative management response in action

CONTENTS

8.1 Introduction *303*

8.2 Reviewing organizational behaviour *304*

8.3 Managing the interfaces *304*

8.4 Individual and group issues *315*

8.5 Organizational issues *318*

8.6 Summary *325*

Questions *326*

References *326*

Map: Chapter 8

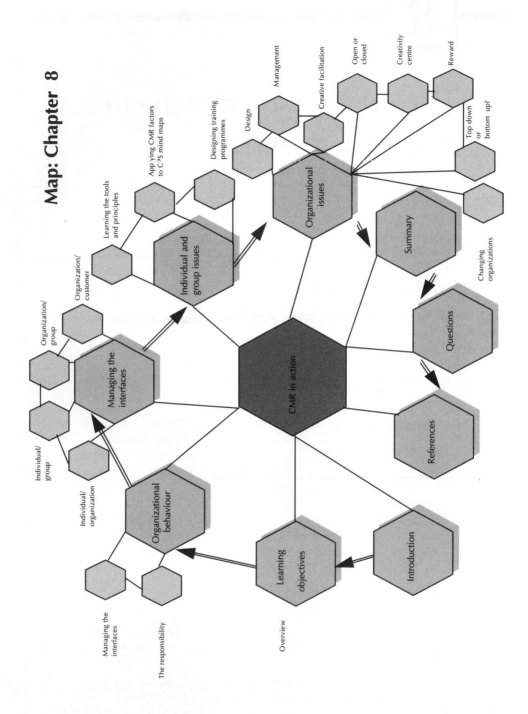

EXAMPLE 8.1

The new ways

To inspire their staff, McDonnell Douglas, the American corporation best known for its interests in the aviation industry, issued an internal document quoting the following remarks made by Mr Matsushita, the founder of the Japanese Matsushita Electrical Group. The way to empower people to change is to help them focus their energies on the *new* ways.

> For us, the core of management is the art of mobilizing the intellectual resources of all employees in the service of the firm.

> Any institution has to be organized so as to bring out the talent and the capabilities within the organization; to encourage men (and women) to take initiative, to give them a chance to show what they can do, and a scope within which to grow.

This message was circulated to McDonnell Douglas staff in 1946! (Belasco, 1990)

8.1 Introduction

This chapter contains a selection of important matters of concern relating to the introduction of the *creative management response approach*. It draws on research and consultancy activities in a wide selection of large and small organizations including private sector, public sector and ex-public sector establishments. The opening section stresses the overall responsibility of general management today. The next examines the importance of effectively managing the internal and external interfaces. The final sections address key issues that our work has shown to be particularly worthy of consideration by those contemplating actioning the *creative management response approach*.

LEARNING OBJECTIVES

After reading this chapter the reader will have an appreciation of the main issues that tend to arise when individuals, groups and organizations experiment with the *creative management approach*, as follows:

- A view of the internal and external interfaces that confront general management.
- An insight into the factors facing management as they tackle these interfaces.
- A review of the main problems that individuals, groups and organizations meet.
- Hints on how to introduce the *creative management model*.

8.2 Reviewing organizational behaviour

8.2.1 The responsibility

The prime task of management, whether at the individual, group or organizational level, is to shape and co-ordinate behaviour to achieve real, predetermined, wealth-creation goals. This will inevitably involve a Matsushita 'people oriented' visionary approach (see Example 8.1), that seeks to deliver quality and value to all publics which interface with organizations. In addition to the need to base operations on sound (up-to-date) contextual considerations, the management response needs to address creatively two sets of interfaces:

1. Internal interfaces between:
   (a) individual/organization;
   (b) individual/group; and
   (c) organization/group.
2. External interfaces between:
   (a) organization/customers;
   (b) organization/suppliers; and
   (c) organization/shareholders/other stakeholders or publics.

This is an awesome challenge that calls for considerable sensitivity to the contextual stimuli and to the management responses to ensure that individuals, groups and organizations work together in unison.

8.3 Managing the interfaces

8.3.1 Context and response

Congruence

A key responsibility for any manager of people is to secure a healthy balance or congruence (Nadler and Tushman, 1988) between individuals in and dealing with the organization to facilitate the successful co-ordination of effort needed to meet wealth-creation targets. This section presents a summary (Tables 8.1–8.3) and brief discussion of the key internal and external interfaces that require management attention. Before reviewing the interfaces it is necessary to take a look at the *CMR context and response* factors (context, management response and creativity – see Figure 8.1) that impact on individuals, groups and organizations.

Contextual factors

Many Western organizations are finding it increasingly difficult to generate revenue in today's difficult operating conditions. Although at first glance it might sound depressing, clients are recommended to undertake an annual *contextual audit* and to publish the

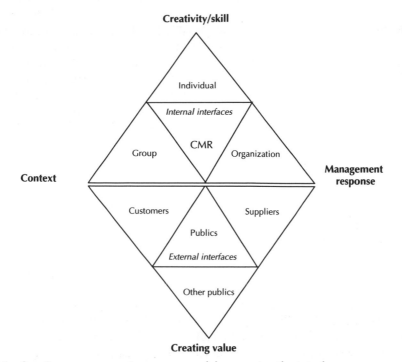

Figure 8.1 Creative management response model: managing the interfaces

results to stakeholders such as employees and trusted suppliers. This ensures that every-one working in and for the organization knows what the business climate is going to be. If it is going to rain, a warning is helpful as it enables individuals to take a coat and so avoid getting too wet. Soothing assurances that all is well when there are reasonable grounds for believing that this is not the case results in disappointment and promotes cynicism. Saying anything to deflect the problem temporarily – false charm – is not clever management. A useful complement to publishing the true contextual position is to hold a series of brief presentations for all staff.

There is little doubt that rapidly changing contextual factors are going to impact on many Western organizations well into the next century. This will certainly cause diffi-culties in traditional operations, but will also promote opportunities. Wise organizations in the West will promote innovation both in *what* they do (new product development) and *how* they function (general management responses). This entails stressing the import-ance of their *brain* power by encouraging the constructive use of the brains on their books and by enthusiastically seeking to acquire any needed additional expertise.

Management response factors

Contextually aware individuals and organizations now have to do something. A *co-ordinated team* usually achieves more than a collection of self-indulgent individuals or groups. Most team games call for both specialized individual and collective effort. Sustained and rapid change in contextual conditions calls for teamwork of the highest quality. If the *what* of the contextual factors are known, then the key factors concerning an efficient response – the *how* – need auditing. Power/authority styles of management do not often encourage creative teamwork. Tough talking autocratic managers, officials, directors and shareholders do not help football teams under pressure to perform on the park. Supportive ones do. The park is the playing field. A BGO (blinding glimpse of the obvious) perhaps. How does your organization shape up in the light of this metaphor?

Effective Traditional Management Competence training needs to be directed towards tackling live issues for individuals and groups in the organization. The traditional skills are important and should be regarded as investment expenditure in support of an organization's goals. When wealth-creating activity is under pressure from fierce domestic and overseas competition, good traditional management skills can make a vital difference. The restrictive mind-set that regards them as 'something it's nice to do when we've got the cash' and readily imposes severe budget cuts when things get tough is depressing. As more and more organizations seek to acquire and sustain high quality standards in the outputs they deliver to their customers, clearly well-trained people can add real value. Highly bureaucratic quality schemes may just deliver bits of paper!

Attitudes towards the playing field, employee training, customers and organizational life in general can easily be affected by individual and organizational *mind-sets*. Clients are recommended to carry out *mind-set audits* every year. Firm, intractable, mind-sets often indicate escalating myopia.

Creativity

The main problem that continues to surface when talking about creativity is usually – 'What is it?' 'Is it like creative accounting?' There are powerful arguments to cope with this question that place the emphasis on logic! If it is accepted that real contextual pressures are making life difficult for wealth creators and cost controllers, it is usually in order to argue that management responses – the *how* – need some help. This being the case, creative management has much to offer to address the real issues facing individuals and organizations. It is relatively inexpensive to install and will generate clear benefits if given freedom to operate, some support, and a base commitment of two to three years. The minimum condition to negotiate is tolerance to try a different approach without having to explain every move beforehand. Given a chance, creative management will prove its worth. It is still depressing to meet individuals who are highly prejudiced and have no intention of changing the *status quo* of their management *how* processes, to give the CMR model a real try.

When given the opportunity 'to have a go', choose one or two real concerns or problems and get to work with a simple selection of *CPS tools*. Resist the temptation to run before you can walk and to indulge in pre-session classifications of the relative 'weirdness' of the tools and principles that you may bring to the task. Never underrate the power of autosuggestion! If you are promoting anything, does it really make sense to fill people's ears with how strange it is? Seeing is believing. See to it that you are judged on the results you achieve and not exclusively on the methods you use.

8.3.2   Interface 1   Individual/organization

Employees who demonstrate low *confidence* levels are invariably going to be holding something back from their jobs. They may be distrustful of management activity both imagined and real. Most individuals are hugely concerned about their personal future. Managers usually are. So too are the managed. Does the organization trust its employees? Does it regularly hire and fire and buy the cheapest it can, and seek to automate processes as much as possible either by machine or paper technology? As behaviour breeds behaviour, evident lack of trust in each other by senior management will be noticed by the corporate rank and file. Most individuals can be persuaded to ride with change as long as it is fairly introduced. Sports teams have to change tactics to win through against difficult competition and playing conditions. It all depends on *how* behaviour is managed.

Individuals and organizations lacking in confidence will find it difficult to introduce significant changes to their general management practices. Confidence develops when a united face is turned toward problems – 'all for one and one for all'. Sacking 20 or 30 per cent of the potential wealth-creating force does not promote confidence in those who are left. Reducing administrative budgets by redirecting labour to wealth creating as opposed to wealth/cost measuring activities would be better. During the course of consultancy work it is not at all unusual to find organizations employing vast armies of administrators to produce and manipulate data. Some boast employee ratios as high as 8 to 1 in favour of administrators to wealth creators.

In reviewing the major difficulties that are encountered in relation to the interface between individuals and organizations, by far the greatest single problem area is that of *trust*. Symptoms of mistrust include:

- *Insecurity*.
- Aggressive attitudes to staff (*emotional* effects).
- Poor *real* (i.e. open) *communication*.
- Excessive power/authority cultures – divide and rule, misuse of patronage, and soon (*culture*).
- Lack of *vision* – would you feel safe in a plane being controlled by a flight deck crew with their eyes closed?
- Lack of *freedom* to act – all work has to be done to a set pattern. Any deviation from this is interpreted as skiving or treachery!
- *Confusion* – as to what the job involves.
- No *recognized influence* over own or other's work.
- No feedback from senior management – no recognition and sustained encouragement. Too much staged 'encouragement' (shallow *communication*), such as organizational Christmas parties, outings and mechanical appraisals.
- Propagation of a working belief that individuals work to live rather than live to work (*culture*).
- Deliberate discriminatory policies regarding standards of working environment.

Sadly, many organizations who requested a *trust audit*, have operated several of the above practices. When confronted with the evidence, most were genuinely shocked and

Table 8.1 **Managing the individual/organization interfaces**

Factor	Individual	Organization
Context		
Time dimension	Aware–unaware	Aware–unaware
Ages, times	Aware–unaware	Aware–unaware
Wealth creation	Aware–unaware	Aware–unaware
Brains	Aware–unaware	Aware–unaware
External factors	Introversion–extroversion	Introversion–extroversion
Competition	Domestic–global	Domestic–global
Management response		
Traditional management	Developed–undeveloped	Developed–undeveloped
competency (business	Supply–demand	Supply–demand
orientation)		
Mind-sets	Aware–unaware	Aware–unaware
Creativity		
Creative awareness	Low–high	Low–high
Creativity level	Residual–enhanced	Residual–enhanced
Total thinking	Low–high	Low–high
Left-brain thinking	Low–high	Low–high
Right-brain thinking	Low–high	Low–high
Creative problem-solving skills	Basic–advanced	Basic–advanced
Individual Responses		
Confidence	Low–high	Low–high
Willingness to change	Low–high	Low–high
Obstacles		
Insecurity	Low–high	Low–high
Perspective	Narrow–broad	Narrow–broad
Emotion	Cold–warm	Cold–warm
Communication	Restricted–open	Restricted–open
Culture	Power/Authority–team/support	Power/Authority–team/support
Vision	Myopic–credible	Myopic–credible
Trust	Low–high	Low–high
Assists		
Work environment	Good–poor	Good–poor
Freedom to contribute	Restricted–open	Restricted–open
Recognized influence	Existent–nonexistent	Existent–nonexistent

have sought to mend their ways having received a powerful message. A minority 'sanitized' the findings before reluctantly communicating the results to their employees.

Trust is a two-way factor that is highly experiential. Management that really are keen to promote it usually succeed. It has to be managed and sustained. Many organizations have the right intention but somehow seem always to be too busy to take care of the detail. Real value-added organizations recognize the importance of all their staff and deliberately set out to promote team spirit. Whilst the world is full of strains and stresses it is obvious to outsiders when an organization is valuing its people. There is a buzz in the air and the rumour-mongers are smiling! All that is needed is the commitment to encourage staff consistently and to really (in the eyes of employees and others) operate a team culture.

Apart from the obstacles briefly discussed above organizations should be aware of the key *assists* that they can implement to boost employee morale. Vast differences in working conditions (*working environment*) that reflect organizational rank or personal or political dislike (a kind of reverse patronage) damage the credibility of organizational 'team music'. The best organizations strive to provide a good working environment for all their employees and recognize the value of an individual's pride of place. Furthermore vibrant organizations mould their 'systems' to encourage individuals to assume direct responsibility for identified tasks. This is a tremendous motivator and promotes *self-confidence* and creativity.

See Table 8.1 for a summary of the chief factors involved in the management of the individual/organization interface.

8.3.3 Interface 2   Individual/group

Individual/group responses

The CMR *approach* to management offers some different process responses than conventional management methods. This provides the determined individual, who is prepared to experiment, with an opportunity to arouse the curiosity of others as he or she performs in groups. Table 8.2 summarizes the main primary, secondary and tertiary CMR factors affecting the individual/group interface.

Effective creative group problem-solving sessions usually begin with the *problem owner* (individual) choosing other individuals to meet informally to assist in progressing a professional concern. As groups are normally established by choice and not compulsion, *problem owners* tend to select those that they feel will approach the exercise in the right frame of mind (*confidence*). This preselection tends to heighten the chances of the group working well as a team. Gradually *group support* builds for the creative management approach, and undeniable successes establish the credibility of the group (*group recognition*).

After group members have attended a few CPS sessions it is amazing how quickly they warm to the natural appeal of the basic tools and principles and willingly begin to explore ways of applying them in their own operations (*willingness to change*). Once again, it is best to keep the approach fairly simple to begin with and to resist the temptation to get too complicated too quickly. There is both power and beauty in simplicity. Individuals often have to be slowed down as they try to race away in an effort to acquire all there is to know about creativity in management practice by the end of the week! The CMR model is a dynamic one and needs to be experienced rather than collected. The 'fast track' to gaining its potential power is to use it on real problems.

Table 8.2 **Managing the individual/group interfaces**

Factor	Individual tendency	Group tendency
Individual/group responses		
Confidence	Low–high	Low–high
Self-confidence	Low–high	
Boss support	Low–high	Low–high
Group support		Low–high
Group recognition		
Willingness to change	Low–high	Low–high
Obstacles		
Vision	Defined–undefined	Defined–undefined
Participation	Low–high	Low–high
Interaction level	Low–high	Low–high
Rule-bound	High–low	High–low
Confusion	High–low	High–low
Insecurity	Low–high	Low–high
Creative problem-solving skills	Low–high	Low–high
Trust	Low–high	Low–high
Assists	Low–high	Low–high
Work environment	Good–poor	Good–poor
Informality	Rule–exception	Rule–exception

As with many new skills there will be difficulties. Many result from the tendency of some to rush into the subject without sufficient thought and preparation and then to attempt to drive the process along themselves. The CMR model is intended to be used as a team-enabling systemic. It is not a 'quick solution' prescription. Overzealous use of domination methods, that are habitually used by the power and authority management players, will result in failure. A real team approach is necessary. Power driving might appear to be heavy on action but is often a hollow performer and can have long-lasting adverse effects on individual and group morale.

A poorly functioning group will display typically low levels of individual participation and consequently generate low levels of interaction. This is often because they are too *rule bound* and readily become confused unless they are directed (*confidence*). A real blockage can sometimes occur when potentially keen contributors are hamstrung by a lack of understanding of where the boundary lines are. This is an understandable difficulty for people used to formal models and procedures but is a mind-set that needs breaking by a sympathetic facilitator. As creative thought is an amazing synthesis (individual and collective) of traditional left-brain thinking and natural (but often typically restrained) right-brain thinking, it is quite common for people to be surprised by joy when they personally rediscover creativity.

Some individuals fight the creative experience preferring to cling on to the known ways of the past. This can ruin their potential contribution to a creative group problem-solving session and may heavily threaten the experiences of others. This can be a tricky problem for a group leader or facilitator to handle, especially if strong emotions are involved. Experience has shown that it is usually best politely to ask difficult, *insecure* characters to leave the group with the promise that they would be welcome if they choose to return at a later date.

Creative management is an activity that is significantly influenced by the *working environment*. It is advisable to hold sessions in a 'quiet' room away from the bustle of organizational life. Constantly ringing telephones and chattering personnel, as experienced in open-plan organizations and busy offices, does not favour CPS sessions. It is useful to find a room that has a window with a view of something more interesting than a brick wall and to take time out to check that the room contains articles of interest to the right brain (flowers, plants, pictures, cartoons, and so forth). Finally, sessions should be run on an *informal* basis – rank, deference, and power/authority habits and practices need to be left outside the room.

8.3.4 Interface 3   Organization/group

Organization/group responses

The last of the internal interfaces is that between the organization and groups. Table 8.3 sets out the leading issues. If groups get the feeling that the 'organization', usually a

Table 8.3 **Managing the organization/group interfaces**

Factor	Organization tendency	Group tendency
Organization/group responses		
Confidence	Low–high	Low–high
Willingness to change	Low–high	Low–high
Obstacles		
Vision	Defined–undefined	Defined–undefined
Staff appreciation	Low–high	Low–high
Culture	Low–high	Low–high
Quick solution	High–low	High–low
Management thinking	Set–open	Set–open
Trust	Low–high	Low–high
Creative problem-solving skills	Low–high	Low–high
Rule-bound	High–low	High–low
Insecurity	High–low	High–low
Confusion	High–low	High–low
Trust	Low–high	Low–high
Assists	Low–high	Low–high
Work environment	Good–poor	Good–poor
Informality	Rule–exception	Rule–exception
Learning organization	Poor–good	Poor–good
Tolerance of mistakes	Good–poor	Good–poor

metaphor for senior management, does not really value their work, much of the good work that has been done to improve the individual/group interface will be wasted. Top managers need to be aware that they need to acknowledge (*encouragement*) the efforts of their staff regularly. If this is neglected, group individuals will lose confidence in the organization (*confidence*). If senior management under pressure starts to lose confidence, then this will be magnified throughout the organization when insufficient attention is given to communicating (both good news and bad) to the troops effectively. Good communication can be used dramatically to rouse the troops. Poor communication often leads to them imagining the worst and losing heart at the very time that extra effort is required.

The degree of confidence that groups and individuals have in the organization has a marked influence on the way that they are likely to greet change. If organizations typically impose rather than openly introduce change, after due and fair consultation, they can expect attitudes of subordinates to harden (negative *willingness to change*). When the going gets tough the tough get going, and tough teams usually do achieve more than tough individuals. Adversity can unite. Power-and-authority-type responses can destroy effective teamwork – especially when high quality standards need to be met and sustained. Customer value is critically dependent in many cases on employee morale. The ability to sustain high levels of customer value is vital to an organization operating in today's *value time*.

The most severe threats to the organization/group interface are listed under the heading 'Obstacles' in Table 8.3. Most are self-explanatory, and most arise from entrenched mind-sets that severely affect the primary contextual, management response and creativity factors. In short, management myopia. A few lost shepherds can lose a lot of sheep. Good shepherds tend *all* their sheep and especially when the conditions get rough. Most individuals look for guidance, support and leadership. Its absence damages the organization/individual and organization/group interfaces. The end result is *confusion*, *insecurity* and mistrust (negative *trust*).

8.3.5 Interface 4 Organization/customers

Without customers, all that organizations have are costs. The pursuit, capture and retention of customers is a prime concern in the present *value time* buyers' markets. When customers (existing and potential) can exercise choice and turn to competing organizations at any time, *customer care* and excellence policies assume a vital importance. These range from basic politeness to effusive cosseting in order to 'delight' the customer. The fundamental rule is that wise organizations equal the best standards in their markets (*customer interface*) and attempt to go one better. Table 8.4 itemizes the main factors.

High standards of *quality* are generally expected these days. To offer anything less is false economy. To offer real, as opposed to paper, quality is a powerful positive discriminatory policy. Accurate and consistent *market research* should then be regularly used to:

- Monitor movements in the contextual factors impacting on the organization.
- Identify key trends, fashions in the marketplace.

Table 8.4 **The organization/customer interface**

Factor	Standards	Tick
Organization/customer interface		
Quality	BS 5750	
	ISO 9006	
Marketing research	Ongoing–*ad hoc*	
Customer care	Satisfactory	
	Excellent	
	Delightful	
Product/service offering	Clear–unclear	
Presentation/promotion	Clear–unclear	
	Consistent–inconsistent	

- Monitor the activities of competitors.
- Monitor effectiveness of own marketing efforts – in buyers' markets all businesses should be professionally marketed. This is no longer an option; it is a real cost and should be budgeted sensibly rather than frugally.
- Enable the organization to understand clearly what product/service 'packages' the market is demanding.

Customers need to be treated with respect and consistently wooed. Sloppy *customer care* – such as the mind-set of taking customers for granted – can easily lead to a successful capture by a competitor. Again this should be budgeted regularly and sensibly and not ignored or switched on and off intermittently. Winning organizations invest seriously to generate excellence in customer care. Similarly, wise management realize the importance of regular and consistent communication with customers and markets. A well-researched, sustained high-quality house style is essential. It is vital that all personnel who may come into contact (interface) with existing or potential customers exercise the highest standards of civility and care. Switchboard mannerisms switch people on or off.

All of the organization/customer interfaces itemized above demand the recognition and involvement of all employees in an organization. High regard in the marketplace is very expensive and difficult to achieve and is easily lost by unthinking individuals. It may sound hackneyed but this basic message needs to be communicated to all employees frequently.

8.3.6 Interface 5 Organization/suppliers

Clark and Fujimoto (1991) investigated and compared the performance of European, American and Japanese auto manufacturers in their bids to reduce product market lead times. They found that the Japanese bettered the Western manufacturers by 30 per cent with less than half the man-hour input! Investigation revealed that the key differences between the respective times to market performances were due to:

- Coherent overlapping of project stages.
- Intensive communication.
- Development of in-house manufacturing capabilities.
- Early involvement of supplier design and engineering.
- Accelerated pre-project planning.

The willingness of the Japanese to involve suppliers early in the new product development cycle is a significant policy. It is true, however, that for an organization to feel comfortable about this it must be satisfied that its suppliers will prove trustworthy. Assured of this, the early inclusion of external parties does much to boost the performance of the internal members of the team – true team spirit rather than a process disjointed by individual and small-group power authority behaviours.

8.3.7   Interface 6   Organization/shareholders/other stakeholders or publics

Open and fair communication with shareholders is another characteristic of the confident, caring organization. Lack of information invariably leads to rumour that is often more damaging to the organization than a fair and open release of the truth.

8.3.8   Winning organizations

Winning organizations are contextually aware and seek to find and then apply relevant management responses. They are prepared to harness suitable approaches, tools and techniques to respond to contemporary challenges. They are not stuck in the past. Increasingly these days, this means that they have to tolerate new ways of doing things and to judge employees, at all levels, on what they achieve rather than seek to police the way in which they think. Difficulties, issues and problems are seen positively and there is a climate conducive to open thought (*freedom*). The *how* to proceed is left to the creative thinking of individuals and groups and not dictated by rigid organizational manuals rigidly codified over previous decades.

Our consultancy and research work clearly shows that winning organizations do more than tolerate such open thinking. They consistently *encourage* it and charge individuals and groups with clear *challenges* to meet. Finally, they provide constant encouragement to personnel rather than hover, every ready, to jump in with carping criticism when problems and difficulties occur. Winning organizations continually strive to find ways in which to add value to their businesses. Losing organizations are usually complacent and often live in costly headquarters, flying their corporate flags to ever fewer buyers. Abandoned and decaying headquarters litter the business and industrial landscape in the West and stand as stark reminders of the dangers of going backwards into the future!

KEY TERMS

Congruence	Mind-set audit	Restrictive mind-sets
Contextual audit	Trust audit	Personality
Customer care	Winning organizations	Behaviour
Interface	Attitude	Constructive mind-sets

8.4 Individual and group issues

The *creative management response approach* is very much an 'action-oriented' process option, so increases in the basic skill abilities depend largely on experience. There are four individual and group issues that seem to crop up repeatedly: learning the tools and guides; applying the CMR factors to CPS mind maps; designing training programmes; and dealing with individual mind-sets. We now outline these issues, together with a few hints to assist learners' progress.

8.4.1 Learning the tools and guides

A common fear that many have with operating the CPS part of the CMR model is that it seems to demand a high level of expertise in applying the tools and guides in order to make any progress. Individuals should not be deterred from 'having a go', as surprisingly good results can be generated from a relatively unsophisticated use of the model. The important thing is to muster sufficient courage to work the model and not succumb to lingering doubts (real or imaginary) that can be used to justify a refusal to give it a try. A car is a sophisticated machine – but you do not have to understand everything about it in order to drive it. Whilst it is true that improved 'technical knowledge' will benefit the ordinary motorist's driving and open up new horizons and challenges, the basic tools that get you moving can be mastered relatively easily. The key issue here is usually one of *attitude*. Faced with any new challenge it is easy to become defeatist. This is not a viable option for wealth creators in the present *value time*.

Start carefully, try out a few of the simple tools and guides, and pace your learning. A word of warning: cognitive understanding of the broad specifications of the CPS component of the CMR model is not enough to achieve results. You must pluck up courage and 'give it a go', and you will probably make some mistakes. When you do, consider the following points and learn from them:

- What was the context?
- What tool did not deliver?
- Was the tool selection too ambitious?
- Was the CPS session pacey enough?
- Were you adequately prepared?

Table 8.5   **CPS starter tool kit**

Function	Tool	CPPS	CGPS
Problem evaluation	Stakeholder analysis	x	x
	5 W's and H	x	x
	'Why?'	x	x
Idea generation	Notebook	x	
	Private brainstorming	x	x
	Analogies	x	x
	Metaphors	x	x
	Mind mapping	x	x
	Reversal	x	x
	Visual outliner (s)	x	
Classification	Clustering	x	x
Selection	Colour code	x	x
	Intuitive judgement	x	x
Realization	Advantage/disadvantage	x	x
	Comfort zones	x	x

Note: (s) denotes software.
Tools drawn from a number of sources (for full details see Chapters 4 and 5) and listed alphabetically by category.

- Did you explain the new approach too much before generating some action?
- Did you indulge in long-winded apologetics ('You might find this strange but . . .')?

There is a learning curve to the CPS component. Most find that they can make rapid progress once they decide to try, and the potential benefits to individuals, groups and organizations are amazing. Put any fear that you may have of making mistakes into perspective. Early mistakes are rarely fatal, and how can you tolerate other people's mistakes – resulting from honest endeavour – if you do not make the odd one or two! The secret to successful CPS at the individual, group or organizational level is to proceed carefully. Start with a simple CPS tool selection and achieve something simple. Table 8.5 presents a cut-down *starter CPS kit* that you may like to try before turning to the expanded kit that is developed in Chapters 4, 5 and 6.

The essential principles are as follows:

- To observe personal propriety at all times – no carping or heavy criticism of others in the room or outside.
- To generate a quantity of ideas *before* applying qualitative arguments.
- To support and build on ideas.
- To suspend all usual boundaries.

8.4.2   Applying the CMR factors to CPS mind maps

Consultancy experience has shown that individual factors of the CMR model (primary, secondary and tertiary components – see Chapter 7) can all stimulate progress in CPS sessions. The six primary factors are particularly useful in this respect and could well be considered as a checklist in their own right, as follows:

1. Context.
2. Management response.
3. Creativity.
4. Creative management response (individual).
5. Creative management response (group).
6. Creative management response (organization).

8.4.3   Designing training programmes

The CMR model component factors can be used to assess individual, group and organizational training needs to empower an organization and its people to meet declared goals. Mounted on cards, the factors can easily be used for the construction of mind maps to aid understanding of the CMR model and to assist with matters such as training needs analysis (see Chapter 7, Appendix 7.3 and Chapter 10 pp. 362–81).

8.4.4   Dealing with individual mind-sets

The first thing to realize about mind-sets is that they are not all negative. So the first step is to assist individuals to map their own and then to help them identify the ones that make it difficult for them to alter their management responses. This is a delicate operation and needs to be conducted carefully and respectfully by a skilled facilitator. A powerful way to deal with individual *restrictive mind-sets* is to persuade their owners that it makes sense for them to:

- acknowledge that they harbour them;
- identify them;
- accept contextual arguments that real-world stimuli have changed; and
- accept that it is logical for them to change too if they do not want to be left behind.

Many know after such a confrontation that they are out of touch or out of step and need to adjust if they are to find their way in contemporary times. However, some genuinely feel that this is impossible as they would need a personality transplant! Confusion between *personality*, which is usually difficult to change, and *behaviour*, which can be changed relatively easily provided that the individual honestly wants to change, is common. Sensitive counselling can easily set people free from this blockage. If they are then encouraged to think openly and suitably trained in *total thinking* continuously (see

Chapter 4), they will, without realizing it, start to practise *creative management*. Setting a series of graduated attainable challenges is a good ploy to stimulate individuals.

Individuals are individuals and as such they are all different. One quick training course will not accomplish the transition in a twinkling of an eye. *Mind-sets* are heavily rooted in fear and mistrust of others and of the assumed and real intentions of the organization. *Restrictive mind-sets* are usually easily exposed. The skill lies in replacing them with new constructive ones and then providing the *freedom* and *encouragement* for them to grow. Restrictive mind-sets are not instantly deleted but remain in the subconscious in a dormant mode that can erupt at any moment. Hence the real need for continuous encouragement and for the setting of achievable *challenges* for people to meet with focused *constructive mind-sets*.

Dominant factors here are *trust* and *integrity*. Whilst creativity is a natural force and is the real trigger of value, it is frequently diluted to a low or *residual level* by an individual's perceived need to 'fight off' others or the organization. *Winning organizations* are fully aware of this and so try to function as teams or extended families or partnerships. They are characterized by flat management structures, employee empowerment policies, sound training budgets and cross-functional team working. The best organizations are enthused from the top down – the very antithesis of common power/authority organizations.

Individual, group and, ultimately, organizational creativity is heavily dependent on *trust*. Somehow this was progressively neglected throughout history and became a very unfashionable subject. Contextual stimuli are constantly altering our lives, sometimes seemingly imperceptibly and sometimes dramatically. The future of wealth creation in the West will demand a different approach that delivers value to discerning customers. This text argues the case for the *creative management approach* and faces up to the importance of the role of trust. Chapter 9 advances some seed thoughts for management debate as the subject assumes a renewed interest.

8.5   Organizational issues

8.5.1   Organizations – palaces or spades?

When the contextual conditions are favourable there is a tendency for organizations to become ends in themselves and for them to be viewed, consciously or unconsciously, as the central palaces of business life. The real purpose of an organization should be to facilitate the creativity of its members to create wealth (a spade). Empire building and rigid power/authority cultures can so easily cause an organization to lose sight of where it is going. Organizations should be like road vehicles suitable for the journey. Chaotic conditions require tailor-made vehicles. As operating conditions change so the organizational specifications should change. Here now is a selection of seven commonly occurring issues that we hope will assist all those who have an interest in seeing that organizations deliver, comprising: means or ends – organizational design; management practice; creative facilitation; freedom of expression; creativity centres; reward and motivation; and activating the creative management response.

8.5.2 Means or ends – organizational design

A hard but vital truth of modern wealth creation or management is that organizations, as well as individuals must critically adjust their *modus operandi* in order to deliver in tough buyers' markets. Nostalgia, whether for the rosier markets or much loved institutions of the past, is dangerous in modern contextual conditions. It blinds the eye and confuses the mind and can easily slip progressively into fully-fledged myopia.

EXAMPLE 8.2

Matrix management at ABB

Percy Barnevik, the chief executive of the Swedish-Swiss engineering multinational ABB, has revolutionized the management style of the group in the last six years by rigorously championing a matrix management approach, so that an organization with in excess of 200,000 employees is run or 'steered' by a head office staff of only 150. The role of management has been altered from the familiar power-broking, control and information processing role up and down the organization to a cross-company function concerned with coaching and the transference of skills and technology. (Source: Lorenz, 1994)

Looking back, as with Lot's wife, is dangerous. It is better to stride out boldly to face the future than to track back in the hope of finding yesterday's comforts. Surrounded by disorder and chaos, individuals often try to minimize the disturbance to the accepted – sometimes publicly maligned but often silently treasured – status quo. In times of accelerating and complex changes in the contextual factors impacting on wealth creation, it is best to accept the inevitable and contemplate that all management responses need to be reviewed. I firmly believe that organizations should serve the requirements of their accepted market needs. They are primarily a means to an end (generating wealth), not an end in themselves. Many an organization has been sunk through overzealous administrators indulging complacent management by trying to preserve the *ancien régime*, as rapidly changing contextual influences (e.g. transition from industrial to neoindustrial age – see Chapter 1) render it redundant.

For over sixty years there has been a tendency for organizations to mushroom as business boomed. Monuments in stone and vast armies of people to enable them to function have characterized Western business activity. The predominantly production oriented, power/authority cultures that operated these organizations liked their status symbols and many tried for too long to edify and preserve them, as business conditions changed. The industrial landscape of the West is now littered with vacant organizational monuments – time and change hold little respect for past dreams and redundant accomplishments. Modern organizations need to serve the visions of current times freed from the nostalgic mind-sets of yesteryear (see Example 8.2).

Large bureaucratic organizations are like the splendid ocean-going liners of the past – splendid but of another time. Today's organizations need to be highly responsive to the market. Typically they need to be smaller craft that are evolving continuously to meet the current and future requirements of the market. So organizations should provide all the necessary services that a wealth-creating or resource stewardship body really needs, as opposed to what they might have been used to in the past. Itemizing the essentials is a fruitful exercise – it is always surprising to discover just what really is necessary. Organizations should be like egg shells, thin but strong, and leaving plenty of room for individuals and groups to get on with the action of wealth creation. Other colourful metaphors that describe the journey which traditional hierarchical organizations must make to prosper in times of rapid changes in contextual conditions include the following:

- From daffodils to dandelions – from large bulbous bottom-heavy organizations to smaller self-contained offspring.
- From closed fields to open country – from closely defined boundaries to the borderless world.
- From the rule book to free expression – from regimentation to imagination.
- From a heavy reliance on hard system quantitative control to soft system qualitative empowerment.

Can you think of any more? How would you express metaphorically the journey that needs to be made by your organization?

8.5.3   Management practice

Staffing should be kept to the minimum consistent with a delivering the business to the right quality standards. The *modus operandi* should encourage all individuals to give of their best to meet the published organizational goals. This means delivering *value packages*, and to be successful means *innovating*. To innovate in process (management), product or service terms means being *creative*. Creativity does not flourish in highly regulated hierarchical organizations. It is the spirit of free enterprise, the lore of the · frontier. Creativity needs freedom, challenge and encouragement. It means *teamwork* of the highest order, and a new direction to management – team management.

Four levels of teamwork can usefully be identified here:

1. minimal;
2. steady;
3. solid; and
4. outstanding or world class.

Minimal teamwork is when the individuals that comprise the group pay lip service to teamwork and just about get on together. The resulting performance is usually pretty disappointing, particularly if the playing conditions have suddenly become more exacting and the competition smarter. *Steady* teamwork demonstrates a marked improvement and there is real evidence of an attempt to develop team skills to achieve a common end. *Solid* teamwork is better still and is the essence of dependable positive differentiation. *Outstanding* or *world-class* teamwork produces impressive results and is the product of dedicated work both on the playing field and behind the scenes. *Winning organizations* tend to display outstanding teamwork and operate a culture of 'all for one and one for all'. The power–authority style of management is frequently the antithesis of the team approach. It is often characterized by personnel ambition, which is seen by the thrusting individual as being separate and superior to the aspirations of the team. The CMR model demands real teamwork.

8.5.4 Creative facilitation

Problems, issues or challenges – however businesses like to see them – will continue to face organizations into the foreseeable future. These events will demand positive interventions and are likely to be difficult to cope with as they will be the fruits of chaos rather than order. In systemic terms, this means disequilibrium rather than equilibrium, soft rather than hard issues. Such problems will be hard to describe and difficult to resolve. There is likely to be more than one answer. As the contextual conditions will change continuously, precedent will not be as reliable a guide as it has been in the past.

This text has exhorted all those interested in management to ensure that they are contextually aware and to acquire and use a kit of problem-solving tools to ply their trade. Against a background of rapid change in the world's wealth-creating arena it is essential for the well-being of the West that our organizations and peoples learn quickly. There is very little time for individuals and groups to get to grips with creative management tools. An important feature of this approach to management is to emphasize the importance of training individuals, groups and organizations to use and apply successfully the CMR model tools and principles. To this end a training programme has been developed which will empower individuals to facilitate organizations to practise the CMR model. This is a subtle, sensitive and professional skill. All the programmes are tailored to meet the requirements of clients, but here is a representative schedule for the purpose of illustration:

Stage 1   One-day introductory workshop – 'capturing creativity'.
Stage 2   One-day follow-up workshop – 'running CPS sessions'.
Stage 3   Consultancy package that features:
   (a) on-site training and support;
   (b) the establishment and continuous up-dating of a *creativity centre* (see below); and
   (c) training consultancy (education and project training).

Further details can be obtained from the author, see also p. 233.

8.5.5 Freedom of expression

Many who have felt oppressed by power cultures have yearned for the freedom to express themselves. Strangely, once set free, many sigh for the good old days when the boundaries were clearly set and managed by firm rule-sets. There is a risk in working for a flatter, leaner organization. Life is full of real challenges where co-operation with others is the watchword, rather than the 'first past the post' competitiveness that is so common today. Status is won on the field and is for the benefit of the individual and the organization.

Open organizations featuring freely floating cross functional teams tend to produce the right conditions for creativity to flourish. Seen in this light the creative manager is very similar to a devoted gardener. He or she fully recognizes that the real power lies somewhere else (with the Creator) and accepts the role of enabler and facilitator. The role of Creativity Centres (see below) is to support and encourage 'would-be gardeners' to achieve excellent results in season.

8.5.6 Creativity centres

A creativity centre provides a focus in an organization for CPS activity. It is both a source of inspiration and a source of excellence. It is best located either within or close to the Training Department. Typically a centre will provide the following services to organizational personnel:

- A counselling service on all aspects of the CMR approach (e.g. how to release personal creativity).
- A forum to discuss CPS issues, such as what tools and tracking designs to consider.
- A library of useful publications.
- Software support.
- Audio library.
- Video library.
- Lunch time and/or evening events.
- Network support to individuals.
- Compilation and issue of bimonthly journal or magazine.
- Provision of short on-site training courses in CPS and applications of the CMR model.

A vibrant *creativity centre* can be established for a modest investment and soon begins to make a positive contribution, as it is focused on live challenges, issues and problems. It also generates a sense of excitement and expectancy that 'sparks' the latent creativity of individuals.

8.5.7 Reward and motivation

A crucial question for many aspiring creative managers is how to continuously stimulate creativity in their organizations. Writing a decade ago Lovelace (1986) addressed the challenge of how to stimulate creativity in research and development scientists. He assumed that stimulating creativity was largely a matter of personal ability and providing the right environmental conditions. He proposed that Maslow's (1943) hierarchy of needs provided an adequate model, maintaining that the urge to be creative was merely the scientist's natural quest to achieve self-actualization.

In common with Wahba and Bridwell (1976), I have found that it is difficult to flatly apply the need hierarchy in organizational contexts. However, I am convinced that management does need to encourage creativity constantly by stressing its importance in both the internal and external interfaces.

Organizations need to provide the room (*freedom*) for creative responses, to issue their staff with real *challenges*, and then to *encourage* them to release their latent creativity. A novel American technique that is starting to receive publicity in the United Kingdom is that of *upward feedback*. This allows employees anonymously to assess the performance of their manager and is directly linked to bonus schemes. BP Oil, Federal Express and W. H. Smith are all reported to be giving it a try.

8.5.8   Activating the creative management response

So far so good, but how can this general approach be adopted by organizations effectively? Whilst there is a rich literature featuring new product development and innovation from a marketing and project planning viewpoint, covering everything from attributes to project systems (e.g. in Tushman and Moore, 1988), changing the behaviour of organizations so that they actively and continuously foster the *creative management approach* is not quite so cut and dried. Sir John Harvey-Jones, a previous chairman of ICI, in an interview in July 1994, was firmly of the opinion from his considerable experience that all such initiatives if they were to last had to be championed firmly from the *top down*. Clearly public and sustained support (real championship) is desirable. If top management is firmly committed, this makes the whole process much easier. At present this seems to be somewhat of a rarity, but recent developments in the West are encouraging. In the United Kingdom progress has been reported at Rover Cars, BP, and British Gas, while across the Atlantic the American management consultant Tom Peters (1993) cites many examples of US organizations that have become committed to such leadership from the top.

By far and away the greater part of case experience has been with organizations whose top management have often just tolerated this approach. Frequently they have been prepared to give it try on a *faute de mieux* basis and after trying a plethora of other management offerings. In these cases the *creative management response* is best introduced in a low-key, unobtrusive way by individuals working in small groups, focusing on everyday matters of concern and obtaining interesting results. As the individuals and groups register undeniable successes, learn from experience (reflective practitioning), and begin to network, so they gradually assume a higher profile in the organization and themselves become powerful agents of change. Provided that the top management are openly supportive, confidence in the creative management response can grow spectacularly from the *bottom up*.

Clearly strong, sustained, *top down* enthusiasm and support provides vital encouragement for the rapid development of the creative management response and significantly boosts corporate teamwork. This involves a transition from the chief executive, managing director or board of directors in the role of hero to that of the whole organizational team believing it enjoys hero status. Experience has shown that where top management are aware of the need for change in the way their organizations are managed, they prefer to proceed slowly. Few, unless faced by a severe externally imposed challenge, such as privatization or acute competition, have been prepared to experiment actively with a real team as opposed to the power/authority style of operation.

Gradually, increasing pressure from the contextual factors impacting on wealth creation and stewardship, as detailed in early chapters, is lowering the barriers to new management response approaches. Experience has shown that once top management 'can find the time' to attend a brief presentation on the *creative management approach*, they have to face up to the issue of whether or not they really want to introduce management changes that will substantially alter the status quo. Talking about cross-functional team working and empowerment is one thing, fostering its growth is another. So in many cases top management becomes 'neutral' or tolerant and agrees to a number of small-scale experiments whilst reserving its total commitment. This is enough to achieve a *bottom-up* launch but insufficient to achieve a rapid real change in management practice. The personal, group and organizational values, as conventionally expressed in the power/authority style, are very resilient and difficult for outside consultants to break. The determination has to come from the client and be backed up by a well-communicated and sustained action plan. Paying lip service to appease fashion, without visible works, produces a poor return. This signals to the organizational rank and file that 'nothing has really changed'. The tragedy for Western organizations is that this is a false position. Not only is it contextually wrong, but it is also a managerial attitude that fosters the growth of restrictive mind-sets. In short, as put by Moss Kanter in May 1989 and quoted by Peters (1993), individuals should: 'Forget loyalty and conformity (to traditional management practices). We can't afford narrow-skill people . . . You've no future unless you add value, create projects (to generate wealth or save resources).'

A basic aim of this text has been to present the case for adopting a new general approach to management and to encourage managers to experiment with the *creative management response* (CMR). The organizations who have gained the most from (CMR) have been the ones that have deliberately sought to effect improvements in the way they manage their internal and external interface by the introduction of team-oriented cultures. Overdependence on specific components of the management problem – for example, TQM, value-added marketing, and so on – will not produce the 'high-performance workplaces' (*The Economist*, 1994) that Western organizations need if no commitment is made to change the general pattern of management response activity. The pursuit of excellence and attendant value are common goals, yet so many organizations try to achieve these goals with management practices whose heyday has long since gone. Every organization is different, as every individual is different, so there is no universally applicable solution. Theory is fine on paper but it is action that counts in today's world.

The creative management response has real potential in the current *value time* and for the opening decade of the next century. The *approach* road is clear but where it ultimately leads is not. Uncertainty is hard to manage, but it's here to stay. The *creative management response* as described in this introductory text offers much but demands commitment. Are you liberated enough to give it a real evaluation?

8.5.9 A trumpet call

You should remember that the creative management response is not a 'quick solution' although early benefits will soon become apparent. Individuals and groups will discover the joy of creativity and the usefulness of CPS, but organizations have historically taken more time to change course. Real effort is now needed by management to be prepared to think 'short term' and address the immediate stimuli affecting wealth creation in their responses. Chaotic operational conditions demand this action, but so often management, whilst adopting 'short-term' thinking for perceived personal aspirations, are happy to adopt 'long-term thinking', as they seek to preserve the temples and observances of outdated organizations. The bottom line is wealth creation and a fair share of prosperity for all. This ideal has been a fervent vision of the democratic dream for years. There is still time to steady and arrest the escalating decline of the West, but only if those who hold management and political positions come to realize that they are important team workers for the greater community. Little further delay can be suffered if Western managers and politicians really do want to build a future for the children and grandchildren of their citizens.

> **KEY TERMS**
>
> | | | |
> |---|---|---|
> | Means or ends | Creativity centre | Upward feedback |
> | Teamwork | Motivation | Top down |
> | Creative facilitation | Rewards | Bottom up |

8.6 Summary

Management is an occupation that concerns us when we work alone, and when we work with others in groups and organizations. Its prime task is to co-ordinate human behaviour to meet declared wealth-creation goals as efficiently as possible in terms of resource usage. To deliver value for money efficiently, individuals, groups and organizations must manage their internal and external interfaces effectively.

The main internal interfaces describe the individual/organizational, individual/group and organization/group relationships. Effective team working and creative expression is critically dependent on the professional maintenance of these interfaces. Each of these interfaces is influenced by the primary , secondary and tertiary factors of the *CMR approach*.

The external interfaces directly affect the way in which individuals, group and organizations are perceived by their publics. Three key interfaces are addressed in this chapter – organization/customer; organization/supplier; and organization/other stakeholders or publics (shareholders, government offices, press, and so on). Maintaining good customer relations is critically dependent on the supply of quality products and services to the right markets with due regard to upholding high standards of customer care and promotion. Attention to the organization/supplier interface results in shorter market (organizational) response times. Adherence to the accurate and frequent release of key information is the best way of preventing potentially damaging rumours spreading round interested publics

Winning organizations achieve their status by the sustained support of sound internal and external interface policies. They are often characterized by their efforts to encourage the release of their employee's creativity.

A selection of individual/group and organizational issues that often follow a decision to introduce the CMR approach closes the chapter. In all times, but especially chaotic ones, the issue of trust assumes great importance.

QUESTIONS

1. What is the prime purpose of general management effort?
2. Describe the main internal and external interfaces that organizations should manage. What CMR factors impact on the internal interfaces and what factors significantly affect the external ones?
3. What are the leading individual and group issues that arise when people adopt the CMR approach? If you were a consultant how would you advise your clients?
4. Organizations – *palaces* or *spades*? Discuss.
5. Briefly describe the role of a *creative facilitator*.
6. What is a *creativity centre* and what benefit does it bring to an organization?
7. Teamwork – fact or fiction in most organizations? How would you improve it in your place of work or study?
8. Discuss the problems associated with activating the creative management response (CMR) in an organization. Top down or bottom up – which is the best way of ensuring a successful adoption? How would you promote CMR from the bottom up?
9. What distinguishes winning organizations? Describe one that is known to you.

References

Belasco, J. A. (1990), *Teaching Elephants to Dance*, London: Century Business

Clark, K. and Fujimoto, T. (1991), 'Reducing the time to market: the case of the world auto industry', originally published in *Design Management Journal* 1 (1), 49–57 (1989), and in J. Henry and D. Walker (eds), *Managing Innovations*, London: Sage.

The Economist, 'New work order', 9 April, 94.

Lorenz, C. (1994), 'Time has come for a revolution in style', *Financial Times*, 22 April.

Lovelace, R. F. (1986), 'Stimulating creativity through managerial intervention', *R & D Management*, 16, 161–74.

Maslow, A. H. (1943), 'A theory of human motivation', *Psychological Review*, 50, 370–96.

Nadler, D. A. and Tushman, M. (1988), 'A model for diagnosing organizational behavior', in M. Tushman and W. L. Moore (eds), *Readings in the Management of Innovation*, 2nd edn, New York: Ballinger.

Peters T. (1993), *Liberation Management*, London: Pan, 216.

Tushman, M. L. and Moore, W.L. (1988), *Readings in the Management of Innovation*, New York: Harper Business.

Wahba, M. and Bridwell, L. (1976), 'Maslow reconsidered: a review of the research on the need for hierarchy theory', *Journal of Personality*, 33, 348–69.

9

Future issues

CONTENTS

9.1   Introduction   *331*

9.2   The purpose of hunter individuals: self-satisfiers or social builders?   *331*

9.3   The purpose of teamwork: fact or fantasy?   *333*

9.4   The purpose of organizations: the big inside or the big outside?   *334*

9.5   The purpose of management: short-termism or long-termism?   *335*

9.6   The purpose of government: redistribution of wealth or increasing national wealth levels?   *337*

9.7   Summary   *340*

Questions   *340*

References   *341*

Map: Chapter 9

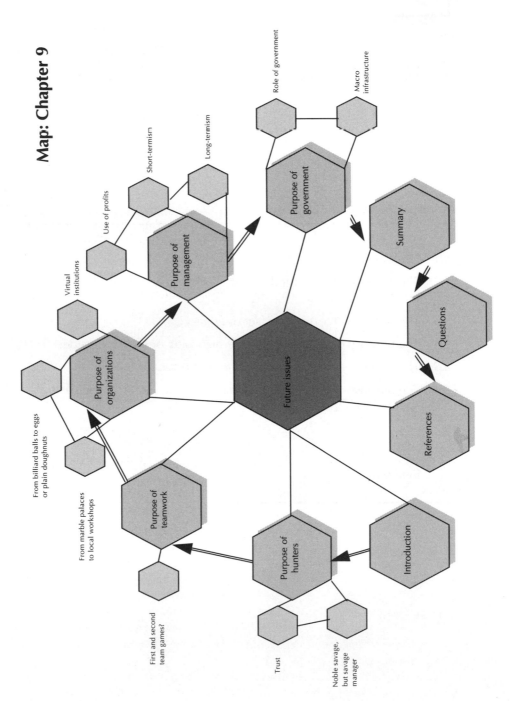

9.1   Introduction

By the time that this text is published the West and everybody else will be in the latter stages of the countdown that will usher in the next century. Although many words have been and will be written that express both optimistic and pessimistic views, the temptation in this penultimate chapter to join in is both apt and repetitive. It is apt to sound yet another *cri de coeur* for sanity to occur rather than self-interest and convenient incrementalism as organizations start to contemplate seriously what the going will be like as the new millennium approaches. Repetitive perhaps, as there is so much comment around that those influencing the affairs of organizations might be forgiven for feeling that they are being bombarded by visionaries. However, well-focused visions are needed for us to have confidence that our economic activities will feed us in the twenty-first century.

In no way is this text intended to be greeted as the last word on the subject or necessarily the most apposite. My sole aim has been to sound the gong – as an academic, practitioner, consultant and parent – out of a deep concern for the fuzziness that seems at present to surround the future of wealth-creating activity in the West.

This chapter raises a handful of issues which in my opinion deserve to be seriously addressed well before the chimes of Big Ben in London and the car horns in New York City's Times Square ring in the new century. The choice of issues is immense but I have selected the following as they seem to be worthy foci for readers on both sides of the Atlantic:

- The purpose of hunter individuals – self-satisfisers or social builders?
- The purpose of teamwork – fantasy or destiny?
- The purpose of organizations – the big inside or the big outside?
- The purpose of management – short termism or long termism?
- The purpose of government – redistribution of wealth or increasing national wealth levels?

9.2   The purpose of hunter individuals: self-satisfiers or social builders?

9.2.1   Noble savages become savage managers

Primitive man made a great step forward when he discovered that by developing social relationships with other groups he could increase his ability to provide for himself and dependants. We were all programmed to live a communal life and most of us do, at least to some extent. We live in separate family shelters (houses) and interact with immediate family and neighbours. We are the perfect noble savage. At work many of us behave differently. The environment is more formal, less friendly and the purpose of our interactions (the game) changes from 'society building' to self-satisfaction. Away from the familiar, co-operative group and its real team activity, we so often become lone hunters in pursuit of self-advantage.

This competitive behaviour can be seen regularly today in the transformation many drivers undergo when they get behind the wheel. Man the noble savage can so easily become man the savage manager, self-reliant, self-directed and frequently vain. Two people living in one body. We saw earlier that behaviour breeds behaviour. Different social cultures (home and work) produce different responses as a direct reflection of opposing trust influences. We have moved from what the German sociologist Tonnies (1887) called *Gemeinschaft* (familiar home environment) to *Gesellschaft* (the organizational environment). From a place where individuals were bound together by common traditions and ties of affection and solidarity to a place where social relations are contractual, rational and nonemotional.

9.2.2   Managing trust

All too often this move across the *Gemeinschaft–Gesellschaft* spectrum is characterized by a progressive decline in the level of trust in our lives. A base quotient of trust is essential for all human interaction. If we are mistrustful of others we will become suspicious and limit the degree to which we are prepared personally to contribute to others. Thus the level of trust has a direct effect on the quality of teamwork that can be achieved. Furthermore, inspired – as opposed to well-drilled – mechanical teamwork is vitally dependent on the willing release of creativity. As we have seen earlier in this text, creativity is vital to secure effective innovation in management responses.

Business is essentially about risk – or is it? In one sense this is clearly true, for any business organization is responsible for the stewardship of its resources and is open to criticism if it places these in danger. So some see the role of management as being essentially concerned with the elimination of risk; thus business is basically simple and entails the rigid control of expenditure and people. However, others argue that business is about taking risks – that is, acceptable ones – in order to achieve increases in the levels of wealth generated by the business. This is the approach of fabled entrepreneurs such as Alan Sugar (AMSTRAD), Anita Roddick (Bodyshop) or Ray Kroc (founder of McDonald's hamburger restaurants), encapsulated in corporate decision making.

As more and more businesses are faced with severe competition, then to survive they will have to contemplate taking entrepreneurial risks. Thus they will need to generate, develop and introduce new products and services to ever tougher value standards. Managing in buyers' markets is a difficult team game that requires both efficiency and flair. Successful teamwork is crucially dependent on extracting the best from the corporate players. Each will have to give more of themselves to the cause. Ultimately this is a matter of trust.

Trust is an attitude that we choose to take and has the following three components:

1. A cognitive element which gives us confidence that the other party is trustworthy.
2. An emotional element that leads us to feel comfortable that we can trust someone else.
3. A volitional element that leads us to act on it.

Trust is a risk that we take as we deliberately surrender control over part of ourselves to others. It demands accountability. If one person accepts another's trust, then a responsibility rests for the exercise of that trust to the trustee. It is a serious business. It is crucial to fostering creativity.

So if we wish to boost creativity, all we have to do is find ways of enhancing trust levels between individuals. However, many find it hard to trust others in *Gesellschaft* relationships. This could be for a variety of reasons. Some of the most common are:

- Breach of confidence.
- Disloyalty – desertion.
- Betrayal – sacrifice of trust for personal gain.
- Dishonesty – the deliberate lie to gain someone else's trust and their subsequent discovery of the deceit.
- Moral weakness – inadequate support given when needed.
- Uncertainty and indecisiveness – sitting on the fence.
- Unreliability and inconsistency.
- Unfairness or injustice.

To boost trust levels amongst the rank and file that work for organizations it is necessary to change typical power/authority cultures to softer, caring cultures. Fostering a climate of trust is a gradual process but the rewards of a true *Gemeinschaft* are:

- increased confidence;
- loyalty in all weathers;
- reliability and dependability;
- consistency;
- honesty and plain speaking; and
- enhanced levels of creativity.

and thus acknowledged integrity. Encouraging managers to assume a responsibility for fostering a climate of trust involves being seen to be:

- reliable in discharging trustworthiness and dependability;
- honest;
- unselfish and self-centred – a real team player; and
- principled under pressure – not compromising trust for the sake of short-term advantage.

In the absence of actions to earn trust managers will continue to find it difficult to foster and increase levels of trust, creativity and performance necessary to consistently deliver value outputs. What is needed is real teamwork to increase the wealth of all by successfully harnessing the potential of human creativity.

9.3   The purpose of teamwork: fact or fantasy?

9.3.1   First and second team games?

On the assumption that management is a team game, it is instructive for many groups and organizations to reflect on the quality of their *real* team play. Whilst most managers would agree that team spirit is in essence a good thing, many harbour the mind-set that it is pure fantasy in their operation. Perhaps there are signs of it in the lower, middle and upper management ranks. It is relatively rare for it to flourish across the rank interfaces. A real commitment to cross-functional team working is critically dependent on the higher view that puts the performance of the team above personal aspirations. Ideally the two coincide and this is seen to be the case in high quality team play.

The key question is *attitudinal*. Whilst good teams are a mixture of players of all abilities and experience they are united by the main cause – winning. Division in the camp is damaging to team performance but may, by some thrusters, be judged as sound individual play. Encouraging not only the first and second teams but all the 'teams' within a business to work harmoniously for the good of the organization is a key and a difficult leadership challenge. Managers in organizations should strive to achieve the right balance between directional and team leadership. For many this will lead to a reshaping of corporate management response styles. Traditional *power and authority* plays will have to give way to a more balanced approach that really seeks to encourage high-quality team play. It is hoped that this text provides some guidelines as to how this might be achieved in readers' group and organizational lives.

9.4 The purpose of organizations: the big inside or the big outside?

9.4.1 From marble palaces to work sheds?

The changing nature of the 'norm' operating conditions for many wealth-creating organizations and resource stewardship bodies is rapidly altering and often revolutionizing their outlook. Senior managers are being faced with complex contextual situations that they have rarely seen, if at all, in the past twenty or thirty years or more. So it is becoming more and more dangerous to respond by triggering precedent responses (past 'norms') or worse still to ignore external challenges altogether and attempt to ride out the storm.

Today's conditions demand organizations that are flexible and creative and that can form and reform to professionally respond to changing stimuli. The day of the solid, central marble hall corporate headquarters has passed. Formalized bureaucracy and power/authority structures, that typified previous suppliers' markets, are too rigid to meet the current operational conditions. Organizations need to get closer to the action, become less preoccupied with ritual, and rediscover the practicality and simplicity of the outside world. Splendid headquarters like magnificent churches and other buildings are fine, as long as they have life. Devoid of movement, spirit and direction, they stand forlorn as museums to the glories of the past.

Those in positions of corporate responsibility are going to have to come to terms with the realities of modern operational contextual factors and discover a new way of managing. This will mean accepting that the old order has to give way to the new. Cherished headquarters will have to be reduced and perhaps abandoned, and the corporate cross-functional teams will have to gather and go out to the market rather than expecting the market to come to them. So organizations will have to change and become support vehicles for the cross-functional teams that will increasingly have to play away from home. Greater emphasis will have to be placed on acquiring and developing the brains, skills and personal back-up services that enable a team creatively to perform to the highest standards.

9.4.2 From billiard balls to eggs or plain doughnuts!

Metaphorically we need to progress from organizational designs that resemble billiard balls to ones that resemble eggs. A billiard ball is solid and dependable – its skin is its centre. In contrast the bulk of the volume of an egg is designed to assist its occupant to develop. The shell provides local accommodation and protection. Organizational administrative and support functions must resemble the concept of the eggshell (protective and nourishing) rather than the billiard ball that is dense and barren.

Professor Handy (1994) sees the organizations of the future as resembling ring doughnuts. The doughnut in the ring supports the corporate activity in the middle. An extension of his basic vision is to imagine a traditional organization as a jam doughnut where the jam symbolizes the creative energies of the organization and the dough the administrative shell. Take your pick of metaphor but think about making your organization change if necessary.

9.4.3 Virtual institutions

Developments in communication and computer technology are hastening the advent of virtual institutions. These could be formed on a temporary basis by a collection (team) of relevant specialists, who may actually be self-employed or be on the books of other organizations, and who are assembled to tackle a particular task. Theoretically they need never meet in the flesh, since teleconferencing can bring them into VDU contact in their host organizations (shells) or home (private shells). Such developments promise exciting possibilities for the future but are further threats to the old style corporate HQs.

9.5 The purpose of management: short-termism or long-termism?

9.5.1 Profit purpose

If the West wishes to maintain, let alone increase, its standard of living, then management must be concerned with more than the annual generation of profits. Business managers must earnestly seek to increase the overall level of wealth of the Western economies. Profit generation, though important, should not be regarded as an end in itself. Profits are indeed needed, not only to reward the risk taking of institutional and private investors but also to provide funds that can be ploughed back into organizations to exploit known opportunities and to research unknown ones. Thus top management should be strong on vision and determined to achieve real and sustained growth for their organizations. This is an active charge that calls for considerable skill in chaotic times.

9.5.2   Short-termism

Cyclical management strategies to generate impressive-looking profits in the short term can seriously damage the future wealth-creation ability of organizations. Tactics such as asset raiding and timely tuning of the books just before the year end are potentially disastrous unless significant proportions of the funds are used to fund medium to long-term growth. Dominant short-term thinking is, to an extent, forgivable in sound prosperous suppliers' markets. In the highly competitive buyers' markets of today it is a dangerous policy for Western organizations.

Frequently banks and money-lending institutions have been blamed for seeking short-term profits and for placing an unhealthy influence on organizations to deliver in the short term at the cost of sound performances in the longer term. The process of wealth creation is of vital importance to Western nations and should not be allowed to become mortgaged to the tactics of short-term speculators.

9.5.3   Long-termism

To safeguard the standards of living of our children and grandchildren requires a determined and sustained investment in the micro infrastructure that facilitates business performance. Investing in the education and training of human talent is necessary but not sufficient to arrest an escalating decline in real living standards. Such talent needs backing with project and research funding that may have a relatively long payback period. Charles Handy (1994) argues powerfully for the need for a greater philosophy that lies beyond much current practice. He advocates a new order in which business organizations are determined to establish an alternative set of practices that address wealth creation from a new perspective, reflecting continuity, connection (virtual integration) and purposeful direction.

Since going their separate ways after the success of *In Search of Excellence* (Peters and Waterman, 1982), it has been Peters (1987, 1993) who has enjoyed the higher profile with his arresting charismatic texts such as *Thriving on Chaos* and *Liberation Management*. Meanwhile Waterman (1987, 1992) produced some equally perceptive works such as *The Renewal Factor* and *Adhocracy: The Power to Change*. In his latest book *The Frontiers of Excellence* Waterman (1994) argues powerfully that today's top companies are the ones that put people first rather than bow to the short-term dictates of vociferous shareholders. Consequently these companies do well and achieve good profit performances that their shareholders applaud. Waterman's text is based on research into the achievements of the top 10 American companies. While the growing appreciation of the benefit of human capital is laudable, Waterman's book largely features successes that have been generated by the rank and file of corporations. He fails, however, satisfactorily to address the critical and more difficult issue of the power and authority games played by middle and senior management.

As a final thought before turning to the role of government authorities, it is appropriate to reflect that the 'free market' economies of the United Kingdom and the United

States have in recent years shown marked declines in relative performance. This has been most evident in a slowing down in the growth of real national incomes that has been characterized by a massive redistribution of wealth to privileged groups in society.

9.6 The purpose of government: redistribution of wealth or increasing national wealth levels?

9.6.1 Role of the government

The actions of the wealth creators are so essential to society that governments must inevitably assume a management role for the benefit of all citizens. This is, at the end of the day, a moral and political judgement. We believe that all have certain inalienable rights that are succinctly summarized in the original American Declaration of Independence. Furthermore it seems desirable that governments should be concerned with improving the lot of all their citizens through the exercise of a consistent, central and moral leadership.

This would seem logically to suggest a degree of planning – a word that is loaded with much false innuendo. After all, most private organizations ought to plan ahead. As many consultants are fond of quoting, 'to fail to plan is to plan to fail'. So the state needs to do some planning and with it some inevitable regulation. Experience since the Second World War has shown that the Communist system of rigid central planning failed disastrously. In comparison, the Western-style market economy has fared demonstrably better. This does not imply that everything should be left to market forces – some regulation is desirable. The trick for politicians is to discover the levers that manifestly benefit the long-term development of their economies. Continuously playing end-game strategies may secure the political future of the parties concerned but at the possible cost of inflicting serious long-term damage to national economies for decades.

9.6.2 Physical infrastructure

Maintaining the standard of the physical infrastructure should be a vital concern to any wealth-creating nation that wants to increase its standard of living. Good roads, railways, airports, harbours and coastal defences, and so on, are all matters of national importance. If these are allowed to decline through inadequate investment then this will damage the ability of countries to compete effectively in the outside world. Planning the maintenance and development of the physical infrastructure fabric is a key responsibility of all governments.

9.6.3 Human capital

The advent of the *value time*, as argued in this text, will place an increased emphasis on people. If the case for creativity becomes accepted, then business leaders and politicians throughout the West will need to adopt a positive approach to 'fostering human capital'. Brains will truly be seen as national assets.

UK perspective – free-wheeling backwards?

From these shores there is every reason for concern over the nation's poor international standing as measured against a selection of key 'world competitiveness factors' (see Table 9.1) in a recent study conducted by *The Economist* Advisory Group (1993). This compared the position of the country with that achieved by 22 other member states of the Organisation for Economic Co-operation and Development (OECD). The findings put the United Kingdom in thirteenth place. For a nation that was once the 'Workshop of the World' the United Kingdom is clearly far from being a world-class outfit now. Especially disturbing was the poor ranking achieved on the investing-in-people factor where the United Kingdom's performance achieved twentieth place.

Since the mid 1980s concern had been mounting in Government circles over the relatively poor international competitiveness of the UK. The Confederation of British Industry (CBI) drew attention to the importance of developing individuals to boost business performance and in 1991 the Government launched the 'Investors in People' initiative. This aims to provide a framework and structure for employers to use in developing their human resources strategies. It has four key principles:

1. An Investor in People makes a public commitment from the top to develop all employees to achieve its business objectives.
2. An Investor in People regularly reviews the training and development needs of all employees.
3. An Investor in People takes action to train and develop individuals on recruitment and throughout their employment.
4. An Investor in People evaluates the investment in training and development to assess achievement and improve future effectiveness.

Table 9.1   Key world competitiveness factors

World competitiveness factor	Position of the United Kingdom
Domestic economic strength	13
Internationalization	8
Government	6
Finance	8
Infrastructure	16
Management	16
Science and technology	14
People	20

The initiative is managed at a local level by the network of Training and Enterprise Councils (TECs). These are private companies contracted to the Government to provide for the training and enterprise in their areas. The key issue is to get the balance right between fostering education and training, and to assist people at all levels to improve their problem-solving skills.

For over 50 years the state has had a tradition of concern for its people from the cradle to the grave. As the country becomes progressively poorer (an inevitable result of a declining ability to compete overseas), so there is less money to spend on the social infrastructure. This has led to efforts to save money in all the main public services. In many cases investigative reports have identified big cost saving opportunities. As long as standards do not drop from actions imposed following these studies, it is clearly sensible to redeploy resources. In the case of wealth creators it is the end customers' opinions and their right of choice that determines whether business moves are successful. It seems that in many cases in the traditional public sector services, cost reduction has become the dominant target imposed by central Government who then act as judge and jury on their initiatives.

Stringent reductions in budgets, followed by severe cost cutting and the imposition of private sector management practice (traditional management response), has taken its toll on the breadth and quality of service coverage. Severe problems are currently facing the health service, local government, the police, the social service, and so on. Unless these bodies adopt the *creative management approach* they have little chance of avoiding serious damage to their service provision. The inevitable consequence will be an escalating decline in the overall social infrastructure of the country. Apart from the human pain and misery this will cause it will heavily damage the ability of the country to compete in overseas markets. Reduced and overstrained public services will ultimately lead to anarchy. It is not an argument as to whether a modern state should be paternal or free for all. Too much state paternalism is bad but so is too little, especially when much of it is to negate the very free enterprise it preaches.

Comment from America

Many of the competitive ills that face the United Kingdom are also evident in the United States. Peters (1993) concludes that two messages emerge from his analysis:

1. Keep the competitive juices flowing (encourage trade and competition).
2. Invest in brains (training, research and social security).

Quo vadis?

The *what* is the same on both sides of the Atlantic (declining competitiveness). It is hoped that this text will provide some insight and inspiration for readers in the West to overcome myopia. To appreciate reality (contextual awareness) and to harness their latent creativity. Understanding and actioning the *creative management response model* is a good start.

KEY TERMS

Gemeinschaft	Profit purpose
Gesellschaft	Short-termism
Managing trust	Long-termism
Attitude	Human capital

9.7 Summary

As the final years of the twentieth century flash by it is hoped that the wealth creators of the West will debate the five issues featured in this chapter. The buyers' markets that have dominated the 1990s are likely to become even more pronounced in the twenty-first century. Western management will need to develop a team-oriented approach in place of the traditional power/authority approach that so dominated the twentieth century. Smaller, flexible organizations will emerge to do battle in a worldwide marketplace.

The role and use of profits will be argued intently in the boardrooms of the West. At the same time, managers will have to think through the difficulty of finding constructive long-term strategies that can accommodate the requirement to maintain a short-term capability. Meanwhile democratic governments will have to grapple with the old chestnut of engineering short-term booms for political advantage or seeking to boost the real longer-term wealth of their countries.

The countdown has started and the new millennium approaches. Our children and grandchildren expect nothing less than our best thinking.

QUESTIONS

1. *Gesellschaft* vs *Gemeinschaft* – where do you stand and why?
2. Why do so many people think that 'politics' is a dirty word?
3. How would you promote and achieve better teamwork amongst wealth creators?
4. 'Organizational stability is traditionally expressed in bricks and mortar.' Why should things change now?
5. Will traditional institutions become virtual institutions? Argue your views.
6. Should organizations live from year to year or seek to take a longer-term view? Comment.
7. More for the few or more for the majority? How do you think that Western governments should approach their economic policies?
8. Human capital . . . will it ever be valued in the West? Your views, please?

References

The Economist Advisory Group (1993), 'Sharpening the competitive edge: the challenge for the UK's economic strategy in the 1990s', report, March, The Economist Publications, London.

Handy, C. (1994), *The Empty Raincoat*, London: Hutchinson.

Peters, T. (1987), *Thriving on Chaos*, New York: Knopf.

Peters, T. (1993), *Liberation Management*, London: Pan.

Peters, T. and Waterman, R. H. (1982), *In Search of Excellence*, New York: Harper & Row.

Tonnies, F. (1887), *Gemeinschaft und Gesellschaft*, Leipzig.

Waterman, R. H. (1987), *The Renewal Factor*, New York: W. W. Norton & Co.

Waterman, R. H. (1992), *Adhocracy: The power to Change*, New York: W. W. Norton & Co.

Waterman, R. H. (1994), *The Frontiers of Excellence*, London: Brealey; published in the United States as *What America Does Right*, New York: Norton.

10

Case studies

CONTENTS

10.1   Introduction   *345*

10.2   Analysis guide   *346*

10.3   Case study 1   Hallstead and Partners   *348*

10.4   Case study 2   Project control: walking on eggshells!   *349*

10.5   Case study 3   T. L. Rose plc   *351*

10.6   Case study 4   NJK plc   *353*

10.7   Case study 5   Millbank Foods plc   *358*

10.8   Case study 6   DHG Products plc   *362*

　　　　Appendix 10.1   Internal and external interface templates   *382*

Map: Chapter 10

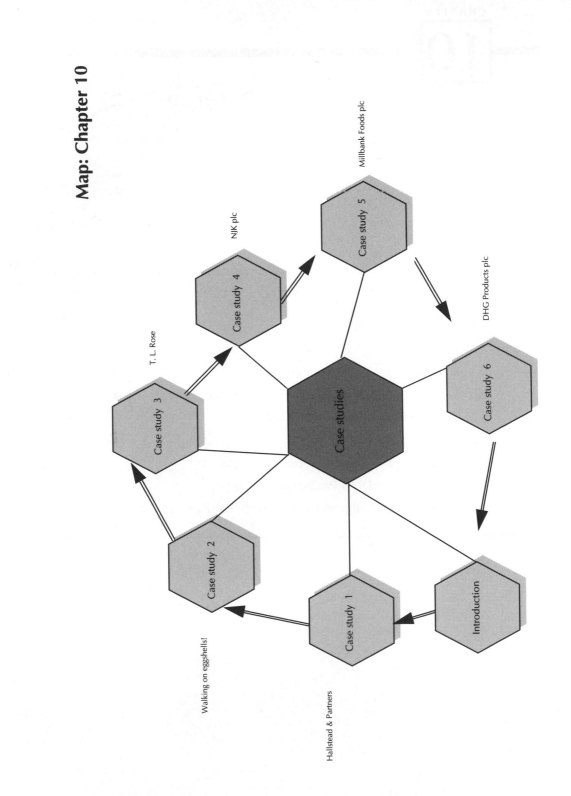

10.1   Introduction

This chapter gives readers an opportunity of applying the *creative management response* to six management situations. To honour confidentiality agreements, both corporate and personal names have been altered . The case studies have been chosen to offer a graded challenge. The first three cases are short presentations and feature three 'everyday' management situations. Case studies 4, 5 and 6 are more complex situations.

Case study 1   Hallstead & Partners

The setting is a regional office of a well-known firm of civil consulting engineers. The problem is one of steadily falling morale.

Case study 2   Project control: walking on eggshells!

This is set in a large corporation and features the frustration of a professional Project Engineer who finds it difficult to elicit a response for a client.

Case study 3   T. L. Rose

A tragic situation in which the professional lives of many are held to ransom by the political ambitions of a self-centred managing director and his friends. A classic case of 'how not to manage'.

Case study 4   NJK plc

This case features the difficulties that befell a determined manager who tried to apply CPS tools in order to give a boost to new product development activity in a small furniture manufacturer.

Case study 5   Millbank Foods plc

An opportunity to carry out an *organizational creativity audit* in a quality supplier in the convenience foods market.

Case study 6   DHG plc

This is a worked example of a consultancy exercise undertaken in a company manufacturing plastic components for the building and DIY markets. The action takes place shortly after the company had fought off a takeover bid.

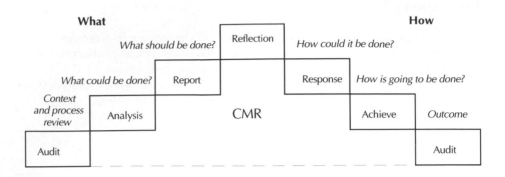

Figure 10.1 Example of a learning process sequence

10.2 Analysis guide

10.2.1 Getting started

Learning process sequence

Now that you have been introduced to the *creative management response approach* it is useful to get in some practice by having a go at applying it to some case material. Every reader of this text will have travelled along several learning curves during their lives. For example, some will have learnt to drive, some to master the rules and moves of a sporting activity, others to achieve excellence in a variety of skills of their choice. Whilst the skills will vary from activity to activity (the *what*), many will follow a similar process-learning approach (the *how*) as they seek to master new skills. Figure 10.1 illustrates an example of a basic learning process sequence.

The what *sequence*

A useful way of approaching this is to follow a three-stage approach: audit; analysis; and report.

Audit

This is a useful procedure to identify the key conceptual and process response (input and output – see Figure E.1 (p. 403) in the Epilogue). In other words, *where* are we now (*context*) and *what* management process skills (*TMC/Management response*) are available. Valuable *contextual* information can be secured by gathering information from the external interfaces (customers, suppliers, other publics – see pp. 312–14). Vital response data can be collected by internal individual, group and organizational audits (see main audits in the appendices of Chapters 4, 5 and 6 and the periodic audit suggestions in Chapters 8 and 9).

Table 10.1 **Case study: management pointers**

Management pointers	Topics	Notes
Audits	Various	See Chapters 4, 5, 6, 8
Problem solving	CPS	Ditto
Response skills input	Traditional management competencies	Appropriate? What training is required?
	Individual creativity	How enhance? See Chapter 4
	Group creativity	How enhance? See Chapter 5
	Organizational creativity	How enhance? See Chapter 6
	Management thinking	Hard vs soft. See Chapter 6
Response skills output	TMC	Sufficient
	CMR	Preferred?
Issues	Individual/group	See Chapters 8, 9
	Organization	See Chapters 8, 9
Interfaces (internal)	Individual/organization	See Chapters 7, 8
	Individual/group	See Chapters 7, 8
	Organization/group	See Chapters 7, 8
Interfaces (external)	Organization/customers	See Chapter 8
	Organization/suppliers	See Chapter 8
	Organization/publics	See Chapter 8

Analysis

Evaluate findings from the internal and external audits taking care to ensure that all crucial points are identified. You may like to use a relevance filter such as:

- What is essential (i.e. the case study material cannot be addressed unless these points are examined)?
- What is useful but not essential?
- What is either of minor importance or irrelevant?

Interim report

Summarize the key points in an interim report and then reflect on your findings, considering how you would progress the problem in question.

The how sequence

This too is a three-stage process: response; achievement; and audit.

Response

Will the prevalent traditional management competencies be sufficient? Do they need to be improved? Whilst they are necessary will they be sufficient to progress the issues in the cases? Is creative management needed and, if so, how might it be applied to the situation?

Achieve

What initiatives, programmes, will be needed to achieve progress? Wherever possible outline a brief action plan:

- How does the individual/group/organization intend to move forward?
- How is progress going to be measured?

Audit

Pick a suitable time period and then review progress since the initial audit exercises. What was good? What needs changing? What has been learnt?

A text guide to these sequences is contained in Table 10.1.

10.3   Case study 1   Hallstead and Partners

10.3.1   Background

Martin Brown holds the position of associate in a firm of consulting engineers that provides a wide range of civil engineering services from a network of regional offices. Martin is based at the Durham office that specializes in highway engineering and supervises a satellite highways team in the Darlington office. Following a spurt in design activity in 1992 the workload of the Durham office diminished and a small number of redundancies were declared. This caused morale to collapse at Durham. Meanwhile at Darlington spirits are high. A small team of 10 staff are ably led by Andrew MacLintock who enjoys a close working relationship with Martin.

News about the Durham office has reached Darlington and the staff have begun to fear redundancy. This has been made worse by the return of Jim Ryan, a 30-year-old technician who specializes in the traffic and economic aspects of the development of highway proposals. Jim has been unable to work regular hours consistently owing to the intermittent attacks of a mystery illness that was diagnosed two years ago as a post-viral syndrome. As a result the quality of his work has suffered. Eighteen months ago he accepted loss of permanent staff status and was re-engaged on a temporary contract basis whereby he is paid for the hours that he works. Martin values Jim's skills and would recommend a return to permanent status if he were able to work normally.

10.3.2   Problems, problems

Martin was alarmed at the falling morale in the Durham office and thought that although this was the symptom it was not the cause. He was aware that, so often, management at Hallstead's, under constant time pressure, tended to snatch at problems, and he suspected that their wish to manage instantly probably turned their attention to the wrong problems. Martin was determined not to fall into this trap and searched for a management method that would enable him to establish the exact nature of this problem.

Soon, fed on rumour from Durham, Martin's permanent staff at the Darlington office began to display mounting fears of redundancy as they were convinced that the permanent staff would be off-loaded before anyone touched Jim. Independently Martin had decided that the time had come to resolve the problem of how to accommodate Jim and felt that it might provide an excellent situation to explore with a basic creative problem-solving kit.

Another pressing personal concern troubling Martin was stress management. He felt under considerable stress when 'placed in the limelight', for example, when he was called upon to take questions following technical presentations. He felt that this would give him a good opportunity personally to explore some right-brain CPS tools and see if he could make an impact on his immediate scepticism, which he was open enough to believe might well be the result of a hard mind-set.

0.3.3 Task

How should Martin seek to discover the underlying causes of the falling morale in the Durham office? Try this exercise yourself using the starter tool kit described in Chapter 8. Now select a suitable CPS tracking design (see Chapter 5) to progress Martin's problem regarding the position of Jim Ryan. Lastly, what right-brain tools would you select to help Martin with his personal stress management concern?

10.4   Case study 2   Project control: walking on eggshells!

0.4.1 Introduction

This case addresses the question of how to get a response from a client during/after a project. The action takes place in a medium-sized company in the energy industry.

0.4.2 Background

Brian Lipton is a senior project engineer whose function is to produce project reports for his senior management to evaluate. Once a project proposal report has been completed and 'sent upstairs' Brian can do nothing until he is informed of the decision. Brian is conscientious and prepares his reports speedily and professionally, so as not unduly to delay his clients. He is frustrated at the amount of time it takes for him to receive an executive decision and hates keeping company consulting engineers and customers waiting a long time for a response. Time costs money and the consulting engineers are constantly ringing him up asking for news of projects that have been 'upstairs' for weeks.

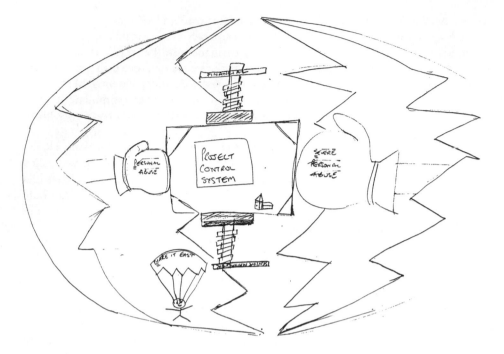

Figure 10.2 Sketching the situation

After yet another 'strong' call from one of the consulting engineers, Brian decides to try and get things moving. The question is how? Senior managers are important people and it is his yearly appraisal in a fortnight. He decides to 'doodle' and draw the situation as he sees it . . . hoping for inspiration. After completing a sketch which reflects his feeling that project control is a sensitive area – walking on eggshells! (see Figure 10.2) – he is startled by a knock on the door . . .

10.4.3 The consultancy

Imagine that you are a creative management consultant and that you have been referred to Brian by the company's training manager who is sympathetic to his plight. How would you advise Brian to proceed? He is anxious to involve other project engineers as the response problem is getting worse, and anyway there is safety in numbers! Brian wants to get some useful ideas. Choose an appropriate idea and then put together a proposal to take to his manager.

Prepare a brief report for Brian that simply sets out a suitable course of action. Explain in detail how it could be implemented.

10.5   Case study 3   T. L. Rose plc

10.5.1   Background

T. L. Rose plc supplies moulded thermoplastic components to the automotive industry. The company was founded 25 years ago when its parent organization, a well-known quality engineering firm, set it up to establish a position in a newly emerging market in the automotive industry for thermoplastic mouldings. Over the last five years the company's profitability has slipped badly and losses have mounted. Currently 90 people are directly employed.

10.5.2   The organization

The company is organized in three departments, as shown in Figure 10.3. The Original Equipment department (OE) supplies components to the surviving British automotive manufacturers and prides itself on the quality of the products that it makes. The Spare Parts department (SP) manufactures replacement parts to a lower standard than the OE Department and markets them to automotive after-sales parts shops and warehouses. The Customer Manufacturing department (CM) procures a range of spare parts and supplies private individual customers through direct marketing programmes.

The current managing director, Brian Whittle, joined the company five years ago from a well-known blue-chip manufacturer of industrial fasteners that had for the past 40 years operated in sellers' markets. His contract expires towards the end of the year. Since joining the company Brian has shaped the organization 'his way' and has deliberately placed his people in the key positions. He appointed Fred Smith, an arrogant, staunchly (upwardly) loyal individual, in charge of the CM department. Roy Waddle, who used to work as a clerk in the of SP department, was given the job of heading up the OE department. Clive White, a very rude man, worked with Brian in his previous appointment and was recruited specially to take charge of the SP department. Clive's behaviour causes everyone but himself to have problems, as does his constant interference in other

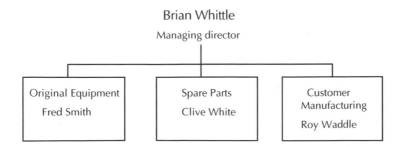

Figure 10.3   Operating departments of T. L. Rose plc

people's jobs whilst neglecting his own. He is firmly of the opinion that the rest of the world, bar one, his boss, is stupid.

10.5.3 The management style

Brian Whittle was a vain man who liked to get his own way and was convinced that his talents and experience were just what was needed by T. L. Rose. He managed by encouraging Clive, Fred and Roy to keep him secretly informed of all the gossip circulating in the company. Key managers working for his trusted lieutenants were encouraged to 'back the boss' by a well-worked patronage system. Staff who were seen as a threat were managed by a 'divide and rule policy' and were subjected to negative patronage (deliberately disadvantaged).

To enforce his position Brian had driven through an ambitious building programme and created a vast bureaucracy that was personally selected by him. By Easter 1994 administrative staff out numbered productive staff by a ratio of 8 to 1.

From time to time (usually after the chairman had requested it) Brian commissioned reports and surveys to discover how the staff felt about the company. The surveys were openly conducted and then sanitized if they failed to sing the praises of Brian's leadership loudly enough.

Brian's view of the company was that it was there primarily for him to build an outside reputation and, if possible, to enable him to achieve associate director posts in other companies. His real aim was to secure enough recognition where it counted to be recommended for an honour such as a knighthood.

10.5.4 The current situation

In the last five years markets for the company's traditional products have been very disappointing. Turnover has fallen and price competition has been getting tougher and tougher. Brian felt that this was just temporary and reassured his chairman and staff that he had already discerned the first clear signs of recovery. Markets would soon pick up and all would be well. Brian's view was that the best way to manage was to give as little information as possible to anyone, since that way 'you keep all your options open'. Pushed by his chairman for up-to-date market information, Brian was irritated to find that the basic statistics indicated a sharp decline in the company's fortunes over the next five years. His response was to encourage his loyal lieutenants to cover this up by issuing a series of 'bullish' reports that he laid before his chairman. If taxed by his boss he could always claim that one of his departmental heads had deliberately misled him or argue that the problem lay with his front-line troops and middle managers.

10.5.5 Task

Alarmed by his sixth sense that all was not as it seemed and in the full realization that Brian might well be presenting a very optimistic picture, the chairman has retained your services to investigate the company. He is intrigued by what he has heard about creative management and secretly hopes that the company can adopt it in time to prevent a crash that would be a serious embarrassment to the parent company. He has asked you to draft a brief, two-page statement explaining how you might apply the creative management model to T. L. Rose.

10.6 Case study 4   NJK plc

0.6.1 Introduction

This case study features a practical application of CPS tools in an environment where such methods are a novelty.

0.6.2 Background

NJK is a small subsidiary of a large international corporation and is a manufacturer of traditional quality upholstery. The company prides itself on its craft tradition and is well respected in the industry and trade. Since 1990 turnover has risen from £20 million to £23 million and there has been a steady decline in 'bottom line' profitability.

Robin Brown had been recently appointed as marketing director on the retirement a year ago of Sid Greenhall who had been a charismatic sales director with the company for over thirty years. Robin had been encouraged by Mark Kendrick, his managing director, to take a fresh look at the business. After conducting some basic survey work Robin began to get increasingly concerned that NJK was badly positioned in the market, with too narrow a product range and an overdependence on a small number of key accounts. He was confident that he could do something to broaden the distribution of the company's products in the short term but he knew that this would only be a holding operation. Substantial changes needed to be made both to the product portfolio and the *modus operandi* of the company.

0.6.3 Part 1   Gentle beginning . . .

Acutely aware of the conservative style of the other board directors and uncertain as to just how much support he could bank on from Mark, Robin decided to test the temperature of the water by seeking his agreement to call in a management consultant for some preliminary discussions. Mark was sceptical of the real need to spend money on this sort of thing but agreed reluctantly to Robin's request as long as he was discreet and did not upset the rest of the board. Aware of the reception that Robin's initiative would receive from his board, Mark decided that there was no need at the present to inform them of this matter.

The consultation

The consultant began by quizzing Robin on six counts:

1. The contextual factors impacting on the business.
2. The company's conventional management response style.
3. The need to introduce creativity to develop a new management response – the creative or contextual management response (CMR) to cope with the new stimuli impacting on the company's markets.
4. How personally to understand this new approach.
5. How to involve others in this approach.
6. How to change organizations by using this approach.

This really opened things up for Robin and confirmed his worst fears. He was convinced that something drastic had to be done to safeguard the medium/long-term future of the company. He knew that this would entail major surgery. Whilst it would not be difficult to convince his boardroom colleagues of the business problem that they were currently facing, it would not be easy to convince them that any big changes were necessary. They had all been closely connected with the industry for a long time and had been directors for 15 years. Two of the four had been on the board of NJK since the early 1970s. Robin knew that they would respond by saying that in times of crises wise organizations stick to their normal routine and that in the past they had seen several slow market periods come and go. All that was necessary was to keep going and the upturn would soon arrive.

Worried, Robin contacted the consultant. He was determined to win over both his managing director and his boardroom colleagues. He was well aware that this was a delicate mission. He was not facing a simple problem that would yield to logic, experience and precedent. This was a messy problem. The situation was characterized by a lack of clear predictive information, contradictory information within the company, complex people issues, and uncertainty as to the nature of the real problem facing the organization. Firm in his belief that an application of the traditional management solutions would not address the key issues, Robin felt that a new approach was needed. The consultant's description of CPS seemed to offer some hope.

Task I

Imagine that you are the consultant. Prepare a brief (maximum three-page) summary of the creative management response model and indicate how it might be applied to NJK.

10.6.4   Part 2   Slowly, slowly, catchee monkey . . .

The consultant cautioned Robin to proceed carefully with CPS in such a traditional company. He suggested that a good start could be made if Robin selected a work problem over which he had complete jurisdiction. This could be a people or a technical issue. He would then facilitate a series of CPS sessions and document the procedures and outcomes. On no account was Robin to try to evangelize his boardroom colleagues. The best way to gain their acceptance of the potential power of CPS was to present them with undeniable evidence of real successes. They would then be more open to consider the use of CPS tools to look at Robin's big concern. CPS is not a religion or a prescription; it is merely an effective way of tackling difficult intractable problems that tend to surround significant company readjustments.

Robin's choice

After long and careful consideration, the problem owner (Robin) chose a nagging departmental issue: 'How to increase the sales volume achieved by salesman A by 20 per cent to that regularly recorded by salesman B.'

Now two key decisions had to be taken:

1. What overall CPS design to use.
2. What individual CPS tools to select.

The consultant recommended the adoption of a traditional three stage model:

1. Problem evaluation/definition.
2. Idea generation.
3. Evaluation and realization.

This should ensure that there is little danger of the CPS exercise running into the idea generation stage before the nature and extent of the problem is fully agreed and understood. Furthermore this simple model can be recycled in any stage and encourages the use of convergent and divergent thinking (see Chapter 4).

The consultant then asked Robin to select a group of people to progress this problem. He nominated Ted Brookes, his sales manager, and himself and asked the consultant to be the third member of the group. The characteristics of the people involved were as follows:

Consultant	Ted	Robin
CPS experience.	No CPS experience.	No CPS experience.
Sound sales experience.	Sound sales experience.	Sales experience.
Positively biased.	Narrowly focused.	Positively biased.
Welcomes new ideas.	Dislikes 'newfangled' ideas.	Open to new ideas.

Robin could only sanction another three hours of the consultant's time before involving his managing director. Therefore selected CPS tools would have to be:

- Simple, requiring no training.
- Time efficient.
- Group CPS tools to take advantage of experience and personality styles of the three men.
- Selected to promote interactive activity.

Task II

Refer to the starter CPS tool kit outlined in Chapter 8. What tools would you select and in what order would you apply them to address the sales problem Robin described? Which master guides would be useful and why (see Chapters 4 and 5)?

10.6.5   CGPS Session One – Problem redefinition

The consultant suggested that it would be useful to use the starter CPS tool kit described in Chapter 8. He decided to use one hour for each stage of the traditional CPS model and to run these sessions on successive days. As Ted had a hard and 'narrow' view of the problem, the consultant used the first session to redefine the problem in order to test Robin's description and help to broaden the definition, as well as share an understanding of the issues. He selected the '*Why?*' and *Stakeholder* tools.

Under the skilled facilitation of the consultant, this session worked well. At first Ted felt that all this 'stuff' was a waste of time as he already knew what the problem was. What was more, some of the discussion and questioning seemed to be naive – especially from his perspective. However, as the session progressed, even Ted had to admit that something interesting was happening. Following the *Stakeholder* tool, the consultant returned to a brief phase of '*Why?*' questioning. Suddenly Ted became less flippant and jocular. He suggested that the problem statement should be changed to: 'How can Ted maintain his bonus at its current level?'

10.6.6   CGPS Session Two – Idea generation

The consultant now needed to progress the idea generating stage of the CPS exercise. Which tools would you advise him to use and in what combination? Make your choice from the tools listed below.

- Notebook.
- Private brainstorming.
- Analogies.
- Metaphors.
- Mind mapping.
- Reversal.
- Visual outliner.

Before you make your final selection you may like to turn to the more extensive Introductory CPS tool kit on pages 193–4. Which tools might be helpful here? By using the tools listed in the Introductory and Starter tool kits the consultant concluded the session with the *Colour code* tool to ensure that one of generated ideas was selected for the next session. One idea emerged as a clear winner: 'Increase the level and structuring of the company sales bonus scheme.' Ted then asked if he could copy down all the ideas on the *Mind map* as he reckoned that several held potential.

10.6.7   CGPS Session Three – Realization

The final session began with Ted making a presentation on how he thought that the winning idea could be realized. Afterwards the consultant introduced the *Advantage–Disadvantage* and *Comfort zone* tools and exposed Ted and Robin to *Force-field analysis*.

Robin was pleased with the outcome, and particularly so at the sudden conversion of Ted. The consultant too thought that the sessions had gone well and stressed that one of the greatest difficulties in introducing individuals to the CMR and CPS was their own reluctance 'to give it a go'. The consultant then encouraged Robin to practise using the introductory CPS tool kit at home and at work. Once he had generated a collection of work 'successes', it would start to become obvious that CPS worked and people would start to ask how he did it.

10.6.8   Follow up

Full of enthusiasm, hope and excitement Robin was pleased when Mark asked to discuss CPS. He felt that this was the time to persuade Mark to ask the consultant to run a CMR course for all board members. He had found his early interviews with the consultant to be particularly incisive and held great hopes that the CMR model could be adopted by TJK and used to change the way in which the company operated. Mark was enthusiastic and agreed to sound out the opinions of the other directors by the end of the week.

In the middle of the following week Mark dropped by to see Robin and said that all board members had flatly refused to take part in any CMR exercise. They were just too busy for this 'newfangled stuff'. It was all just too academic. 'That's not what I and others have found,' said Robin. 'I'm sorry, Robin, but no and that's my last word on the subject,' replied Mark.

Comment

The CMR model is an active one that demands an open mind and an initial commitment to try it. It is not an instant solution. Sometimes organizations appear to want to change and make all the right noises as long as it does not entail any commitment to change. This is sad, but it is their decision. In these circumstances the Robins of this world can do little except leave and join an organization with a more promising culture or resolve to act as a slow agent of change by adopting as much of the CMR approach as they can within the jurisdictions of their departments. This case study has indicated that CPS does have a positive payback. To maximize this, it is sensible to see that trusted individuals are educated in the basics of CMR and then trained in CPS facilitation skills.

The consultant noted the performance of TJK until it collapsed four years later. Interviewed on local radio the managing director put the blame on fierce domestic and global competition and added that 'the market doesn't seem to appreciate craft companies any more'. The only director to leave during this time was Robin Brown who joined an engineering company more in tune with his way of thinking.

End note

In recent years there has been a tendency for some top managers to ascribe the blame for their failure to carry through change in the organizations to the intransigence of their front-line and middle management personnel. Curiously enough, there have been a number of recent high-profile executive departures from some leading corporations including Digital, General Motors, IBM and Kodak in the USA and Midland Bank in the United Kingdom. (See article by Chistopher Lorenz, 'Top dogs bark up the wrong tree', published in the *Financial Times* on 3 June 1994).

Task III

1. Why do you think that TJK failed to take advantage of CMR and CPS at what turned out to be a critical time in its history?
2. Imagine yourself as Mark Kendrick. How would you have explained the advantages of the CMR model to the board? How would you have won them over?

10.7 Case study 5   Millbank Foods plc

10.7.1 Background

This company is a subsidiary of a large, fast-moving goods corporation and manufactures a wide range of convenience foods. Millbank distribute their products to a wide variety of customers including airlines, cafés, fast food restaurants, hotels and guest houses, supermarkets and a host of other contract markets including schools, rest homes and universities. Over the last 10 to 15 years the company has been very successful and has enjoyed a healthy growth in profits and turnover. However, the directors are concerned that many of their traditional 'bread and butter' lines are now meeting stiffer and stiffer competition, placing a considerable strain on profit margins.

The company have just received a report from the market research agency that they commissioned to carry out some *ad hoc* research. The findings were disturbing as they indicated that the company, whilst good at manufacturing and supplying standard lines, had a disappointing record in the introduction of new 'winner' products into the marketplace.

As might be expected from a respected 'name' in the industry, the company used the best conventional management practices and had a competent new product development department. Several new product ideas were generated every year by the department but few passed right through their system into the marketplace, and those that did often seemed to arrive just behind the opposition.

The market research agency's report sparked off heated debate in the boardroom, as the agency had severely questioned not the technical expertise of the company but their management style. Worried by pressure from the parent company to sort itself out, the board decided to retain the services of a new management consultant. The traditional consultancies all seemed to sing similar songs and they were looking for a fresh approach. They wanted to sharpen their 'market edge' and be well positioned to do well in the next five years.

10.7.2 Fear of flying or fear of falling

The consultant's proposal indicated that it would be necessary for them to:

- Conduct a complex set of audits.
- Key/direct learning to specific company projects.
- Design and run an introductory weekend for the directors.
- Design and run an introductory course for key senior managers.
- Design and run introductory courses for key middle managers.
- Design and run CPS facilitation courses for nominated personnel.
- Provide a backstop or support facility for two to three years.

The Millbank board were caught in two minds. To agree to the consultant's programme would draw him close to the company and would expose the complete organizational executive. There were bound to be people problems to cope with as a result of this, and some of the board were very uneasy as to the wisdom of letting an outsider get an inside track into the company. However, to refuse this opportunity would possibly be a mistake. It was clear that the company were under pressure with their traditional lines and on reflection they admitted that there was a problem introducing new products. After a rigorous debate the managing director put the proposal to retain the services of the consultant to the vote and gained the board's approval. Sitting in his office after the meeting he wondered what the consultant was going to find. It had been a difficult year since he joined the board and he was secretly pleased that what had started out as a market research exercise had rung so many of the right bells. Furthermore this consultancy programme would impress his corporate masters.

10.7.3 Reviewing the situation

Millbank Foods was regarded in the market as being a solid, quality manufacturer that had built up a strong brand name. As such, competitors regarded them as a target and over the past two to three years the company had been losing market share in many of its standard lines. The company viewed itself as an old-fashioned firm that included only the very best ingredients in all its products. The market research agency had rigorously argued the case for the introduction of a range of new cheaper products that would reach parts of the market which Millbank had always sought to avoid in the past. Low-cost products would lower the tone of the company.

The company was established in 1927 by a farmer Thomas Millbank as a supplier of quality tinned foods. After the Second World War the snacks and convenience foods output began to take off and the company moved very successfully into dried, vacuum-packed ('boil in the bag'), and frozen products by a deliberate policy of making their well-advertised leading lines available in a number of different convenience formats. Gradually the traditional tinned-food trade declined but a comprehensive range of quality, basic 'cook's' products are still sold in large numbers to institutional markets. Since an impressive automation programme in the mid-1960s, which was ahead of its time, the company had invested in up-to-date technology on a regular basis. Ever since most people in the company could remember, the business had maintained a country-fresh–country goodness projection. This had featured strongly in the advertising and promotional programmes and was seen as a strong plus factor that had built up the brand's quality image.

Thomas Millbank had given the company a strong sense of duty and had established a benevolent but essentially autocratic approach to management. Until his retirement in 1967 he had insisted on personally signing off all new products to be sure that they were up to the Millbank standard. His son succeeded him and rigidly maintained this practice until illness forced him to leave the business in 1985. The next managing director was an internal appointment who held the position for two years and left suddenly after the company was taken over by a large multinational food corporation in 1987. The current managing director, a bright youthful man in his late forties, was appointed in 1993.

At the time of the takeover the new owners decided to leave the management of the company alone as it had been achieving very respectable 'bottom line' performances. The Millbank management style had been set by the founder Thomas Millbank who instituted an essentially autocratic but benevolent style. The early success of the company had led progressively to the strongly held belief within Millbanks that people would still queue for its products because they represented the very best of their kind. Times might change, but people still needed to buy quality food products. All competition was seen as inferior by definition and foreign products just had to have a 'freshness problem'!

Millbanks had built up a reputation for being a hard but fair employer. Staff were encouraged to develop themselves to their full potential and the Training Department was well funded. It was expected to provide quality education and training but not to encourage individuals to challenge the company lore. Annual appraisals were seen as important and every manager was expected to take a real interest in the development of their people. Efficiency was a key company word and the Training Department had gained a reputation for the excellence of its traditional management courses in assertiveness and meetings, stress, and time management. The newly appointed training manager was trying to interest the personnel director in problem-solving courses.

The company enjoyed an excellent reputation for the standard of its training and for the quality of its promotional programmes. However, it remained essentially a power/

authority, supply-based business that tended to take customers for granted. After all, the Millbank name was so good and people would always want good products. The company had achieved BS 5750 and ISO 9006 approval and even the Training Department had been awarded BS 5750.

Whilst these quality successes were genuine, they all helped to harden the mind-set that Millbanks were simply the best. Team working was actively encouraged and cross-functional teams operated in many aspects of the business. Despite this, many felt constrained from doing anything that could be construed by staff senior to them to be critical. There was a clearly defined pecking order in the company and people were expected to know their place. Promotion to and through the management ranks was generally from within. Most employees welcomed the chance to belong to a cross-functional team, such as Quality Circle, but many were frustrated in their inability to influence events personally if participation or 'sign off' was needed by any of the senior management team. Whilst individuals in theory had the scope to exercise their specific flare and talents, few did for fear of 'crossing' the management. As the competition that the company was facing increased in severity and product coverage, the paternalistic style of the management was damaging Millbank's market responses.

Accordingly, the overall level of creativity in the company was low to basic, except for those in the Marketing Department who were paid to be creative. However, most employees regarded the company as a good place to work. Fringe benefits were excellent and the company put generous amounts of money into its Sports and Social Club and into local community clubs and functions.

The personnel director was particularly pleased to hear of the retention of the consultant, as for some time he had harboured a growing concern that the company management style needed changing to reflect the challenges of the present. Currently he felt that it largely reflected the successes of the past. He was sympathetic to the arguments presented by his training manager for the introduction of companywide courses on problem solving but was somewhat unsure as to how to explain the need, as he saw it, to his fellow directors.

The senior management were a close-knit team and genuinely respected each other's talents, and felt overall that the company was in safe hands as long as they were in charge. The view from the boardroom window seemed rosy. As far as they could tell the interfaces between individuals in the company seemed sound and the organization was lending considerable time and resource support to the working of the cross-functional teams and other group activities. Looking beyond the factory complex, Millbank's policy of building up excellent relationships with its customers and suppliers over the years had proved a sound investment. The present troubles were merely 'blips' that would disappear as the economy picked up. It was a time for solidarity and for riding out the choppy water, not a time to expose the company to a new management craze.

The view of the rank and file was of a company that had been ascendant in the past and was now in danger of keeling over and sinking. Fear of redundancy was high and confidence in the managerial skills of the board was waning fast. There was a growing concern that although Millbanks had always been a model employer, the company's business problems would prompt the holding corporation to take drastic action. They welcomed the news that a consultant was going to take a real hard look at the 'way we do things' and make recommendations to sharpen up their responses. Cynics felt that this amounted to legalized job cutting, but most hoped secretly that the board would 'come alive' and respond appropriately, for they liked working for Millbanks.

10.7.4 Task

1. Imagine that you are the consultant that has been retained by Millbank. Using the case study material and the primary and secondary factors of the CMR model developed in this text carry out a creativity audit of the company. What other audits might be useful and why?
2. Now write a brief report, say, two to three pages, presenting your recommendations to the company and make some rough notes that will help you to explain and justify them at a specially convened meeting of the board.
3. Finally prepare an outline of a two- or three-year programme that will introduce the CMR model to the company. What problems would you anticipate and how do you intend to handle them?

10.8 Case study 6   DHG Products plc

10.8.1 Background

The company

DHG Products are one of the leading manufacturers of plastic products for the building and DIY markets in the UK. Since 1990 the company have returned an excellent financial performance despite the relatively depressed state of the UK economy. The senior management of the company are determined to maintain DHG Products' performance in the latter half of the decade and are becoming increasingly worried by the escalating competitive pressure on their business. The company is based in the Midlands in a modern factory complex and has additional sites in the North and Home Counties. It has an excellent national reputation for its staff training programmes. At present 500 people are employed on the company's main site. There are 10 directors who head up five divisions that are managed by a total of 40 managers.

For years DHG Products has been regarded nationally as a quality company. It has won many accolades both for its business performance and for its generous employee benefits. The board are aware of the importance of maintaining excellent relations with the local community and are an enthusiastic sponsor of a variety of local events.

Aware of the need to retain their profits in rapidly deteriorating business conditions the directors decided to build on the successes of their Quality Programme by seeking to improve the management performance of the organization at every level. To this end they scoured the market for a reputable firm of management consultants who could help them to sharpen up their management skills over the next two to three years.

The personnel director, who had just completed his first year with the company, whilst settled and generally quite happy in his job, sensed that all was not well with the company's approach to general management. He knew that his managing director had similar feelings. After searching the market for three weeks he strongly recommended to the board that they retain the services of a new consultancy firm that had generated some genuine results and enthusiasm by introducing organizations to creative management.

10.8.2 The brief

Warwick Consultants were asked to submit a proposal for a programme to update the general management skills of the entire company in order equip them to deal successfully with the severe competitive pressures that were expected to impact on DHG Products in the latter half of the 1990s.

After visiting all the sites of the company Warwick Consultants submitted the following proposal:

1. To undertake a comprehensive audit of the general management approach of the board of directors, all middle managers, and a sample of 60 rank-and-file employees.
2. To analyze the results and present a report to the board summarizing the findings.
3. To provide a brief presentation indicating how they would propose to develop DHG Products' staff.

The proposal was accepted and Warwick Consultants were retained to the excitement of the personnel director, the expectation of the managing director, and the apprehension of most of the rest of the board and a substantial number of the middle managers. Meanwhile, the rank and file remained sceptical. Whilst the consultants' approach seemed novel, 'Would our lot really change their ways?'

10.8.3 The audit

Warwick Consultants gained board approval to:

1. Carry out an organizational creativity audit.
2. Analyze the results.
3. Examine critical component factors affecting the management responses of the organization at all levels.
4. Examine the internal and external interfaces of importance to the company.

Organizational creativity audit

The organizational creativity audit (see Chapter 6, Appendix 6.1) statement sheet was given to:

- all directors (10);
- all middle managers (40); and

Table 10.2 **Organizational summary audit results**

Factor	Directors	Middle managers	Factory and office workers (FOWs)
Context	70 : 30	68.5 : 31.5	73.7 : 26.3
Management response	90 : 10	38.5 : 61.5	33.7 : 66.3
Creativity	48 : 52	17.0 : 83.0	12.6 : 87.4
CMRI	80 : 20	32.0 : 68.0	24.0 : 76.0
CMRG	68 : 32	49.5 : 50.5	28.0 : 72.0
CMRO	90 : 10	30.5 : 69.5	14.3 : 85.7

- a sample of 60 factory and office workers spread over the company's operating sites (hereafter referred to as 'FOWs'.)

The audit addressed the six primary creative management factors:

1. Contextual awareness and understanding of the company's market position (see Chapters 1 and 2).
2. Management responses of the organization (see Chapter 3).
3. Creativity – awareness and understanding (see Chapter 4).
4. Individual creative management response (CMRI) – attitudes and perceptions (see Chapter 4).
5. Group creative management response (CMRG) – attitudes and perceptions (see Chapter 5).
6. Organizational creative management response (CMRO) – attitudes and perceptions (see Chapter 6).

Table 10.2 summarizes the responses to the six primary creative management factors.

Explanation of scoring system

The figures declared for each factor and each group of employees are percentages that indicate the degree of positivity/negativity to the creative management response model primary factors. A score of 50 : 50 indicates a neutral response to a factor. If the number on the left is greater than 50 it indicates a positive response. The larger the number, the stronger the response. Similarly, the larger the number on the right, the weaker the perceived factor response.

Summary results

Taking *context*, it appears that the directors were very aware of its importance (70 per cent score), the middle managers were slightly less aware (68.5 per cent score) and the FOWs recorded the greatest degree of awareness (73.7 per cent score). Looking at the *management response* factors reveals some interesting points. The directors felt that they were very positive about the general management direction they were giving to the organization (90 per cent score). However, the middle managers (38.5 per cent score) and FOWs (33.7 per cent score) were by no means as impressed. As far as promoting *creativity* was concerned, the directors were roughly evenly split on their achievements (48.0 : 52.0 per cent score) and the middle managers (17 per cent score) and FOWs (12.6 per cent score) were in no doubt as to their lack of success on this factor.

The *CMRI* ratings reveal that the directors felt that they were encouraging creativity (80 per cent score) but it is clear from the audit that the middle managers (32 per cent score) and FOWs (24 per cent score) had a very different view. Turning to group management activity (*CMRG*) the results reveal that even the directors recognized their failings (40 per cent score). The ratings for the middle managers was better (47.5 per cent score) but still unexciting. The FOWs (33.3 per cent score) were clearly not at all impressed. Lastly, the *CMRO* scores. The directors are firm in their conviction that the organization is serving the company well (90 per cent score). Both the middle managers and the FOWs seemed disillusioned and demotivated. It is clear that the view from the executive suite was seriously out of line – an indication, perhaps, of a large degree of general management myopia. A dangerous condition for a company that was engaged in tough competitive battles in the market.

10.8.4   Taking a closer look

Context

A quick scan down the data in Table 10.3 shows that all three groups of employees were broadly in agreement over the *context* statement set, though, surprisingly, two-thirds of the middle managers did not know how the market regarded the company.

Management response

However, a very different story is revealed from the findings of the *management response* statement set. All three groups agree that the company offered standard training programmes (Statement 2 in organizational creativity audit – see p. 234) but disagreed over

Table 10.3   **Contextual appreciation**

Statement	Positive regard	Negative regard
Supply-oriented	All	
Service-oriented	All	
Domestic organization	All	
External factor influences	All	
Know what market thinks of company	Dir./FOWs	

Note: Dir. = directors; MM = middle management; FOWs = factory and office workers.

Table 10.4 **Management response findings**

Statement	Positive regard	Negative regard
Standard training programmes	All	
Belief in tailor-made training	Directors	MM/FOWs
Hard systems thinking	Directors	MM/FOWs
Customers first: organization second	Directors	MM/FOWs
Open management system	Directors	MM/FOWs

Note: MM = middle management; FOWs = factory and office workers.

the principle that training programmes should be individually tailored to employees' needs (Statement 8). Further questioning of the directors revealed that they viewed training on the basis of a budget figure (5 per cent of turnover), and from the broad principle that everyone ought to receive the same package according to their level within the organization. The middle managers and FOWs felt that training should be individually tailored as employees had different needs.

Further differences between the directors and the other two groups were evident from the responses to the management thinking probe (Statement 14). All the directors reckoned that they used hard systems thinking whereas the other groups, though subjected to the hard control systems from the executive suite, preferred to use softer systems on the shop floor and in the company's offices. The difference between the directors and the other groups widened still further when the audit probed the basic purpose of the organization. The directors felt that their organization put the customers first; the other groups thought that the senior management seemed to go out of its way to preserve the special status and practices of the executive. Finally, the top management believed that they practised an open management style (Statement 25). The middle managers and FOWs saw it completely the other way round. Table 10.4 summarizes the variances between the perceptions of the three groups.

Creativity

On the point of awareness (Statement 3) the audit showed that all three survey groups recorded negative responses. However, the board indicated that they valued it (Statement 9), but this was not the impression that the other two groups had formed. The directors stated that they were prepared to evaluate new methods of management thinking (Statement 15). The other groups registered strong negative responses – 'We don't believe that anyone will change the way we do things here!' On the matters of the provision of space for CPS sessions (Statement 20) and the provision of funds for a creativity centre (Statement 26) the replies were largely negative but top management was evenly split on the funding issue. Table 10.5 summarizes the views of the three groups.

The first set of CMR model factors mainly reflected the current practices of the organization (the *what*) whereas the second set of factors (see below) provided indicators as to *how* the organization might change.

Table 10.5   **Creative awareness findings**

Statement	Positive regard	Negative regard
Awareness of creativity		All
Value creativity	Directors	MM/FOWs
New management thinking	Directors	MM/FOWs
Space for CPS		Dir./MM/FOWs
Creativity centre funding	Directors	Dir./MM/FOWs

Note: Dir. = directors; MM = middle management; FOWs = factory and office workers.

Table 10.6   **Summary of CMRI findings**

Statement	Positive regard	Negative regard
Encouraging creativity		All
Open communication	Directors	MM/FOWs
Provide secure jobs	Directors	MM/FOWs
Cultivate trusting environment	Directors	MM/FOWs
Provide good working conditions	Directors	MM/FOWs

Note: MM = middle management; FOWs = factory and office workers.

CMRI

On the question of whether individual directors actively encouraged creativity amongst their staff, the responses (Statement 4) largely indicated that they did not. This was echoed in the replies drawn from the middle managers and FOWs. When it came to communication the top management team were convinced that they practised a policy of open communication (Statement 10) which stood in stark contrast to the perception of the other groups. DHG Products had traditionally had a policy of seeking to provide secure employment. This was currently under a great deal of strain as market conditions for the company's products became more and more difficult. Nonetheless the directors felt that they were doing their best (Statement 16). The other groups, in contrast, were becoming increasingly concerned as to the security of their jobs. Top management believed that they enjoyed the trust of their employees (Statement 21) and were very upset to discover that this was definitely not the case. However, all three groups agreed that the organization did provide a good working environment (Statement 27). Table 10.6 summarizes the CMRI findings.

CMRG

The directors were aware that good teamwork counts for much in any organization and had tried to promote it across the traditional management divides in the company. After installing a 'tweaked' standard quality package they had also invested heavily in a

Table 10.7   **Summary of CMRG findings**

Statement	Positive regard	Negative regard
Support group working	Dir./MM	FOWs
Provide suitable training	Directors	MM/FOWs
Provide time for creative work	Directors	MM/FOWs
Open communications	Directors	MM/FOWs
Reward creative groups		Dir./MM/FOWs

Note: Dir. = directors; MM = middle management; FOWs = factory and office workers.

Table 10.8   **Summary of CMRO findings**

Statement	Positive regard	Negative regard
Value staff	Directors	MM/FOWs
Service organization for people	Directors	MM/FOWs
Learning organization	Directors	MM/FOWs
Tolerating mistakes	Dir./MM/FOWs	MM

Note: Dir. = directors; MM = middle management; FOWs = factory and office workers.

re-engineering exercise. Conscious of the dangers of overmanaging these programmes, they had decided unanimously to sit back and let the staff manage the programmes themselves. The audit revealed that both the directors and the middle management were actively supporting team working (Statement 5). The FOWs responded very negatively to this probe. On the question of the suitability of the training provision, only the directors believed that the company was providing the right packages (Statement 11). Whilst the top management team believed that they were gifted management technicians, they admitted that they did not provide time for creative group work. In contrast the middle managers and FOWs frequently found that they had awkward problems to solve on the shop floor and did provide time for individuals and groups to contribute creative solutions (Statement 17). On the communication issue (Statement 22), the directors felt that they used open channels, the middle managers were roughly equally divided on the issue and the FOWs admitted that their communications were closed. Lastly, all three groups admitted that the fruits of group creativity were rarely rewarded (Statement 28). Table 10.7 summarizes the CMRG findings.

CMRO

The directors felt that they did value the staff (Statement 6), but this was not the perception of the other two groups. They also believed that they tried to match the organization to the needs of the employees (Statement 12) and this too was not how the middle managers and the FOWs saw it. This was also the case on the learning organization probe (Statement 23).

However, the pattern changed on the tolerance probe (Statement 29). Both the directors and the middle managers tolerated mistakes but the FOWs did not. Lastly, on the question of loyalty upwards and downwards the results indicated that the directors and FOWs encouraged it and the middle managers were split on the issue (Statement 30). Table 10.8 summarizes the CMRO audit findings.

10.8.5   Probing deeper

Given the findings from the organizational creativity audit Warwick Consultants decided to take a closer look at the secondary and tertiary factor components of the CMR model (see Chapter 7).

Context

The audit confirmed the general air of anxiety around the company regarding trading conditions as all could see that the volume and value of orders were slumping. DHG Products was a paternalistic company that was used to firm order books for its products and set great store on its constructive role in the local communities of its factory sites. They were not the sort of company that would panic in a hurry. Surely things would get better soon, but a number of the directors were starting to get seriously worried.

Management response

Whilst the company had carried out a detailed survey of their marketing prospects they had not reviewed *how* they managed their affairs. There was increasing evidence to suggest that in the light of difficult, ever more frequent, changes in the external factors impacting on their operations, they needed to review their management process responses. They were already a market-oriented company but could probably be more imaginative in their marketing activity. However, Warwick Consultants' brief was to review their management approach and skill sets. Basic education in the fundamentals of the traditional management competencies was firmly installed in the company. The problem clearly identified by the consultants was that once educated, individuals were often 'culturally dissuaded' from practising 'management' on the shop floor and in the offices. Furthermore there appeared to be an unwritten convention that the extent to which an individual was expected to manage depended on the size of the office that they were allocated. Good management theory needed to be coupled to a steady stream of project work for the theory to come alive. The whole organization was littered with mind-sets. Traditional shop floor workers did not want to waste their time doing 'management', they just wanted to get on with their jobs and earn their wages. Management were seen as people you turned to when you were in trouble. They were then seen as the people who caused the trouble. They were a despised class. Some groups – usually technical ones and informal day-to-day ones convened to tackle immediate issues – did work well on the shop floor. The quality and re-engineering initiatives of the management were essentially seen as irritants and as tinkerings with the organizational process architecture, with no real direction from management. What made matters worse was that both of these programmes had resulted in an escalation in paperwork and administrative tasks.

Individual middle managers were worried about the future of their jobs and did not want to be seen to be rocking the boat with any new initiatives; they complied with instructions from above and moaned in the cafeteria and the toilets. The directors were getting very concerned, but tried to keep their thoughts and fears to themselves. The feeling that the company was having a lean time sped through the organization at breakneck speed, whilst the top management maintained stiff upper lips and made periodic 'assurance announcements'.

Creativity

This was largely misunderstood in the organization at all levels. The top management were just somewhat more polished in the expression of their puzzlement! Warwick Consultants were convinced that a release of guided creativity would come to the aid of the organization. Real teamwork needed to be demonstrated and that meant breaking through the cultural barriers. Some managers privately realized that the ship was in danger of going down but preferred to dine in the manager's canteen rather than do their stint at manning the pumps!

The company also seemed to waste a lot of time by repeated application of conventional methods that had worked in the past, trial and error activity, and in endless searches for textbook formulas for resolving difficult and increasingly messy problems. The whole company would benefit from some basic CPS instruction, but before that could be done successfully all employees would need some basic education and training to trigger their appreciation of the potential of CPS sessions.

10.8.6 Interim report

Warwick Consultants expected no difficulty in making the academic argument for the introduction and release of creative management. They did expect some awkward and probing questions from the board as to *how* it might be done. Assuming that the cognitive argument on the contextual, management response and creativity counts would not present too much trouble, Warwick Consultants turned to the issues surrounding the introduction of the CMR model.

They proposed an experiential approach that would address the matter from the following three perspectives: individual; group; and organization. In each case this would involve tackling such live issues as *confidence* and *willingness to change* and would need careful handling if a successful path was to be cut through some heavy individual, group and organizational obstacles. The key to working the CMR model lay in the key management interfaces (see Chapter 8):

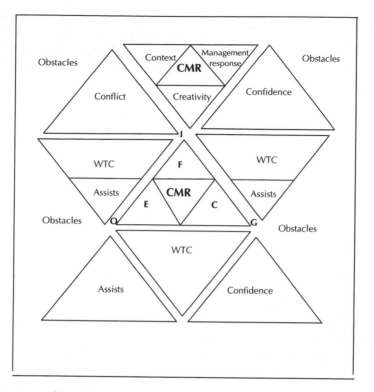

Figure 10.4   Internal interfaces

Internal	**External**
Individual/organization	Organization/customers
Individual/group	Organization/suppliers
Organization/group	Organization/other publics

and by the attention to some important individual/group and organizational 'how to' issues. Figure 10.4 illustrates the complete set of internal interfaces.

10.8.7   Exploring the internal interfaces

Individual/organization (I/O in Figure 10.4)

Confidence
Faced as they were with difficult operating conditions in their traditional markets, DHG Products had suffered a drop in corporate morale. This in turn had caused a drop in group and individual confidence. For any new management process system to take off it

is essential to bolster the confidence of all employees. Introducing a new system in these relatively depressed times was bound to present problems. The organizational creativity audit had highlighted serious discontinuities in the existing management response system. These would have to be addressed to foster a recovery in *self-confidence*. Further work would need to be done to build a new culture in order to lower the barriers, real and imagined, between the rank and file and middle management, and between them and the directors, providing the board retained their commitment to funding a broad range of activities for their employees and, in the local area (*organizational benevolence*), for their staff and the local area. *Confidence* has to be tended carefully and steadily and takes a long time to show firm growth. Clumsy, ill-timed decisions and poor communications in the heat of a crisis can severely damage confidence in a few seconds.

Willingness to change (WTC)

Experience has shown that even after the above factors have been addressed, it may still be impossible to progress any real change. A lot of people moan about things in organizations and, curiously enough, many just like to be able to moan about something. Taking the best 'moanies' away can actually make some people more stubborn over accepting change. The attraction of the old ways is that at least they are known. However, if individuals can be *freed* from a restrictive system and directly challenged to achieve (hopefully creatively), the adrenaline rises and creativity starts to be released. The important thing though is to sustain *encouragement*. If this is neglected, then at the first sign of its absence the whole process becomes vulnerable and may collapse at the first hurdle.

Obstacles

Obstacles can be many and varied. The most common ones encountered in change programmes using the CMR model are:

- insecurity;
- perception;
- emotion;
- communication;
- culture;
- vision; and
- trust.

These are a formidable collection of potential blockages in their own right. Interacting with others they can assume a mighty drag on progress. It is impossible to neutralize all these downdraught forces. The aim must be to weaken as many of them as possible whilst generating a firm and steady updraught of creative activity. *Communication, culture, vision* and *trust* are key topics for executive attention.

Communication

Communication needs to be regular and informative, and must reach the whole of the intended audience. Many a boardroom in the past has thought that it has communicated properly, only to find that a message that should have circulated widely has got lost in some middle management drawer. Poor communication is often the symptom of deeper ills. People need communication and if it is denied it will be invented. If this happens it rarely flatters managers and organizations.

Culture

Whilst it is true that culture evolves over time, decisive adaptations or revolutions need to be purposefully and confidently introduced. This is especially true of management systems; they must be seen to be managed. DHG Products need to acquire a team culture and, what's more, a cross-functional one. The old familiar power/authority culture needs to give way to a softer organizational structure.

Vision

DHG Products saw itself as one of the leading manufacturers of plastic components for the building and DIY trades. Whilst it was true that they did command a substantial market share, they were also under attack from competitors, both domestic and foreign, who were equalling their quality standards but at cheaper prices. The company used its brand name in the fight against these competitors, but were a little naive in their belief that established brand names can see organizations through most business droughts. The crucial question was how the market perceived them. The reflected view of others is always more realistic than internal beliefs and judgements.

Trust

The results of the opening creativity audit revealed a huge trust problem (see Chapters 8 and 9). What is more, when things get tough trust obstacles assume ever greater heights. At DHG Products a substantial number of employees were living in fear regarding their jobs. So introducing a new system of management was likely to be identified as legalized headcount reduction even if this was not the case. Unless there is a certain level of residual trust in an organization (the degree varies from organization to organization), it is difficult to create the right conditions for the release of creativity.

Individual and group (I/G in Figure 10.4)

Confidence

The individual/organization interface provides both the individual and the organization with a set of bearings. The individual looks for a sense of support from the organization in that acceptable 'hygiene' factors are supplied together with a sense of corporate membership. To manage effectively within the organization usually requires interacting with other individuals and this raises a new set of confidence dynamics in addition to those of *self-confidence* and *boss-support*. Individuals need to feel assured that the groups that they associate with are supported meaningfully by the organization when they are on organizational business. This implies that groups should have clearly defined aims and objectives which relate to the overall published corporate vision. Groups are suboperating units of the organization that need to be supported by the greater organization in much the same way as the basic support that individuals require (*group support*).

Furthermore the deliberations and achievements of groups need to be recognized and rewarded (*group support*).

Willingness to change (WTC)

To benefit from the creative management approach groups should be given the *freedom* to cross departmental and management rankings. True cross-functional teams are one of the highest expressions of teamwork. Employees assume both an individual and team identity and concentrate their energies and talents on the problems at hand rather than in 'pecking order' distractions. Contrary to the fears of many managers, being willing to play a team role is very rewarding and tends to raise individual managers' reputations in the eyes of the rank and file. Team games really demand a *challenge* and need some focus for their activities. Sports teams have the primary *challenge* of winning but also second-ary ones such as holding their own under difficult circumstances. Without a realistic *challenge* teamwork can so easily disintegrate into loose uncoordinated associations. DHG Products had many cross-functional teams but several had no real sense of purpose. They just met to shift bits of paper around. This seemed to be a strong grouse from all those connected with the Quality Programme. This was a pity because good Quality programmes should be more than administrative exercises. Lastly, groups – as with individuals – need to be *encouraged* all the time.

Obstacles

The ones that seem to crop up time and time again are:

- vision;
- perception;
- interaction level;
- rule-bound;
- confusion;
- insecurity;
- CPS skill level; and
- trust.

Good *visions* contain freedom for expression, a challenge, and encouragement to suc-ceed. They are dynamic expressions of intent rather than limp slogans such as 'our aim is to be the best', which is a *what* statement that does not give any direction as to the *how*. Furthermore visions should be defined at the individual, group and organizational levels. Some potentially creative groups flounder because individual members find it difficult to respond when challenged by unfamiliar stimuli such as right-brain thinking. This is normally a *perceptual* problem that requires gentle attention from the team leader. Some individuals are just shy in public and easily lose their *perceptive* skills as they seek the comfort of well-known interventions. Strange as it may seem, it is common for individ-uals to long for a chance to escape the system and its associated procedures (*rule-bound*), but then to feel the need (if something does not happen in a twinkling of an eye in a CPS session) to revert to organizational mode. *Confusion* and *insecurity* often go together and frequently are the result of poor *creative facilitation* skills. Another regular obstacle to creative group work occurs as the result of real or imagined poor CPS skills. The quite joyous truth is that most individuals and groups can make amazing headway by keeping things simple. The starter tool kit (described in Chapter 8) should help most people straight away. Lastly, the trust issue again. Sensitive creative facilitators should be aware that individuals take to CPS tools and creative management concepts in their own time. Overforcing the pace can lead to a breakdown of trust within the group as individuals lose their trust in the facilitator.

Organization/Group (O/G in Figure 10.4)

Confidence

Organizational support and reward are mighty motivators at the organization/group interface. Groups need to know that their work is appreciated by the organization. Some organizations expect groups to report regularly on their progress in the company broad-sheet or newspaper. This may seem like college stuff but regular information updates on group activities are good news items. In these days of sophisticated desktop publishing software, most organizations should be able to produce in-house news-sheets. As a powerful statement of the two-way support flow between organizations and groups, organizations can give groups the choice as to whether they wish to be identified as official or fringe entities. If they opt for the former, the organization can provide them with stationery that carries both the corporate and working group address. At DHG Products the estimating group is referred to as the DHG Products Estimating Group. This may sound like badge engineering but it has its place in organizations, where it is important to demonstrate adoption.

Willingness to change (WTC)

The main problems here tend to arise at the organizational end, especially when groups petition for a change in the operating system to accommodate an urgent group need. In this case, if the freedom can be won and a target performance agreed (the *challenge*), it is up to the group to sustain the *encouragement* to achieve.

Obstacles

Obstacles caused by *vision, culture, trust, CPS skills, rule-bound, insecurity* and *confusion* problems affect all three interfaces. The obstacles that have emerged as being particularly relevant to the organizational/group interface concern:

- staff appreciation;
- quick solution; and
- management thinking.

There have been cases where individuals who have given their services freely to groups have later felt excluded from the limelight upon the successful completion of a project because all the appreciation has been directed at the group or the leader or the facilitator of the group, or even at the department or manager that has sponsored the group. It is important for organizations to remember that even team players need to feel valued as individuals (*staff appreciation*). From time to time organizations have adopted part answers and ideas from groups as '*Quick solutions*', and then ceremoniously dropped them later, and, in the worst cases, maybe criticized the groups for any problems that might have arisen. This is largely a question of judgement and sensitivity. If the entire organization is converting to a softer systems approach, repeated returns to the old hard *management thinking* for short-term gains can severely damage organizational/group relations.

Appendix 10.1 carries a set of completed templates for DHG Products' internal interfaces plus a set of blanks for your own use.

10.8.8 Exploring the external interfaces

External interfaces cover the relationships between the organization and its customers, suppliers, and other publics. Figure 10.5 demonstrates these external interfaces and the factors that influence them.

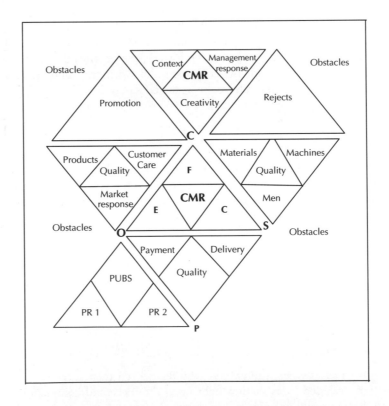

Figure 10.5 External interfaces and the factors that influence them

Organization/customers

Quality
Maintaining quality standards has always been important but is particularly so in these days of buyers' markets. DHG Products have installed a respectable quality package and after some initial difficulties things seem to be improving, except that the rank and file are constantly complaining that the directors do not seem to be working the systems themselves! Behaviour breeds behaviour and so observance breeds observance.

Market research
Before the initial visit of the consultant, the marketing director was at odds with his boardroom colleagues over the need to increase his expenditure on market research during the turndown in business expectations. Retaining firm market information is important at all times but particularly when things are rough.

Customer care
Conscious of the need to do all he could to retain his customers, the marketing director of DHG Products had just increased his customer care budget. Though he was getting increasingly worried at his ability to compete on value terms with his leading competitors.

Product/service offering
The marketing director was at odds with the sales director over the basic product offering. His colleague thought that the company's products were just the best and that was that. The business would come back. The marketing director doubted this and repeatedly asked for increased effort from the sales department only to be met with accusations that the marketing target were just unrealizable. The marketing director felt aggrieved, as he believed that the sales director was basically an 'order taker' rather than a 'sales achiever'.

Promotion
Tightening finances had meant that the marketing director had to lose some of his promotion budget in order to maintain his market research programme. The next few months were going to be very difficult. If ever there was a time for creative marketing it was now!

Organization/Suppliers

For several years DHG Products had pursued an enlightened policy of getting close to their main suppliers. There were no obvious material shortages on the horizon but the cost of raw materials continued to rise as the pressure mounted on market prices. To escape this financial pinch the technical director had been trying for some time to involve a number of suppliers in a new product development programme he was masterminding. He was hopeful that the CMR approach would help him speed up the new product development turnround time. A slight but mounting irritation he had was that the financial director was slowing down the *payments* to suppliers as part of his effort to manage the company's cash flow. The technical director was concerned that this might prejudice *deliveries* and material *quality* standards.

Organization/publics

DHG Products had been at the centre of a recent takeover battle and had just managed to fight off the bid. This had drained its cash reserves and subjected the company to hostile scrutiny by the City. It was as a result of this that the company had sought the services of a consultant to review their management systems. This they hoped would result in an improved performance that would attract the attention of the City observers.

As previously mentioned, the company had earned a very favourable reputation as a result of its activities in the local communities near its sites. To boost the overall image of the company they employed a *press relations* consultant (*PR1*) and a *public relations* (*PR2*) expert whom they had found in the midst of the takeover battle.

Customers/suppliers

As stated above, maintaining customer quality was of paramount importance. Recently there had been some poor-quality material deliveries that had escaped the company quality control procedures and gone right through its activities into the market. So far several return loads had to be accepted owing to poor finished-product quality standards. This had caused a double shock as the faulty product runs had not been picked up at either the material input or product output end of the production line. A rigorous review was in progress to discover how these quality failings had occurred.

10.8.9 The diagnosis

DHG Products was clearly in need of some professional help to revamp its management processes. The consultants reported that the company needed to sharpen up its affairs if it wished to hold its own in the marketplace. Most of the board were of the opinion that all that was needed was a little patience as they battled to hold down costs during a temporary turndown in the marketplace. The consultants had changed all this powerfully by their explanation of the CMR model. Now the board could see that there had been a far-reaching set of changes in their markets and that continuing change was going to be the norm rather than an exception to the rule. At first they were very sensitive when the consultants started to look at their management performance. They were convinced that they had to address their management responses in the light of these changing market stimuli. The managing director had felt this in his bones for the last two years but it had taken the takeover crisis to trigger the approach to the consultants.

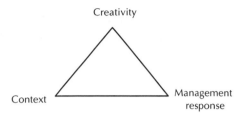

Figure 10.6   Slide 1: Creative management (the *what*) primary factors

The presentation

Warwick Consultants presented the essentials of their findings in a sequence of four slides.

1. Creative management response (*what*) primary factors.
2. Creative management response (primary factors – *what* plus *how*).
3. Creative management response change model.
4. Creative management response training model.

In today's very competitive buyers' markets DHG Products will have to become highly contextually aware. This means keeping a close eye on all the main global influences that affect the business. These contextual forces are not a temporary phenomenon but will be a permanent feature of the business world facing the company for the foreseeable future. In the light of these changing external forces the company will have to reorientate its management approach and sharpen up its traditional management competencies. To survive in the last half of the 1990s and to generate acceptably healthy profits will call for a sustained commitment to innovation. This will entail a complete re-examination of the company's product and market portfolio and a complete reorientation of the management process architecture. Innovation is needed in both the traditional new product development sense and in the process sense. To compete successfully in the market, DHG Products will have to earn a strong positive differentiation in crowded markets. Such a market edge will depend on the company's ability consistently to deliver value packages to customers. Creativity is required to 'imagineer' (see Chapter 5) the products and services that the company offers. Its capture and use will call for a totally new perspective regarding management practice (see Figure 10.6).

Creativity is a personal quality that for long has been heavily constrained by hard management systems. As it is imperative that creativity is encouraged, supported and rewarded, it will be necessary to educate and train the complete workforce to rediscover and harness its potential. Additional training will be needed to smooth the introduction of creative thinking into the operations of company groups (see Figure 10.7).

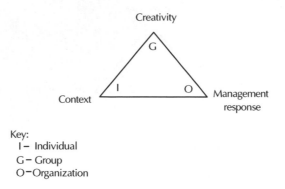

Figure 10.7 Slide 2: Creative management response (primary factors)

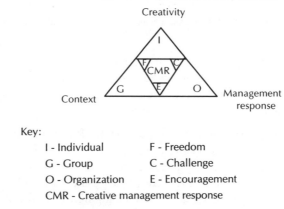

Key:

I - Individual	F - Freedom
G - Group	C - Challenge
O - Organization	E - Encouragement
CMR - Creative management response	

Figure 10.8 Slide 3: Creative management response change model

Further training will be required to change the organizational culture from that of a paternalistic, benevolent, power/authority operation to a creatively managed, team-based operation.

The contextual or creative management approach is a complex soft system that is a function of contextual, traditional management responses and creativity inputs. The output depends on:

- the release of creative talent in individuals;
- and then into the group situation;
- and so into the architecture of the organization.

Creative management is energized by creating conditions in which individuals, at all levels within the company, experience the *freedom* to release their creativity in peer group sessions where every individual enjoys the same status. This process requires ambitious

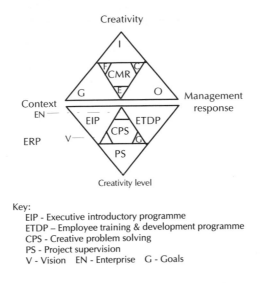

Figure 10.9   Slide 4: Creative management response training model

but realizable targets to be set (*challenge*) and for the organization to grant continuous support and *encouragement* (see Figure 10.8).

This will entail an executive introductory programme (EIP) for senior management as the introduction and fostering of the creative management process needs to be positively managed. On completion of the initial EIP programme every employee should be positively encouraged to attend a staggered series of employee training and development programmes. (ETDP). This includes the senior management and is designed to acquaint and equip the DHG Products staff with the necessary concepts and operational tools. In addition it will be necessary for nominated employees to be trained in the techniques of creative facilitation in order to lead creative problem solving sessions (CPS). It is strongly recommended that the entire training package is 'earthed' in a series of company projects that will be run under the process supervision (PS) and guidance of Warwick Consultants. These sessions will generate the innovative effort that will translate the corporate vision sets (individual, group and organizational) into value product and services packages which are necessary if the company is to survive. In modern market conditions, the realization of the DHG Products goals is dependent on the adoption of a different, softer management process approach that will maximize the creativity of its operations. The CMR approach has the potential to deliver, but it requires a sustained commitment (see Figure 10.9).

APPENDIX 10.1

Individual/group interface – 1

CMR factors		Individual	Group
Confidence	Self-confidence	Low, but varies from day to day	Some groups OK, others very gossipy
	Boss support	OK, but what is going on upstairs?	Team is holding together
	Group support	My groups are all OK	Not too bad, but things could be better
	Group recognition	Yes, my groups are all OK	Would like more interest from above
Willingness to change	Freedom	I'm not sure now	We must change
	Challenge	To keep my job	We must get the company back into good profits
	Encouragement	Not a lot	Individuals' heads are down
Assists	Freedom to contribute	Yes, but why should I?	Yes, but some people are inhibited especially now
	Recognized influence	They pay my wages	Yes, most groups are valued, I think
	Work environment	Very good	More places to sit and discuss things would be appreciated

Individual/group interface – 1

CMR factors		Individual	Group
Confidence	Self-confidence		
	Boss support		
	Group support		
	Group recognition		
Willingness to change	Freedom		
	Challenge		
	Encouragement		
Assists	Freedom to contribute		
	Recognized influence		
	Work environment		

Individual/group interface – 2

CMR factors		Individual	Group
Obstacles	Insecurity	Mounting . . . We just do our jobs now	We are doing what we can
	Perception	The company is dying	We're Ok. We will pull through
	Emotion	Depression	Worried but determined
	Communication	Awful and getting worse	It's hard to know what to tell them . . .
	Vision	Is there one?	Trying to find it
	Cultural	Fine, we get on OK	Groups layered like the dining rooms
	Work environment	Good	More places to talk and think would be nice
	Low participation	Because of poor morale	A problem but we're trying
	Poor interaction	Low morale	Problem-solving skills needed
	Rule-bound	Not really, but hide behind them	We make our own rules
	Trust	I don't	A difficult one . . .
	Confusion	I'm Ok, but top management seem confused	No, we know where we are going
	Informality	Best really	Pulling rank can be a problem

Individual/group interface – 2

CMR factors		Individual	Group
Obstacles	Insecurity		
	Perception		
	Emotion		
	Communication		
	Vision		
	Cultural		
	Work environment		
	Low participation		
	Poor interaction		
	Rule-bound		
	Trust		
	Confusion		
	Informality		

Individual/organizational interface – 1

CMR factors		Individual	Organization
Context	Time dimension	Supply and buy	Traditional?
	Wealth creation	Product supply	Product supply
	External factors	Market quiet	Aware of competition and STEP factors
Management response	TMC	Confusion between directors, managers and rank and file	Benevolent power/authority. Good name for training
	Business orientation	Marketing/supply?	Traditional old fashioned sales director – order taker?
	Mind-sets	Amongst rank and file, middle managers and directors	Widely held belief that company are the best in the country
Creativity	Creative awareness	Minimal – practically non-existent	Directors – yes; others – no
	Creativity level	Base/residual	Basic – little real usage
	CPS	Basic	No formal CPS but some semi-active
	Total thinking	Unaware	Unaware; directors partially aware

Individual/organizational interface – 1

CMR factors		Individual	Organization
Context	Time dimension		
	Wealth creation		
	External factors		
Management response	TMC		
	Business orientation		
	Mind-sets		
Creativity	Creative awareness		
	Creativity level		
	CPS		
	Total thinking		

Individual organization interface – 2

CMR factors		Individual	Organization
Confidence	Self-confidence	Low, individuals concerned for jobs	Morale low, exhaustion after takeover battle
	Boss support	OK within peer groups, but up and down in the company?	OK with top management
	Organization support	Still basically OK, but rumours around	Directors determined to hold the line
	Benevolence	Benefits appreciated but more management expected	Board want to keep things steady
Willingness to change	Freedom	Prisoners of the system	Change needed, but how?
	Challenge	To save job. Looking for a challenge	Saving the company; don't want to downsize
	Encouragement	Looking to the senior management	After surviving the takeover bid
Assists	Freedom to contribute	Not sure. Think that it is a time to keep head down	Why don't employees make good suggestions?
	Recognized influence	Does the organization know that I work here?	More recognition required?
	Trust	Until recently	Need to build it up
	Work environment	Good	Amongst the best
	Informality	Between mates, but not with management	Believe managers are approachable
	Tolerance of mistakes	Got to be careful these days	Yes, we are a learning company

Individual/organization interface – 2

CMR factors		Individual	Organization
Confidence	Self-confidence		
	Boss support		
	Organization support		
	Benevolence		
Willingness to change	Freedom		
	Challenge		
	Encouragement		
Assists	Freedom to contribute		
	Recognized influence		
	Trust		
	Work environment		
	Informality		
	Tolerance of mistakes		

Individual/organization interface – 3

CMR factors		Individual	Organization
Obstacles	Insecurity	Yes, most feel very insecure	We're trying to improve things
	Perception	What's going on?	Market difficult, business poor, problems
	Emotion	Running, but not running well	The bid was an emotional time for us all
	Communication	What communication?	Information flow needs looking at
	Vision	Are we the best? Why the takeover attempt?	To be the best in the business next year again
	Cultural	Management is too tight and too remote	Yes, we need to change but how?
	Work environment	Pretty good – we just need top management	Try to maintain good standards
	Staff appreciation	I wish they did	We value all our staff
	Quick solution	All the time	Only when we have to
	Management thinking	I wish they would see the real world	Theory sound but I wish practice would fit in with it
	Rule-bound	All over the place!	Yes, we've systems, but people can think too!
	Trust	I used to be Ok on this one, but now . . .	OK, we think. We've not declared any huge redundancies yet

Individual/organization interface – 3

CMR factors		Individual	Organization
Obstacles	Insecurity		
	Perception		
	Emotion		
	Communication		
	Vision		
	Cultural		
	Work environment		
	Staff appreciation		
	Quick solution		
	Management thinking		
	Rule-bound		
	Trust		

Organization/group interface – 1

CMR factors		Organization	Group
Confidence	Organization support	Support all groups	Generally OK
	Benevolence	Money is tight but our benefit policy does boost confidence	Benefits are pretty good
	Group support	We value them	Yes, but we'd like a better budget
	Group recognition	Yes, all are recognized	Yes
Willingness to change	Freedom	Yes, I think so	Which way?
	Challenge	We need to issue some	Let's have some
	Encouragement	We do	Sometimes not very obvious
Assists	Work environment	Our factories are pretty good	More places to think
	Informality	We are approachable	Yes, but top management never come down and see us. We always have to group to them
	Tolerance of mistakes	Yes, we are	Yes, as long as they are not too serious

Organization/group interface – 1

Responses	Factor influences	Individual	Organization
Confidence	Organization support		
	Organization benevolence		
	Group support		
	Group recognition		
Willingness to change	Freedom		
	Challenge		
	Encouragement		
Assists	Work environment		
	Informality		
	Learning organization		
	Tolerance of mistakes		

Organization/group interface – 2

CMR factors		Organization	Group
Obstacles	Staff appreciation	We'd like to do more	Top management needs to show it values group work
	Vision	To be the best	To innovate and meet high-quality standards
	Cultural	Seen as hard and systems-driven	Softer cultures
	Quick solution	We have to from time to time	We seem to do a lot of fire-fighting
	Management thinking	We are all MBAs	Too many theories
	Rule-bound	Within reason	Imprisoned
	Confusion	No, not exactly	What are they up to?
	Insecurity	No	Yes
	Work environment	Fine	Not bad, but not good. Need more thinking space
	Low participation	We keep to ourselves	No, not really
	Poor interaction	We are very busy	We wish that they would come out of the cupboard
	Informality	Yes	We don't wear suits every day!

Organization/group interface – 2

CMR factors		Organization	Group
Obstacles	Staff appreciation		
	Vision		
	Cultural		
	Quick solution		
	Management thinking		
	Rule-bound		
	Confusion		
	Insecurity		
	Work environment		
	Low participation		
	Poor interaction		
	Informality		

Organization/customer interface

Primary factors	Secondary factors	Findings
Quality	BS 5750	
	ISO 9006	
	Other	Quality package installed
Marketing research	Ongoing	Marketing Director finding it difficult to persuade Board of the importance of market research
	Ad hoc	
Customer care	Satisfactory	No need to be improved to counter competition
	Excellent	
	Delightful	
Product/service offering	Clear/unclear	Marketing Director at odds with the Sales Director over basic product offering.
Presentation/ promotion	Clear/unclear consistent/ inconsistent	Weakened recently as the Marketing Director has transferred funds to pay for market research

Organization/customer interface

Primary factors	Secondary factors	Findings
Quality	BS 5750	
	ISO 9006	
	Other	
Marketing research	Ongoing	
	Ad hoc	
Customer care	Satisfactory	
	Excellent	
	Delightful	
Product/service offering	Clear/unclear	
Presentation/ promotion	Clear/unclear consistent/inconsistent	

Organization/other publics interface

Primary factors	Secondary factors	Findings
Press relations	Continuous	
	Frequently	
	Infrequently	Marketing Director anxious to improve
Public relations	Continuous	
	Frequently	
	Infrequently	Ditto
Publics	Shareholders	City Observers expect better management performance
	Local community	Relationships excellent
	Local government	OK
	National government	OK
	International	Company not very export minded
	Environmental	Awareness and response improving

Organization/other publics interface

Primary factors	Secondary factors	Findings
Press relations	Continuous	
	Frequently	
	Infrequently	
Public relations	Continuous	
	Frequently	
	Infrequently	
Publics	Shareholders	
	Local community	
	Local government	
	National government	
	International	
	Environmental	

Organization/supplier interface

Primary factors	Secondary factors	Findings
Quality	BS 5750	Key suppliers all have BS 5750
	ISO 9006	
	Other	Some have other packages
Delivery	JIT	
	Delayed	
Project policy	Early involvement	In new product development – Technical Director
	Continuous involvement	Company aware of systems in supplier's companies
Communication	Casual	
	Continuous	Generally good but could be improved
Payment	Poor	
	Up to 90 days	
	Over 90 days	Finance Director trying to lengthen payment – quality risks?

Organization/supplier interface

Primary factors	Secondary factors	Findings
Quality	BS 5750	
	ISO 9006	
	Other	
Delivery	JIT	
	Delayed	
Project policy	Early involvement	
	Continuous involvement	
Communication	Casual	
	Continuous	
Payment/Prior	Up to 90 days	
	Over 90 days	

Epilogue

The daily pattern of our lives can become so familiar, so normal, that we can easily slip into a routine that for many becomes a Monday to Friday ritual. Then the weekend arrives and there is a two-day break in the pattern before the next week begins. Although most of us try to resist it, the majority lead programmed lives and we adapt our behavioural responses accordingly. In a sense we become robots occupying ourselves with the modern equivalent of man's age-old occupation of hunting, gathering and exchanging material wealth. In this preoccupation it is so easy for even the liveliest of minds to get stuck in a rut.

If sudden changes occur in the context of our lives we do our best to adapt our behaviour to cope with the disturbance. If repeated and progressively violent change occurs our responses will come under increasing strain. Some will win through but others, sadly, will become casualties to the cold, impersonal, forces of change. In this scenario, sadness, depression and deprivation affect us all and totally overwhelm many. In such a situation, the natural wealth-creating aspirations and talents of the community are blighted and frustrated. If things do not improve relatively quickly, then this despair will threaten community life, and, if not checked, will eventually lead to degradation in the social order.

Change is inevitable; the real issue is how to adapt our behaviour. This requires giving due consideration to our real contextual position and to the response mechanism we have to hand. If the external factors impacting on our wealth-creating activities are chaotic, then we need to address how we might change our responses. This text has been an excursion in search of a new management approach that will preserve and prosper wealth creation in the West, and so protect and enhance the living standards of the people (see Figure P.1 in the Prologue).

To this end, the text (see Figure E.1) journeys through some dark and threatening places (*stimuli*) but also travels through some bright and challenging country where individuals, groups and organizations are experimenting with new (in normal business usage) creative response patterns (*process skills input*). Halfway through, the text stops to review progress and to define a new response for managers – the creative management response (*process skills output*).

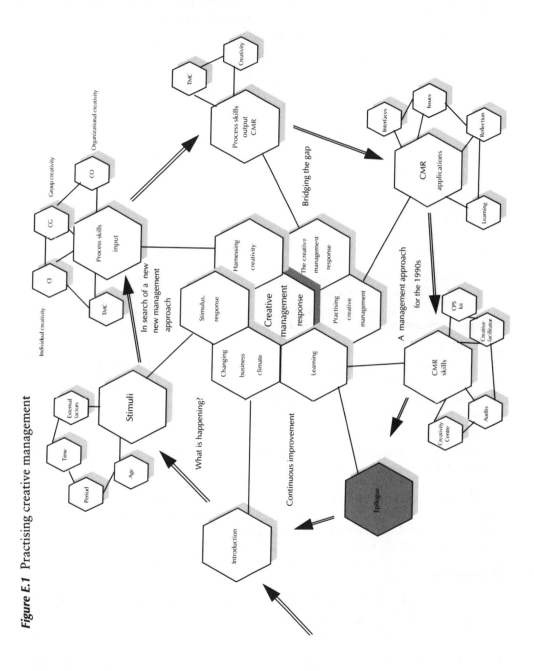

Figure E.1 Practising creative management

At this point readers are given the opportunity of following a new path that has been cut by individuals, groups and organizations who have experimented with the CMR approach (*CMR applications*). As the reader returns to everyday life, he or she is presented with a CMR skill set that includes:

- A basic creative problem-solving kit (CPS).
- An introductory CPS kit.
- Personal, group and organizational creativity audits.
- A set of CMR component factor cards.
- A guide to creative facilitation.
- A description of a creativity centre.

I hope that readers will have found the personal freedom to use these resources as they respond to their own challenges.

End note

Some quotations from recent issues of the *Harvard Business Review*:

> Most layoffs at large companies have been the fault of managers who fell asleep at the wheel and missed the turn off for the future.
>
> If managers don't have detailed answers to questions about the future, their companies can't expect to be market leaders. (Hamel and Prahalad, 1994)

> If all competitors fight with the same weapons, the natural result is commoditization and declining profit margins.
>
> Creative Managers must bring insights and expertise to their customers' problems. (Gouillart and Sturdivant, 1994)

> Many successful management innovations have come from companies that have adapted not adopted ideas. (Nohria and Berkley, 1994)

Finally, for further information please contact the author at: Durham University Business School, Mill Hill Lane, Durham DH1 3LB, UK, Tel (0191) 374 2211, Fax (0191) 374 3748, Email M.R.V. Goodman@durham.ac.uk.

References

Gouillart, F. J. and Sturdivant, F. D. (1994), 'Spend a day in the life of your customers', *Harvard Business Review*, 72 (1), Jan.–Feb.

Hamel, G. and Prahalad, C. K. (1994), 'Competing for the future', *Harvard Business Review*, 72 (4), July–Aug.

Nohria, N. and Berkley, J. D. (1994), 'What ever happened to the take-charge manager?', *Harvard Business Review*, 72 (1), Jan.–Feb.

Author index

Ackoff, R. L. 212, 214–215
Adair, J. 94, 147
Amabile, T. M. 156
Argyris, C. and Schon, D. 217
Armstrong, M. 132

Baden-Fuller, C., and Stopford, J. 55
Barnard, C. 70, 232
Baron, F. 98
Bass, B. M. 71, 81
Bate, R. and Morris, J. 31
Belasco, J. A. 303
Belbin, M. 94, 97
Bennis, W. and Nanus, B. 81
Blake, R. R. and Mouton, J. S. 76
Beer, S. 71, 232
Belasco, J. A. 81
Berle, A. and Means, G. 70
Boden, M. A. 132
Boulding, K. 207
Briggs-McCaulley 94
Briggs-Meyer 97
Brown, M. 55
Buxton, T., Chapman, P. and Temple, P. 248
Buzan, T. 131
Buzan, T. and Buzan, B., 114 118

Carey, S. 133
Case, R. 133
Caulkin, S. 225
Chandler, A. D. Jr. 55
Checkland, P. 214–215
Churchman, C. W. 214
Clark, K. and Fujimoto, T. 313
Clark, R. 232
Crosby, P. B. 44, 46, 55, 228

deBono, E. 87, 132
DE Geus, A. 232

Delbecq and Van de Ven 116
Drucker, P. 18, 33, 55, 71, 218, 232
Dumas, A. 148, 214

Eberle, R. 169
Economist, The 23, 324, 338
Ekvall, G. 156
Encyclopaedia Britannica 87,101

Fayol, H. 70–71
Feigenbaum, A. V. 228
Fiedler, F. 71
Financial Times 248
Firestein R. L. and Treffinger, D. J. 189
Flood, R. and Carson, E. 232
Follett, M. P. 70–71
Foremski, T. 174
Fortune, 18 29
French, W. 216
French, W, and Bell, C. 216
Freud, S. 95
Fritz, A. 171
Fukuyama, F. 55

Garnham A. and Oakhill, J. 88, 156
Gawain, S. 189
Gazis, D. C. 24
George, C. S. 81
Getzels, J. W. and Csikszentmihalyi, M. 89
Getzels, J. W. and Jackson, P. W. 98
Glouberman, D. 189
Goman, C. K 88, 120, 121, 151
Gordon, W. J. 164
Gouillart, F. J. and Sturdivant, F.D. 404
Guilford, J. 89

Hamel, G. and Prahalad, C. K. 81, 404
Handy, C. 22, 33, 50, 335–336
Harvey-Jones, Sir, J. 81
Hayes, R. and Aberbathy, W. 218, 224

Heimal, C. 99
Hellriegel, D. & Slocum, J. W. 88
Hertzberg, F. J. 71
Hill, W. E. 109
Honey, P. and Mumford, A. 94
Hout, T., Porter, M. E. and Rudden, E. 33
Hudson, L. 89

Imai, M. 42
Isenberg, D. J. 133

Janis, I. L. 149
Jensen, J. V. 112
Johnson, P. 33
Jones, D. E. H. 133
Jones, L. 190
Jung, C.G. 95–97
Juran, J. M. 42–43, 228

Kaletsky, A. 46
Kanter, R. M. 81, 324
Kaufmann, G. and Gronhaug, K. 133
Kennedy, C. 232
Kennedy, P. 55
Kerr, C. 33
Kilman, R. 232
Kim, D. 201, 217
King, N. and Anderson, N. 181
Kipling, R. 164, 167, 169
Kirton, M. J. 94, 96–97
Koch, J. V. 33
Koestler, A. 87
Kolb, D. 94, 97, 117, 166
Kosslyn, S. M. 190
Kotter, J. P. 81
Kreitner, R. 88, 117, 126, 160
Kwak, N. and DeLurgio, S. 232

Lerner A. J. and Lowe, F. 115
Levitt, T. 33, 40
Loon, H. W. 33
Lorenz, C. 245, 319
Lovelace, R. F. 322

McClelland, D.C. and Winter D. G., 71
McGregor, D. 218
McKenney, J. L. and Keen, P. C. W. 131
McShane, J. 133
MacKinnon, D. W. 89
Maier, N.R.F. 189
Maier, N.R.F., Julius, M. and Thurber, J. 86, 88
Majaro, S., 71 168–169
Maleki, R. A. 42
March, J. G. and Simon, H. A. 71
Maslow, A. 71, 247
Mayo, G. E. 70
Meakin, R. 224
Mintzberg, H., 71 133

Mitroff, I. I. 205
Monden, Y. 46
Morgan, G 71, 171
Morland, R. L. and Levine, J. M. 190
Myers-Briggs 95
Myers-Briggs McCaulley, M. H. 94

Nadler, D. A., and Tushman, M. L. 81, 304
Nilson, T. H. 48
Nohria, N. and Berkeley, J. D. 404
Nonaka, I. 232
Nystrom, H. 133

OECD 338
O'Neil, J.R. 55
Ohmae, K 25–26, 33
Ohno, T. 45
Osborn, A. F. 126, 166, 169
Ouchi, W. 232
Ouchi, W. G. and Price, R. 220

Parkinson, C. N. 81
Pascale, R. and Athos, A. 232
Pedler, M. J., Burgoyne, J. G. and Boydell, T. H. 217
Pentagram 108–111
Perkins D. N. 132
Peters, T. 55, 214, 251, 323–324, 336, 339
Peters, T. and Waterman, R. H. 214, 336
Porter, M. E. 25, 31

Quinn, R. 232

Reich, R. B. 17, 324
Rickards, T. 71, 116, 118, 120, 164, 167–169, 179, 181
Rosenhead, J. 216

Schon, D. 232
Schonberger, R. J. 45
Senge, P. 205, 217
Senn, J. 232
Simon, H. A. 160
Simonton, D. K. 81
Sperry, R. W. 103
Spooner, P. 132, 166
Stalk, G. and Hout, T. 44, 48
Sternberg, R. J. 88
Stevens, M. S. 117, 120, 126, 164, 166, 168–169
Stewart, R. 71

Tannenbaum, R. and Schmidt, W. H. 76
Tardiff, T. Z. and Sternberg, R.J. 89
Tarr, G. 190
Taylor, F. W. 20, 70–71
Thomson, R. 110
Toffler, A. 17
Tonnies, F. 144, 332

Torrance, E. P. 98
Tushman, M. L. and Moore, W. L. 323

Urwick, L. 70–71

VanGundy, A. B. 116, 151, 153, 160–161,
    164–165, 172, 174, 178

Wahba, M, and Bridwell, L. 323
Wallas, G. 89, 90

Walton, M. 42–43, 232
Waterman, R. H. 336
Weber, M. 69
Weisberg, R. W. 132
Weisbord, M. 212
West, M. A. 189
Womack, Jones & Roos 24, 29
Wrege, C.D. 33

Zeithaml, C. P. and Zeithaml, V. A. 33

Subject index

ABB 29, 319
Administrators 205
Aero Engines 30
Ages
   agricultural age, 14–15
   industrial age, 15–16, 200
   neoindustrial age, 16, 39
Amoco 227
Arkwright, Richard 15
Assumptions 203
Audits
   16PF, 97
   Belbin (team inventory), 94, 97
   contextual, 304
   personal creativity (PCA), 94, 97, 133–136
   group creativity, 146, 190–193
   KAI, 96, 97
   Kolb learning cycle, 97
   MBTI, 95, 97
   management styles, 92, 133
   organizational creativity, 230, 233–236
   trust, 307

BP
   Oil 323
   top down commitment 323
BMW 30
Beethoven, L. 172
Beatles, The. 172
Bell, Canada 227
Benchmarking 44, 218, 227
Berol 223
Beliefs and attitudes 205
Black & Decker 225
Body Shop 228, 332
Boeing 29, 56
Bonas 223
Borderless World 22, 26–27, 199, 205, 209
Bosch 30
Branson R., 85, 110

Brain
   assets, 77, 338
   physiology, 101–103
   power, 49–51, 210, 305
   working, 103
British Aerospace 30
Buyer's market (see demand gap)

CBI 338
CIM, see production systems
Cajal, R. 103
Canon 25
Cartwright, Edmund 15
Case studies 343
   analysis guide, 346–348
   DHG Products, plc., 362–381
   Hallstead and Partners, 348–349
   Millbank Foods, plc., 358–362
   NJK, plc., 353–358
   Project control: walking on eggshells,
      349–350
   T L Rose, plc., 351–353
Casio 25
Causality
   linear, 201, 205
   loops, 201
Cause and effect 201, 206, 250
Change
   coping with, 212
   lasting, 214–215
Clinton, Pres. 26
Copland 172
Columbus, C. 107
Congruence, 304
Context, audit 304–305
Creative facilitation 147–149, 151, 155–158,
      212, 227, 311, 321
Creative management response (CMR) 58–59
   approaching I – the diagnosis, 246–250
   approaching II- the journey, 250–252

early sketch, 78
individual and group issues, 315–318
organizational issues, 318–325
text innovation, 249
Creative management response (CMR) model
component codes, 266–273
factor codes, 254–261, 274–278
factor code cards, 278–295
organizational implications, 253–254
metaphorical view (top dog), 261–265
mindmaps and tables view, 254–261
summary formula view, 261
three dimensional view, 252–253
Creative problem solving (CPS)
basic CPS tool kit, 121
building up a kit, 158–163
introductory CPS tool kit, 193–194
learning CPS, 315–316
stages, 160
starter CPS tool kit, 316
template, 117
tracking, 162–163
Creativity
audits, 89–90, 93–101, 190–193
capturing, 93–101
centre, 159–160, 227, 322
characteristics (people), 88
creative spark, 19–21, 50
definition, 86–87, 306
encouraging, 90–93
enhanced, 254
establishing climate, 155–158
explaining, 87–88
force, 85–87, 125, 150–151, 156, 251
helping others, 150–155
intelligence, 98
natural gift, 101
obstacles (group), 185–186
obstacles (personal), 125–128
residual, 254
responses (personal), summary map, 129
sources, 107–111
summary maps, 129, 188, 229
Crompton, Samuel 15
Cummins Engines 223
Customer care 48–49, 312–313
Cybernetics 218

daVinci, L. 88
Daimler Benz 30
Demand gap (buyer's market) 39, 51, 77,
    250, 252, 332
Determinism 200
Digital Equipment 46
Downsizing 228
Du Pont 29

EC 24–25
Edison, T. 88, 113,

Factor sets
cultural, 202
personal, 202
psychological, 202, 204–205
social, 202
Federal Express 323
Fiat 30
Flexible manufacturing systems (FMS) 41
Ford 29, 44
Fordism 41
Freedom
expression 322
Freud, S. 95
Future issues 331–340
backwards into, 37–48
forwards into, 48–50
purpose of government, 337–339
purpose of hunter individuals, 331–333
purpose of management, 335–336
purpose of organisations, 334–335
purpose of teamwork, 333–334

GEC, 30
General Electric, American 28
General Motors 29, 49
Gilbert & Sullivan 149
Global factors 26–32
borderless world, 26–27
organizational response, 27–31
Government, role 337
Greenhouse effect 31
Grofe 172
Group behaviour 143–150
basic dynamics, 146–147
definition, 202
managing, 148–150
organizing, 147–148
participation, 143–146

HIM see production systems
Hadyn, J. 172
Hall, Sir, John 85, 110
Handel, G. 172
Hargreaves, James 15
Harley-Davidson 46
Helicopter vision 200
Hewlett-Packard 24, 223, 228
Honda 25, 28, 30
Human relations 41–42, 46–51
Brainpower, 49–51
Kaizen, 42
SPC, 42

IBM 24, 29, 223, 246
ICI 246
ICL 225,
IRI 29
IT 74, 206
Imagery

alternative dimension, 170–178
Imagineering 171–178
  active approaches, 173–178
  bridging approaches, 172–173
  passive approaches, 171–172
Industrial Revolution 15, 20, 23, 25, 69,
  199–200
Infrastructure (physical) 337
Innovation, managing 228
Institute of Economic Affairs 33
Institute of Mechanical Engineers 23
Investors in people programme 338–339

JVC 25
Jobs, S. 113
Johnson, Pres. Lyndon 172
Jung, C.G. 95, 97
Just in case (JIC) 41, 44
Just in time (JIT) 43–46

KIA 29
Kaizen 42, 210
Kanban 45–46
Kay, John 15
Kodak, Eastman 227
Kroc, Ray (McDonald's) 332

Labour, division 15
Leadership 147
Learning
  psychological factor set, 205
  networking, 58
  reflective practice, 58
  skills, 104–105
Learning organization 211, 217, 224–225,
  227
Lerner and Lowe 115
Long-termism 336–337

3M, 46, 228
McDonnel Douglas 303
Machiavelli 69
Machine assisted manufacture 15
Man
  noble savage, 331–332
  savage hunter, 331–332
Management,
  competitive skill, 16
  definition, 68, 72
  long-distance skill, 16
  planning cycle, 71–72
  practice, 320–321
  prime task, 304
  process skills, 16, 75–76
  responses, 46–48, 52–53, 56–58, 77–78,
    199–200
  styles, 75–76
  thought, evolution, 67–71
  traditional competencies, 52–53, 71–75,
    79–80, 254, 306

Management interfaces
  individual/group, 309–311
  individual/organization, 307–309
  organization/customers, 312–313
  organization/group, 311–312
  organization/shareholders etc., 314
  organization/suppliers, 313–314
Management, Japanese 210, 218–223
Management, re-engineering 226–227
Management style
  power/authority, 306
  team based, 306
Management, Western 223–225
Marketing,
  customers, wooing, 41, 48–49, 312–313
  market research, 312–313
  niche marketing, 41
  promotion, 40, 313
  product offering, 49, 313
  relationship, 48
  strategic, 43
  valued added, 49, 324
Marks & Spencer 223–224, 228–229
Matsushita 30, 303–304
Mazda 29
Measurement 47, 207
Metaphor
  bridging the gap, 111–113, 172
  definition, 112
  tool, 167
Metro Centre 85
Microsoft 49, 228
Mind-sets, 201–206
  audit, 306
  challenging, 204
  group, 202–203
  organizational, 203, 248, 306
  personal, 202, 250, 306, 317–318
  psychological factor sets, 204–205
  thinking-pattern factor sets, 202
Motivation and reward 322–323
Motoren Turbinen Union 30
Motorola 44, 224
Mozart, A. 110, 172

NEC 25
Newcastle college 176–177
Newcastle General Hospital 180–181
Newton, Sir I. 87
Nikon 25
Nissan 28, 218
Nominal Group Technique 116, 121
Nordstrom 214
Northern Electric 120, 173–174, 176
Notebook 121

Office of information 227
Olympus 25
Organization Development (OD)

description, 216
objectives, 216–217
Organization, winning 314, 318, 321
Organizational behaviour interfaces (see
      management interfaces)
external, 304, 312–315
internal, 304, 307–312
managing, 304–306
Organizational design 319–320
Organizational Learning 217
Organizational responses
Japanese approach, 218–223
Owen, R. 69–70

Pacific rim,
countries, 25–26, 77, 209, 223, 246
Pasteur, L. 88
Perception 204–205, 208, 251–252
Period 11–16
Plato 69
Philip Morris 29
Positivism 200
Problem
definition, 106–107, 158
statement, 153
Problem solving (group-creative)
idea generation, 160–162, 167–179
principles (master guides), 182–185
problem evaluation, 160–161, 164–166
problem owner, 309
realization, 160, 161–163, 179–181
reflection, 160, 163
selection, 154, 178–179
Problem solving (organizational-creative)
benchmarking, 227
creativity centres (office of information),
      227
creative facilitation (learning organization),
      227
management re-engineering, 226–227
principles (master guides), 228–229
quality initiatives, 227–228
Problem solving (personal-creative),
discovering, 114–116
idea generation, 117–121
principles (master guides), 121–125
selection, 121
stages, 117
Problem solving (techniques)
advantage-disadvantage, 178, 180
analogies, 118, 167–168, 172
attribute listing, 168–169
brainstorming, 117,
broadsheet, 176–177
checklists, 168
clustering, 118,
colour code, 178
comfort zones tool, 181
creative evaluation, 178

cut and connect, 168 .
excursion, 167
force-field, 181
forcefit, 153–154, .
gut feel (intuitive judgement), 179
Kipling's questions (5W's & H), 164, 165,
      169–170
metaphors, 172
mind mapping, 118, 153,
multimedia, 173
notebook, 121
picture, 174
picture book, 174–176
punning, 173
relaxation, 171
reversal, 120, 153, 167
round robin, 117, 153
SCAMPER, 169
shaping, 120, 154,
software packages, 170
sounds inspirational, 172
stakeholder analysis, 165
Synectics, 164, 166–167
timeout, 120, 154
virtual reality, 173–174,
why?, 164–165
wildest idea, 167–168
wishful thinking, 165–166
Procter & Gamble 223
Production systems 41
Benchmarking, 44
CIM, 43
Flexible manufacturing systems (FMS),
      41
Fordism, 41
HIM, 43
JIC, 41, 44
JIT, 43–46
Lean production, 49
TQM, 43
Pratt & Witney 30
Proctor & Gamble 29
Profit purpose 335

Quality 312

Reality
contextual, 250
coping, 51–52
geographical, 209
natural, 209
perceived, 208
recognizing, 50–51
universal, 209
virtual, 204, 207, 250
Reductionism 200
Rice & Webber 149
Risk 332
Roddick, A. 85, 110

Rolls-Royce 30
Rover 30, 224–225, 323

SPC (see human relations)
SSM (Checkland's soft systems
    methodology) 215–216
Salk, J. 112
Seller's market (see supply gap)
Sharp 18, 25
Shell, Royal Dutch 29
Short-termism 336
Sinclair, Sir C. 110, 169
Smetana 72
Smith, W. H. 323
Socrates 69
Software packages
    Harvard Graphics, 170
    Microsoft Powerpoint, 170
    Think thunder, 170
    Visual outliner, 170, 254
Sony 25, 218, 228
Sperry R. W., 103
Standard parts, assembly 15
STEP factor 21–26
    economic and political factors 24–26
    social expectations 22–23
    technological factors 23–24
Sugar, Alan (AMSTRAD) 332
Supply chain 224, 228, 313–314
Supply gap 25, 38–39, 77, 208, 249, 252
Synectics 164–166

TEC 339
TQM 43–44, 224, 227–228, 3324
Taylorism 20, 41, 210, 212
Teamwork 306, 309–310, 312, 320–321,
    324, 332–335
Therapy 177–178
Thinking
    Cybernetics, 218
    Left-brain, 104, 158, 171, 310
    Hard systems, 69, 206–208, 249
    Hard vs. soft, 210–210
    long-term, 325, 336–337
    Management, 199–206
    Rational analytical, 69, 200, 205–207

Right-brain, 87, 103, 107–111, 158,
    170–178, 310–311
Short-term, 325, 336
Soft systems, 69, 200–201, 208–209,
    211–212, 215–216
Total, 105–106, 111–113, 147–149, 158,
    160, 170–171, 249, 317
Three-way-stretch 212–214
Triad, global 25, 28, 30
Time dimensions 14, 39
    task-oriented, 16, 39–41
    product/service design-oriented, 16, 39,
        41–42
    systems-oriented, 16, 39, 42–46
    value-oriented, 16, 20, 39, 48–50, 76, 201,
        208, 223, 252,–253, 312, 325, 337
Toyota 24, 28, 45
Training programmes
    designing, 317
Trust 90–93, 113, 252, 202, 307–308, 318,
    332–333

Union Carbide 227
Unipart 225
Upward feedback 323

Vicious circles 200
Virgin Airways 223
Virtuous circles 200
Vision 215
Virtual institutions 335
Vivaldi 172
Volvo 223

Watt, James 15
Wealth creation 16–19
    agricultural sector, 16–17
    external influences, 21–31
    industrial sector, 16–17
    knowledged-based sector, 17–18
    service sector, 16–17
Weberism 210
Whitney, E. 69

Xerox 227

Yamaha 25